AMNESTY
INTERNATIONAL
REPORT
1984

**This report covers the period
January to December 1983**

AMNESTY INTERNATIONAL is a worldwide movement which is independent of any government, political grouping, ideology, economic interest or religious creed. It plays a specific role within the overall spectrum of human rights work. The activities of the organization focus strictly on prisoners:

—It seeks the *release* of men and women detained anywhere for their beliefs, colour, sex, ethnic origin, language or religion, provided they have not used or advocated violence. These are termed *"prisoners of conscience"*.

—It advocates *fair and early trials* for *all political prisoners* and works on behalf of such persons detained without charge or without trial.

—It opposes the *death penalty* and *torture* or other cruel, inhuman or degrading treatment or punishment of *all prisoners* without reservation.

AMNESTY INTERNATIONAL acts on the basis of the United Nations Universal Declaration of Human Rights and other international instruments. Through practical work for prisoners within its mandate, Amnesty International participates in the wider promotion and protection of human rights in the civil, political, economic, social and cultural spheres.

AMNESTY INTERNATIONAL has more than 500,000 members, subscribers and supporters in over 150 countries and territories, with over 3,000 local groups in more than 50 countries in Africa, Asia, Europe, the Americas and the Middle East. Each group works on behalf of at least two prisoners of conscience in countries other than its own. These countries are balanced geographically and politically to ensure impartiality. Information about prisoners and human rights violations emanates from Amnesty International's Research Department in London. No section, group or member is expected to provide information on their own country, and no section, group or member has any responsibility for action taken or statements issued by the international organization concerning their own country.

AMNESTY INTERNATIONAL has formal relations with the United Nations (ECOSOC), UNESCO, the Council of Europe, the Organization of American States and the Organization of African Unity.

AMNESTY INTERNATIONAL is financed by subscriptions and donations of its worldwide membership. To safeguard the independence of the organization, all contributions are strictly controlled by guidelines laid down by the International Council and income and expenditure are made public in an annual financial report.

AMNESTY INTERNATIONAL REPORT 1984

Amnesty International Publications
1 Easton Street ● London WC1 X 8DJ ● United Kingdom

First published 1984 by Amnesty International Publications
1 Easton Street, London WC1X 8DJ, United Kingdom

© Copyright Amnesty International Publications 1984

ISBN 0 86210 071 2
AI Index: POL 01/01/84
Original Language: English

Printed, designed and typeset in Great Britain by
Redesign, 9 London Lane, London E8

Regional maps have been included in this report to indicate
the location of countries and territories cited in the text and for
that purpose only. It is not possible on the small scale used to indicate
precise political boundaries. Larger territories whose disputed
status is a matter of unresolved concern before relevant bodies of
the United Nations have been indicated by striping.
Amnesty International takes no position on territorial disputes.

Contents

vi

viii

Preface

I

This report places on record the work of Amnesty International in the year 1983. It is therefore a public account of efforts to identify and free prisoners of conscience, to secure fair and prompt trials for political prisoners and to end torture and executions throughout the world.

The details cited in this account are evidence of the extent to which governments have ordered or permitted the arbitrary detention, torture and killing of their own citizens. No government is justified in claiming that such acts carried out by its agents can be condoned or that Amnesty International has no right to intercede on behalf of the victims. The activities of the organization are inspired by fundamental principles adopted by the member states of the United Nations and, in many cases, ratified as legally binding by international treaty. These principles include the right to life, the right not to be tortured, and the right to freedom of thought, conscience and religion.

II

Human rights are an international responsibility; in this area governments are accountable not only to their own citizens but to the world community as a whole. Other governments, intergovernmental organizations, like the United Nations (UN) and the International Labour Organisation (ILO), and also non-governmental organizations must have the right to ask questions, observe trials and visit prisons and detention centres. These standards, however, continue to be violated by some governments. Special representatives appointed by the UN were not allowed to visit Chile and Poland. The Government of Uruguay continued to ignore recommendations by the International Human Rights Committee thereby making a mockery of its ratification of the International Covenant on Civil and Political Rights. The Government of Guinea, under former President Sekou Toure, repeatedly failed to appear when called to the same committee. The undermining of such International efforts to implement agreed principles has also hampered the work of Amnesty International. Some governments still do not respond to its inquiries, some refuse fact-finding missions and avoid serious discussion of Amnesty International's concerns.

III

Governments have attacked local groups formed to defend freedoms and fundamental rights, often under the pretext that they constitute a threat against national security. People working peacefully for human rights in their own countries have been taken to clandestine detention centres and tortured. They have been sentenced to long prison terms in secret trials. They have been accused of "subversion" and held without charge or trial. In some countries they have been assassinated.

In some cases, spies have worked to infiltrate human rights networks, disrupt communications, and identify contacts, aiming to destroy the credibility of entire human rights programs. Activists' homes have been raided, their papers confiscated and their families intimidated. Some governments have directed their efforts against people who have tried to circulate information about human rights violations inside their countries or who have sent such accounts abroad. The attacks on those who defend human rights are an attempt not only to deter dissent, but to eliminate the very exercise of conscience. When individuals expose the crimes of the state they are punished as if they were criminals. By demanding respect for the dignity of the human person, it is they who have acted in accordance with international human rights commitments accepted by their governments, while their governments act with contempt.

The names are numerous; a few must stand as symbols for the rest. Like many of those who have suffered the same fate they have become victims because they defended or tried to help others.

In Guatemala, labour lawyer América Yolanda Urizar has "disappeared". A former victim of death threats for her work with local trade unions, she was abducted in March 1983 by heavily armed men and driven away in an army Jeep. She has never been seen again.

Levko Lukyanenko is one. A lawyer, he is serving a 15-year prison sentence in the Soviet Union for his activities as a member of the Ukrainian Helsinki monitoring group – one of a number of unofficial groups assessing the government's compliance with the human rights provisions of the Final Act of the 1975 Conference on Security and Cooperation in Europe. It is the second 15-year term to which he has been sentenced for the non-violent exercise of his human rights. Wei Jingsheng is another. Wei was a leading campaigner in the "democracy movement" that started in China in late 1978. An electrician at Beijing Zoo, he became the editor of the unofficial journal *Exploration*. In October 1979 he was sentenced to 15 years' imprisonment and is reported to have been held in solitary confinement since then, including a period in a prison block where prisoners under sentence of death are held.

These cases are not cited because they are of greater significance than others; they are simply three among the thousands of prisoners of conscience around the world. Amnesty International works for the release of all such prisoners who are detained solely because of their political, religious or other conscientiously held beliefs or because of their ethnic origin, sex, colour or language. The organization has presented an Appeal for a Universal Amnesty for All Prisoners of Conscience to all governments and to the UN. The appeal, signed by more than one and a half million individuals from 122 countries, was handed over to the UN in a special ceremony on the eve of Human Rights Day, 10 December 1983. Slightly abbreviated texts of the statement made by Amnesty International on that occasion and the responses by the President of the UN General Assembly and the UN Secretary-General follow the Introduction (pages 13 to 15).

IV

Work for the release of prisoners of conscience is one part of Amnesty International's mandate, which also includes endeavouring to ensure fair and prompt trials for political prisoners and an end to torture and executions. In pursuing this mandate Amnesty International is strictly impartial. It does not work against governments but against human rights violations. It does not take sides in political or other conflicts. It neither supports nor opposes any political, social, or economic system. It applies a single, universal standard – the body of human rights principles elaborated by the member states of the UN – to all countries, regardless of the ideology of the government or the views of the victims. Amnesty International believes this impartial approach to be vital, not merely as a means of obtaining concrete results in its work for prisoners, but also because human rights are absolute and the defence of such rights should not be dependent on political convenience. This commitment to impartiality demands a consistent effort to seek further information about alleged violations and evaluate these reports in a scrupulously non-partisan manner. Thorough and unbiased research is crucial for the human rights movement.

4

V

Abuses have been committed by opposition groups in various countries. Amnesty International adopted a resolution in 1983 making clear that it condemns, as a matter of principle, the torture and execution of prisoners by anyone, including opposition groups. It reiterated its view that governments are responsible for dealing with such abuses, acting in conformity with international standards for the protection of human rights.

VI

Amnesty International is often asked to compare and contrast the human rights record of different countries or of successive governments. It does not and cannot do this. Government secrecy and intimidation obstruct the flow of information from many countries and can impede efforts to corroborate allegations; this fact alone makes it impossible to establish a reliable and consistent basis for comparison. Furthermore, prisoners are subjected to widely differing forms of harassment, ill-treatment and punishment, taking place in diverse contexts and affecting the victims and their families in different ways; this fact would render any statistical or other generalized comparison meaningless as a real measure of the impact of human rights abuses. Finally, it is Amnesty International's experience that the comparison of governments' human rights practices is frequently open to political manipulation and misuse. This is a disservice to human rights and has nothing to do with helping the victims.

The reader must therefore bear in mind that a report such as this is not comparative and can never be comprehensive – in many instances Amnesty International simply does not have the resources to carry out the research or activities it might wish to. In some cases, no country entry in this report has been possible, but this should not be interpreted in any way as indicative of Amnesty International's assessment of the human rights situation prevailing in the country. Among the countries where the information available to Amnesty International was insufficient to allow an entry in this report were: Botswana, the Dominican Republic, Ecuador, Jordan, Liberia, Mongolia, Qatar, the Seychelles, United Arab Emirates, Venezuela and the Yemen Arab Republic.

Within these limits the report reflects an international effort to make progress in ensuring respect for certain of the inalienable rights of all members of the human family. The pages that follow show clearly how much more needs to be done before that object is secured.

Amnesty International — a worldwide campaign

Twenty-three years ago Amnesty International began as an idea – a publicity campaign to highlight the "forgotten prisoners". It got underway with only a handful of dedicated volunteers, virtually no funds and few opportunities to present its case to governments or the public. Today there are more than 500,000 members, supporters and subscribers in over 160 countries; many of them are often out on street corners or at public markets collecting signatures to petitions, asking for donations and distributing information.Amnesty International has missions are able to visit a range of countries each year.

Public support has been the key to this extraordinary development. From the very beginning Amnesty International has relied on ordinary citizens to build a movement that would reflect the worldwide concern for human rights. It has deliberately organized itself so that anyone, anywhere can take part in some way in the vital work for prisoners. It has insisted on being an open, democratic movement. It has chosen to rely on members' fees, donations and public fund-raising to ensure that its political independence is matched by financial independence. This financial integrity is essential to keep the movement free from pressure and to maintain its impartiality. Amnesty International's accounts are open to public scrutiny and copies are available from the International Secretariat.

Work for individual prisoners

Amnesty International members are organized into small groups in over 50 countries doing practical work to protect prisoners held around the world. Research is carried out at the International Secretariat where dossiers on individual prisoners are compiled. When Amnesty International determines that a prisoner of conscience is being held the prisoner is "adopted" by one or more groups which then try to achieve his or her immediate release. Group members appeal to the authorities holding the prisoner and mobilize public and professional interest in the case. Government and prison officials are faced with insistent, continuous and informed appeals urging the prisoner's release. When a case is being investigated because there is not enough evidence to determine whether or not the prisoner is a prisoner of conscience, the group will ask the authorities for details about the case, such as the charges involved. Groups work for prisoners held in countries other than their own. The cases – generally two are allocated to a group – are balanced politically and geographically to reflect the movement's impartiality. Groups also send material assistance to adopted prisoners and their families, such as money, medicine or clothing. In 1983 there were over 3,221 groups in 52 countries, working on behalf of over 5,000 prisoners (some of whom had been adopted by more than one group).

Networks have been set up to respond rapidly in cases where prompt action is essential. During 1983 there were 276 urgent action appeals on behalf of individuals and groups of prisoners in 66 countries. The cases included prisoners in need of immediate medical treatment, prisoners who had "disappeared" in unacknowledged custody and prisoners threatened with torture or facing execution.

Each month the *Amnesty International Newsletter* highlights the plight of three prisoners of conscience and asks its readers to send direct personal letters or telegrams on their behalf. During the year Amnesty International members and groups cooperated in special actions to help prisoners in several countries. On 23 March 1983 Amnesty International initiated a campaign to expose unlawful political killings by government forces or officially sanctioned "death squads".[1] Participation in the campaign, which ran for eight months, was worldwide. In a major report, *Political Killings by Governments,* published to start the campaign, Amnesty International detailed evidence that hundreds of thousands of people were killed by the political authorities in their countries in the previous 10 years. In all these cases, the victims were denied any protection from the law and were killed because of their real or suspected beliefs or activities, or their origins. Through letters, petitions and visits to embassies, Amnesty International members called on the relevant governments to set up official inquiries into the killings and to publish the findings.

Each year the movement organizes Prisoners of Conscience Week to draw public attention to Amnesty International's work on a particular

---

1 Political killings by governments have certain common features. These are summed up in the definition that Amnesty International uses: "unlawful and deliberate killings of persons by reason of their real or imputed political beliefs or activities, religion, other conscientiously held beliefs, ethnic origin, sex, colour or language, carried out by order of a government or with it's complicity".

concern: the 1983 week was devoted to human rights activists in prison. In many cases, human rights activists are jailed because they defended or tried to help people who had been harassed or detained for their beliefs. In some countries, people working for human rights have been taken to clandestine detention centres and tortured. They have been sentenced to long prison terms in secret trials. They have been accused of "subversion" and held without charge or trial. Their efforts have been officially denounced, their houses have been raided, their papers have been confiscated and their families intimidated. In various countries, human rights activists have been assassinated. Human rights activists in prison stand, in a sense, as symbols for all prisoners of conscience everywhere.

Amnesty International members and groups continued to work to expose and prevent the torture or ill-treatment of all prisoners, without reservation. This effort is to be stepped up in 1984 when Amnesty International is to launch a major campaign, involving its worldwide membership, against these gross violations of human rights.

Amnesty International is unconditionally opposed to the death penalty and works for its total abolition throughout the world. Amnesty International regularly monitors death sentences and executions around the world. It appeals for clemency whenever it learns of a case in which imminent execution is feared.

On 15 December 1983 the House of Representatives (parliament) of Cyprus adopted a bill abolishing the death penalty for premeditated murder, the only common crime for which it remained in force.

Under the new constitution which came into force in El Salvador on 20 December 1983, the death penalty was abolished except for offences under military law in time of international war.

By the end of the year 26 countries had abolished the death penalty for all offences and 18 for all but exceptional offences, such as war crimes. A number of other countries have not abolished the death penalty but do not carry out executions in practice.

During 1982, 1,699 prisoners are known to have been executed in 39 countries, and 1,160 sentenced to death in 63 countries. These figures include only cases known to Amnesty International: the true figures are certainly higher.

Refugees

Amnesty International's statutory objectives relate exclusively to prisoners. However, its work towards achieving those objectives leads it to oppose the forcible return of anyone to a country where he or she might reasonably fear being imprisoned as a prisoner of conscience, tortured or killed. It presents information about the risks refugees face in their countries of origin to specialized refugee organizations and to governments considering applications for political asylum. With respect to prisoners of conscience whose only alternative to continued imprisonment is exile, Amnesty International may call upon governments to admit individuals who seek this alternative.

Amnesty International regularly submits information to the United Nations High Commissioner for Refugees regarding refugees who face becoming victims of human rights violations within Amnesty International's mandate upon being returned to another country or within the country where they are seeking refuge.

Relief

During 1983 the International Secretariat of Amnesty International distributed £202,557 in relief payments to help prisoners of conscience and their families and to assist the rehabilitation of torture victims. Sections and Amnesty International groups also sent help to many thousands of prisoners and their families. The relief program is not a substitute for the primary objective of securing freedom for prisoners of conscience and an end to the use of torture, but aims to alleviate suffering. When relief payments are distributed by bodies outside Amnesty International or through intermediaries, the organization takes care to stipulate the precise prisoner-related purpose for which the payments are intended, and wherever possible obtain receipts from the beneficiaries. The relief program of the International Secretariat is supervised by a sub-committee of the International Executive Committee which also advises sections on relief activities. Amnesty International's relief accounts, like its general accounts, are audited annually and are available from the International Secretariat.

International Organizations

Amnesty International continued to urge all governments to become parties to the major international human rights instruments relevant to its mandate, in particular the two international covenants on human rights and the Optional Protocol to the International Covenant on Civil and Political Rights. During 1983 Amnesty International welcomed ratification of the covenants by Afghanistan, Belgium, Congo and Gabon; and ratification of the Optional Protocol by Congo and

Luxembourg. By the end of 1983, 80 states were parties to the International Covenant on Economic, Social and Cultural rights, 77 states were parties to the International Covenant on Civil and Political Rights and 31 states were parties to the Optional Protocol.

During 1983 Amnesty International submitted to the UN information on Argentina, Pakistan, Turkey, Uruguay, the Soviet Union and Zaire for consideration under the procedure created by Economic and Social Council Resolution 1503 (XLVIII). This procedures provides for the confidential consideration by the competent UN bodies of reports that appear to reveal "a consistent pattern of gross and reliably attested violations of human rights". Information on Benin, the German Democratic Republic and Haiti was submitted pursuant to ECOSOC Resolution 728F (XXVIII).

During 1983 Amnesty International submitted to the UN Working Group on Enforced or Involuntary Disappearances information on cases of "disappearances" in 16 countries: Angola, Argentina, Bolivia, Colombia, Costa Rica, East Timor, Ecuador, El Salvador, Guatemala, Haiti, Honduras, Iran, Mexico, Paraguay, Peru and the Philippines. The Working Group was created in 1980 by the UN Commission on Human Rights to investigate "disappearances" in any part of the world. In its annual report of December 1983 the Working Group stated that the number of new "disappearances" in 1983 was about the same as in 1982. The Working Group said that during the past 12 months it had transmitted reports on some 2,390 "disappearances" to the governments of 15 countries. In an oral statement to the 39th session of the Commission on Human Rights Amnesty International drew the Commission's attention to the fact that, in spite of the Working Group's persistent efforts, less than five per cent of the cases so far transmitted to governments had been clarified. Amnesty International therefore suggested that the Working Group should be asked to make public the information on cases in which government responsibility had been clearly established but in which the government refused to cooperate with the Working Group.

During 1983 Amnesty International submitted to the UN Special Rapporteur on Summary and Arbitrary Executions information on extrajudicial executions, and death penalties pronounced after inadequate trials, in 22 countries.

Under different UN procedures Amnesty International submitted written information on its concerns in Afghanistan, Chile, East Timor, Guatemala, Iran, Kampuchea, Poland, and on the repression of indigenous peoples in Latin America. At the request of various UN bodies it submitted information and views on the independence of judges and lawyers; the right of conscientious objection to military service; the human rights of prisoners and detainees; the abuse of psychiatry for political purposes; and violations of human rights under states of emergency. Amnesty International representatives made oral statements to various UN bodies on the organization's concerns in Brunei, East Timor and Namibia; and on "disappearances", summary or arbitrary executions, and states of emergency.

During 1983 Amnesty International submitted information to UNESCO's Committee on Conventions and Recommendations on violations of the human rights of writers, teachers and others in El Salvador, Kenya, Laos, Paraguay, Viet Nam, and Yugoslavia. Pursuing its concern for increased UNESCO activity in the field of human rights education, Amnesty International participated in a number of UNESCO meetings, in particular the General Conference where Amnesty International's Secretary General explained the concrete proposals that Amnesty International was making, such as the need for a dynamic program of dissemination of international human rights standards and mechanisms and for increased budgetary priority for UNESCO's plan for human rights teaching. Amnesty International continued to participate as coordinator of the Non-governmental organization (NGO) side in the UNESCO Secretariat/NGO Joint Working Group on Education for the Promotion, Application and Defence of Human Rights.

Amnesty International has no formal status with the International Labour Organisation (ILO) but it continued to make information available on such issues as forced labour and violations of the right to freedom of association to organizations which do work formally within the ILO.

Amnesty International continued to send appropriate information on countries where human rights violations within its mandate occurred to the Inter-American Commission on Human Rights (IACHR), the specialist human rights organ of the Organization of American States (OAS). The countries included Chile, Guatemala, Mexico (in respect of refugees from Guatemala), Paraguay and Suriname.

Representatives of Amnesty International attended the 13th regular session of the OAS General Assembly after being granted an invitation as a "special guest" by the OAS Permanent Council. In advance of the assembly, Amnesty International had addressed an open letter to heads of delegation indicating the organization's continuing concern that within the OAS region could be found violations of human rights under all aspects of Amnesty International's mandate. In the letter Amnesty International urged that "the rights enshrined in the American Convention on Human Rights be respected in law and practice."

The African Charter on Human and Peoples' Rights was adopted unanimously by the Organization of African Unity (OAU) in 1981 and Amnesty International continued to monitor the incidence of ratifications of the Charter. Instruments of ratification were deposited by five states during 1983 – Congo, Gambia, Nigeria, Rwanda and Tunisia – bringing to 10 the total number of ratifications on deposit. In addition Sierra Leone ratified in September 1983, although its instrument of ratification had not been deposited by the end of the year. A majority of the 50 OAU member states must become a party for the Charter to come into force.

All 21 member states of the Council of Europe are parties to the European Convention on Human Rights. On 28 April an additional protocol to the European Convention abolishing the death penalty for peace time offences was opened for signature. Amnesty International urged all member states of the Council of Europe to become parties to this protocol. By the end of 1983 the protocol had been ratified by Denmark and signed by Austria, Belgium, France, Federal Republic of Germany, Greece, Italy, Luxembourg, Netherlands, Norway, Portugal, Spain, Sweden and Switzerland. Turkey was the only member state of the Council of Europe which continued to carry out executions during the year.

On 1 July the Council of Europe's Committee of Ministers announced that it had awarded the European human rights prize to Amnesty International's "medical section", "because of its exceptional contribution to the cause of human rights". The award was presented to Amnesty International at a ceremony in Strasbourg on 28 September.

On 27 September the Parliamentary Assembly of the Council of Europe adopted without a vote a resolution in support of Amnesty International's campaign for a universal amnesty for all prisoners of conscience and solemnly called on all the nations of the world to release all prisoners of conscience.

The Inter-Parliamentary Union, a non-governmental organization composed of members of parliament from 100 countries, maintains a special committee which investigates reported violations of human rights of parliamentarians. During 1983 Amnesty International submitted to the special committee information on detained members of parliament in 15 countries: Bangladesh, Gabon, Ghana, Indonesia, Iran, Kenya, Republic of Korea, Mauritania, Singapore, Somalia, Sudan, Turkey, Uganda, Viet Nam and Zimbabwe.

A Universal Amnesty for All Prisoners of Conscience

Presentation address by Suriya Wickremasinghe

"We have come to the United Nations to speak on behalf of the thousands of men and women whose governments have imprisoned them because of their political or religious beliefs or because of their colour or ethnic origin, none of whom has used or advocated violence. These are prisoners of conscience. Their imprisonment violates the Universal Declaration of Human Rights.

Most prisoners of conscience are detained for trying to exercise their rights to freedom of expression, association, assembly, or movement. Trade union activity or participation in strikes or demonstrations is a common cause of imprisonment. Members of religious groups are jailed for religious practices which contravene restrictive limits set by the state. Some prisoners of conscience are held for actions taken as individuals; others for belonging to a group or movement. Some acted in direct opposition to the government in power, while others worked within the country's political system without seeking confrontation with authority. Some are held simply because of the political activity of members of their family, or for belonging to a national minority.

Few governments are willing to admit that they detain people in violation of internationally agreed norms. Some choose to give a very narrow interpretation to these standards. Other governments assert that they do not send people to prison for their beliefs, but only for criminal acts – while their legislation makes even the peaceful expression of dissent a crime. Some governments define the concept of national security so broadly that almost anyone suspected of being critical of the government can be detained.

Many prisoners of conscience in the world today were arrested because they themselves worked for the release of persons who should not be in jail, or because they tried to publicize facts about other human rights abuses.

A year ago, we felt that renewed effort was needed to have these people freed. The result was the launching of the present Appeal for a Universal Amnesty for All Prisoners of Conscience.

The appeal has been signed by former presidents and heads of government, by scientists and artists, by newspaper editors and writers. But by far the majority of signatures are not from the leaders and makers of public opinion, but from the public itself – from men and women of all walks of life, from many cultures, speaking on this issue with one voice.

While we speak to you now, thousands of prisoners of conscience around the world are spending this day deprived of their basic human right to liberty, often in appalling conditions. They should be freed unconditionally.

Asking that prisoners of conscience be freed does not mean that we identify ourselves with the views of those whose liberty we seek. What is at stake is the fundamental right freely to hold opinions and freely to express them. No person and no government has the right to a monopoly of truth or to deny to others the right to voice their ideas. This principle is an important part of the international agreements on human rights.

While we speak to you now, thousands of prisoners of conscience around the world are spending this day deprived of their basic human right to liberty, often in appalling conditions. They should be freed unconditionally. Such an amnesty would have implications far beyond the restoration of the individual freedom of the men and women concerned. It would be an historic step in the implementation of solemn obligations. It would advance respect for the dignity and worth of the human person everywhere."

Responding to the presentation of Amnesty International's appeal, the UN Secretary-General, Pérez de Cuéllar, said:

"I accept this appeal with deep concern. The story which it tells and which you have just related is indeed disturbing. In our day and age people should not have to suffer for their conscience, their beliefs or their opinions.

The Charter of the United Nations preaches tolerance and understanding among nations and peoples, and the Universal Declaration of Human Rights requires that this very tolerance and understanding be practised between individual human beings as well as between governments and their people.

It is very distressing that, notwithstanding these commitments, there are still many thousands of political prisoners in the world today.

In drawing attention to this issue, Amnesty International has once again rendered a valuable service to the entire international community. Your previous campaigns against torture, the death penalty, arbitrary and summary executions, and now against political imprisonment, have served to focus world opinion on these problems in a very special way.

I want you to know that we at the United Nations are grateful for the work which you are doing with such dedication and skill. The world owes you a debt of gratitude for your efforts.

I should also like to assure you that the Commission on Human Rights will be appropriately informed of this appeal.

Please rest assured that you have my full understanding and support even if, for reasons which you will appreciate, I sometimes must operate in ways that are different from yours.

I thank you very much for your courageous efforts and strongly encourage you to continue your good work."

In a statement made after Amnesty International's appeal was presented at the UN, the President of the General Assembly, Jorge E. Illueca, said:

"The movement to protect human rights and fundamental freedoms is sponsored by the United Nations Organization under the powers given in Article 1 and other provisions of the United Nations Charter. However, it is evident that the formulation of binding general rules of international law for the protection of human rights and fundamental freedoms by adequate machinery for their enforcement still remains more a promise than an achievement.

The worldwide appeal for A Univeral Amnesty for All Prisoners of Conscience presented today by Amnesty International is in harmony with the Charter, the Universal Declaration of Human Rights, the General Assembly Declaration on the Protection of All Persons from Being Subjected to Torture and Other Cruel, Inhuman or Degrading Treatment or Punishment, and other human rights instruments proclaimed by the United Nations.

Without passing judgement as to the merits of any particular case, the appeal addressed to the General Assembly and to all governments, endorsed by more than one million signatures, is giving effectiveness to the popular participation recommended by the General Assembly as an important factor in development and in the realization of human rights, and among them the fundamental right of the self-determination of peoples and nations.

Let me express to Amnesty International how grateful we are at the United Nations for the outstanding work it is performing to advance the ideals of the United Nations and the movement for the protection of human rights and fundamental freedoms. Amnesty International is making effectively good the rule that 'eternal vigilance is the price of liberty'."

Africa

Angola

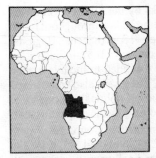

Amnesty International was concerned about the long-term detention without trial of real or suspected opponents of the government and allegations of torture of detainees. The organization considered that a major political trial in March fell short of internationally accepted standards. The organization was concerned about the use of the death penalty and the government's continued failure to account for a number of people who "disappeared" in detention in 1977 and 1978. Amnesty International was also concerned about the arbitrary detention by armed opposition groups of civilians who had not been involved in the armed conflict.

Widespread armed conflict persisted throughout the year affecting much of the country. South African forces based in Namibia occupied the southern part of Cunene province and in December launched an attack further north into Huíla province, ostensibly against Namibian guerrilla fighters based in Angola. The South African forces were believed to have taken a number of prisoners, although no information was made public about them.

The government was also under increasing pressure from the *União Nacional para a Independência Total de Angola* (UNITA), National Union for the Total Independence of Angola, an armed opposition group active particularly in the southeast and centre of the country. In January an attack organized by UNITA guerrillas took place on Tari detention camp in Kwanza-Sul province, where a considerable number of detainees accused of supporting the UNITA or other armed opposition groups were held. About 100 of the detainees chose to accompany the guerrillas and left the camp. Tari camp was subsequently closed and some of its inmates were transferred to another camp near

Negage, in Uige province; however, many of those who had not accompanied the UNITA guerrillas were released from detention during the first half of the year.

Several hundred alleged members or supporters of the UNITA were reportedly captured or detained during the year and some were put on public display at political rallies, but none of them were known to have been tried by the end of the year. In October 79 detainees appeared at a public rally in Huambo, accused of helping the UNITA. One of them was detained for allegedly receiving a letter from a UNITA guerrilla soliciting supplies and failing to inform the appropriate authorities. He and 70 others accused of minor offences were subsequently released, while the remaining eight detainees were kept in custody.

In late July, following a wave of attacks by the UNITA on towns and railways, the government introduced martial law throughout much of the country. In at least 10 of Angola's 18 provinces, Regional Military Councils were established to take charge of the administration and the jurisdiction of military courts was extended to include a wide range of political and "economic" offences. They were also empowered to try civilian defendants. However, no trials of political opponents of the government had taken place in military courts by the end of the year.

Alleged members of another armed opposition group, the *Frente Nacional de Libertação de Angola* (FNLA), National Front for the Liberation of Angola, which remained sporadically active in the north of the country were also arrested. However, in March several former leading members of the FNLA were permitted to return from exile in Zaire and were not imprisoned.

The authorities continued to detain without trial many alleged UNITA and FNLA supporters who had been arrested in previous years. Unofficial sources suggested that there were as many as 1,000 or more political detainees. They were said to be held in Luanda and in other provincial centres or at rural detention camps such as the one at Bentiaba, in Namibe province, which was formerly known as São Nicolau camp. No official figures were issued on the number of political detainees. Amnesty International did obtain information about some of the detainees, many of whom had been held without charge or trial for several years. For example, Lucas Tshisumba, an alleged UNITA supporter who was arrested in Huambo when he was 16 years old, had been detained without trial since 1979.

Other long-term political detainees included a number of asylum-seekers. A Sao Tomean national, António Trovoada, who was recognized as a refugee in Portugal, was held in custody for 12 months after he was arrested when he arrived in Luanda in November 1982. In November 1983 he was summarily repatriated to Sao Tome and

Principe, where he was immediately arrested and apparently accused of supporting a Sao Tomean opposition group.

A small number of people were detained for having criticized government policies or officials. A group of four officials and supporters of the ruling *Movimento Popular de Libertação de Angola – Partido de Trabalho* (MPLA-PT), Popular Movement for the Liberation of Angola – Labour Party, were arrested in December 1982 and January 1983 and accused of being involved in the production of a satirical play which had reportedly criticized the authorities. Three of those arrested were released in late January, but one, Fernando Costa Andrade ("Ndunduma"), the Secretary General of the Union of Angolan Journalists at the time of his arrest, was kept in custody. He was adopted by Amnesty International as a prisoner of conscience and had not been either tried or released by the end of 1983.

Detainees who were suspected of supporting armed opposition groups were reportedly tortured during interrogation, particularly in a prison on the Catete road in Luanda where most political detainees who were arrested in the capital appeared to be held for questioning. Under the terms of a June 1980 law such detainees may be held incommunicado for questioning for three months and may be detained for a total of seven months before being charged.

Several detainees who were reportedly tortured in Sumbe, the capital of Kwanza-Sul province, in early 1982 were brought to trial at the end of March 1983. Statements allegedly made under duress were reportedly used as evidence against them. They were among 27 defendants who were tried by the People's Revolutionary Tribunal in Sumbe on charges relating to their alleged activities in support of the UNITA. The prosecutor at this trial requested the court to sentence 12 of the defendants to death. At the end of the week-long trial, however, only one of the defendants, Tomás Pinto Vidro, was sentenced to death. He was a school teacher and official of the Congregationalist Church in Wako Kungo, where he was arrested in December 1981, shortly after UNITA guerrillas had been active in the area. He and several others arrested at the same time in Wako Kungo were reportedly tortured, and it appeared that he was convicted and sentenced to death for having been involved in clandestine activities in support of the UNITA partly on the basis of statements he allegedly made under torture.

The authorities did not publish details of the precise offences alleged to have been committed by Tomás Pinto Vidro or the 14 other defendants who were convicted at the same time. Amnesty International received no response to its requests to the court and to other officials for details of the charges against them. Three defendants were sentenced to prison terms of 26, 18 and 16 years respectively, four to 12 years and seven others to two-year prison terms.

Amnesty International was concerned that at this trial, as at previous trials before the People's Revolutionary Tribunal, defendants may not have been given adequate opportunities to defend themselves; at previous trials defendants had to present their defence in a written statement and often appeared to have received little real assistance from legal counsel during their trials. Amnesty International was also concerned that all but two had no right to appeal against their conviction or sentence. Sentences of death or prison terms of more than 20 years are reviewed by a special Appeals Tribunal, but it was not known what the results of any such review were. When Amnesty International learned that Tomás Pinto Vidro had been sentenced to death, the organization appealed for his sentence to be commuted. No replies were received to these appeals and no subsequent announcement was made to indicate whether the death sentence had been carried out.

Amnesty International continued to seek information from the authorities about some 20 people who were among a number of political prisoners who "disappeared" from detention after being arrested in 1977 and 1978. They were believed to have been executed in secret on account of their alleged ties with the UNITA or their alleged involvement in an unsuccessful attempt to overthrow the government in May 1977, but the government consistently refused to confirm this or to account for them. In September, apparently in response to Amnesty International's inquiries, Angola's national press agency stated categorically that no prisoners had "disappeared" or been "shot in the middle of the night" in Angola. No information was, however, supplied about the individuals who were the subject of these inquiries.

Benin

Amnesty International's main concern was the imprisonment of prisoners of conscience and other political prisoners, some of whom had been detained without trial for several years, others having been sentenced to prison terms after unfair trials. There were also disturbing reports of ill-treatment of prisoners.

Amnesty International continued in 1983 to seek the release of 42 untried detainees who were held for their real or suspected involvement in non-violent protests against government policies. Thirty-five of them, mainly students and teachers, had been arrested between 1979 and

1981 following protests against the government's education policy at the university and in schools in Benin's major towns. They remained in detention as "administrative internees", without any right to a trial or to access to a lawyer; the authorities continued to deny them knowledge of any charges against them and of the reasons for their detention. In late December 1983, 20 of these detainees received the first official document concerning their detention, signed by the Minister of the Interior and Public Security, Lieutenant Colonel Michel Alladaye, in the form of a renewable order of "administrative internment" of six months' duration, retroactively applied from August 1983. These documents stated that the detainees were held because their activities were "liable to disrupt public order and security". Twenty-six of the detainees, including Firmin Awadon, Alassane Issoufou and Leon Yelome, had been arrested between March 1979 and October 1980, in the wake of demands by students to be allowed to form an independent students' organization and to have improved educational facilities. All continued to be held throughout the year in prisons in Porto Novo and in the capital, Cotonou. Two of these long-term detainees, Sébastien Adjakpa and Mathias Dognon, were released in September and November 1983 respectively. The latter, who had reportedly suffered serious psychological disorders during his detention, had been held in a psychiatric hospital for almost a year prior to his release.

Amnesty International also sought the release of nine detainees, including several technical workers and teachers, who had been held without charge or trial since March 1981 when they were suspected by the authorities of distributing leaflets critical of government policy. They were reportedly held in poor conditions in Parakou military barracks.

The organization also appealed to the Benin authorities for the release of Paul Koudoukpo, a teacher who was arrested in September 1982, apparently being suspected by the authorities of distributing leaflets which called for the release of the students and teachers who were arrested between 1979 and 1981. One group of four pupils and another of two teachers, who were arrested in April and June 1982 respectively in connection with the distribution of leaflets, were released in mid-1983, shortly after they had been adopted as prisoners of conscience by Amnesty International.

Amnesty International continued to appeal for the release of five prisoners of conscience and for a review of the cases of eight other political prisoners, all of whom were arrested in 1975 and convicted in March 1975 or February 1976 of participating in or being in complicity with alleged attempts to overthrow the government. Their trials before an executive body, the *Conseil national de la révolution* (CNR), the National Council of the Revolution, did not conform to the most basic international legal standards for a fair trial. The defendants were not permitted to know the charges against them, to be present at the hearings or to be represented by defence counsel. They were not permitted to bring evidence or call witnesses in their defence. The prisoners were not informed by official sources that they had been convicted and sentenced, three of them being sentenced to death and the remainder to long terms of imprisonment. They were denied the right of appeal. Three of them – Grégoire Agbale, Benoît Hounsou and Abbé Alphonse Quenum – were reported during the year to be suffering from very poor health and were admitted to hospital. The first two underwent serious operations and were then returned to prison.

Amnesty International's investigations into the cases of Claude Midahuen, Léonard Maboudou and André Oke Assogba were pursued throughout 1983. All were senior government officials when they were arrested in 1975 and 1976, apparently in connection with the alleged 1975 coup attempts. They continued to be held without charge or trial and the authorities reportedly continued to deny them any information as to the reasons for their detention.

Amnesty International was also investigating the cases of Colonel Alphonse Alley and Major Jean-Baptiste Hacheme, who were both sentenced to 20 years' imprisonment in early 1973, for alleged involvement in a coup attempt. Their trial, also before an executive body, was grossly unfair and displayed the same deficiencies as the political trials in March 1975 and February 1976. Another alleged plotter, Paul Kponou, was released from prison in April 1983 after serving a 10-year sentence.

In June 1983, Michel Bamenou Toko was released; he was the last senior official of the government of Hubert Maga, which was overthrown in 1972, to remain in detention. His case had been investigated by Amnesty International. At the time of his arrest he had apparently been accused of misappropriating state funds, but he was never tried and reports had suggested that the reasons for his arrest were primarily political.

In a letter sent to Amnesty International in March 1983, the government invited the organization to send a mission to Benin to undertake fact-finding into the cases of detainees and prisoners of concern to the organization and to hold discussions with government representatives. In their letter, the government also expressed the view that political detention or imprisonment in Benin was carried out according to the laws and regulations in force in the country. In its reply to the government in April 1983, Amnesty International accepted the invitation to visit Benin and suggested dates when it might send representatives. By the end of 1983, no reply had been received from the government.

Amnesty International continued to be concerned about the generally poor conditions in which political detainees were being held. Crowded and insanitary conditions were reportedly common, and the available medical facilities were grossly inadequate in all places of detention. These unacceptably low standards of cleanliness and medical care were believed to have encouraged the spread of many infectious diseases among detainees, including skin, stomach and eye complaints. Conditions in the many police stations in Cotonou where political detainees were reportedly held, and at Parakou military barracks, were believed to be particularly inadequate, due to overcrowding, lack of exercise facilities and poor food and sanitation. The authorities continued to fail to supply food to any of those political detainees arrested since 1979, thereby forcing them to rely on the generosity of their families or fellow prisoners. However, in Cotonou prison, such detainees were provided with less cramped quarters and were granted more time to meet and talk with visitors.

Burundi

Amnesty International's concerns centred on the situation of refugees and asylum seekers from Zaire; two were forcibly repatriated to Zaire and several others were detained without trial for short periods. Amnesty International also sought information about two school teachers who had been suspected of criticizing or opposing the government and were arrested in 1981 and 1982.

The arrests of Zairian asylum-seekers was initially reported in April, when three were arrested in Rumonge and taken to the border with Zaire to be repatriated. One of them escaped from custody, but two others, Kalenga and Kitungano, were handed over into the custody of the Zairian national security service at Uvira. They were detained in Zaire and reportedly subjected to severe beatings, but were released uncharged after several weeks.

Two Zairian refugees remaining in Burundi, Mukadi Walengamina and Musafiri Ramadhani, both of whom had previously been detained in Zaire for political reasons, protested to the Burundi authorities about the April repatriations and were arrested on 1 June. Amnesty International made inquiries about the reasons for their arrest and the grounds for their detention, but received no reply from the government.

In August Amnesty International appealed for their release and the organization subsequently learned that they had been released uncharged in September.

In November 22 Zairian refugees were arrested after staging a demonstration outside the Bujumbura office of the United Nations High Commissioner for Refugees. They were apparently protesting because they had still not been resettled in a neighbouring country of their own choice despite lodging requests several years earlier. Several of those arrested had previously been detained for similar reasons in 1981. All of them were released uncharged in December after spending six weeks in custody.

Amnesty International continued to inquire about two school teachers who were reportedly still being detained without trial at the beginning of the year. One, Juvénal Kubegusa, was arrested in October 1981 apparently because the authorities learned that he was writing a political critique of Burundi. He had previously been held without trial from June 1980 until early 1981, when a number of students who had criticized government policies were detained. Daniel Bacinoni, the other detained teacher, was arrested in March 1982 apparently because he was suspected of having links with an opposition political party based outside the country. By the end of the year, neither of the two was known to have been brought to trial; however, it was unclear if they were still being detained or if they had been released.

Amnesty International was also concerned about a number of short-term detentions which appeared to be politically motivated. The wife of a former political prisoner was arrested and held for several months when she returned to Burundi after living abroad and a former political detainee who had been out of the country for several months was reportedly arrested when he returned in January. However, he escaped from custody shortly after his arrest.

Cameroon

Amnesty International was concerned about the continuing detention without trial of one prisoner of conscience who had been held since 1976, and investigated the cases of 10 other untried detainees considered likely to be prisoners of conscience. The organization was also concerned about reports of beatings inflicted on both criminal and political prisoners after a riot at Yaoundé central prison.

President Biya's authority as Head of State was contested by former President Ahmadou Ahidjo, who resigned from office in favour of President Biya in November 1982 but remained President of the ruling party, the *Union national camerounaise* (UNC), Cameroon National Union, until September 1983. In August 1983, President Biya announced the detention of Commandant Ibrahim Oumarou (an administrative officer) and Captain Salatou Adamou, an aide-de-camp on the staff of former President Ahidjo, who had left Cameroon shortly before the arrests. All three were accused of plotting to assassinate President Biya. They had not been formally charged or tried by the end of the year.

Amnesty International continued to appeal throughout the year for the release of Martin Ebele-Tobbo, a prisoner of conscience who was still held at Tcholliré *Centre de ré-education*, "re-education" centre, at the end of the year. He was the sole remaining prisoner from a group of 200 students, teachers and workers who were detained in July 1976 apparently on suspicion of distributing anti-government literature. On 10 November 1983 Amnesty International wrote to President Biya to clarify whether or not Martin Ebele-Tobbo had been released. However, no reply was received.

Amnesty International also continued to appeal for the trial or release of Jean Kona and Thomas Mabong, who had both been detained since January 1982. They were close friends who, after a long period of residence in France, were detained when they returned to Cameroon on holiday. They were held apparently because an article considered to be critical of Cameroon had been found in Jean Kona's possession. This was believed to be an article by Jean-François Médard entitled "De l'Etat sous-développé au Cameroun" ("On the Under-development of the State in Cameroon"). Jean Kona was reportedly held at Tcholliré and Thomas Mabong at Yoko *prison de production*, labour camp.

Among the cases taken up for investigation as possible prisoners of conscience by Amnesty International were those of Winston Fonyonga, Vincent Nteh, Ferdinand Langsi and a man named Fokemba. They were among a group of 21 people who were detained in October 1982 in connection with a riot which had occurred during a public meeting concerning a land dispute between the villages of Bali and Mbengwi. They were subsequently released uncharged. The four were then re-arrested in March 1983, apparently to punish them for opposing local politicians and a member of the National Assembly in the dispute. They reportedly remained uncharged at the end of the year. The second arrest was carried out by officers of the *Brigade mixte mobile* (BMM), a paramilitary police force. Amnesty International had received reports in previous years that people arrested by the BMM had often been detained for considerable periods without trial. The organization repeatedly asked the authorities for information as to the basis for the arrest of the four detainees, but received no reply.

On 18 February prisoners at Yaoundé central prison rioted after a rumour had spread that they had been deliberately excluded from an amnesty (Law no. 82-21 of 26 November 1982) which in fact applied to people convicted of only minor criminal offences. As a result of the riot, several prisoners were reportedly beaten and doused with urine and human excrement in the presence of senior government officials. Some of those alleged to have participated in the riot, including political prisoners, were subsequently reported to have been transferred to administrative detention centres or camps, including Yoko, as a punishment. On 6 July Amnesty International wrote to Jean Fouman Akame, the Minister of Territorial Administration, asking whether the government had initiated an inquiry into the alleged ill-treatment of prisoners in connection with the riot. However, the organization had received no reply by the end of the year.

Cape Verde

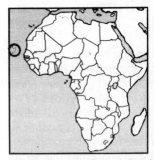

Eleven prisoners who were convicted in March 1982 of committing offences against the security of the state and sentenced to prison terms ranging from three to 10 years were released during the year. Seven other people convicted at the same trial had already been released by the end of 1982. These civilians had all been convicted by a military court but Amnesty International believed that insufficient evidence was produced at their trial to prove their guilt (see *Amnesty International Report 1983*).

Seven of the prisoners, who had received sentences of between three and five years' imprisonment, were released as a special act of clemency on 15 January. One of them, Osvaldo João Oliveira Rocha, died three weeks later. Members of his family claimed that his death had been caused by ill-treatment during his imprisonment, but the authorities denied this.

Three other prisoners were released some months later after their seven and nine-year prison sentences were reviewed in Praia by a *Tribunal de Execução de Penas*, a court which examines the implementation of sentences. The last of the 11, Albino Ferreira Fortes ("Bibino"), who was serving a 10-year sentence, was reportedly released in November on the orders of the same court.

In late 1982 Amnesty International had expressed concern about various aspects of the March 1982 trial to the authorities. The organization had concluded that some of the defendants had been convicted and given relatively severe sentences in part, at least, because of criticisms which they had made of government policies and because of their alleged links with an opposition political party.

The government replied by providing details of safeguards available to protect human rights and by claiming that all those convicted in March 1982 had been found guilty of committing criminal acts. In May, in reply to a further communication by Amnesty International, the government provided details of the various releases which had taken place. In the same month a new law was enacted restricting the jurisdiction of military courts, which were previously empowered to try all cases involving offences against the security of the state, to specifically military offences and offences considered to have an essentially military objective.

Central African Republic

Amnesty International was concerned about the imprisonment of prisoners of conscience and by the long-term detention without trial of suspected opponents of the government. A number of Chadian nationals who sought political asylum in the Central African Republic were among those detained. Amnesty International was also concerned that some aspects of the procedures at the trials of political prisoners did not accord with internationally recognized standards and about allegations of harsh prison conditions. No reports of executions were received during the year but three prisoners who were convicted of political offences in May 1982 remained under sentence of death at the end of 1983.

The military government headed by General André Kolingba remained in power and continued to maintain the ban on political activities which it imposed when it seized power in September 1981.

At the beginning of the year there were more than 100 untried political detainees at Kassaï military camp in Bangui. Some had been arrested in 1981 following a bomb explosion in Bangui, others being arrested in March 1982 when there was an alleged attempt to overthrow the government. Two opposition party leaders arrested in August 1982 and accused by a government minister of involvement in subversive activities were also in custody.

In all, some 65 of these detainees were brought to trial in 1983. Most of the others were released uncharged.

At the beginning of January five members of the banned opposition party, the *Mouvement de libération du peuple centrafricain* (MLPC), Central African People's Liberation Movement, were released apparently on the orders of a judge, after being held without trial for 12 months for attending a political meeting.

In February, the wife of the MLPC leader, Lucienne Patasse, who was arrested after her husband evaded arrest in March 1982, was released, together with Agnès M'Baïkoua, the wife of a Minister who had also evaded arrest, and Charlotte Fayanga, a member of the MLPC's Political Bureau.

Most of the releases, however, occurred in September, when President Kolingba announced a partial amnesty to celebrate the second anniversary of his military government's accession to power. Amnesty International learned that 40 political prisoners were released, all but four of them untried detainees. By the end of the year, only a few political detainees remained untried.

Further arrests took place of suspected opponents of the government. In February, 17 people were arrested after workers in the private sector went on strike in Bangui to protest against a government directive ordering them to contribute five per cent of their salaries to a "Fund for National Recovery". Those held included Théophile Sonny-Cole, the former Secretary General of the *Union générale des travailleurs centrafricains* (UGTC), Central African Workers General Union, which had been dissolved on government orders in May 1981. Amnesty International appealed for the release of these detainees. They were freed, uncharged, in May.

Several asylum seekers from neighbouring Chad were also detained during the year although in most cases they were later released and permitted to leave the country. However, at least two Chadians were still being held at the end of the year. Ousmane Gam, a former close associate of Chad's President Hissène Habré, who had been detained in Chad for political reasons, escaped from prison in May and entered the Central African Republic in June. He was immediately arrested and both he and another Chadian, Baradine Adoum, were reportedly for a time at risk of forcible repatriation.

Trials involving some 65 political prisoners altogether took place in April, June, October and November before the Special Tribunal. This court, which was established shortly after a bomb explosion in July 1981, has jurisdiction over all cases of a political nature. It is composed of three judges: the court president is a civilian judge but the other two judges are army officers. Legal representation is permitted but there is no right of judicial appeal from the Special Tribunal, as there is from other criminal courts. Defendants may not even challenge the legal grounds of their conviction before the *Cour de cassation*, cassation court.

In April, two leading members of the *Front patriotique oubanguien – Parti du travail* (FPO-PT), Oubangui Patriotic Front – Labour Party, and the brother of one of them, went on trial in Bangui. The trial was attended by an Amnesty International observer. Abel Goumba, the FPO-PT leader, and Patrice Endjimoungou, the party's spokesperson in France, allegedly infringed the ban on political activities and were responsible for writing articles for a party publication which were critical of the government. They were also accused of having contact with a foreign power after the authorities discovered a number of letters which Abel Goumba had addressed to politicians in France. Abel Goumba and Patrice Endjimoungou were both convicted and sentenced to five-year prison terms. Patrice Endjimoungou's brother was convicted on a lesser charge of insulting the head of state in a private letter and was fined and released. All three defendants had been adopted as prisoners of conscience by Amnesty International following their arrest in August and September 1982. Abel Goumba and Patrice Endjimoungou were freed in September when President Kolingba granted a partial amnesty to political prisoners.

Twenty-two other detainees, including several members of the MLPC, were also brought to trial in April to face charges arising from an alleged coup attempt in March 1982. At this and subsequent related trials it became clear that there had been no violent action against the government on 3 March 1982, but that an announcement by one government Minister, General François Bozize, who had claimed on the radio that an attempt was being made to overthrow the government, had itself been interpreted by the authorities as a coup attempt. In all, 15 of those tried at the end of April were acquitted. Six others were convicted and imprisoned for periods of one to three years; three on charges of impeding official attempts to arrest one of the alleged ringleaders of the March 1982 coup attempt and three others for impeding an official search of the house of Ange Patasse, the MLPC leader, five months before the coup attempt, in October 1981.

A further trial occurred in June when 23 people appeared before the Special Tribunal accused of responsibility for a bomb explosion in July 1981, which had resulted in a number of deaths. In May 1982 six people had been tried on related charges of possessing explosives and five had been sentenced to death, two of them *in absentia*. At the trial in June 1983 one defendant admitted complicity in the bomb explosion but all the others denied involvement. Thirteen defendants were convicted. There appears to have been little evidence to connect some of those convicted with the bomb attack and Amnesty International believed that some may have been convicted on account of their membership of the *Mouvement centrafricain de libération nationale* (MCLN), Central African Liberation Movement, whose leader, Iddi Lala, had publicly claimed responsibility for the explosion. The MCLN was banned after the explosion. Three received life sentences and the others were sentenced to 10 years' imprisonment. Ten of the defendants were acquitted.

In October and November, 17 people, including former leading MLPC members, appeared before the Special Tribunal at a series of separate trials on charges of complicity in the alleged March 1982 coup attempt. An Amnesty International observer attended the four-day trial of four civilian MLPC members who were charged with complicity in the coup attempt. Two of them, both members of the MLPC's Political Bureau, were eventually convicted, but not on charges relating to the coup attempt. Instead, they were sentenced to two-year prison terms for "advocating disobedience to the government's orders": their alleged offences had consisted of signing a letter sent to President Kolingba in

January 1982, in which the MLPC Political Bureau had complained about the harassment of MLPC members and had called for his resignation. Both had been adopted by Amnesty International as prisoners of conscience. The two other defendants were not convicted, but had their cases referred back to the prosecution for further inquiries. One was accused of MLPC activities after the military government banned all political activities in September 1981. He was adopted by Amnesty International as a prisoner of conscience. The other was accused of provoking violence shortly after the alleged coup attempt, when members of the security forces tried to arrest one of the ringleaders.

Five of the other 13 defendants who were tried in October and November were acquitted. None of the remaining eight were convicted for involvement in the coup attempt. However, an army officer, Michel-Paulin Bondeboli, who had been a member of the military government in March 1982, was convicted of failing to reveal his alleged prior knowledge of a plot against the government and was sentenced to three years' imprisonment. He had apparently failed to report for duty when summoned by the head of state shortly after General Bozize had claimed there was an impending coup attempt. Two other former members of the military government were tried on similar charges but were not convicted: the court referred their cases back for further inquiries. The cases of all three prisoners were taken up by Amnesty International for investigation.

The Amnesty International observer who attended two trials, in April and November, reported that defendants were given adequate opportunities on both occasions to present their defence. However, Amnesty International was concerned that at both trials defendants were convicted for having exercised their basic right to freedom of expression without having used or advocated violence and that neither the defendants convicted at these trials, nor any others convicted by the Special Tribunal had the right to appeal against their conviction or sentence. The organization was also concerned that at these and other trials, some defendants were convicted of relatively minor offences, but had been kept in pre-trial custody for 18 months on the grounds that they had committed serious offences against the security of the state.

Amnesty International was concerned about various aspects of the conditions in which political prisoners were held, particularly the lack of medical facilities and the infrequency of family visits. At the end of May Mathieu Gonda, a political detainee being held in pre-trial custody on suspicion of involvement in the March 1982 coup attempt, died after being denied appropriate medical attention. He had been suffering from generalized oedema for some time. At the same time two other political detainees were reported to be seriously ill after being refused medical attention.

Political detainees at Kassai military camp, where conditions were said to be cramped and very uncomfortable, were transferred to Bangui's central Ngaragba prison in March. Although some aspects of their conditions were said to be better at Ngaragba prison, detainees continued to complain about the difficulty of obtaining medical attention or of seeing relatives, lawyers or priests. In August, President Kolingba apparently intervened to ensure that political detainees were allowed weekly family visits. Amnesty International was also concerned about reports that a number of inmates of Ngaragba prison who were accused of committing non-political offences had been severely beaten by prison guards. The 13 prisoners convicted by the Special Tribunal in June were reportedly held in particularly harsh conditions in the prison's "Birao" block, along with the three others sentenced to death in May 1982. Temperatures are particularly high inside this block. The inmates were reportedly sleeping on the floor without mats or mattresses and were not allowed any exercise in the prison courtyard, nor any visits from their families. Amnesty International was concerned that their conditions of imprisonment were being made particularly harsh as a deliberate form of punishment.

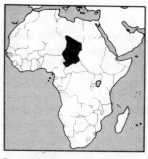

Chad

Amnesty International was concerned about alleged extrajudicial executions and by the detention without trial of real or suspected political opponents of the government headed by President Hissène Habré.

There was renewed fighting between forces loyal to Hissène Habré, who took control of the capital, N'Djamena, in June 1982 and whose government was officially constituted in October 1982, and those supporting former President Goukouni Oueddei's *Gouvernement d'union nationale de transition* (GUNT), Transitional Government of National Unity. During the year the GUNT's military forces were organized into the *Armée nationale de libération* (ANL), National Liberation Army. The GUNT came under the command of a new political body, the *Conseil national de libération* (CNL), National Liberation Council. The most serious armed clashes between forces loyal to President Habré and ex-President Goukouni occurred between May and August. By the end of that period GUNT forces occupied virtually the entire northern part of the country centred on the town of Faya-Largeau, which changed hands several times. There was foreign involvement in the conflict: the GUNT received Libyan support and Libyan aircraft flew missions in support of GUNT forces, although Libya denied having any troops on Chadian soil. French and Zairian troops were deployed in support of President Habré's government.

Both government forces and those supporting the GUNT were alleged to have extrajudicially executed prisoners taken in the course of the conflict. Both sides claimed to have taken over 1,000 prisoners. Most of the allegations of extrajudicial executions were made against President Habré's forces, which allegedly committed them for political reasons not only in areas of armed conflict but also in other parts of the country under government control. In such areas there was evidence to suggest that some victims were real or suspected critics or opponents of the government who were not involved in armed conflict. On 3 March Amnesty International expressed its concern to President Habré about these alleged killings, citing individual cases of people who had reportedly been killed or who had "disappeared" in 1982, and calling both for an inquiry and for urgent measures to be taken to prevent further such killings.

In November, members of President Habré's administration in a meeting with Amnesty International delegates referred to two of the cases mentioned by Amnesty International. In the case of Raymond Matha, an engineer, they claimed that he had died of illness on the night of 29–30 August 1982 while in detention. They denied that he had been extrajudicially executed. They also claimed that the former Prefect of Moundou, Karhyom Ningayo, had been a victim of armed conflict rather than having been extrajudicially executed as Amnesty International had reported. The Chadian delegation undertook to inquire into the whereabouts of other prisoners whose names were submitted by Amnesty International.

There were other reports of political killings by government forces in 1983, particularly in southern Chad. In April, as many as 40 civilians were reportedly killed in the Doba region in retaliation for attacks carried out in the area by armed opponents of President Habré's government. In July, eight police officers were reportedly the victim of extrajudicial executions at Kélo after they had been suspected of being connected with an attack on installations of the national cotton company, Cotontchad. Yacob Bawoyeu Langue, Police Commissioner of Laï, was taken to N'Djamena and detained in connection with the same attack. His body was reportedly found in N'Djamena on 15 August bearing signs of torture. In November, Chadian delegates agreed that Yacob Bawoyeu Langue had died while in custody on that date but denied that his death had resulted from torture or other deliberate ill-treatment.

Forces loyal to ex-President Goukouni may have extrajudicially executed up to 15 suspected political opponents at Abéché between 8 and 10 July, but Amnesty International was unable to confirm whether such executions had taken place. On 9 September the organization wrote to ex-President Goukouni requesting further information about the allegations but received no reply.

On 10 October, after it had addressed several inquiries to President Habré's government without response, Amnesty International publicly expressed its concern about more than 160 reported extrajudicial executions since mid-1982. In response, the Information Minister Mahamat Soumaila reportedly declared on 11 October that Amnesty International's information was based on the testimony of "people of bad faith" and that the organization was welcome to send a mission to Chad to investigate its concerns. He said it was possible, however, that some people had been killed accidentally during the armed conflict between government and GUNT forces. He also reportedly called on Amnesty International to denounce alleged killings by GUNT forces. Mahamat Soumaila did not mention any of the specific cases cited in Amnesty International's previous communications to the government. On 8 November, Amnesty International wrote to Mahamat Soumaila stating that the organization had received unconfirmed reports that civilians had been extrajudicially executed by GUNT forces, but that Amnesty International considered that such reports did not diminish the responsibility of the government to uphold the fundamental rights of government-held prisoners. Amnesty International also requested that the government indicate a suitable date for an Amnesty International mission. The organization had not received a reply by the end of the year.

Amnesty International was also concerned about reports that the government security forces detained suspected political opponents. Some of these detainees may have been prisoners of conscience. There were fears for the physical safety of some of those thus detained. Pierre Ousmane Touadé, a lawyer and journalist and a former leader of the *Parti national pour le développement du Tchad* (PNDT), National Party for the Development of Chad, was arrested in Moundou in August 1982 and transferred to a place of detention in N'Djamena, where he was reportedly still detained in March. Although the authorities are reported to have stated that he was still alive after that date, Amnesty International was unable to establish his whereabouts and was concerned that he might have "disappeared". Maurice Lapia, the former parliamentary Deputy of Bongor, was also reported to have been arrested in late 1982 and to have been transferred to N'Djamena. Neither Maurice Lapia nor Pierre Ousmane Touadé were known to have been charged, both apparently being detained because they were suspected of being actual or potential opponents of the government. Amnesty International made several appeals for further information about them but received no reply.

Amnesty International received reports from several towns and villages in southern and eastern Chad that people had been detained by government troops either because they were suspected of complicity with anti-government forces or held as hostages for members of families known to be opposed to the government. At Abéché, over 150 people, including the Imam of the central mosque and members of the family of the Sultan of Abéché, were detained in July apparently because they had made contact with advancing GUNT forces, pleading with them not to bombard the undefended town. Amnesty International considered that the 150 were probably prisoners of conscience. Possible prisoners of conscience detained in other southern towns included Babouh Yakouma and Kimitine Tangoïna at Eré, who were detained apparently because they were related to people who were suspected of having launched a guerrilla attack in the area in July.

On 7 June, the first anniversary of the capture of N'Djamena by his forces, President Habré announced an unconditional amnesty for people imprisoned for offences against state security and a reduction of sentences for some common law prisoners. At the same time the authorities announced that all Chadians in exile were free to return. Between 21 and 23 June, 223 prisoners were officially said to have been released in accordance with this amnesty. They comprised 113 civilians whom the government announced had been detained for crimes against state security, and 110 people said to have been combatants. Although the government published the names of those released, Amnesty International was unable to establish under what circumstances they had been detained or where they had been held. However, the organization noted that a number of prisoners whose names had been reported to the organization in preceding months, such as Maurice Lapia and Pierre Ousmane Touadé, were not included among the names of those released under the terms of the amnesty. The organization was unable to establish whether or not they had been released by the end of the year.

Comoros

The principal concerns of Amnesty International were the short-term detention or imprisonment of suspected political opponents of the government and the beating or ill-treatment of political detainees, some of whom may have been prisoners of conscience.

Between 8 and 12 January, 10 or more people including members of the *Front démocratique*, Democratic Front party, were detained on suspicion of having written or distributed a newspaper article accusing President Ahmed Abdallah of corruption. Amnesty International received reports that some or all of those detained may in fact have had no connection with the article in question and that they may have been detained on account of their membership of an opposition political party. On 5 February, four of those arrested were acquitted by the *Tribunal correctionnel de Moroni*, Moroni Criminal Court, while the six remaining defendants were convicted of libel and insulting the Head of State and sentenced to up to four months' imprisonment. In response to an inquiry from Amnesty International, the Minister of Justice, Saïd Tourqui, wrote to the organization on 11 March confirming the names of the six people convicted. He stated that their trial had been public and that the defendants had been able to choose their own counsel. At an appeal hearing on 23 March the sentences passed on the six were increased to eight months' imprisonment of which five months were suspended. Amnesty International was unable to ascertain the nature of the evidence presented either at the original trial or the appeal hearing. On 30 May, a new Minister of Justice, Mohammed Moumini, confirmed in a letter to the organization that the six were released between 11 and 13 April after serving three months in prison.

Between 20 and 50 people suspected of membership of the *Front démocratique* were reportedly arrested in mid-July apparently because some of them had applied to contest local elections on 24 July. They included at least two people who had previously been held in January: Abdou Mhoumadi – who was one of those convicted on 5 February – and Aboubacar Boïna. Some of the detainees were reportedly beaten by officers of the federal police prior to their release on 4 August. One woman was reportedly raped by police officers while in their custody. A former minister, Hadji Hassanali, was released on 10 August after being held for some three weeks at the headquarters of the *gendarmerie* in Moroni. It was not known whether his arrest was connected with the arrest of the suspected members of the *Front démocratique* in July.

President Abdallah reportedly announced a partial amnesty of both political and common law prisoners on 13 May, the fifth anniversary of his accession to the presidency. Amnesty International wrote to the authorities to seek further information about the precise terms of the amnesty but received no reply. However, unofficial reports indicated that no prisoners of conscience were being held immediately after the amnesty.

Congo

Most of the approximately 50 political detainees whose cases were known to Amnesty International were released during the year, although former President Joachim Yhombi-Opango continued to be held without trial. Two people associated with him were released from detention but were subject to restriction orders.

Congo acceded to the International Covenant on Economic, Social and Cultural Rights, the International Covenant on Civil and Political Rights (ICCPR), and the Optional Protocol to the ICCPR in October.

Congo celebrated the 20th anniversary of the *Trois Glorieuses*, Three Glorious Days, revolution in which the country's first head of state was deposed in August 1963. The occasion was marked by the release of most political detainees known to Amnesty International. They included more than 30 Angolan nationals from the Cabinda enclave who had been detained without trial since January 1977 on account of their alleged links with the *Frente de Libertação do Enclave de Cabinda* (FLEC), Cabinda Enclave Liberation Front. Thirty-four of them had been taken up for investigation by Amnesty International.

Several people who were detained in May 1982 and others who were arrested later in 1982 after two bomb explosions in Brazzaville were released in September. None of them had been charged or brought to trial. They included Abel Thauley-Ganga, a former trade union leader. Government sources also informed Amnesty International of the release of Bernard Kolelas, a former government official who had been detained for political reasons on previous occasions and had been formerly adopted as a prisoner of conscience by Amnesty International. However, according to reports received at the end of the year, Bernard Kolelas and one other political detainee were still being held.

Two people arrested with former President Yhombi-Opango in March 1979 after he had been deposed a month earlier, were also released from detention in August. However, they were restricted by being sent into internal banishment. Their cases were taken up for investigation by Amnesty International. Former President Yhombi-Opango was not released.

Earlier, in March and April, several refugees from Zaire who had been arrested in 1982 when they sought asylum in the Congo were released from custody. They included Kabeya Tchiang and Mupesse Impobakut, both of whom had left Zaire after being imprisoned there for political reasons. There were fears, however, that two other refugees from Zaire might have been repatriated against their will. Egbongo Mangongo and Tumba, both former military officers in Zaire, were detained in May when they sought asylum in Congo. Subsequently, there were unconfirmed reports that they had been sent back to Zaire.

Djibouti

Amnesty International was concerned about allegations of torture of detainees including former political refugees who had returned to Djibouti from exile.

Amnesty International received detailed allegations that two people were tortured in January at the Villa d'Ambouli, an interrogation centre, by officers of the *Brigade spéciale de recherche de la gendarmerie*, the Special Research Department of the *gendarmerie*. One of the alleged victims claimed after his release that he had been detained and tortured as a result of a personal dispute with an officer of the *gendarmerie*. He claimed to have been beaten while suspended from an iron bar and to have had his head repeatedly immersed in water to the point of suffocation. He also alleged that another detainee, Ahmed Abdallah, was transferred to Gabode prison after being tortured at the Villa d'Ambouli at the same time. However, Amnesty International was unable to confirm these detailed allegations.

In October the organization received reports that Ali Mohamed Houmed (known as "Moyale"), Hussein Houmed Ahmed, Ibrahim Mohamed (known as "Nahouda") and at least one other person suspected of belonging to the clandestine *Mouvement populaire de libération* (MPL), Popular Liberation Movement, were tortured at the Villa d'Ambouli by officers of the same security service. The four, who were apparently suspected of having perpetrated acts of political violence in 1979, were detained after returning from four years' exile in Ethiopia. Amnesty International was not aware of the circumstances of their return from Ethiopia. On 21 October Amnesty International urged President Hassan Gouled Aptidon to establish an official investigation into these reports of torture, recalling the undertaking to abolish torture which President Hassan Gouled Aptidon had made to an Amnesty International delegate in January 1980. Amnesty International had not received any reply by the end of the year, although the four were reportedly still being held at Gabode prison. It was not known whether charges had been brought against them.

On 1 February, the governments of Djibouti and Ethiopia entered into a tripartite agreement with the United Nations High Commissioner for Refugees which provided for the voluntary repatriation from Djibouti of some 35,000 refugees from Ethiopia. Amnesty International investigated allegations of the forcible repatriation of some of the refugees but was unable to confirm that any refugees had been repatriated to Ethiopia against their will. Over 7,000 refugees had apparently returned voluntarily and safely to Ethiopia by the end of the year.

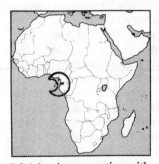

Equatorial Guinea

Amnesty International was concerned that a trial of 26 people accused of plotting to overthrow the government may not have been conducted in accordance with internationally recognized standards for a fair trial, and was concerned about the use of the death penalty.

Between 30 and 80 people are believed to have been arrested in May, mostly in Malabo, in connection with an alleged plot to overthrow the government. There was no official announcement of the arrests at first but after several weeks the authorities confirmed the arrest of some 20 to 30 soldiers and civilians allegedly implicated in the plot to kill the head of state and overthrow the government. The authorities alleged that Pablo Esono Obama Eyang, a former member of the military government, had been responsible for promoting the conspiracy. He was apparently among those arrested.

In mid-May, Sergeant Venancio Mikó, one of those arrested,

escaped from Blabich (Black Beach) Prison in Malabo and sought asylum in the Spanish embassy. He alleged that he had been severely beaten while in custody. However, he was handed back to the Equatorial Guinean authorities at the end of May after the Spanish Government apparently obtained an assurance that he would neither be executed nor subjected to torture.

On 1 July 26 people were brought to trial before a military court in Malabo charged with plotting to kill the head of state and overthrow the government. Others arrested in connection with the plot were apparently released uncharged. Three of the defendants, Venancio Mikó and two former military government ministers, Carmelo Owono Ndongo Andeme and Gregorio Micha Ela Obono, faced the most serious charges of directly planning to assassinate President Obiang Nguema Mbasogo and overthrow his government. The 23 others, who apparently included Pablo Esono Obama Eyang, were accused of aiding and assisting them. The trial lasted three days and was open to the public. The three principal defendants were convicted and sentenced to death. However, Amnesty International was unable to obtain further information about the verdicts or sentences of the other defendants.

Two of those sentenced to death, Carmelo Owono Ndongo Andeme and Gregorio Micha Ela Obono, were executed on 6 July, the day after their sentences were announced. Venancio Mikó was not executed apparently because of the assurance given to the Spanish authorities in May. However, his sentence was not commuted and at the end of the year he remained under sentence of death at Blabich Prison. Following the executions on 6 July, Amnesty International appealed to the government to extend clemency to Venancio Mikó and any other prisoners who might be sentenced to death.

The trial in July of Venancio Mikó and other prisoners appears to have failed to conform to internationally recognized standards in certain respects. Neither the three prisoners sentenced to death nor others who may have been convicted were able to appeal to a higher court against their conviction and sentence. It also appeared that the two prisoners who were executed had been given no opportunity to submit formal pleas for clemency to the head of state.

Ethiopia

Amnesty International was concerned about the imprisonment of prisoners of conscience. It was also concerned that real or suspected opponents of the government were being detained indefinitely without charge or trial, some having been held for over nine years. The authorities continued to fail to account satisfactorily for some 15 political prisoners and an abducted church leader who "disappeared" in 1979. Amnesty International received allegations of the widespread use of torture and harsh conditions of imprisonment.

There was continued armed conflict between the government and armed opposition organizations in Eritrea, Tigray, the Ogaden and other regions. In these areas civilians were reportedly subjected to violations of their human rights, including arbitrary imprisonment and executions, although independently verified details were often difficult to obtain. On two separate occasions, in April and August, the opposition Tigray People's Liberation Front abducted several people, including foreign nationals, but released them some weeks later.

Amnesty International was not able to make any reliable estimate of the total number of prisoners of conscience or other political prisoners in the country. The political prisoners known to the organization were only a small proportion of the several thousand believed to be imprisoned in 1983. Details concerning those imprisoned and the grounds for their imprisonment were difficult to obtain because the authorities disclosed no information on political prisoners and because relatives and friends of those arrested feared reprisals if they publicized arrests. Arrests were made without legal formalities and prisoners had no legal recourse. Many arrests were not officially acknowledged and some of those arrested were feared to have "disappeared". The majority of political prisoners were detained for an indefinite period without charge or trial. Their cases were subject to review by a committee of police, security and justice officials but the findings of the committee were not published and were not binding on the government.

Amnesty International continued to appeal for the release of 19 close relatives of the late Emperor Haile Selassie who had been detained without trial since 1974, and 21 members of the Oromo nationality (or ethnic group) who had been detained without trial since 1980. All were adopted as prisoners of conscience. The late Emperor's relatives were apparently being held for their family connections with the overthrown government. They had been arrested in Addis Ababa during the 1974 revolution and were transferred in 1975 from house arrest to *Alem Bekagne* ("End of the world") prison, where they were still being held in 1983. Nine of them were freed in an amnesty in September 1983 when the government announced the release of 117 political prisoners among a total of 1,163 prisoners freed on the occasion of the ninth anniversary of the revolution. Among those released was Rebecca Asrate. Amnesty International had appealed to the authorities for her to be allowed specialist medical treatment for a severe skin disease. Those still detained at the end of 1983 included Tenagnework Haile Selassie, the late Emperor's daughter, and her four daughters, one of whom, Hirut Desta, underwent surgery for skin cancer during 1983 and was reportedly still ill and seriously underweight at the end of the year.

The 21 Oromo prisoners of conscience had been detained without trial since February 1980, when large numbers of Oromos in Addis Ababa were arrested for allegedly having links with the opposition Oromo Liberation Front. Amnesty International believed that they had been arrested principally because of their nationality (ethnic origin) and had not used or advocated violence. Five of them were released during 1983. The others, who included Zegeye Asfaw, who was Minister of Law and Justice when he was arrested, Tsehai Tolessa, the wife of the Reverend Gudina Tumsa (see below), and Martha Kumsa, a journalist, were still detained at the end of the year.

Among others believed to be imprisoned for their non-violent beliefs were over 30 officials of the Ethiopian Evangelical Mekane Yesus Church, which is a member of the Lutheran World Federation. Desta Buba, the Secretary of the Church's Central Synod, who was arrested in April 1979, and Reverend Olana Lemu, President of the church's Western Synod, who was arrested in September 1982, were still being held uncharged at the end of the year in Nakamte prison in Wollega region, in western Ethiopia. Many other pastors and lay officials of the church had been arrested between 1979 and 1982 and further arrests, particularly in Wollega region, were reported in 1983. The authorities, while reiterating the official policy of freedom of religious worship, appeared nonetheless to suspect members of this church of having links with the opposition Oromo Liberation Front, which the church authorities denied. Members of smaller protestant churches such as the Meserete Christos Church, Kale Hiwot Church, Baptists and Jehovah's Witnesses, were also reportedly imprisoned in 1983. Some members of the Beta Yisrael community (known as *Falashas* or Ethiopian Jews) were allegedly imprisoned for their religious activities or for trying to evade the severe restrictions on emigrating to Israel. Leaving the country illegally is a serious political offence in Ethiopia punishable by lengthy imprisonment or even under certain circumstances the death penalty.

Five employees of the United Nations Economic Commission for Africa in Addis Ababa continued to be held at the beginning of 1983 after being arrested on political grounds on separate occasions between 1979 and 1982. Two were released during 1983 but at the end of the year Azeb Abaye, a secretary, and two others were still held in incommunicado detention without having been charged. Amnesty International was investigating whether they were prisoners of conscience.

Reports were received in December of a new wave of arrests in Addis Ababa of alleged political opponents of the government. The government subsequently announced that Asegahegn Araya, a former senator, and 17 other alleged leaders and sympathizers of the clandestine opposition Ethiopian People's Democratic Alliance had been arrested on 8 December and were being held for investigation into anti-revolutionary activities.

Several hundred political prisoners were reportedly held in the Central Revolutionary Investigation Department known unofficially as the "third police station"', in Addis Ababa. Those arrested on political grounds in the capital were reportedly first taken there for interrogation. Some detainees were said to have been held there for three years or more. In *Alem Bekagne* prison, over 1,500 of the 5,000 or more people imprisoned (who were said to include convicted criminal prisoners and prisoners captured in armed conflict situations) were said to be political prisoners arrested in recent years on suspicion of belonging to or collaborating with clandestine political opposition groups, such as the Ethiopian People's Revolutionary Party or the All-Ethiopia Socialist Movement (*Me'isone*), or armed opposition organizations such as the Eritrean People's Liberation Front, the Tigray People's Liberation Front or the Oromo Liberation Front. Political detainees were also being held in regional prisons around the country, particularly in Asmara, Gondar, Dessie, Dire Dawa and Harar.

Amnesty International was also investigating allegations that people were arrested in 1983 for attempting to leave the country illegally for political reasons, for allegedly having been in contact with opposition organizations while studying or travelling abroad, or for refusing to join the militia.

A Voluntary Repatriation Program for Ethiopian refugees in Djibouti was initiated on 1 February under a tripartite agreement between the Governments of Ethiopia and Djibouti and the United Nations High Commissioner for Refugees. The Ethiopian Government had promulgated a decree granting amnesty to refugees returning to Ethiopia from Djibouti. Amnesty International was investigating during the year whether any Ethiopian refugees in Djibouti were returned to Ethiopia against their will or whether any refugees were imprisoned on their return. However, the organization was unable to verify any cases of forcible repatriation or of the imprisonment of returning refugees. By the end of the year over 7,000 of the 35,000 Ethiopian refugees in Djibouti had apparently returned voluntarily and safely to Ethiopia.

The authorities provided no further clarification on the fate or whereabouts of 15 political detainees who "disappeared" in July 1979 after being taken from the prison where they had been held. The government denied that they had "disappeared" but by the end of 1983 had not provided any evidence that they were still in detention. Their relatives had had no knowledge of their whereabouts or fate since their "disappearance". Most were widely feared to have been secretly executed soon after their "disappearance". They included nine members of the former government who were arrested in 1974; the former Patriarch of the Ethopian Orthodox Church, *Abuna* (Archbishop) Tewoflos, who was arrested in 1976; and five leaders of *Me'isone* who were arrested in 1977 for opposing the military government.

No further information was received concerning the fate of the Reverend Gudina Tumsa, General Secretary of the Ethiopian Evangelical Mekane Yesus Church, who "disappeared" after being abducted in July 1979. His abduction appeared to have been carried out by people acting for the government but the authorities denied responsibility and claimed that he had left to join the opposition Oromo Liberation Front.

Amnesty International received new reports of torture of political prisoners in 1983. Torture was reportedly routinely used to interrogate prisoners in the "third police station" in Addis Ababa and elsewhere. Torture methods reportedly included beatings on the body and on the soles of the feet while the victim was suspended upside down; crushing of the bones of the hands; and electric shocks. The detainees under interrogation were held incommunicado in overcrowded unhygienic conditions – their detention in many cases not being officially acknowledged. Several prisoners allegedly died following torture or the denial of appropriate medical treatment.

Prison conditions in *Alem Bekagne* prison and other prisons where political detainees were held were said to be poor, although detainees were allowed to receive their daily food, basic necessities, some correspondence and occasional visits from relatives. Medical treatment was reportedly often inadequate and delayed.

Gabon

Amnesty International was concerned about the continued imprisonment of 18 prisoners of conscience, 17 of whom were sentenced to long prison terms in November 1982 after a trial which was not in accordance with internationally recognized standards for a fair trial. The organization also received disturbing reports of prisoners being subjected to cruel, inhuman and degrading treatment.

Gabon acceded to the International Covenant on Civil and Political Rights on 21 January.

On 11 March, the eve of the 15th anniversary of the establishment of the *Parti démocratique gabonais* (PDG, Gabonese Democratic Party, President El-Hadj Omar Bongo announced a five-year reduction in the sentences imposed in November 1982 on 29 prisoners who had been convicted of threatening state security and insulting the head of state. All were adopted as prisoners of conscience by Amnesty International. The organization believed that, following the clemency decree announced on 11 March, all but 17 of those convicted in November 1982 had been released. The 17 remaining, however, continued to be imprisoned throughout the year. They included Jean-Marc Ekoh, a prominent educationalist and former government minister, and Michel Ovono, a mining engineer. They had all been accused of belonging to an illegal political group, the *Mouvement de redressement national* (MORENA), Movement for National Recovery.

An Amnesty International delegate, who had observed the trial of suspected members of MORENA in November 1982, reported that the trial was unfair, notably in that no substantive evidence was produced before the court to support the charge of threatening state security. Amnesty International informed the government of its findings in relation to the trial on several occasions and repeatedly appealed for the release of the 17 prisoners.

The other prisoner of conscience known to Amnesty International was Serge Edouard Etsine who was reportedly sentenced to three years' imprisonment by the *Tribunal correctionnel de Libreville*, Libreville Criminal Court, on 5 December 1981, having been accused of writing a document which criticized the Minister of Public Works. He was allegedly beaten and held in chains for some time while in pre-trial detention.

Amnesty International investigated the cases of three prisoners who may have been prisoners of conscience. Abbé Noël Ngwa-Nguema, a

Catholic priest and philosophy teacher, was reportedly sentenced to one year's imprisonment, subsequently increased to four years at an appeal hearing on 10 June. Three other people were believed to have been sentenced to similar terms, although their names were not known to Amnesty International. All four were apparently convicted of organizing opposition to the government. Two other prisoners whose cases were being investigated were Bidza Bonaventure, who had been sentenced to eight years' imprisonment in 1981 apparently for writing a magazine article critical of the government, and Jean-Marie Mbieleu Fosso, a Cameroonian sentenced to one year's imprisonment increased to 10 years' imprisonment on appeal. He was convicted of conspiracy and possession of firearms, but information received by Amnesty International suggested that he had no connection with the alleged conspiracy and may have been implicated simply because of his non-violent association with another defendant.

Amnesty International continued to receive reports of harsh conditions of imprisonment in the cases of both political and criminal prisoners at Libreville's main prison, Gros Bouquet, where all the prisoners of conscience known to Amnesty International were believed to be held. It was alleged that some prisoners who became ill received inadequate medical attention and that some prisoners, both criminal and political, were held in chains for considerable periods as a form of punishment. In October Amnesty International wrote to President Bongo to draw these allegations of the chaining of prisoners to the government's attention. The organization sought to clarify whether the use of chains as a form of punishment constituted government policy. Such practices are contrary to the provisions of the United Nations Standard Minimum Rules for the Treatment of Prisoners. However, no reply had been received from the government by the end of 1983.

Gambia

The trials of over 60 prisoners charged with treason in connection with the failed coup attempt of July 1981 continued in 1983 before the Special Division of the Supreme Court. Prior to their trials, which began in late October 1982, 127 other individuals had been tried before this court since its constitution in late 1981, on charges such as treason, kidnapping, robbery, murder and rape. Of these, 111 were convicted and sentenced, 35 receiving the death sentence. In late December 1983, the court was reported to have pronounced judgment on 34 of the 60 cases on trial. One death sentence and 10 prison terms of between seven and 10 years were imposed, while 23 other defendants were reportedly acquitted and discharged. All of those on trial were defended by counsel, and no procedural irregularities or other shortcomings at the trial were reported to Amnesty International. The trials of nearly 30 others had reportedly not been concluded by the end of the year.

In August 1983, the Gambian authorities announced the release of the remaining 51 detainees who had been arrested in connection with the failed 1981 coup but against whom no prosecution was eventually brought. Most were believed to have been arrested in late 1981 and, although their cases were reportedly reviewed by a semi-judicial body shortly after their arrest, none was apparently charged with an offence. One of the recommendations made in the report of Amnesty International's observer to the trials before the Special Division of the Supreme Court in January 1982, which was submitted to the authorities in June 1982 and made public in June 1983, was that the policy of holding detainees without charge for long periods should be ended. It was recommended that the authorities should promptly charge remaining detainees or release them.

During the year eight of the 35 death sentences imposed in 1982 were confirmed on appeal, bringing to 24 the number of such appeals which were rejected. However, two appeals were reportedly successful in May 1983, one apparently on the grounds of conflicting evidence and the other on the grounds that the offence committed was not treasonable and should not carry the death sentence. The first of the two prisoners was reportedly released. In November 1983, following an appeal for clemency from Amnesty International, the authorities informed the organization that the Advisory Committee on the Prerogative of Mercy, established according to law to advise the President on the use of his power of commutation, had been convened and would be making its recommendations to the President once all the trials before the Special

Division of the Supreme Court were concluded. None of the prisoners sentenced to death by the Special Division of the Supreme Court had been executed by the end of 1983.

In October 1983, the Gambian authorities announced the return to the Gambia, and subsequent detention, of three individuals who had fled the country following the failed 1981 coup attempt and had reportedly been granted asylum in Cuba. Their names were reported to be Fansu Camara, Bonakieu Jod and Seed Alias Gomez. They had apparently flown from Cuba to France in mid-September 1983, where, after a 24-hour stop-over, they boarded a plane for Senegal, where they were arrested and subsequently transferred to the Gambia. At the end of 1983, Amnesty International was investigating the circumstances of the return of the three Gambians to determine whether there had been an infringement of their internationally recognized right to non-repatriation to a country where their life or freedom would be threatened on account of their politically-motivated activities. The organization was also investigating the reported arrest and detention of 12 people between late October and early November 1983, apparently following statements which the three returned individuals had made while in custody. These included Sam Sarr, a teacher, Amie Sillah, a social services employee, Halifa Sillah, a sociologist, three other civilians and six police officers. By the end of the year Amnesty International was still attempting to establish the reasons for these apparently politically-motivated detentions and the legal basis for them.

Ghana

Amnesty International was concerned about the detention without trial of real or suspected opponents of the government and by trials before the Public Tribunals which did not conform to internationally recognized standards of fairness. There were allegations that detainees, particularly those detained in military custody, had been beaten, and disturbing reports of extrajudicial executions, notably after unsuccessful attempts to overthrow the government in February and June. However, the government was known to have prosecuted people, including public officials, who were suspected of carrying out political killings. Thirty-two people were reportedly sentenced to death by Public Tribunals, 19 of them *in absentia.* At least eight people were executed as a result of their conviction by Public Tribunals.

The government, headed by Flight-Lieutenant Jerry John Rawlings, had taken power on 31 December 1981 and continued in office throughout the year, despite several attempts to overthrow it. Apparently the most serious coup attempt occurred on 19 June when political prisoners, including people who were detained on suspicion of previous such attempts, escaped from prison in Accra and tried to overthrow the ruling Provisional National Defence Council (PNDC). Dozens of people were reportedly killed in the ensuing fighting.

The action the government took to investigate the murder of three judges and a former army officer in June 1982 remained controversial. The Special Investigation Board appointed by the government to investigate the murders issued its final report on 30 March, recommending the prosecution of 10 people on charges of murder or conspiracy to murder. The 10 included Joachim Amartey Kwei and Sergeant Alolga Akata-Pore, who were both members of the PNDC at the time of the murders, and ex-Captain Kojo Tsikata, the Head of Security and Special Advisor to the PNDC. In May, Attorney General George Aikins stated that, notwithstanding the recommendation of the Special Investigation Board, there was insufficient evidence to prosecute five of those named including Sergeant Akata-Pore and Captain Tsikata. Supporters of the government alleged that the Special Investigation Board's final report was politically biased and that its authors were determined to implicate Captain Tsikata in particular. Opponents of the government alleged that, in refusing to prosecute Captain Tsikata and Sergeant Akata-Pore, the government was attempting to hide the guilt of some of its own members.

Throughout the year individuals and groups of people were detained on suspicion of opposing the government. The largest such groups were of people arrested in the aftermath of alleged conspiracies or attempts to overthrow the government. After the jailbreak and coup attempt of 19 June, some hundreds of people, including lawyers, soldiers and students, were detained on suspicion of involvement in the attempted coup, or because they had welcomed the apparent overthrow of the PNDC. Most were released within a few days, but Amnesty International took up for investigation the cases of others who were held for longer periods, including Tommy Thompson, John Kugblenu and Mike Adjei, respectively the managing editor, the editor and the leading journalist of the *Free Press* newspaper, which had frequently criticized the government. The three were arrested in late June. The organization also investigated the case of Sam Okudzeto, a lawyer who was detained on 26 June. He was National President of the Association of Recognized Professional Bodies, an association of professional groups which had frequently criticized the PNDC. All four were held under Section 4 of PNDC Law 42, which gave the government wide powers of detention. Although the government stated that they were being investigated for possible subversion, and particularly for their alleged connection with the 19 June coup attempt, Amnesty International considered that they might be prisoners of conscience. They remained uncharged at the end of the year.

Amnesty International also took up for investigation as possible prisoners of conscience over 20 prisoners who had been detained since 1982. They included former members of the government of Dr Hilla Limann and former officials of the People's National Party who were held without trial. Among cases of people imprisoned apparently on suspicion of attempting to overthrow the government or of incitement to mutiny, Amnesty International investigated the case of Sergeant Alolga Akata-Pore, who was detained in November 1982 but remained uncharged at the end of 1983. The organization also investigated the case of Andrews Asare Kwame Pianim who had been convicted after an unfair trial of preparing to overthrow the government.

Amnesty International investigated the cases of several members of left-wing political organizations who had been detained in 1982 apparently for criticizing or opposing the government. Most were members of either the Movement on National Affairs (MONAS) or the June Fourth Movement (JFM). Both organizations were established in 1979 by supporters of the first government headed by Flight-Lieutenant Rawlings, the Armed Forces Revolutionary Council (AFRC). Two members of MONAS, Kwesi Agbley and Kweku Baako Kakraba, had been held without trial since February 1982, apparently because they were suspected of association with leading members of the opposition in exile. Some JFM members, including Kwame Agyeman and Vadis Kwasi Kamassah, were detained apparently because of their support for former members of the PNDC who had resigned or been dismissed, and on account of their criticism of the government's economic policy.

Several political detainees whose cases were being investigated by Amnesty International were released during the year. Former President Hilla Limann and former Vice-President Joseph de Graft Johnson were released on bail by the end of the year. However, nine former ministers or former members of parliament were still being held at the end of 1983 including George Garbrah, former Deputy Minister for Defence, and Dr John Nabila, former Minister for Presidential Affairs. Two members of the JFM, Tata Ofusu and Nicholas Atampugre, were reportedly released uncharged in November after being held for a year apparently on account of their association with Sergeant Akata-Pore and their criticism of government policy. In August five former ministers and members of parliament who had been held without trial since January

1982 were released uncharged. They included J. E. Adarkwa Yiadom and Roland Atta-Kesson. On 31 December, the second anniversary of the establishment of the PNDC, the government announced the release of at least one person whose case was being investigated by Amnesty International, former Minister of Fuel and Power, Franz Wulff Tagoe.

The Public Tribunals, established in August 1982 to try in particular cases of subversion, smuggling or corruption, heard a clearly political case for the first time. On 14 March, Major Seïdu Musah and 21 others appeared on charges relating to an attempted coup on 23 November 1982. On 11 March, Amnesty International urged the authorities to ensure that the trial was fair. Although Amnesty International had not at that point been able to observe the Public Tribunals at first hand, it was concerned about aspects of their structure, including the absence of internationally recognized safeguards such as the right of appeal. This suggested that they might not be fair. Amnesty International drew the authorities' attention to its previous unanswered requests for a visa for a delegate to observe sessions of the Public Tribunals. However, the organization received no reply.

The trial of Seïdu Musah and others ended on 3 August when the Public Tribunal sentenced one defendant, Kwame Pianim, to 18 years' imprisonment. All the other defendants were either acquitted or were sentenced *in absentia*. Amnesty International was especially concerned that Kwame Pianim was convicted solely on the testimony of one person who had apparently secured immunity from prosecution in connection with the 23 November coup attempt. Amnesty International also noted that one member of the five-member panel which heard the case against Kwame Pianim was not present during the delivery of the verdict and did not sign the judgment. This panel member later claimed that the Public Tribunal had been directed by the political authorities to deliver a guilty verdict against Kwame Pianim.

In August an Amnesty International observer was able to attend sessions of the Public Tribunals. The observer arrived in Ghana on 15 August, the day that Joachim Amartey Kwei and four others were sentenced to death after being convicted by a Public Tribunal of the murder of three judges and a former army officer in June 1982. Amnesty International was concerned not only about the death sentences but also about the fact that Joachim Amartey Kwei and his four co-defendants were not represented by legal counsel. The observer transmitted to the authorities a letter from Amnesty International expressing the organization's concern about the execution on 13 August 1983 of four people who were sentenced to death between 3 and 5 August.

During his mission, from 15 to 18 August, Amnesty International's delegate was able to observe sessions in cases then being heard by two

Public Tribunal panels. He also discussed the Public Tribunals with relevant officials including George Kwaku Agyekum, Chairman of the Board of Public Tribunals, and Kwamena Ahwoi, PNDC Coordinator for Investigations, Vetting and Tribunals. The delegate noted that, although the PNDC was empowered to review all death sentences passed by Public Tribunals, the review appeared to be extremely summary in the case of Amartey Kwei and others executed on 18 August.

On 26 October, taking into account the report of its trial observer, Amnesty International submitted to the authorities a memorandum on the Public Tribunals. The memorandum examined the operation and constitution of the Public Tribunals and proposed 10 specific amendments. Amnesty International concluded that there should be a right of appeal and that every Public Tribunal should include at least one qualified lawyer who should have the right to decide questions of law put to the panel. Amnesty International also called on the authorities to specify in any amendment to PNDC Law 24, the fundamental law governing the Public Tribunals, that proof was to be established "beyond all reasonable doubt". Amnesty International received no reply to its memorandum. However, the authorities published a revised version of the law governing the Public Tribunals in December, which had been in preparation since July. Amnesty International was unable to examine the revised law by the end of the year.

In some prisons warders beat criminal inmates, although the senior prison authorities sometimes acted to prevent such ill-treatment. The most severe beatings occurred at military detention centres including Burma Camp near Accra, and the military guardroom at the Castle, the government headquarters. Amnesty International was particularly concerned about reports that suspected political opponents of the PNDC were beaten at the Castle with the apparent knowledge of senior members of the government. Those reportedly beaten at the Castle included Kofi Ashiboe-Mensah, former PNDC Secretary for Trade.

At least 32 people were sentenced to death during 1983 for crimes including attempting to overthrow the government, murder, armed robbery, fraud and smuggling, all of them being convicted by Public Tribunals. Eight of the 32 were subsequently executed and one had his sentence commuted by the PNDC. Nineteen others were sentenced *in absentia*.

There were continuing reports of beatings and killings carried out by members of the armed forces, although the government condemned such actions on numerous occasions. Several members of the armed forces were prosecuted for murder or assault. However, Amnesty International was also concerned about reports that suspected political opponents of the government, including many suspected of armed opposition, were extrajudicially executed following attempted coups. In February, Lance Corporal Fitih was shot by soldiers at the Air Force Station near Accra after he had been suspected of involvement in a coup attempt. He later recovered from three bullet wounds. By the end of the year Amnesty International also received reports that between 30 and 70 people were extrajudicially executed by the security forces between 19 and 21 June, following the jailbreak and attempted coup of 19 June. They included people who had escaped from prison and had been recaptured: Kwame Agyeman, a civilian, and Sergeant Matthew Aawaar, a soldier, were reportedly shot at the Border Guards' guardroom. Amnesty International interviewed one civilian who was detained on 19 June and was subsequently shot without being killed at the Air Force Station guardroom. Although he reportedly had no connection with the 19 June coup attempt he was suspected of opposition to the government.

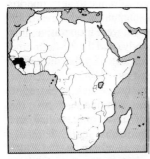

Guinea

Amnesty International's main concerns were the detention without trial of suspected political opponents of the government, the government's continued failure to account for a large number of political detainees who "disappeared" from custody in previous years, the torture of detainees and harsh prison conditions.

There were many reports in 1983 of detentions for political reasons but Amnesty International was often unable to verify them or to estimate the number of political detainees held at any given time because of the high level of official censorship affecting all communication between Guinea and the outside world and official secrecy regarding detentions. On the basis of information received in 1983, it appeared that Camp Boiro in Conakry, the main detention centre, contained an average of about 200 political detainees over recent years although this figure was occasionally temporarily increased by several hundred. Most detainees were apparently held for several months and then released or moved to another prison. Political detainees were also reportedly held during the year at the Alpha Yaya and Samory Toure military camps in Conakry and at several police stations in the capital, at Camp Keme Boureima in Kindia, and in police stations or prisons in at least seven other major towns. Reliable estimates for the number of political detainees held in these locations were not available. Exiled opposition sources provided estimates of the total number of political detainees which varied from several hundred to several thousand, but the accuracy of these claims was difficult to assess.

Many people were detained for openly expressing some form of dissent, however minor, from directives by local officials of the only authorized political party, the *Parti démocratique de Guinée*, the Guinean Democratic Party, or for criticizing some aspect of party policy. Others were reportedly detained for participating in student protests against obligatory agricultural work or because they were suspected by the authorities of attempting to leave Guinea without official permission. Many others appeared to have been arrested because they were suspected of having been connected with a grenade explosion at the *Palais du peuple*, People's Palace, in May 1980 or attempted sabotage at Conakry airport in February 1981.

None of those who were known to have been detained for political reasons in 1983 were believed to have been charged or tried by the court; arrests and subsequent detentions were often ordered by minor party officials or local administrators without reference to any superior authority, and the constitutional and legal safeguards which exist in Guinea to protect citizens against arbitrary arrest were inoperative. The 48-hour legal limit on *garde à vue* (police custody) and the 72-hour limit on preventive detention apparently were not respected by the authorities when arrests were made for political reasons. Political detainees received no protection from the judicial structure, which appeared to have no power to intervene in such cases. Detainees were often interrogated first by members of the *milice* (militia) or of the police, and then by political officials. In 1983, as in previous years, detainees branded as "counter-revolutionaries" or as members of the "fifth column" were usually transferred to Camp Boiro in Conakry and interrogated by the *Comité révolutionnaire* (Revolutionary Committee), a body which consisted of senior political officials and relatives of President Ahmed Sekou Toure and had sweeping powers of arrest and detention. The *Comité révolutionnaire* was believed by Amnesty International to make use of coercion and duress including torture to extract "confessions" from political detainees.

Amnesty International continued to investigate the case of Bah Mahmoud, a food technology engineer who had been detained without trial since August 1979 in connection with an alleged plot to destroy public buildings with explosives. At least 10 other people arrested at the same time as Bah Mahmoud are believed to have been extrajudicially executed by the authorities shortly after they were taken into custody, by means of the *diète noire*, "black diet" (total deprivation of food and water). Investigations were also made by Amnesty International into the case of Barry Mouctar, who was repatriated forcibly and extra-judicially from the Ivory Coast in April 1981. He was detained on arrival at Conakry and taken to Camp Boiro, where he was apparently interrogated in connection with the May 1980 grenade explosion. He reportedly continued to be held there without trial in 1983. Amnesty International made further inquiries in 1983 about two other Guineans, Cheik Mohamed Kone and Jack Soumah, who were forcibly and apparently unlawfully repatriated from Liberia in November 1981, where they had reportedly been linked to an exiled opposition grouping. Both were reportedly held in Camp Boiro.

The authorities continued to withhold information on the fate of some 2,900 political detainees who were arrested between 1969 and 1976 and reportedly "disappeared" in prison. Among the detainees were many former government ministers and senior civil servants, army officers, teachers, lawyers and medical personnel who were arrested in a series of purges and accused of "counter-revolutionary" or "fifth column" offences. Many of them were killed in prison, often by means of the "black diet", or died as a result of malnutrition and disease. Amnesty International sent appeals to the authorities throughout the year to end their policy of secrecy regarding political detainees and to supply information on the fate of 78 named "disappeared" detainees. In December 1981, at the time of an Amnesty International mission to Guinea, the authorities had agreed to provide information on the fate of those individuals, but they failed to do so in either 1982 or 1983.

There were eye-witness reports that torture and other forms of ill-treatment were regularly being used in many military camps, prisons and police stations as a means of intimidating individuals taken into custody and of extracting "confessions" from them. Beatings appeared to be administered as a matter of routine against newly-arrested detainees suspected of either criminal or political offences, often with several guards using rifle butts, sticks or truncheons. In many cases, suspects were bound tightly with rope or metal wire, a practice which often resulted in temporary paralysis. Many suspects were denied food and water for several days in order to weaken them and to facilitate the extraction of confessions. Individuals arrested on suspicion of serious political offences were usually held at Camp Boiro or at Camp Keme Boureima in Kindia. In both these camps victims were regularly beaten and deprived of food and water, burned with cigarettes and had electric shocks applied to the head, limbs and genitals. Standards of sanitation, nutrition and medical care remained unacceptably low. Most detainees were believed to be held in small, poorly ventilated cells and to be deprived of exercise. Conditions in the *tête de mort* ("death's head") quarter at Camp Boiro were described as particularly cruel, with detainees being held in grossly overcrowded and absolutely dark cells. All political detainees in Guinea were believed to be held incommunicado.

Guinea-Bissau

Amnesty International's main concern was the continued detention without trial of former government officials arrested after the coup which brought President João Bernardo Vieira to power in November 1980. By the end of the year all but two of these detainees had been released uncharged, although President Vieira had earlier accused some of them of being responsible for secret extrajudicial executions which had been committed by the previous administration of President Luiz Cabral.

Thirteen former officials of the Cabral government were in detention at the beginning of 1983. However, nine of them, all former members of the national security service, were released in May. Two others, both former senior members of the armed forces, were freed in November. None of them were charged or brought to trial despite government allegations that they had been responsible for secret extrajudicial executions carried out on government orders between 1975 and November 1980.

Only two of the long-term detainees were still believed to be in custody at the end of the year. They were Umaru Djalo, who was Minister of Defence before the coup of November 1980, and former Interior Minister Constantino Teixeira, who was arrested a few weeks after the coup when he returned from an overseas visit. However, official sources claimed that they were not imprisoned but that they were living under a form of house arrest. The authorities said that Raphael Barbosa, a political prisoner whose case was being investigated by Amnesty International and who had previously been in prison for political reasons prior to the November 1980 coup, was also no longer in prison but was living under house arrest.

In May the government released Leopoldo Alfama (known as "Duki Djassi"), who had been arrested in June 1982 in connection with an alleged plot against the government. Two other detainees who had been arrested at the same time, Honorio Fonseca and João da Costa, were released in November. After these releases, President Vieira claimed that there were no longer any political prisoners in Guinea-Bissau.

In May 38 people who had been sentenced to death in the mid-1970s reportedly had their sentences commuted to terms of imprisonment. They had apparently been convicted on charges relating to offences against the security of the state. All 38 were believed to have been subsequently released from prison.

Kenya

Amnesty International was concerned about the detention of prisoners of conscience and continued to investigate the cases of several people convicted of sedition who might be prisoners of conscience. The organization was also concerned about poor prison conditions; the "disappearance" and subsequent *refoulement* (involuntary repatriation) of several refugees; and the imposition of the death penalty.

Nine prisoners of conscience who had been adopted by Amnesty International continued to be held at the beginning of 1983, all having been arrested in 1982 and detained without trial under the Preservation of Public Security Act which permits detention without trial for an unlimited period (see *Amnesty International Report 1983*).

The conditions under which these detainees were held gave cause for concern. Visits from relatives were permitted only rarely and in some cases not at all. There were fears for the health of Al-Amin Mazrui, a university lecturer, and other detainees. In May Amnesty International wrote to President Daniel arap Moi to express concern about the continued detention of these prisoners of conscience and renewed its appeal for their release. Amnesty International also called for an investigation into the conditions under which they were held, but there was no reply from the government. However, in October, Oginga Odinga, a former Vice-President, and three others – John Khaminwa, a lawyer, Al-Amin Mazrui and university law lecturer Willy Mutunga – were freed soon after President Moi's inauguration for a second presidential term of office, following general elections in the country. The five other detainees were still held at the end of 1983.

Amnesty International continued to investigate the cases of Wang'ondu wa Kariuki, a journalist, and Maina wa Kinyatti, a university lecturer, both of whom were convicted in 1982 for possessing seditious literature and sentenced respectively to four-and-a-half and six-year prison terms.

In May 1983 Maina wa Kinyatti's appeal was rejected by the High Court.

Three new detention orders of indefinite duration were imposed in April, following the withdrawal of treason charges, on three people accused of involvement in an abortive attempt by members of the Kenya Air Force (KAF) to overthrow the government in August 1982. Raila Odinga, the son of Oginga Odinga, and Otieno Mak'Onyango, a newspaper editor, were still being held without charge or trial at the end of the year but Alfred Otieno, a university professor, was released in October. All three had remained in custody without official explanation after charges against them were dropped in March before their trial could begin. Amnesty International had issued an international appeal for their trial or release.

More than 60 university students were also arrested following the attempt to overthrow the government in August 1982 for allegedly demonstrating in support of the coup attempt. They were charged with sedition; however, all but six of the students were granted presidential clemency in February and were freed without standing trial. The other six were all tried, convicted and sentenced to five- or six-year prison terms. Three of the trials were attended in part by an Amnesty International observer, who reported that the proceedings appeared to have been conducted in accordance with internationally recognized standards. However, as Amnesty International subsequently informed President Moi, the observer expressed some doubt as to whether sufficient evidence had been produced to justify the students' conviction on charges of sedition.

The trials by courts-martial of former KAF personnel accused of involvement in the coup attempt of 1 August 1982 came to an end in March. Over seven months some 1,000 defendants were convicted of various offences and sentenced to prison terms ranging from six months to 28 years. Eleven of the defendants were sentenced to death for treason but two of these were subsequently released after the High Court quashed their convictions in late 1983. Appeals by the nine others were rejected by the High Court, which confirmed the death sentences imposed at the courts-martial. More than 550 former KAF personnel who had been arrested but not court-martialled were freed between February and June. Two civilians and the former Police Commissioner Ben Gethi, who were arrested in connection with the coup attempt, were also released after several months' detention without trial.

In early November up to seven Tanzanians who had earlier fled to Kenya to seek asylum were arrested and subsequently "disappeared" from police custody. They were apparently returned secretly to Tanzania against their will even though three of them had previously been recognized as refugees by the Kenyan authorities. Another of them was a naturalized Kenyan citizen. At the end of the year they were reportedly still being held by the Tanzanian authorities, although this had not been officially acknowledged.

In exchange the Kenyan authorities were believed to have received at least 16 Kenyan nationals who had fled to Tanzania to seek asylum and who were returned forcibly and secretly by the Tanzanian authorities. They were said to have included two self-confessed leaders of the August 1982 coup attempt, other former KAF personnel, two former members of parliament and some university students. At least 10 of them had reportedly been granted asylum in Tanzania; their return and detention had not been acknowledged by the Kenyan authorities by the end of 1983. These secret exchanges of alleged political opponents, (some of whom were recognized as refugees under the United Nations Convention and Protocol relating to the Status of Refugees), took place shortly before the meeting on 16 November between the Presidents of Kenya, Tanzania and Uganda, when they reportedly reached agreement on a number of political matters affecting all three East African states.

On 25 November Amnesty International expressed its serious concern to the Kenyan authorities about the alleged arrest and forcible return to custody in Tanzania of Tanzanian refugees in Kenya and inquired into the situation of refugees forcibly returned from Tanzania and detained in Kenya. The organization also urged President Moi's government to reaffirm its stated commitment to the protection of refugees in accordance with the United Nations Convention and Protocol Relating to the Status of Refugees, which Kenya has ratified. The authorities did not reply and by the end of the year had not disclosed the legal basis for the continued detention of those returned from Tanzania.

As described above, sentences of death were confirmed on nine former KAF personnel convicted of treason after the 1982 coup attempt. The death sentences had not been carried out by the end of the year. It was not known how many people were under sentence of death at the end of 1983 after being convicted of homicide or violent robbery, or whether any executions were carried out during the year. In August Amnesty International appealed to President Moi to commute the death sentences on the nine former KAF personnel and other condemned prisoners. In May, in his capacity as Chairman of the Organization of African Unity, President Moi had appealed to Malawi's Head of State to grant clemency to Orton and Vera Chirwa after they had been sentenced to death for treason.

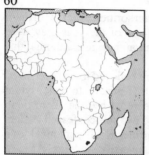

Lesotho

Amnesty International was concerned about the detention without trial of political detainees and the death in detention of one such political detainee. The organization remained concerned about the government's failure to reveal the cause of death of another political detainee who died in custody in late 1981 and to investigate thoroughly alleged extrajudicial executions committed in September 1981.

There was a continuing high level of tension between the governments of Lesotho and South Africa throughout the year, following a South African military incursion into Lesotho in December 1982 which resulted in more than 40 deaths. The Lesotho Government alleged on several occasions that new attacks had been made or were about to be launched from South Africa, and in mid-1983 the country was for some weeks under a virtual blockade as South African authorities imposed stringent controls at the borders.

As a result of South African pressure on the government, many South African refugees were obliged to leave Lesotho. More than 100 were reportedly air-lifted to Mozambique in January and others left later in the year. In August, the Lesotho Government appealed for international assistance with the resettlement outside Lesotho of South African refugees still resident there.

There were also further acts of sabotage attributed to the Lesotho Liberation Army (LLA), the military wing of one faction of the Basutoland Congress Party (BCP). In March, there was an apparent assassination attempt on the Minister of Agriculture and the government alleged on two occasions, in June and in August, that opposition forces had attempted to assassinate the Prime Minister. In December, the government announced that a new plot had been uncovered and that several people had been detained for questioning.

Amnesty International learned of several new detentions during 1983, but received insufficient information to be able to estimate how many people were detained for political reasons. Most of those held were believed to have been detained under the Internal Security (General) Act which empowers all members of the police to detain people whom they suspect of subversive activity and to hold them incommunicado for 14 days. Thereafter, the Commissioner of Police may authorize detention for another two weeks, following which the government minister responsible for security matters may sanction detention for a further 14 days, thereby permitting a maximum 42 days' detention.

Amnesty International received information which suggested that several political detainees had been kept in custody beyond the legally permitted period. Thakane Mohapi, a 30-year-old pregnant mother of two who was reportedly arrested on 13 April, was held in incommunicado detention and not released until 1 June. Amnesty International inquired in early May into the reasons for her detention incommunicado and subsequently received confirmation of her release from the government. Other uncharged detainees were allegedly held incommunicado for three months or more.

On 16 April, the authorities announced that Henry Khahlanyetso Masheane, a political detainee, had been found dead in custody three days earlier. They said that he had been detained for four days before his death for questioning about an act of sabotage committed in February near his workplace. They stated that he had been found hanged with a belt around his neck in his cell at Maseru Central Prison. An inquest into his death began in December and had not been completed by the end of the year. At the inquest it was alleged by the pathologist who carried out a post-mortem examination that Henry Khahlanyetso Masheane could not have committed suicide by hanging given the position in which his body had been found. It appeared therefore that his death by hanging may have been faked to simulate suicide.

Amnesty International remained concerned about the government's failure to disclose the circumstances in which another political detainee, Setipa Mathaba, had died in custody in November 1981. A post-mortem examination was reportedly carried out after his death but its findings were never disclosed and no formal inquest was known to have been held to determine the cause of death. At the time of Setipa Mathaba's death, Amnesty International received substantial information about the torture and cruel, inhuman or degrading treatment of political detainees being held under security legislation. The organization brought these reports to the attention of the Prime Minister, but the government did not respond substantively to Amnesty International's communication.

In December, Amnesty International learned that an inquest would be held early in 1984 into the killing of Edgar Motuba, a prominent newspaper editor, and two others in September 1981. Following the deaths, an Amnesty International mission had visited Lesotho to inquire into allegations that the killings had been politically motivated and had been carried out by a pro-government "death squad" known as *Koeeoko*. No investigation was known to have been initiated into the case of Benjamin Masilo, a leading cleric and, like Edgar Motuba, a well-known critic of the government, who had been the victim of an attack by armed men within days of the other killings in 1981. His grandson had been killed in the attack but he escaped and subsequently alleged that those responsible for it had been members of the paramilitary Police Mobile Unit, some of whose personnel were allegedly connected with *Koeeoko*. No inquest was known to have been held into the death of his grandson, a young child.

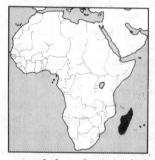

Madagascar

Three prisoners of conscience whose cases had been taken up by Amnesty International were released. One had served a one-year prison sentence, while another had been held without charge for eight months, and the third was released after receiving a suspended sentence of five years' imprisonment on charges of threatening state security. Sixty-four people were tried on charges relating to state security between September and the end of November, in four separate trials. Three defendants appearing in one of the cases had been held for six years without trial and Amnesty International received allegations that the trial might not have been fair. Amnesty International also received reports of poor prison conditions, particularly at Antanimora prison in Antananarivo.

Manana Bosthène Ratsimandresy, a medical student who had been adopted as a prisoner of conscience by Amnesty International, was apparently released from prison on 10 August although the organization was unable definitely to confirm his release. He had been sentenced to one year's imprisonment on 11 August 1982 after he had been overheard criticizing President Ratsiraka while waiting for a flight at Ivato airport. Another prisoner of conscience, Monja Jaona, the leader of the *Madagasikara Otronin' ny Malagasy* (MONIMA), Madagascar for the Malagasy Party, one of seven permitted political parties, was released uncharged in August. He had been detained in December 1982 after calling for a general strike in protest against alleged ballot-rigging during the presidential election of November 1982, when he had stood as a candidate in opposition to President Didier Ratsiraka.

At least 17 other prisoners whom Amnesty International considered to be prisoners of conscience or whose cases were being investigated by the organization were released as a result of court decisions.

In April, four members of the *Mpitolona ho amin' ny Fanjakan' ny Madinika* (MFM), the Party for Proletarian Power, who had been convicted of threatening public security during riots in March 1982, were released after their sentences had been reduced upon appeal. The four – Gilles Lejamble, Rajoanesa, Yves Dzaozara and Paul André – had originally been sentenced to four years' hard labour by a criminal court in Hellville, on Nossi-bé island. At their appeal hearing their sentences were reduced to three years' suspended imprisonment.

In October, a further 13 people were released after five had been acquitted and eight had been sentenced to suspended terms of imprisonment by an Antananarivo criminal court on charges of threatening state security. The 13 had been detained since January 1982 after being accused of plotting to assassinate President Ratsiraka and overthrow the government. They included Colonel Auguste Rasolofo; a student; a Catholic priest; a civil servant; and a woman accused of being a sorceress. At least one of the 13 was beaten while being interrogated at the headquarters of the security police, the *Direction générale de l'information et de la documentation* (DGID), the General Directorate for Information and Documentation, in its headquarters at Ambohibao, near Antananarivo. The evidence against the defendants consisted almost entirely of statements made while they were being held by the DGID, many of which were subsequently retracted by the defendants in court. After allegations had been made during the hearing that the DGID had acquired information from the defendants illegally, the public prosecutor applied for the case to be heard by an appeal court, reportedly so that the value of evidence obtained by the DGID could be re-examined. At the end of the year the appeal was still pending.

On 5 October, a political trial opened before a military tribunal involving three defendants whose cases had been taken up by Amnesty International for investigation. Richard Andriamaholison, a former government minister and officer of the *gendarmerie*; Jean-Astier Rakoto-Abel, also a *gendarmerie* officer; and Marson Rakotonirina, a former army officer, had been detained since October 1977. On 12 October Richard Andriamaholison and Marson Rakotonirina were sentenced to deportation for life, probably to the Nossi-lava prison island, after being convicted of threatening state security, conspiracy, and possession of firearms. Jean-Astier Rakoto-Abel was sentenced to 10 years' hard labour. At the end of the year Amnesty International was studying reports which indicated that the trial might not have been fair. All the witnesses renounced, at least in part, statements which they had made to the DGID, allegedly because their initial statements had been made under duress. Amnesty International was also concerned about the length of time which the defendants had been detained before the hearing.

At the end of the year, Amnesty International knew of only one untried political detainee. The organization had taken up for investigation the case of Rakotomalala, a journalist who had been detained without trial since 1979 apparently for writing a newspaper article criticizing the government.

Amnesty International received disturbing reports of poor prison conditions at Antanimora prison in Antananarivo where prisoners were held in grossly overcrowded conditions. The diet was reported to be inadequate and many prisoners suffered from scabies or other diseases contracted because of poor sanitary conditions or malnutrition. The population of Antanimora prison reportedly included people who had been detained without trial for up to 10 years, although people held on political grounds were not known to be among such detainees.

Malawi

Amnesty International was concerned about the detention without trial of suspected political opponents of the government, including some prisoners of conscience, and about alleged extrajudicial executions. The organization was also concerned about the trial of Orton Chirwa, a leading political opponent of the government, and his wife, Vera Chirwa, before the Traditional Court. They were sentenced to death and were under threat of execution at the end of the year.

Three cabinet ministers and a member of parliament were reported by the authorities in May to have died in a car accident. Unofficial sources, however, claimed that the four men were victims of political killings carried out by agents of the government.

Two months earlier, the Malawi authorities had publicly denied responsibility for the death of Dr Attati Mpakati, the leader of the Socialist League of Malawi (LESOMA), who was murdered in Harare, Zimbabwe. The LESOMA leader had earlier been severely injured by a letter-bomb in February 1979 when he was resident in Mozambique, and on that occasion had accused the Malawi authorities of sending the bomb.

In February, six students at Chancellor College, one of the constituent colleges of the University of Malawi, were arrested at the campus apparently because they were suspected of wanting to form a new political party in opposition to the Malawi Congress Party (MCP), the only political party permitted by the constitution. Two were released after about two weeks and apparently sent to their home villages but four others – Zangaphe Chizeze, Edge Kanyongolo, Mack Willie Killion, and Tubby Chibwana – remained in detention without trial and were still being held at the end of the year. All four were adopted as prisoners of conscience by Amnesty International, and the organization appealed for their release in April and again in December if they were not to face criminal charges. There was no official response to these appeals. At first, the students were held at Lilongwe Prison but Amnesty International later learned that they had been moved to Mikuyu detention centre, northeast of Zomba, where in the past many uncharged political detainees had been held incommunicado for several years.

The authorities also refused to disclose any information about the legal status or whereabouts of another adopted prisoner of conscience, Fumbani Chirwa. He was arrested together with his parents, Orton and Vera Chirwa, in December 1981, but unlike them was not charged or brought to trial. He was rumoured to be detained incommunicado at Zomba Prison but repeated inquiries about him by Amnesty International and others elicited no response from the authorities. In November, Amnesty International made concerted new appeals to the government to clarify his situation after receiving unconfirmed reports that he had died in custody, but again without response.

At the end of the year, Amnesty International was investigating several other reported political detentions. Those held reportedly included a journalist and a former cabinet minister but the organization was unable to estimate the total number of detainees.

Amnesty International also continued to press for the release of Sofiliano Faindi Phiri, a former nominated member of parliament. He was adopted as a prisoner of conscience after being imprisoned for five years in March 1981 for expressing views about development in the Chikwawa area which were interpreted to be insulting to Life-President Kamuzu Banda.

The trial of Orton and Vera Chirwa on charges of treason, which began in July 1982, continued in the Southern Region Traditional Court at Soche until February. Judgement was then reserved until 5 May, when the panel of five chiefs who presided as judges brought in guilty verdicts against both defendants and sentenced them to death. Amnesty International, which had earlier sought unsuccessfully to send an observer to the trial, considered that it had not been conducted in accordance with internationally accepted standards for fairness. Like all defendants in the Traditional Courts, but unlike those appearing before the High Court, Orton and Vera Chirwa were denied legal representation. They were also refused permission to call certain witnesses from abroad or to arrange for their evidence to be taken on commission. In addition, the normal rules of evidence observed in the High Court do not apply in Traditional Courts. The latter have as their judges chiefs who are not required to have formal legal training and have no security of tenure, thus calling into question their judicial independence.

The executive, not the judiciary, has the discretion to decide whether a particular case should be heard in the High Court or the Traditional Court.

The circumstances in which the Chirwas were detained by the authorities in December 1981 remained unclear. Both Orton and Vera Chirwa alleged at their trial that they and their son had been forcibly abducted from Zambia but the Malawi authorities continued to assert that they had entered Malawi clandestinely immediately prior to their arrest.

In late May, there were unconfirmed reports suggesting that Orton and Vera Chirwa were to be executed on 9 June. Amnesty International issued an international appeal to Life-President Kamuzu Banda urging him to prevent their execution. Public appeals for clemency were also made by President Daniel arap Moi of Kenya and President Shehu Shagari of Nigeria. The Church of Scotland, of which both Orton Chirwa and Life-President Kamuzu Banda are members, sent a representative to Malawi to seek clemency. In response, the authorities announced that Orton and Vera Chirwa were not in danger of imminent execution and said that they had lodged an appeal before the National Traditional Court of Appeal.

In June, unofficial sources reported that Paramount Chief Mumbelwa, the chairperson of the National Traditional Court of Appeal, had refused to preside over the Chirwas' appeal out of respect for Orton Chirwa, with whom he had been long acquainted. The same sources claimed that Chief Mumbelwa had gone into hiding or had been detained but Amnesty International was not able to confirm this. However, he was not among the judges when the National Traditional Court of Appeal began hearing Orton and Vera Chirwa's appeals in September. In late October, it was reported that Chief Mumbelwa had died in hospital at Lilongwe though the cause of death was not known to Amnesty International.

In late September, an Amnesty International delegate visited Malawi in an attempt to observe the appeal proceedings in the National Traditional Court of Appeal. The delegate was admitted to the country but was specifically denied permission to enter the court and was therefore unable to observe its proceedings. However, the court did not sit *in camera* and members of the public were allowed to attend. The appeal proceedings concluded on 25 November, when the prosecutor called for both death sentences to be confirmed. The court reserved judgment and had not delivered its verdict by the end of the year.

In December, Amnesty International made renewed appeals for clemency on behalf of Orton and Vera Chirwa in view of fears that they might be executed with minimum delay if their sentences were to be upheld by the National Traditional Court of Appeal.

Mali

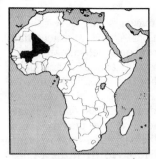

Amnesty International was concerned about reports of cruel, inhuman and degrading treatment of political prisoners and others held for common law crimes at Taoudenit and Kidal prisons, both of which are situated in remote desert locations in northern Mali. Two political prisoners who had been held for many years at Taoudenit Prison died in custody, and other political prisoners due for release in September were reportedly not released at that time.

Some 28 political prisoners and an apparently larger number of criminal prisoners were held at Taoudenit and Kidal throughout most of the year. The political prisoners had all been tried and convicted in October 1978 in connection with an alleged plot to overthrow the government by force. Seventeen of them received five-year prison terms and were due for release in September 1983. Nine others received sentences of up to 20 years' imprisonment and two were sentenced to death.

The two prisoners sentenced to death – Lieutenant Colonel Kissima Doukara, a former Minister of Defence, Interior and Security, and Lieutenant Colonel Tiecoro Bagayoko, former Director General of the Security Services – were not executed but imprisoned for several years at Taoudenit. In October, Amnesty International learned that both prisoners had died in custody, one in late August 1983 and the other in mid-September 1983. Amnesty International appealed to the authorities in October to institute an official inquiry into the reported deaths and to make public the findings of the inquiry. No reply was received from the authorities.

The majority of the 17 prisoners due for release in September 1983 were reportedly not released at that time. In November 1983, Amnesty International appealed to the authorities to release these prisoners, if no further charges were to be brought against them. No reply was received.

Prisoners at Taoudenit and Kidal were reportedly held in total isolation from the outside world throughout their detention and were permitted no visits. At Taoudenit, they were made to undergo forced labour under particularly harsh conditions. They were employed in salt mines several miles from the prison to which they were forced to walk barefoot each day in temperatures up to and exceeding 50° Celsius. At both prisons, hygiene and sanitation standards appeared to be very low and prisoners received a grossly inadequate diet lacking vegetables, fish or meat. At Taoudenit, in particular, a high salt content in the local water reportedly caused recurrent and serious ill-health among prisoners, and medical facilities were virtually non-existent.

Amnesty International issued an international appeal to the authorities in October 1983 to express its concern about such alleged cruel, inhuman and degrading treatment of prisoners at Taoudenit and Kidal. The organization also called on the authorities urgently to improve prison conditions there and to authorize an inspection of the prisoners by an internationally recognized humanitarian organization. Amnesty International appealed to the authorities to close both prisons, and to transfer the inmates to other prisons, if the suggested improvements were not made. No response had been received from the Malian authorities by the end of the year.

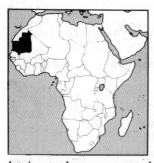

Mauritania

Amnesty International's main concerns were the imprisonment of prisoners of conscience, trials of political prisoners which fell short of internationally accepted standards, the detention without trial of real or suspected opponents of the government, torture and the death penalty.

Throughout the year, Amnesty International sought to obtain the release of detainees who were arrested in August 1981 and March 1982, when as many as 150 people were taken into custody, including a number of women and children, on suspicion of being members of a pro-Iraqi Ba'athist party in Mauritania. Many were believed to have been tortured at the time of their arrest by being beaten severely and hung up by their feet. Some of the detainees were released within a few days of their arrest, but approximately 90 remained in detention without trial until late July 1983 when further releases reportedly took place. However, in late September 26 of those released and 29 of those who had remained in detention were tried by the *Cour Spéciale de Justice*, Special Court of Justice, a court composed entirely of military officers, at the remote military barracks at Jereida. They all faced charges of "complicity with a foreign power" and "membership of a banned organization" on account of their alleged creation of an Arab Socialist Ba'ath Party in Mauritania (all political activity having been outlawed in July 1978 when the ruling military authorities took power). The defendants were represented by legal counsel but their trial suffered serious shortcomings. The defendants were not permitted access to lawyers prior to their trial and the latter were not given adequate time to prepare their defence. The authorities do not authorize appeals to a higher court against convictions by the Special Court of Justice. The trial ended on 1 October. Five defendants were acquitted but the remainder were convicted. In all, 38 received suspended five-year prison sentences, and 11 were sentenced to either 10 or 12 years' imprisonment with hard labour. A 10-year sentence was also passed on another defendant who was tried *in absentia*. More than half of the 11 prisoners sentenced to terms of hard labour had been adopted as prisoners of conscience by Amnesty International in 1982. New appeals for their release, and for the release of the other prisoners sentenced to hard labour in October 1983 and who were also adopted as prisoners of conscience by the organization were sent to the authorities after the trial. Those sentenced included the former government minister Mohamed Yehdih Ould Breidelleyl, Memed Ould Ahmed, a history teacher, and Mohamed Ould Hamady, a journalist and prominent trade unionist. The organization also expressed concern about the possible lack of independence of the Special Court of Justice from the executive and about the restrictions on the rights of the defence. In a reply to Amnesty International in November 1983, the Director of the Presidential Cabinet stated that the court's judges had no political responsibilities and that the rights of the defence had, in the opinion of the government, been fully respected at the trial. However, the reply provided no additional information on the workings of the court or on the trial, and Amnesty International informed the authorities that it remained concerned about the fairness of the trial.

Shortly after their trial, the 11 prisoners who had been sentenced to long prison terms were transferred from Jereida barracks to other places of detention apparently in remote towns or villages. The precise locations were not disclosed, even to prisoners' relatives. The authorities reportedly did not release Yemhelou Ould Sidy Khattary, who had received a suspended five-year prison sentence in October 1983. He had reportedly been absent from the trial having been crippled when he was tortured shortly after his arrest in March 1982. He was adopted by Amnesty International as a prisoner of conscience.

Amnesty International remained concerned about the continued detention without trial of Mohamed Lamine Ould Hormatallah, a former National Assembly deputy, who had been held since October 1979, and three other prisoners of conscience who were being held either because of their links with ex-President Moktar Ould Daddah or because they were suspected of opposing the government's decision to withdraw from its alliance with Morocco in the conflict in Western Sahara. Mohamed Lamine Ould Hormatallah, who was in his 60s, was held at Boumdeïd prison and was in poor health with a stomach ailment. The other detainees, Abderrahmane Ould Mouloud Ould Daddah, a businessperson who was also arrested in October 1979, and Naval Lieutenant Dahane Ould Ahmed Mahmoud, a former Foreign Affairs minister who was arrested in August 1981, were held at Nouakchott Central Prison and at Chinguetti respectively. In late 1983, Amnesty International appealed for the release of the prisoner of conscience Zeini Ould Moulaye Ould Hassan, a magistrate who was arrested in March 1981 and sentenced to two years' imprisonment for his alleged involvement in an armed coup attempt. He was rearrested shortly after he had completed his term of imprisonment in March 1983, apparently because the authorities suspected that he had criticized government policy concerning the Western Sahara. The detention without trial of these four prisoners of conscience was not thought to have any legal basis, and appeared to have taken place simply on the order of the executive.

Amnesty International appealed on several occasions to the authorities to institute a judicial review of the cases of five prisoners against whom heavy prison sentences had been imposed in March 1982 by the Special Court of Justice. Four of them had received sentences of 10 years' hard labour, a fifth being sentenced to five years' imprisonment for allegedly being involved in a coup plot which the authorities claimed to have uncovered. During the trial severe limitations were believed to have been placed on the right to adequate defence and the prosecution apparently failed to advance any evidence of involvement in the alleged plot on the part of the prisoners. Among those convicted were former Head of State, Lieutenant-Colonel Moustapha Mohamed Ould Saleck, the former Prime Minister, Sid'Ahmed Ould Bneijara, and the former government minister Baham Ould Mohamed Lagdaf. In a response in November 1983 to an Amnesty International inquiry concerning the case of Sid'Ahmed Ould Bneijara, the Director of the Presidential Cabinet declared that the accused had confessed to charges of subverting state security and to violence. Amnesty International was continuing to investigate both this case, and the cases of the other four prisoners sentenced at the same trial at the end of the year. The prisoners were believed to have been tortured after their arrest.

Following their conviction in March 1982, these five prisoners were reportedly held in extremely harsh conditions in an old fortress at Jereida which had been built during the colonial period. They were apparently held in underground cells so small that the prisoners were unable to lie down or to stand up fully; the cells were insanitary, without any light and extremely poorly ventilated; food was reportedly very poor and prisoners were denied exercise, visits or correspondence. According to reports received by Amnesty International, most of the five prisoners became very ill during their imprisonment at Jereida. The organization had appealed to the authorities in August 1982 to improve their conditions substantially and to bring them into conformity with international standards relating to the treatment of prisoners, but no answer was received from the authorities. In early 1983, two of the five prisoners were apparently transferred from Jereida to different locations in Mauritania, where their conditions were thought to be improved, and the other three were apparently given better quarters in Jereida barracks.

In September 1983 Amnesty International requested information from the authorities regarding the legal basis for the detention of Ladji Traore, the Managing Director of Pharmarim, the state-owned pharmaceuticals distribution company. He was arrested in March 1983 and apparently accused of poor management of the company, but several reports were received by Amnesty International which suggested that the real reason for his arrest lay in differences of views about the administration of Pharmarim which existed between Ladji Traore and higher governmental authorities. Amnesty International received no reply from the authorities, but continued to make inquiries to establish whether Ladji Traore was a prisoner of conscience.

Five detainees whom Amnesty International had adopted as prisoners of conscience were released in the course of the year. Two of these, Tijani Ould Kerim and Abdallah Ould Bah, had been arrested in April 1980 and April 1979 respectively, apparently because of their political activities during the Ould Daddah administration. The other three released detainees were arrested in March 1981, in the wake of an abortive armed coup attempt, but were not among the nine prisoners brought to trial in the same month on charges of involvement in the plot, four of whom were sentenced to death and later executed. These three detainees were apparently held for their political views alone, and were neither charged nor tried.

In July, Amnesty International publicly appealed to the ruling military authorities to grant an amnesty to all political prisoners on the fifth anniversary of their assumption of power on 10 July 1978 and take action to end the use of torture. The organization drew attention to the imprisonment of several prisoners of conscience and said that unconfirmed reports suggested that there might be as many as 100 political prisoners. Amnesty International also referred to allegations that suspected Ba'athists had been tortured in 1982 by being hung up by their feet and beaten with fists and sticks.

One death sentence was known to have been carried out during the year. In March, a police officer convicted of murder by a *Shari'a*, Islamic law, court was sentenced to death and executed in public by firing squad. Following his execution, Amnesty International protested to the government and called for an end to the use of the death penalty.

Mozambique

Amnesty International was concerned about the long-term detention without trial of suspected opponents of the government, unfair trial procedures, and allegations of beatings and ill-treatment of prisoners. The organization was also concerned about the infliction of floggings on more than 100 people, by the use of the death penalty and by the carrying out of a number of extrajudicial executions.

The country experienced serious political and economic problems. The southern half of the country was affected by a severe drought and famine and guerrilla fighters in the same area belonging to the *Resistência Nacional Moçambicana* (RNM), Mozambique National Resistance, were particularly active in opposition to the government. Government forces mounted a series of offensives in various parts of the country against the RNM and by the end of the year had apparently freed many people detained by the RNM, although at least 15 foreign nationals were still being held by the RNM. In December the authorities offered an amnesty to all RNM guerrillas who surrendered with their weapons and announced the remission or reduction of prison sentences of many convicted prisoners, excluding those convicted of political offences.

In March, smuggling and black marketeering were made capital offences and flogging was introduced as a punishment in addition to imprisonment for offences against the security of the state, for "economic" offences such as smuggling and for various other offences, such as armed assault. In June, a campaign known as "Operation Production" was launched to clear the main towns of unemployed people and others who did not have official permission to reside in them. The authorities subsequently admitted that the operation had resulted in many arbitrary arrests and other excesses by the security forces.

Amnesty International learned of several cases in which people were arrested for criticizing government officials or policies. For example, a priest in Tete province was detained without trial and held in incommunicado detention for six months after writing to the Provincial Governor about problems of food shortages. He was released uncharged in October.

Long-term detention without trial continued to be used on an extensive scale against real and suspected critics or opponents of the government. The detainees included a number of alleged opponents of the *Frente de Libertação de Moçambique* (FRELIMO), the Mozambique Liberation Front, which in 1977 became the ruling Frelimo Party. They were arrested before independence in 1975 and were reportedly held at isolated "re-education" camps in northern Mozambique although no information about them appeared to have been made available to their relatives by the authorities in recent years. None were known to have been released during 1983.

Suspected members and supporters of the RNM constituted by far the majority of uncharged political detainees. They included captured guerrilla fighters, people alleged to have provided them with information or supplies, and others found in possession of tracts expressing sympathy with the RNM's aims. In December President Samora Machel stated that there were some 3,500 detainees in custody who were suspected of supporting the RNM in some way.

Relatively few such detainees were charged and brought to trial. Most were apparently held by the security police, the *Serviço Nacional de Segurança Popular* (SNASP), National Service for the People's Security. No independent body existed to review detainees' cases. Detainees were frequently held incommunicado for many months in harsh conditions, some reportedly being severely beaten or tortured during interrogation.

Amnesty International received information about a considerable number of detainees arrested during the year against whom no specific charges were known to have been brought. They included a number of expatriate workers, mainly of Portuguese nationality, who were arrested in Beira in April and May, apparently because they were believed to be associates of a British citizen, Dion Hamilton, who was convicted in February by the Revolutionary Military Tribunal on charges including involvement in the RNM.

The trial in February was one of two political trials reported during the year, involving a total of 49 defendants accused of offences against the security of the state. Amnesty International was concerned that the trials did not conform with internationally recognized standards. The first trial was held *in camera* in Beira and involved 40 defendants. They included Dion Hamilton, his wife and eight Portuguese nationals, all of whom were arrested in December 1982 and January 1983 after an explosion had wrecked petroleum storage tanks in Beira on 9 December 1982, and 30 other people who were accused of fighting with the RNM or of supporting the RNM in other ways. Hearings lasted three days and involved several groups of prisoners who appeared before the court separately and whose cases do not appear to have been related. All 40 defendants were defended by the same legal counsel, a SNASP officer, who appeared to have had no time to consult many of his clients before the trial.

At the end of the trial 23 of the defendants were convicted and 17 were acquitted. This was the first time that defendants tried by the

Revolutionary Military Tribunal, which was set up in March 1979, were known to have been acquitted. Five people were sentenced to death after being convicted on charges relating to attacks and killings which the RNM had carried out. Of the remaining 18 defendants who received prison sentences, 15 Mozambicans were convicted of involvement with the RNM and were sentenced to terms of between six and 12 years' imprisonment. Dion Hamilton was sentenced to 20 years' imprisonment after conviction on charges including complicity with the RNM, having prior knowledge of the attack on Beira's petroleum storage tanks and possession of weapons. Two of the nine Portuguese nationals on trial were also convicted for failing to reveal prior knowledge of the attack to the authorities and were sentenced to terms of four and eight years' imprisonment.

In mid-March Law No. 2/79 concerning Crimes against the Security of the People and the People's State was amended to extend the number of offences punishable by death to include non-political offences, notably murder, smuggling and black marketeering. On 31 March a further law, No. 5/83, introduced flogging as a punishment for a wide number of offences, both political and non-political. These new penalties could be applied to prisoners who were already in custody and sentences of flogging were subsequently imposed on one group of prisoners whose trial before the Revolutionary Military Tribunal in Maputo had begun at the end of March, before the law introducing flogging was enacted.

This trial ended on 3 April and according to official sources involved 17 defendants, eight of whom were accused of non-political offences. All the defendants were convicted and six were sentenced to death. Two of these, Gulam Nabi and José Manderero, were convicted of economic offences. Two others were sentenced to death on murder charges and two more were convicted on charges relating to involvement with the RNM.

The 11 other defendants received prison terms ranging from two to 12 years and were sentenced to be flogged. Six of them were students from the Faculty of Education at Maputo's Eduardo Mondlane University who were convicted on charges of agitation and were each sentenced to eight years' imprisonment and 45 lashes. They were accused of having written two letters which allegedly urged students to disrupt their classes in the Faculties of Education and Law. Amnesty International subsequently took up the students' cases for investigation to establish whether they were prisoners of conscience. The organization also took up for investigation the case of a school teacher, Leonardo Mabunda, who was sentenced at the same time to eight years' imprisonment and 45 lashes for insulting the Frelimo Party and the State.

At the trials before the Revolutionary Military Tribunal in both February and March, Amnesty International was concerned that defendants had inadequate opportunities to defend themselves and were not properly defended by the state-appointed legal counsel, that tenuous evidence was accepted by the court and that those convicted had no right of appeal. The organization was also concerned that many of the sentences announced on 3 April were imposed under the terms of laws which had been enacted after the defendants had committed their alleged offences.

Sentences of death were reportedly carried out by firing-squad within several weeks of their announcement at both the trials. Although prisoners sentenced to death by the Revolutionary Military Tribunal may in theory appeal to the head of state for clemency, no death sentences are ever reported to have been commuted. On both occasions, Amnesty International appealed for all the death sentences to be commuted. The six death sentences imposed on 3 April were carried out on 8 April in front of a crowd consisting of several hundred Frelimo Party supporters.

In January official sources reported seven executions in towns near Maputo of suspected RNM guerrillas who were shot by firing-squad without any form of trial or other legal procedure. No provision for such executions exists under Mozambican law. Four people were executed at Macia on 13 January and three more at Magude on 18 January. In both cases the executions took place after the prisoners had appeared in public at political rallies which were attended by senior government officials. Amnesty International appealed to the government to prevent any further such killings.

The introduction of flogging at the end of March was justified in the preamble of Law No. 5/83 on the grounds that existing penalties, particularly imprisonment, had proved inadequate to stem a serious crime wave. The new law made flogging mandatory for all political offences, for economic offences such as black marketeering, for armed assaults, robbery, rape and child molesting. It also permitted the imposition of flogging on a non-mandatory basis for offences such as murder and drug smuggling. Sentences of up to 90 lashes may be imposed in addition to prison sentences and fines. The law stipulates that floggings are to be carried out in public and that up to 30 lashes may be administered in each session, following which a period of eight days must elapse before a subsequent session.

In many cases, floggings appeared to have been carried out at well-publicized meetings some days or weeks after sentences were imposed.

Immediately after the new law was announced, a considerable number of sentences of flogging were imposed by the courts: 11 sentences of between 10 and 45 lashes were imposed by the

Revolutionary Military Tribunal on 3 April. The first public floggings reportedly took place in Quelimane on 9 April, when the victims were two dock workers convicted of theft by the Provincial People's Tribunal. By 26 April, less than a month after the new law was introduced, 20 people were reported to have been flogged in Maputo alone, mostly for black market offences and theft.

Although fewer flogging sentences were apparently imposed in May, they continued to be imposed and carried out later in the year. Although no official statistics were available, it appeared that more than 100 people had been publicly flogged by the end of the year.

Namibia

Amnesty International was concerned about the detention without trial of political detainees and by allegations that some of them were tortured and ill-treated. More than 100 long-term political detainees remained in custody throughout the year at a special military detention camp in the Mariental district. Courts ruled during the year that the deaths in custody of two political detainees in November 1982 and the "disappearance" of another in August 1980 were directly attributable to unlawful acts by South African security force personnel.

Amnesty International continued to press for the removal of administrative restriction orders imposed on former uncharged detainees and remained concerned about the South African authorities' failure to review the cases of political prisoners convicted and sentenced to long prison terms after a trial in 1968 which did not conform to internationally recognized standards. The organization also remained concerned about the use of the death penalty and by allegations of extrajudicial executions of civilians.

There was further conflict throughout the year between South African security forces and nationalist guerrillas supporting the South West Africa People's Organization (SWAPO). Both sides accused the other of killing civilians. In December, a major new incursion by South African military forces into Angola resulted in clashes between them and both SWAPO guerrillas and Angolan military forces.

Amnesty International received many reports of detentions for political reasons, particularly in the north, but was unable to estimate their number. Those detained and held without charge or trial included at least four church ministers, several lay preachers in the Evangelical Lutheran Ovambo-Kavango (ELOK) Church, the Secretary of the Catholic Justice and Peace Commission, teachers, farmers and a member of the Kavango Legislative Assembly. Most arrests occurred in Ovamboland and Kavango or in the capital, Windhoek.

Proclamation AG.9 of 1977 constituted the legal basis for most detentions and was used in areas designated as "security districts": these embrace most of the northern half of the country, the area where most of the population live. The proclamation, which was introduced by administrative decree, empowers all members of the South African security forces with the rank of non-commissioned officer or above to detain people on suspicion and hold them incommunicado without charge or trial for an initial period of 30 days following which an unlimited period of detention can be authorized by the Administrator-General. Detainees' relatives are not informed of their arrest or of their place of detention. Proclamation AG.9 indemnifies security force personnel from civil or criminal prosecution for acts committed "in good faith".

Amnesty International investigated the cases of some 60 political detainees during 1983 and called repeatedly on the authorities for all detainees to be brought to trial or released and to be safeguarded against possible torture or ill-treatment while in custody. One such detainee was Kosmos Kalat Makanga, a member both of the Namibian Christian Democratic Party (NCDP) and of the Kavango Legislative Assembly. He was arrested in late July in Kavango and held incommunicado for about three months, during which he was allegedly ill-treated. Following his release, he took up residence in Windhoek allegedly because he had been threatened with re-detention if he should return to Kavango. In late November, security police in Windhoek again detained him under Proclamation AG.9 after he and other NCDP officials walked out of a local conference on Namibia's future. He was still believed to be held at the end of the year.

Amnesty International also took up the case of the Reverend Johannes Sindano, an ELOK pastor at Rundu in Kavango. He was arrested on 19 October, taken to the local security police office, and then transported, blindfold, to a secret camp where he was imprisoned for some three weeks. He was not permitted to see or be seen by any other detainee until shortly before his release. He was held for some three weeks, during which he was interrogated but not tortured, and then returned, blindfold, to Rundu. However, before being released he was put into a cell briefly with another detainee, Amos Shirongo, who told him that he had been in solitary confinement for almost four months and had been severely assaulted.

Some of those whose cases were taken up by Amnesty International were among more than 100 long-term detainees who have been held at a special military camp in the Mariental district under Proclamation AG.9 since May 1979. The had been forcibly abducted from Angola by South African military forces in May 1978 at the time of an attack on a camp for Namibian refugees at Kassinga (see *Amnesty International Report 1983*). The detainees at Mariental were not at Kassinga at the time of the attack but at another camp; their names were not published by the South African authorities and it was not until late 1982 that they were first permitted visits from their relatives. Amnesty International publicized the cases of the Mariental detainees in April 1983, calling for the immediate release of those who were prisoners of conscience and for the trial or release of others.

Amnesty International remained concerned about the lack of institutional safeguards against torture and ill-treatment of detainees. In late 1982, the organization had written to the South African Prime Minister calling on the South African Government to repeal legislation permitting unlimited incommunicado detention and to allow frequent and regular access to detainees. However, the organization received no reply and a press statement publicizing this appeal was banned by the government in early January. In November 1983, a commission of inquiry into security legislation was established by the Administrator-General but it had not completed its work by the end of the year.

Four separate court actions during the year emphasized the need for concern. In June, the Windhoek Supreme Court ruled that a political detainee, Johannes Kakuva, who "disappeared" from security police custody in August 1980, had been killed in detention. Several people who had been detained at the same time as Johannes Kakuva at Opuwa in the Kaokoland area had testified that they had been severely assaulted and locked up for long periods in very confined spaces. The security police had claimed that Johannes Kakuva had become their informer, and that he had been released and had subsequently disappeared. An appeal by the government against the judgment had not been heard by the end of the year. The security police officer accused of responsibility for Kakuva's death in detention reportedly remained on active service despite the court judgment.

In October, an inquest was held at Rundu into the death in detention of Jona Hamukwaya, a teacher. He had been arrested on 18 November 1982 by members of *Koevoet* (Crowbar), a special police counter-insurgency unit under the direct authority of the South African Minister of Law and Order. He died within hours of his arrest. At the inquest, his wife testified that he had been beaten with rifle butts when he was taken from his home. Members of *Koevoet* who had detained him claimed that he had died after he had slipped and fallen down a flight of stairs while in custody. This account was not accepted by the presiding magistrate as it was contradicted by medical evidence of severe back and head injuries which were probably the result of a severe assault. The magistrate ruled that Jona Hamukwaya's death had occurred as a result of an "unlawful act or omission" on the part of *Koevoet* personnel, but he declined to make any finding about the identities of those responsible. No further action in this case was known to have been taken by the South African authorities.

The death of another detainee, Kudimo Katanga, also on 18 November 1982, resulted in the prosecution of four members of *Koevoet*. They were not charged with murder but with the lesser offence of culpable homicide. Their trial opened in October and concluded in November: two of the defendants were acquitted; two others were convicted of assault and fined. Earlier, the court had heard that Kudimo Katanga had been forced by his captors to run in front of their vehicle for several kilometres and had been beaten with sticks while he ran until he fell exhausted and died. Kudimo Katanga was reportedly a deaf mute and would therefore have been unable to answer questions put to him by his *Koevoet* interrogators.

Following a new wave of detentions in Kavango in October and early November, relatives of three of the detainees – Reverend Heikki Ausiku, Gideon Nestor and Severinus Siteketa – made an urgent application before the Windhoek Supreme Court for an order restraining members of the security police or *Koevoet* from assaulting or ill-treating the three men. Lawyers representing the families laid before the court several sworn statements from former detainees who alleged that they had been tortured or beaten while held in solitary confinement. Their statements, which referred to incidents which had occurred over a period of two years, revealed the existence of at least one secret interrogation centre where torture was apparently common.

The authorities opposed the families' application, which also sought legal and medical access to the three detainees, but permitted a doctor to examine them. He reported that they alleged assault and were in poor health as a result of their detention. Reverend Ausiku and the two other detainees were released on 14 December, by which time the court had still not delivered the verdict, despite the urgent nature of the application. More than 20 other detainees from Kavango were released at the same time but a number remained in incommunicado detention at the end of the year, when the Windhoek Supreme Court had still given no ruling at all on the urgent application brought before it in early November.

Further details of torture of political detainees were given at a press conference at Tsumeb on 4 November by Hans Röhr, leader of the NCDP, and four former detainees who had recently been released. The former detainees alleged that they had been held incommunicado for three months and had been beaten and tortured with electric shocks. They said that before their release they had been made to sign statements while blindfold. Hans Röhr alleged that another man, Ndara Kapitango, aged 63, had been beaten and hung up over a fire when he was detained in June by two members of the security forces. He had sustained serious burns which had resulted in the amputation of his right arm. He had been left unconscious by those who tortured him who had then, according to Hans Röhr, raped his wife.

Late in 1982, Amnesty International had called for an impartial inquiry into allegations of torture. In January 1983, such an inquiry was publicly rejected by a security police representative but later in the year there were several announcements about investigations by senior security force personnel into allegations made against the security forces. A few members of the security forces were reportedly prosecuted but the investigating authorities apparently held most allegations to be exaggerated.

Amnesty International learned of two executions during the year. The victims were two brothers who had been convicted of murder. In another case in December, Jonas Paulus, a member of *Koevoet*, was sentenced to death for murder. He and another *Koevoet* member were alleged to have committed acts of robbery and rape in Ovamboland. During their trial, it was submitted in evidence that *Koevoet* personnel had masqueraded as SWAPO guerrillas and that they were paid bonuses according to their success in killing SWAPO guerrillas. There were a number of reports that *Koevoet* personnel might have been responsible for extrajudicial executions of civilians but Amnesty International was unable to confirm such allegations in individual cases.

In February, Amnesty International submitted information on human rights violations in Namibia to the United Nations Commission on Human Rights. The organization gave further detailed information in mid-1983 to a Working Group established by the Commission.

Niger

Amnesty International was concerned about the imprisonment of prisoners of conscience, some of whom had been detained without trial or restricted under house arrest for almost 10 years, and the detention without trial of other suspected opponents of the government. There were allegations of ill-treatment of detainees, at least one of whom died in custody, and prison conditions were reportedly poor.

The former President, Hamani Diori, and Djibo Bakary, the former leader of the *Sawaba* (Freedom) Party, continued to be restricted under house arrest in Niamey throughout the year. They had both been placed under house arrest in April 1980 when they were released from several years' detention without trial in remote military camps, and both were adopted as prisoners of conscience by Amnesty International.

Seven other people related to Hamani Diori or closely associated with his administration, which was overthrown in April 1974, remained in detention throughout 1983. They included Ibrahim Issa, formerly a senior government official, and two relatives of the former President, Ganda Diori and Boubacar Moussa Diori. They were all arrested in April 1974 and detained without trial since then, mostly in Tillabery and Agades prisons. Amnesty International repeatedly called on the government to bring them to trial or release them and was concerned about their continued detention in view of the internationally-recognized right to trial within a reasonable time.

At the beginning of May, there was a nationwide strike by university students and school pupils in protest against the closure by the authorities of the *Ecole supérieure d'agronomie*, School of Higher Studies in Agronomy, after a dispute between staff and students over the method of evaluating students' performance. On 3 May, security forces entered the university campus in Niamey and arrested some 300 students who were taken to the nearby Tondibia military barracks. Many of those arrested were reportedly beaten with rifle-butts, truncheons or sticks and some appeared to have been seriously injured. One of the detained students, Amadou Boubacar, died in custody in the days following his arrest on 3 May, apparently as a result of ill-treatment. His body was returned by the authorities to his family.

Following reports that no official investigation into the circumstances of Amadou Boubacar's death had been instituted, Amnesty International wrote to President Seyni Kountche and several senior government officials in August 1983 calling for such an investigation urgently to take place. The organization also called on the authorities to initiate appropriate legal action against anyone who might be found responsible for his death. No response was received from the authorities and by the end of the year it appeared that there had been no inquest or official investigation into Amadou Boubacar's death. In 1983 the organization had still not received any response from the authorities to appeals it had sent to them in 1982 to establish an official inquiry into two other deaths in detention that year.

All but 14 of those arrested in connection with the May strike were released uncharged after several days in custody. The authorities announced that the remaining detainees would be charged with committing violence and inciting others to do so, but none of them had been brought to trial by the end of the year. They included Ali Chekou, Saïdou Moussa and Harouna Abass, all of whom apparently had been leading members of the student bodies involved in the strike. A lecturer at the university in Niamey was also reportedly among those detained. Their cases were taken up for investigation by Amnesty International.

In June, several more arrests were made, apparently in connection with the strike. Those detained included two students and several university teachers. The authorities did not reveal where they and the other 14 detainees were held but unconfirmed reports suggested that they were detained at a remote military outpost in the desert at Bilma.

An unsuccessful attempt to overthrow the government of President Seyni Kountche took place on 7 October. In the aftermath, at least 26 people were detained on suspicion of involvement in the plot, including two former government ministers, senior civil servants and army officers. However, no charges were reported to have been brought against them and none had been brought to trial by the end of the year.

The conditions in which detainees were being held in Agades and Tillabery, the main centres for long-term political detention, were understood to be poor. The quality of food provided by the authorities was reported to be very inadequate, as was the standard of sanitation. Medical facilities were understood to be grossly inadequate. Political detainees held in these centres were reportedly only rarely allowed visits or letters from friends and relatives.

Nigeria

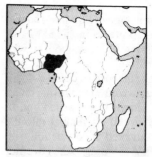

Amnesty International was concerned about reports that large numbers of people were detained during national elections in August, although it was not clear whether any of those detained were held solely on account of non-violent political opinions or activities. At least three people were sentenced to death during 1983 but it was not known how many executions took place.

Presidential and legislative elections took place in August. President Shehu Shagari was re-elected to a second four-year term, and his National Party of Nigeria (NPN) won a majority of seats in the Federal House of Representatives. However, there were widespread allegations that voting had been rigged in several states of the federation. Some results were successfully challenged in the courts. On 31 December, President Shagari's government was overthrown in a coup led by Major-General Muhammadu Buhari.

Over a thousand people were detained in August during the national elections, which were disrupted by political violence. Arson, intimidation and ballot-rigging were widely reported, and hundreds of people were killed in clashes between supporters of rival candidates. There were allegations that several candidates for election to the office of state governor maintained private armies of hired thugs. The most serious violence was reported in Oyo and Ondo states, both of which were won by NPN gubernatorial candidates against incumbent candidates from the Unity Party of Nigeria (UPN). However, a UPN candidate was eventually declared to have been elected as governor of Ondo after the Supreme Court had overturned the election of the NPN candidate. Over 600 people were reportedly detained in Ondo state alone in August and September, while other detentions were reported from almost every state in the federation. Most of those detained were held on suspicion either of electoral fraud or of crimes of violence including arson and murder. Representatives of the UPN and the Nigerian People's Party (NPP) alleged that some of their supporters had been detained on account of their party affiliation and that many detainees were held without charge. Both federal and state police authorities reportedly denied these allegations, stating that all those held in connection with offences during the August elections had been formally charged before a magistrate. Some reports estimated that the number of people held on political grounds in October, including those who had not been charged, may have been up to 150 in Niger state, 200 in Borno, 100 in Imo, 600 in Oyo and 500 in Ondo. In late October, the national press reported that two senior officials of the opposition UPN had been prevented by security officers from boarding a flight to London, and had had their passports confiscated. They had reportedly intended to give Amnesty International information concerning UPN supporters who had allegedly been arrested for political reasons.

Three people were known to have been sentenced to death in 1983 after being convicted of murder. It was not known how many other death sentences were imposed or how many executions were carried out. In Oyo state, the authorities instituted an inquiry in November into the imposition of death sentences on people convicted in connection with violent protests against heavy taxes in 1980. According to the governor of Oyo, Dr Victor Olunloyo, there were fears that some of those sentenced to death may have been wrongfully convicted.

Rwanda

Amnesty International was concerned about the continued imprisonment of 24 people whom the organization had adopted as prisoners of conscience. Some prisoners of conscience, along with other political prisoners, were apparently subjected to deliberately harsh conditions of imprisonment which amounted to cruel, inhuman and degrading treatment. Amnesty International was also concerned that trials of political detainees fell short of internationally recognized standards and that political detainees, some of whom were eventually acquitted by the courts and released, were being kept in pre-trial detention for long periods, sometimes exceeding two years.

In addition to the 24 people adopted by Amnesty International as prisoners of conscience, the organization also received information during the year concerning some 25 prisoners who were accused of having committed offences against the security of the state, although the total number of people imprisoned for political reasons was believed to be somewhat higher. Fourteen of these prisoners, some of whom had apparently been in custody since April 1980, were acquitted and freed in April 1983.

Nineteen of the prisoners of conscience on whose behalf Amnesty International worked had been convicted by the State Security Court in November 1981 and were serving sentences of between two and 12 years' imprisonment. They had mostly been convicted of distributing tracts which criticized senior government officials and were interpreted by the authorities to be subversive, although they did not advocate the use of violence against the government. Amnesty International considered that they and five other prisoners sentenced at the same time to long prison terms did not receive a fair trial. In April Amnesty International set out its concerns in this regard in a letter to the Minister of Justice, Charles Nkurunziza. The concerns included the tenuousness of some of the evidence presented by the prosecution, allegations that four defendants had been tortured in order to make them "confess" to certain offences, and the fact that none of the defendants had been assisted by legal counsel, although several had asked for defence lawyers. Amnesty International received no response to this letter.

Between 18 and 29 April, 27 people were tried by the State Security Court at Ruhengeri on charges connected with an alleged plot said to have been led by the former head of the security police, Théoneste Lizinde in 1980. However, only three of the defendants were convicted of offences against the security of the state. Three others were convicted of insulting President Juvénal Habyarimana. The other 21 defendants were alleged to have distributed subversive tracts but 14 of them were acquitted. Those acquitted included people who had apparently been in custody awaiting trial for almost three years. Two of the seven who were convicted of distributing subversive documents, Froduald Gasamunyiga and Prosper Mubera, had been held in Ruhengeri prison for more than a year before the trial and had apparently been subjected to incommunicado detention in completely unlit cells, *cachots noirs*, for long periods. They both received four-year prison sentences and were subsequently adopted by Amnesty International as prisoners of conscience. Three of the other defendants convicted with them were not arrested before the trial but received summonses and were informed of the charges against them only a few days before the trial. One was sentenced to three years' imprisonment and the other two to four-year terms. They too were adopted by Amnesty International as prisoners of conscience.

The three defendants convicted of insulting President Habyarimana were not accused of having been involved in the alleged plot in 1980. Two were sentenced to three years' imprisonment and one to a two-year prison term.

Three of the trial defendants were convicted on more serious charges relating to an alleged conspiracy to overthrow the government. One was sentenced to 20 months' imprisonment, one had 10 years added to a previous 25-year prison sentence and the third was sentenced to life imprisonment. Stanislas Biseruka, a former army officer who was sentenced to 25 years' imprisonment at the trial in November 1981, had a further 10 years added to his sentence. In 1980, he had sought asylum in Uganda but was forcibly repatriated and allegedly tortured in 1981 after being kidnapped by Rwandese security agents. In November 1981 he was convicted of conspiring to overthrow the government and in April 1983 he was convicted of having contacted other opponents of the Rwandese Government while in Uganda. Donat Muvunanyambo, another defendant who had been forcibly repatriated from Uganda, was sentenced to life imprisonment for allegedly contacting opponents of the Rwandese Government while in Uganda, founding an opposition political group and writing insulting remarks in his personal diary about President Juvénal Habyarimana.

The State Security Court which heard political cases was composed of five judges, two of them members of the armed forces. Although rights of defence were in theory respected, in practice defendants were not given an opportunity to appoint defence lawyers. Although prisoners convicted by the court have no right of appeal, they can challenge the legal grounds of their conviction in a submission to the *Cour de cassation*, Cassation Court, if they do so within 10 days of being sentenced. In most cases reported to Amnesty International prisoners had not received a copy of their judgment within this time and none of those convicted in April was known to have lodged an appeal.

In February and March large numbers of arrests took place in Kigali of men and women whose identity papers were not in order or who did not have proper jobs. In particular, more than 100 women were arrested and summarily sent to Nsinda "re-education" camp near Rwamagana on the grounds that they had been engaged in prostitution. Amnesty International was concerned about the case of four of these women and made inquiries with the authorities about the reasons for their detention. They appeared to have been arrested because they had been in close contact with European expatriate workers. They were reportedly questioned by members of the national intelligence service who apparently suggested that they were working as spies on behalf of their European friends. Following international publicity surrounding these cases, the four women concerned were released and confined to their home villages for several months.

Amnesty International remained concerned about conditions in Ruhengeri prison's "Special Section", a high security wing in which political prisoners were held. It contained six "black cells" which have no no windows or artificial light and in which prisoners were held for long periods. In January Amnesty International urged the authorities to move five prisoners then reportedly being held in these cells. They included Immaculée Mukamugema, who was adopted by the organization as a prisoner of conscience after being sentenced to 10 years' imprisonment in November 1981. She had apparently become ill after being held in a "black cell" in total darkness for most of the second half of 1982. At the end of February, she was reportedly transferred to Kigali prison, where she was placed in an ordinary cell in the women's section of the prison.

Many political prisoners in the "Special Section" at Ruhengeri prison were held incommunicado even after they had been sentenced, although some of those convicted in November 1981 were apparently permitted at least one family visit. Some prisoners' relatives who had received official permission to visit them in July were not allowed by the prison authorities to do so, despite an assurance by President Habyarimana in July that convicted prisoners would be permitted to receive such family visits.

There were some improvements in prison conditions during the year although it appeared that political prisoners were still generally subjected to harsher treatment than ordinary criminal prisoners. In June, President Habyarimana announced that the Minister of Justice and Vincent Nsengiyumva, the Roman Catholic Archbishop of Kigali, had been asked to investigate allegations of harsh conditions of imprisonment. However, by the end of the year no results of this investigation had been made public. In July, the President also announced that the International Committee of the Red Cross had been granted facilities to inspect conditions in Rwanda's prisons.

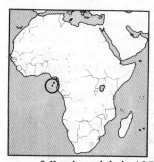

Sao Tome and Principe

Three prisoners of conscience who had been adopted by Amnesty International and two others whose cases were under investigation were released on 12 July on the eighth anniversary of the country's independence. The five had been sentenced to prison terms ranging from 16 to 22 years following trials in 1977 and 1979 which Amnesty International believed did not accord with internationally recognized standards for a fair trial (see *Amnesty International Report 1983*).

Amnesty International was investigating the imprisonment of a primary school teacher, Lucia Carvalho, who was apparently arrested on Principe island at the beginning of the year and accused of preparing pamphlets which criticized the government. She was reportedly tried in June by the Special Tribunal for Counter-Revolutionary Acts on charges relating to the preparation of these pamphlets and was sentenced to two years' imprisonment.

A Sao Tomean citizen who had been granted political asylum in

Portugal, Antonio Trovoada, was forcibly repatriated from Angola to Sao Tome in November and immediately arrested on his arrival. He was apparently suspected of having been in contact with an opposition political group in Portugal and was still in detention at the end of the year. Amnesty International made inquiries about the reasons for his arrest and was concerned that he might have been detained on account of his non-violent political views.

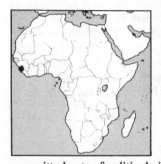

Sierra Leone

Amnesty International was concerned about the detention without trial of suspected political opponents of the government or of the ruling All People's Congress Party (APC), inadequate conditions of detention and the judicial death penalty.

Over 100 people were reportedly in detention in the Pujehun area at the end of the year, apparently on suspicion of having committed acts of political violence. Many of them, possibly including some who were detained in 1982, had not been charged by the end of the year. They were arrested as a result of a dispute between rival factions in the Pujehun East parliamentary constituency which arose when the incumbent member of parliament, Mana Kpaka, was defeated in the general election of May 1982 by another candidate, Solomon Demby. Mana Kpaka's supporters claimed that Solomon Demby's election had been irregular and instituted court proceedings to overturn his election. Following the murder of the chief witness on behalf of Mana Kpaka in October 1982, there were violent clashes between supporters of Mana Kpaka and Solomon Demby. At least 10 people, and perhaps as many as 50, were reportedly killed as a result of political violence in the area in May 1983 alone. Those detained in connection with the dispute were reportedly held at police stations at Bo and Pujehun where they were said to have received insufficient food. At least five people detained on political grounds reportedly died in Pujehun police station during the year from malnutrition or diseases related to it, while others were transferred to Pujehun hospital suffering from malnutrition.

On 20 September Amnesty International wrote to President Siaka Stevens expressing concern about reports that agents of government security forces or of the APC had been responsible for, or had deliberately failed to prevent, acts of political violence including political killings in the Pujehun area. The organization urged the authorities to act to prevent such abuses and to institute an inquiry into the disturbances. On 17 November President Stevens replied to Amnesty International, stating that the security forces had inflicted casualties only when defending themselves against armed opponents. He also stated that all the murders which had taken place in the region and which had been cited in Amnesty International's letter of 20 September were being investigated, that those responsible would in due course be brought to trial by the appropriate authorities, and that the government was doing all in its power to maintain law and order in the area.

In May, Amnesty International learned that 17 people were awaiting execution after having been condemned to death by the courts in previous years. Nine death sentences were reportedly imposed by the courts during the year. However, no executions are believed to have been carried out for more than three years. On 5 July, Amnesty International appealed to the President to commute the death sentences passed on Ahmed Turay, Saliu Bangura and Michael Turay, who had all been convicted of armed robbery. The organization expressed the hope that the commutation of death sentences in recent years might imply a step towards total abolition of the death penalty.

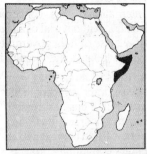

Somalia

Amnesty International was concerned about the detention of prisoners of conscience; the detention of other political opponents of the government; the imprisonment of others after unfair trials; harsh prison conditions; and allegations of ill-treatment of prisoners. More than 30 people were sentenced to death and there were a number of executions during 1983.

The government of President Mohamed Siyad Barre continued to face armed opposition from the Democratic Front for the Salvation of Somalia and the Somali National Movement, both based in Ethiopia. Following an attack by the Somali National Movement on 2 January in the northern town of Mandera, near Hargeisa, a state of emergency was imposed in the area. However, the emergency was lifted on 13 February, when an amnesty was declared for an unspecified number of prisoners, including some of those arrested during the emergency. There was further activity by opposition guerrilla organizations throughout the year in border areas and in other parts of the country, including the capital, Mogadishu.

At the beginning of the year seven former members of parliament and of the central committee of the Somali Revolutionary Socialist Party (the only political party permitted in the country), who had been arrested in June 1982, were still being detained incommunicado in Labatan Jirow prison, near Baidowa. They were charged with treason soon after their arrest but by the end of 1983 no date had been set for their trial before the National Security Court. They were apparently arrested for opposing the re-election of President Siyad Barre for a further five-year term of office. They included Ismail Ali Abokor, a former Vice-President of Somalia, and Omar Arteh Ghalib, a former Foreign Minister. All seven were adopted by Amnesty International as prisoners of conscience.

Amnesty International learned of the death in detention of one of them, Warsame Ali Farah, on 20 July, after he had apparently been refused admission to hospital and continued to be denied access to his family. The organization expressed concern about his death and requested details from the authorities about the cause of death and about his medical treatment in detention. Amnesty International also sought assurances that all prisoners would be given adequate medical treatment. The Attorney General later sent the organization a copy of the post-mortem report, which indicated kidney failure, but provided no further information or guarantees about the provision of medical attention to other prisoners.

Amnesty International investigated the cases of 20 people who had been arrested in Hargeisa at the end of 1981 and were tried by the National Security Court in February 1982. They were convicted of various offences under national security legislation, the main charges being organizing or participating in a subversive association. They were sentenced to prison terms ranging from three years' imprisonment to life imprisonment. They included Mohamed Barud Ali, a businessperson; Aden Yusuf Abokor, medical director at Hargeisa hospital, and other doctors, businesspeople, teachers and engineers. All had belonged to an unofficial organization engaged in local voluntary community projects. The prosecution at their trials alleged that this organization was subversive and engaged in publishing anti-state propaganda. Amnesty International was investigating the possibility that they had in fact been imprisoned for their non-violent opinions and activities. The organization was also concerned that they did not appear to have received a fair trial. Although defendants were permitted legal representation and access to lawyers shortly before the trial, they had no right of appeal to a higher court or to a civil court. The verdict and sentence of the court are subject to review by the President but it had not been announced by the end of the year whether the President had reviewed these cases.

Prisoners of conscience for whose release Amnesty International continued to appeal during 1983 included Yusuf Osman Samantar ("Barda'ad"), a left-wing politician who had been detained without trial since 1978 for his opposition to the government, and Saida Botan Elmi, who had been detained without trial since 1978 in reprisal for her husband's political opposition activities in exile. They remained in detention at the end of 1983. Amnesty International continued its investigations into several other cases of political imprisonment. They included Ahmed Abdi Hashi ("Hashari"), a lawyer and former ambassador, and Abukar Hassan Yare, a university lecturer, who were arrested with other alleged left-wing critics of the government in January 1981. By the end of the year, they were still detained and the government had given no indication whether they would be charged and brought to trial.

Amnesty International learned of a number of arrests during the year apparently made on political grounds. A number of people in Mandera and Hargeisa were reportedly arrested for allegedly collaborating with the Somali National Movement's attack on 2 January, which resulted in the escape from Mandera prison of a number of political and non-political prisoners. The majority of those arrested were released in an amnesty on 13 February, but others were among 55 or more people who were reportedly tried by the National Security Court in Hargeisa in mid-November. Eleven of those tried were sentenced to death on charges alleging their involvement in criminal violence, while a further 39 were sentenced to terms of imprisonment on other charges. Amnesty International appealed for the commutation of the 11 death sentences and sought further details about the trials.

In mid-January, Ubah Arteh Ghalib, the daughter of Omar Arteh Ghalib (see above), was arrested in Mogadishu allegedly in connection with her father's imprisonment. Amnesty International requested details from the Attorney General about the grounds for her arrest and her legal status. In March the Attorney General informed the organization that she had been released.

The treatment of political detainees was reportedly harsh. Those held in the maximum security prisons of Lanta Bur (near Afgoi) or Labatan Jirow (near Baidowa) were held incommunicado. Some were said to be held in prolonged solitary confinement, either in cells that were in permanent semi-darkness, or in cells permanently lit by artificial light. Medical attention in these prisons was reportedly poor, with only irregular visits by qualified medical doctors. Access to specialist treatment was difficult to obtain and often long delayed, with hospital admission usually being denied. Political detainees held in other prisons, such as Mogadishu central prison or regional prisons, were generally better treated, with family visits usually being allowed. Conditions, however, were poor, with a poor diet and little medical attention being available. Those arrested on political grounds and held for interrogation by the National Security Service in Mogadishu and the larger towns were reportedly subject to beatings and were held incommunicado in poor conditions.

The use of the death penalty also gave cause for concern. During 1983, Amnesty International learned of the imposition of over 30 death sentences by the National Security Court, which has jurisdiction over both political and non-political offences carrying the death penalty, including treason and other national security offences, homicide and embezzlement of large amounts of public funds. Some of the death sentences were reportedly carried out, often within days of the sentence being imposed. On 9 June Amnesty International protested to President Siyad Barre about the execution in public in Mogadishu of a former army officer convicted of homicide a few days earlier. On three separate occasions between September and November Amnesty International appealed to the President for clemency for a total of 21 people condemned to death for national security offences, homicide or embezzlement. The organization received no replies to its appeals and did not know whether any of the sentences and executions were carried out. The total number of death sentences and executions during 1983 was not known to Amnesty International.

South Africa

Amnesty International was concerned about the imprisonment of prisoners of conscience. They included people detained without trial, sentenced to terms of imprisonment by the courts, restricted under banning orders or imprisoned for refusing to undertake military service for reasons of conscience. The organization was also concerned about the widespread detention without trial of other political prisoners, the death in detention of two political detainees and the death in custody of certain alleged criminal suspects. Many uncharged political detainees were allegedly tortured or ill-treated and there were substantial allegations of gross ill-treatment of convicted criminal prisoners at Barberton Prison. The government continued to use banning orders to restrict certain political opponents. The death penalty continued to be used on a substantial scale and three political prisoners and many criminal prisoners were executed. Amnesty International was concerned about the imprisonment of large numbers of black people under so-called "pass laws" which discriminate on the grounds of race.

Amnesty International intervened during the year on behalf of more than 200 detainees, many of whom it considered to be prisoners of conscience. They included officials of black trade unions, students, church workers, and political activists suspected of opposing the South African Government or the administrations in the African "homelands" such as Ciskei, Transkei and Venda, which have been declared "independent" but which are not recognized internationally. Most were held under security legislation permitting unlimited incommunicado detention without charge or trial. Such detainees were often held in solitary confinement for prolonged periods and allegedly tortured or ill-treated during interrogation by security police.

Two political detainees died in security police custody. On 8 March, Tembuyise Simon Mndawe, an alleged member of the banned African National Congress (ANC), was reportedly found hanged in a police cell at Nelspruit. He had been arrested some two weeks before but had not been charged with an offence by the time of his death. No inquest had been held by the end of 1983.

Another political detainee, Paris Malatji, aged 23, was arrested on 4 July and killed the following day while in custody at Protea Police Station in Soweto. Medical evidence indicated that his death was due to a gunshot wound in the forehead inflicted at point-blank range. In October, a security police officer, Sergeant Jan Harm van As, was charged with his murder and remanded on bail for trial in February 1984.

Two earlier deaths of political detainees were also the subject of legal action. In February, two members of the Venda security police were tried in Sibasa on charges of murdering Isaac Tshifhiwa Muofhe, who had died in detention in November 1981. An inquest in July 1982 decided that his death had been caused by an unlawful assault by Captain Muthuphei Ramaligela and Sergeant Phumula Mangaga of the Venda security police. However, they were acquitted and discharged after the trial judge refused to admit as evidence their testimony before the Muofhe inquest, which had incriminated them and which differed in certain respects from the testimony which they then gave at their trial. In March, Amnesty International wrote to the Attorney General of Venda to ask whether there had been an official inquiry into allegations of torture made by other detainees arrested at the same time as Muofhe, including allegations by three Lutheran Church ministers that they had been beaten severely and tortured with electric shocks. There was no reply to Amnesty International's inquiry.

An inquest into the death in security police custody of Ernest Dipale, aged 21, was held in June. He was allegedly found hanged in a cell at the Johannesburg security police headquarters in August 1983. The inquest ruled that he had hanged himself and that no one could be held responsible. However, a statement which Dipale had reportedly made to security police shortly before his death apparently was not made available to the inquest or to lawyers representing his family.

In May, two members of a black farming community threatened with forcible resettlement to an African "homeland", died in police custody in disturbing circumstances within two days. Themba Manana, aged 38, was arrested together with his father apparently for suspected cattle theft. However, neither man had been charged by 3 May when Themba Manana's death occurred at Dirkiesdorp Police Station. On release, his father, Absalom Manana, alleged that he had personally been punched and tortured with electric shocks, giving rise to concern that Themba Manana's death might be attributable to ill-treatment. A second death occurred at Dirkiesdorp Police Station on 4 May when Zephaniah Sibanyoni, a 33-year-old man apparently held as a witness, reportedly collapsed and died. Subsequently, it was reported that the authorities were treating Manana's death as murder but believed, on the basis of a post-mortem report, that Sibanyoni's death was due to natural causes.

A month before these two deaths, Saul Mkhize, the leader of the same community had been shot dead by a white police officer while addressing a meeting to protest against the forcible resettlement plans. In September, the authorities announced that a police officer would be charged with Saul Mkhize's murder but his trial had not started by the end of the year.

New allegations of torture were made by former detainees and by defendants and witnesses in political trials. In February, Cedric Mayson, a former Methodist Church minister who had been adopted as a prisoner of conscience by Amnesty International when he was restricted under a banning order in 1977, alleged in court that he had been stripped naked and made to stand for 48 hours, had had some of his hair pulled out forcibly and had been verbally abused during security police interrogation in late 1981. The judge accepted Mayson's account and ruled that he had made incriminating statements which led to his prosecution for treason only under duress. He was granted bail and subsequently left the country. In another case, four people who had been charged under the Terrorism Act were acquitted in April after a trial lasting nine months when the presiding magistrate accepted allegations from several state witnesses, including one woman aged 57, that they had been assaulted in detention and subjected to solitary confinement to induce them to make statements implicating the accused. However, in several other cases allegations of torture and ill-treatment of detainees and witnesses were not accepted by the courts and evidence extracted from them allegedly under duress was used as a basis to obtain convictions.

Particularly serious allegations of torture were made in the second half of 1983 following many detentions in Ciskei. These occurred after residents of Mdantsane launched a boycott of local bus services in protest against an increase in fares. The Ciskei authorities subsequently declared a state of emergency in Mdantsane, detained more than 100 people for interrogation under the Ciskei National Security Act and arrested hundreds more for allegedly infringing curfew regulations. Those detained included many black trade unionists, particularly officials and supporters of the South African Allied Workers' Union (SAAWU), which was banned in Ciskei on 3 September. Many university and school students who joined in the boycott were also detained, as were several journalists and lawyers. Father Smangaliso Mkhatshwa, General Secretary of the Southern Africa Catholic Bishops' Conference, was also detained in late October. Most of the detainees were released before the end of the year but Father Mkhatshwa and a number of students were still being held incommunicado at the end of 1983.

A number of those detained in August were taken to the local Sisa Dukashe sports stadium where they were held in severely cramped and overcrowded conditions. Many were allegedly assaulted severely by Ciskei security personnel or people assisting them including Mvuyo Malgas, a 19-year-old school student who was brutally assaulted with a *sjambok*, a rhinoceros-hide whip.

Allegations of gross ill-treatment of criminal prisoners were made in September during the trial of eight prison warders at Barberton Prison. They faced three charges of murder and more than 30 charges of assault as a result of incidents in late December 1982 when prisoners were forced to undertake strenuous physical labour during a heatwave and had then been attacked by prison staff using rubber truncheons. Three prisoners died and more than 30 others were injured. During the period between this incident and the end of the warders' trial some nine months later there were renewed acts of violence at the prison which resulted in several more prisoners' deaths. The warders were all acquitted of murder but six of them were jailed for assault for terms ranging from one to eight years. After the trial, the government established a commission of inquiry into prison conditions at Barberton but its outcome was not known to Amnesty International by the end of the year.

There was a substantial reduction in the number of people restricted under banning orders. With one exception, all banning orders in force at the end of June 1982, numbering more than 50, were withdrawn in accordance with a provision of the Internal Security Act of 1982. This stipulated that all such orders should be withdrawn one year after 2 July 1982, the date on which the act took effect. However, 10 of those whose banning orders were lifted were almost immediately rebanned for further terms ranging from two and a half to five years, including Nonzamo Winnie Mandela, who has been almost continually restricted or detained without trial since the early 1960s. Their cases were taken up by Amnesty International.

Amnesty International was concerned about the introduction of new legislation which significantly increased the penalties for refusal to undertake military service for reasons of conscience. The Defence Amendment Act for the first time provided an alternative form of service for those who object to military service on strictly religious grounds, but it stipulated that those whose objection was based on moral or political factors would be liable to imprisonment of up to six years.

The death penalty remained a major concern. There was a continued high rate of executions: no official figures were available by the end of the year but it appeared that the number of executions might be comparable to the 1982 total of 101. Most of those sentenced to death and most of those executed were convicted of criminal offences. However, in June three alleged members of the ANC who had been convicted of treason and other offences were hanged at Pretoria Central Prison. Marcus Thabo Motaung, Jerry Semano Mosololi and Thelle Simon Mogoerane had all been convicted in 1982 of guerrilla activities which resulted in loss of life. They were the first prisoners convicted of treason to be executed in South Africa for almost 70 years.

The organization deplored the executions that took place but welcomed the government's decision to commute the death sentences of three other alleged ANC members convicted of treason, apparently because there had been no loss of life as a result of their actions. In December, Amnesty International appealed for clemency for Benjamin Moloise, another alleged member of the ANC, who was sentenced to death in June after being convicted of a political murder and who had exhausted all judicial appeals by late November. He had not been executed by the end of the year.

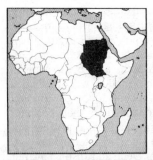

Sudan

Amnesty International's concerns were the large scale detention without trial of political opponents of the government, many of whom were believed to be prisoners of conscience; allegations of torture or ill-treatment of political prisoners; the introduction and application of laws permitting the penalties of amputation and flogging; and the death penalty.

During the year, the government re-divided the country's formerly semi-autonomous southern region into three separate regions, despite strong local opposition, and provided for the creation of elected regional assemblies in each of the country's eight regions. Security in the south deteriorated considerably during 1983, with several violent incidents, including armed attacks on both military and civilian targets by *Anyanya II*, an opposition guerrilla organization.

Abuses by both sides to the conflict were reported, including abductions of civilians by *Anyanya II*. Tens of thousands of people fled the country as a result of these disturbances.

The possible introduction of Islamic (*Shari'a*) law in Sudan, where up to two-thirds of the people are Muslim, had been under consideration by the government for several years. As a result of a presidential decree on 9 September, later ratified by parliament, the previous secular penal code was replaced by a new Islamic penal code. New penalties were introduced for certain offences, to be inflicted after completion of civil judicial procedures providing the right to legal representation and appeal. The new penalties of concern to Amnesty International were those of amputation and flogging. The introduction of Islamic law was followed by the release of all criminal prisoners in the country, numbering about 13,000, who had been convicted under the previous secular penal code and sentenced to prison terms. Few political prisoners, however, were released on this occasion.

At the beginning of 1983, an estimated 300 or more political opponents of the government were detained under the State Security Law. This law provides for indefinite detention without charge or trial on the grounds of state security. The government does not publish the names and number of detainees and to Amnesty International's knowledge there is no formal procedure for independent and regular review of detentions.

Further political arrests under this law took place during 1983. In January several prominent southern politicians were arrested for opposing the government's plan for the re-division of the south. Those arrested included William Ajal Deng, a member of the national parliament. Opposition continued to be expressed against this measure and further arrests took place in 1983; Dhol Achuil Aleu, Vice-President of the High Executive Council for the south (the southern regional government), was detained in March, and Bona Malwal Madut, a journalist and former Minister of Information, was detained in May. Amnesty International issued urgent appeals to the government for the release of these and other people detained for their peaceful opposition to the re-division measure and adopted them as prisoners of conscience. Some of these prisoners were released later in the year without being charged, such as William Ajal Deng and Justin Yac, but the majority remained in prison at the end of 1983.

Other political opponents of the government arrested in 1983 included alleged members or sympathizers of banned opposition organizations. Since 1975, the only political party permitted has been the Sudanese Socialist Union. Suspected members of the banned Sudan Communist Party, Arab Ba'athist Socialist Party, and a section of the Democratic Unionist Party were arrested on several occasions in 1983.

Ustaz Mahmoud Taha, the leader of the Republican Brotherhood, an Islamic organization, and over 50 of its members, including Abdullahi Ahmed al-Naim, a law lecturer, Ahmed Mohamed el-Hussein, a political science lecturer, civil servants, students and others, were arrested in May and June 1983. The organization had reportedly published leaflets accusing certain government officials of promoting religious conflict. Amnesty International appealed for their release as prisoners of conscience. At the end of 1983 they were still being detained without charge.

On 25 September, Sadiq el-Mahdi, a former Prime Minister, was arrested with over 100 of his followers from the Ansar sect after he had publicly criticized the introduction of Islamic law earlier in the month. The prominent Ansar members Nasreldin el-Hadi and Mubarak el-Mahdi were also arrested. Amnesty International expressed concern to the government that they appeared to be imprisoned for their non-violent opinions and called for them to be released if they were not to be charged with any criminal offence.

Mario Muor, leader of the African Nationalists' Organization, an organization of southern students at Khartoum university, was detained for about two months after addressing an open letter to President Numeiri condemning the imposition of Islamic law on non-Muslims.

Amnesty International also continued to appeal on behalf of prisoners of conscience who had been detained at various times in the previous four years. Some of them were released during 1983, such as Sidgi Kaballo, a postgraduate student detained in 1981; Mahgoub Sharif, a poet detained in 1982 and Saudi Daraj, a former trade union official, also detained in 1982. By the end of 1983, Amnesty International believed that over 500 people were detained in Sudan on political grounds, including a considerable number of prisoners of conscience.

Amnesty International was concerned about allegations that some political prisoners were tortured or ill-treated. Several teachers and others arrested in the southern town of Rumbek in August and September 1983, for example, were said to have been beaten and to have had hot pepper put in their eyes. State Security Service officials in October 1983 reportedly beat several prisoners from the south during interrogation, including David Dak Gash, who had been held in Kober prison in Khartoum since 1982. Amnesty International received reports that certain other prisoners held by the State Security Service in Khartoum were similarly ill-treated, but was unable to confirm the reports.

Delays were reported in the provision of medical treatment for prisoners held in civil prisons, such as Kober prison. In December Amnesty International appealed to the authorities to ensure the immediate provision of the necessary medical treatment for nine political prisoners who were reportedly seriously ill. They included Youssif Hussein, a former Communist Party official who was arrested in 1979, and who was said to be suffering from rheumatoid arthritis and a duodenal ulcer.

In October, Amnesty International expressed its deep concern to the government about the introduction in September of the judicial penalty of amputation. Under the new Islamic penal code, theft of items worth more than 250 Sudanese pounds (about $US 200) was made punishable by amputation of the right hand. Amputation of both the right hand and the left leg was made the punishment for armed robbery and persistent theft. Amnesty International called for an urgent review of this law on the grounds that amputation is a cruel, inhuman and degrading punishment and as such is prohibited by international law.

The first two amputations under the new law were carried out publicly on 9 December when two prisoners who had been convicted of theft had their right hands publicly severed by an official executioner at Kober prison. Several others who had been convicted of theft were awaiting infliction of the same penalty at the end of the year.

Following the amputations, Amnesty International protested to the government and called for the practice to be immediately discontinued. The organization reminded both the government and Sudanese medical authorities that any participation by medical personnel in preparations for amputations would breach international codes of medical ethics which clearly forbid medical personnel from participating in or condoning any form of cruel, inhuman or degrading punishment.

Amnesty International was also concerned about the introduction at the same time of the penalty of flogging for adultery by an unmarried person, brewing or selling alcohol and false accusation of an offence against Islamic law. By the end of 1983 over 100 floggings of between 25 and 100 lashes each were believed to have been carried out in public following conviction before the courts.

The new penal code made adultery by a married person a criminal offence punishable by death, with execution to be carried out by stoning, and also required that all executions be carried out in public. A person condemned to death for premeditated homicide could, however, be pardoned and released if the victim's family accepted compensation for the murder. This change was also made applicable to all those condemned to death under the previous penal code. No executions were known to have taken place under the new penal code instituted in September. Amnesty International had no knowledge of the number of people under sentence of death at the end of the year or the number of people who had been executed between January and September under the previous penal code. On 9 June Amnesty International made inquiries to the government about the reported execution of a number of soldiers following their conviction by court martial for mutiny in connection with disturbances within the army at Bor, but no reply was received.

Swaziland

Amnesty International was concerned about the detention without trial of suspected opponents of the government and about the introduction of a new and more severe sedition law which provided for people to be tried before an administrative tribunal without adequate procedural safeguards. The organization was also concerned about the execution of eight people in July. There was also concern for the safety of South African refugees resident in Swaziland after one was shot dead by unknown assailants.

There were two major government changes. In March, Prince Mabandla Dlamini, the Prime Minister, was ousted from office following the arrest of two leading members of the *Liqoqo*, Supreme Council of State, Prince Mfanasibili Dlamini and Chief Mfanawenkosi

Maseko, who were charged with sedition. Their arrest brought to a head a struggle within the government and led Queen Regent Dzeliwe, the Head of State, to dismiss the Prime Minister and release the two members of the *Liqoqo*. However, in August, the Queen Regent was herself deposed by the *Liqoqo* and replaced by Queen Ntombi, another wife of the late King and the mother of Prince Makhosetive, a minor, who was simultaneously named as heir to the throne.

Queen Dzeliwe brought a court application to contest the constitutional legality of her deposition. At the hearing in mid-August before Chief Justice Charles Nathan she was represented by Douglas Lukhele, a leading lawyer and a former Attorney General and High Court judge. After both sides had argued their case, the court adjourned for a few days while the Chief Justice considered whether to allow the application to proceed to the Appeal Court, which alone has jurisdiction on constitutional issues. However, before the court could resume, the government issued an extraordinary decree which excluded from the jurisdiction of the courts all matters affecting royalty and the succession. As a result, the Chief Justice withheld his ruling and Queen Dzeliwe was unable further to challenge her deposition.

After issuing the extraordinary decree, the government also took action against Queen Dzeliwe's advisers. Arthur Khoza, a senior civil servant who had acted as her interpreter, was detained on 22 August. The next day, Douglas Lukhele was arrested. Two members of the Royal Family, Prince Sulumlomo Dlamini and Prince Thunduluka Dlamini, were also detained. All four detainees were held under legislation which permits the Prime Minister to authorize detention without charge or trial for up to 60 days. Their detention orders were then renewed in October after the first 60 days had elapsed, and again in December. They were still being held at the end of the year. All four detainees were adopted as prisoners of conscience by Amnesty International.

In the weeks before new national elections in late October, a number of leaflets were circulated which apparently urged people to boycott them. Several people alleged to have prepared or distributed the leaflets were arrested and charged with sedition, though none had been brought to trial by the end of the year. In mid-October, two weeks before the new elections were due to be held, the government recalled parliament and introduced the Sedition and Subversive Activities (Amendment) Act, which increased the maximum penalty for sedition from three years' to 20 years' imprisonment and provided for the appointment of a special tribunal to try alleged offenders. The Amendment stipulated that the tribunal should sit *in camera* if the prosecution requested closed session and conferred on the tribunal the power to make its own rules of procedure.

There were further arrests at the time of the elections in late October and early November. Those detained included Chief Dambuza Lukhele, who had opposed the deposition of Queen Regent Dzeliwe; Susan Dlamini, the wife of Prince Sulumlomo Dlamini; and two daughters of Douglas Lukhele. Africa Mhlanga and Kislon Shongwe, two former prisoners of conscience who were adopted by Amnesty International when they were detained without trial between May 1978 and May 1980, were also among those arrested. Initially, those arrested were apparently held illegally because they were neither charged nor formally detained. In early December, Kislon Shongwe applied to the courts to rule his imprisonment illegal and to order his release on a writ of *habeas corpus*. However, before this application could be decided he was charged with sedition and 11 others, including Chief Dambuza Lukhele, were charged with treason. By mid-December, some 15 people were known to be in custody for political reasons, in addition to the four detainees who had been held since August. Several of those who were charged with treason then brought an application for bail before the High Court, which discounted government assertions that they would pose a threat to state security and ruled that they should be released pending trial. However, none of the defendants were freed on bail. They were held in custody for some days after they had been granted bail, again apparently without legal sanction, and were then served with 60-day detention orders signed by the Prime Minister. They were still being held at the end of the year. Their cases were taken up for investigation by Amnesty International.

On 2 July, eight people were hanged at Matsapha Central Prison in what were believed to be the first executions for almost two years. All of those executed, seven men and a woman, Phillipa Mdluli, had been sentenced to death after being convicted of ritual murder. At least three other people were sentenced to death for similar offences during the year, but they were not believed to have been executed by the end of 1983.

In February, Amnesty International wrote to Prime Minister Mabandla Dlamini to express concern about the use of the death penalty, following the imposition of at least 14 death sentences during 1982. The organization called on the government to recommend that the Queen Regent should extend clemency to all prisoners whose sentences might be confirmed by the Appeal Court. In July, following the executions at the beginning of the month, Amnesty International made a further appeal to the government to discontinue the use of the death penalty. However, the organization received no response to these appeals.

There was renewed concern for the safety of South African refugees in Swaziland following the killing in November of Zwelakhe Nyanda, an alleged member of the banned African National Congress (ANC) of South Africa, and a Swazi national who occupied the same house. There was no evidence to attribute responsibility for the killings but they apparently gave rise to fears in the refugee community that they had been committed by South African security agents. In December, Amnesty International received information that a number of South African refugees, including some who had long had residence rights in Swaziland, were taken into custody and placed at Mawelawela Camp, near Mbabane. It appeared at the end of the year that some of them might be held pending resettlement in other countries.

Tanzania

Amnesty International was concerned about the indefinite detention without trial of alleged political opponents of the government and the *refoulement* (involuntary repatriation), of refugees.

Following numerous arrests in January 1983, 30 people were remanded in custody and charged with treason. The government announced that a plot to kill President Julius Nyerere and overthrow the government had been uncovered. All but seven of those charged with treason in this connection were members of the armed forces. They were granted access to legal counsel and relatives. However, when the two principal defendants escaped from custody and fled to neighbouring Kenya in June, the authorities withdrew the treason charges against the other 28 defendants but served them with detention orders of unlimited duration issued in accordance with the Preventive Detention Act. They were still being detained on this basis at the end of the year. Amnesty International was concerned that they could be detained indefinitely without legal recourse.

The Preventive Detention Act, in addition to being applied to suspected political opponents of the government, had been used in previous years to imprison alleged "economic saboteurs" without charge or trial. Particularly in view of criticisms among judges and lawyers in Tanzania of the use of presidential detention powers for this purpose, the government introduced new temporary legislation in May 1983 for a period of one year – the Economic Sabotage (Special Provisions) Act – which was made retroactive to 4 March 1983. The act permits police officers to arrest alleged "economic saboteurs" and detain them for investigation for up to 60 days. At the end of the 60-day period, detainees must be formally charged before the new National Anti-Economic Sabotage Tribunal and remanded for trial, or otherwise released. Each of the four tribunals is headed by a High Court judge, and includes two other members appointed by the President. It can impose sentences of up to 15 years' imprisonment. Defendants have no right to legal representation or appeal. Over 2,000 people were reportedly detained under this act between March and December for a wide range of alleged economic sabotage offences. By the end of the year, according to the authorities, almost 400 had been tried; over 600 others had been released without being tried. As many as 1,000 people were still imprisoned while awaiting charge or trial. Amnesty International was monitoring the possible use of this act for political purposes and was concerned about certain aspects of the act – its retroactivity and the denial of the right to legal representation and appeal – which were incompatible with international standards for fair trial.

During 1983 Amnesty International learned of the imprisonment of 25 alleged political opponents of the government in Zanzibar, who were detained without charge or trial for an indefinite period under Zanzibar's separate Preventive Detention Act. Six of the detainees, including Othman Mzee Muqadam "Bapa", had been arrested in early 1981, when they were publicly accused of plotting to overthrow the Zanzibar Government. Another detainee, Ali Sultan Issa, a former prisoner of conscience, was arrested in October 1982 for selling T-shirts bearing the slogan *Maendeleo Zanzibar*, "Forward Zanzibar", which was used by Zanzibar political opponents abroad. Amnesty International received no reply to its inquiries to the authorities about the grounds for the arrest of Ali Sultan Issa or to its expression of concern that he might be imprisoned for his non-violent political opinions. He was, however, released on 5 October 1983 without being charged. A further 18 people were reportedly detained in August for allegedly conspiring to overthrow the Zanzibar Government and establish an Islamic republic. Amnesty International was seeking further details about these detainees in order to determine whether they were prisoners of conscience.

In early November 1983, 20 or more Kenyan nationals, who had fled to Tanzania after the coup attempt in Kenya by elements of the Kenya Air Force on 1 August 1982, were arrested in Tanzania. At least 16 of those who were arrested, including the two self-confessed leaders of the coup attempt, other former air force personnel, two former members of parliament and some university students, were reportedly secretly returned to Kenya against their will and detained. Tanzania had earlier granted asylum to at least 10 of those returned.

Up to seven Tanzanian refugees in Kenya were arrested at about the same time and were reportedly secretly returned to Tanzania and detained. One of them, Hatty McGhee, an Air Tanzania pilot, had earlier escaped from prison in Tanzania in June 1983; he had been charged with treason in connection with the January 1983 coup conspiracy. Three others had reportedly been formally recognized as refugees under the United Nations Convention and Protocol Relating to the Status of Refugees. Another, Said Lamke, a businessperson, was a naturalized Kenyan citizen.

These secret exchanges of alleged political opponents took place shortly before the meeting on 16 November between the Presidents of Kenya, Tanzania and Uganda, when they reportedly reached agreement on a number of political matters affecting all three East African states. On 25 November Amnesty International expressed its concern to the Tanzanian Government about reports of refugees being arrested and forcibly returned to Kenya, where they were immediately detained. Amnesty International also inquired into the situation of a number of Tanzanian refugees who had at the same time been forcibly returned to Tanzania by the Kenyan authorities and detained. Amnesty International urged the government to reaffirm its stated commitment to the protection of refugees in accordance with the United Nations Convention and Protocol relating to the Status of Refugees, which Tanzania has ratified. No response was received. By the end of the year there had been no official comment on the incident, nor confirmation of the detention of those who had been returned from Kenya and whose legal status was not known. Amnesty International continued to investigate this serious violation of international law and to seek details about those who had been returned from Kenya. The organization was concerned in particular that Said Lamke, and possibly others, could be prisoners of conscience.

Togo

Amnesty International was concerned about the detention without trial of suspected opponents of the government, one of whom apparently "disappeared" in custody, and by the continued imprisonment of three political prisoners who were sentenced after a trial which fell short of internationally recognized standards. There were allegations of torture of detainees and prison conditions were reported to be harsh.

Amnesty International continued to receive reports in 1983 about the detention without trial of significant numbers of individuals apparently suspected by the authorities of political opposition. The reported reasons for arrest varied greatly, and were often seemingly trivial. Mere suspicion of possessing leaflets critical of the government or of having made critical statements about its policies was often apparently sufficient reason for the authorities to detain individuals, sometimes for several years. In such cases, detainees had no access to the courts and no means by which they could seek redress. In the majority of the 50 or so cases reported to Amnesty International during the year, the detainees had been arrested in 1982 or 1983 but, in some cases, they had reportedly been held without trial for as long as seven years. The authorities maintained a rigorous censorship on correspondence with the outside world and generally did not publicize arrests and releases. However, it was possible to confirm that seven people whose arrest appeared to be motivated at least partially by political concerns had not been released from detention during 1983. In September and November 1983, Amnesty International requested the Togolese authorities to provide information on the reasons and legal basis for these detentions. Those detained included M'ba Kabassema Hankpade, a former government minister who was arrested in April 1981 and reportedly "disappeared" shortly after his transfer from the capital, Lome, to Niamtougou, and Idrissou Antoine Meatchi, a former Vice-President of Togo, who was arrested in June 1982, officially in connection with the alleged mismanagement of public funds some 10 years earlier. No reply was received from the authorities.

Amnesty International continued throughout the year to seek a judicial review with respect to the cases of Kodjovi Emmanuel de Souza, Kouao Stéphan Sanvee and Kwassi Jean Savi de Tove, who were convicted by the State Security Court in August 1979 on charges of conspiracy to overthrow the government. Death sentences imposed by the court against the first two were later commuted to life imprisonment. Kwassi Jean Savi de Tove received a 10-year prison sentence. The report of Amnesty International's observer, who attended the two-day hearings in Lome, concluded that the trial fell short of internationally recognized standards and was unfair. In particular, the report expressed the view that the state had failed to adequately establish the guilt of the accused, who were denied access to their counsel at all stages of the judicial process. The cases of the three convicted prisoners were being investigated by Amnesty International, which called on the authorities to supply information on the whereabouts of Kodjovi Emmanuel de Souza, whose place of detention was unknown. Amnesty International also expressed concern to the authorities about the state of health of Kouao Stéphan Sanvee, who was reportedly ill throughout the year. No reply was received from the Togolese authorities to Amnesty International's appeals.

Many political detainees in Togo were reportedly tortured and ill-treated after being taken into custody. Beatings, the administering of heavy slaps to both ears causing pain and occasionally permanent damage to detainees' hearing, and electric shocks were all reported to have been used to obtain confessions at various political detention centres in Lome. Conditions of detention in the quarters of the *gendarmerie* known as the *Petite porte* ("small doorway") and *Grande porte* ("big doorway") were described as harsh. The food supplied to detainees was inadequate, in both nutritive value and in quantity. The standard of sanitation was reported to be extremely low, and many detainees were reported to be ill. Medical facilities were said to be poor, and detainees were apparently denied exercise. Amnesty International also received unconfirmed reports that political detainees were being held in very difficult conditions in Temedja military camp and the prison at Mango, both in northern Togo.

Uganda

Amnesty International was concerned about the wide-ranging detention without trial of alleged opponents of the government. Several hundred were detained by the civil authorities under the Public Order and Security Act, in many cases without full observance of their legal rights. Many others were detained unlawfully by the military authorities and reportedly tortured. Some reportedly "disappeared" in military custody or were killed. Amnesty International was also concerned about reports of extrajudicial executions of civilians by soldiers and about the use of the death penalty.

President Milton Obote's government continued to face armed opposition in central and northwestern Uganda from the National Resistance Army, Uganda Freedom Movement and Uganda National Rescue Front. Many unarmed civilians were allegedly killed by the army but the government denied these allegations. Amnesty International also received reports of killings by opposition guerrilla organizations. As a result of the insecurity and violence, several thousand people fled to neighbouring countries. Some 150,000 other people were placed in "displaced persons" camps under army control where many were reportedly ill-treated by soldiers.

In April, Amnesty International published the correspondence with the government that followed a mission to Uganda in January 1982. Amnesty International had submitted recommendations for the protection of basic human rights but few of these recommendations appeared to have been implemented. In particular, the government had not initiated an independent inquiry into allegations of torture or killings and had not taken steps to end arbitrary executions by the army.

Large numbers of people were arrested during 1983 on suspicion of supporting armed opposition organizations. In Kampala, hundreds of people at a time were detained in a number of *panda gari* ("get in the lorry") operations, carried out by police and military officials. Although most such detainees were believed to have been quickly released, a considerable number were reportedly detained for further interrogation.

Several hundred people were detained under the Public Order and Security Act, which provides for indefinite detention without charge or trial. They were held at Luzira Upper Prison, a maximum security prison administered by the Prison Service. On 12 August the government acknowledged that 92 people had been detained under this act in the first half of 1983, when it published a list of 359 people who were still in detention following their arrest between 1979 and 1983. Amnesty International, however, believed that the actual number of detainees was much higher and that the government had failed to observe the constitutional requirement that all those detained under the act should be named in the government gazette within one month and thereafter at six-monthly intervals. The constitution also requires that all detentions should be reviewed within two months by an independent Detention Review Tribunal, at which detainees may appear with legal representation, and thereafter at six-monthly intervals. The findings of the tribunal are not binding on the government and are not published. The tribunal reviewed a small proportion of detentions in early 1983 but many detentions were allegedly not reviewed at all during the year.

Several prisoners detained under this act in 1983 were members of the legally permitted opposition Democratic Party and were apparently arrested for their non-violent political activities. Among them was the Reverend Francis Kizito, a Roman Catholic priest from Mpigi district, who was arrested in January and publicly accused of having visited guerrilla camps in 1981. He was released uncharged in October. Another prisoner who was still detained without charge at the end of 1983 was Ambrose Okullo, a former deputy Minister of Education and an unsuccessful Democratic Party parliamentary candidate. The government made no reply to Amnesty International's inquiries into the grounds for his detention and about the detention of several others whom Amnesty International believed could be prisoners of conscience.

Yoweri Kyesimira, a Democratic Party member of parliament and former university professor, was arrested on 12 March and charged with treason for allegedly having met guerrilla leaders in 1981. By the end of 1983 no date had been set for his trial. Amnesty International was investigating whether he had been detained because of his non-violent political activities.

Amnesty International received information that large numbers of other people were arrested by the army ostensibly for having links with the guerrillas. Details were difficult to obtain but the organization received information indicating that many people were held without official acknowledgement and incommunicado in military custody, although the army has no power in law to detain civilians. It was alleged that people arrested by the army in the Kampala area were usually taken initially to military interrogation offices in Nile Mansions in Kampala, and then transferred to Makindye, Mbuya or Malire barracks in Kampala or certain private houses in Kampala under military control. It was also alleged that torture and ill-treatment of such detainees in military custody were common and some were alleged to have "disappeared" in military custody, although such reports were invariably difficult to verify. Former detainees, including alleged torture victims, told Amnesty International that other detainees had been arbitrarily executed or had died in custody as a result of torture, starvation or the denial of medical treatment.

In July Amnesty International made urgent appeals on behalf of Pius Kawere, a lawyer and Democratic Party member, who was held without official acknowledgement in Mbuya barracks. He had been arrested in Mukono on 22 April by a military intelligence officer. He was released in August after being held in harsh conditions together with almost 100 other civilian detainees, many of whom had been tortured.

Amnesty International made inquiries to the authorities about several other prisoners who were reportedly tortured while in military custody. Amnesty International later learned of the transfer of some of the detainees to detention in civil custody and the release of certain others, reportedly after their relatives had paid bribes to military officials. A number, however, were feared to have "disappeared". In one case documented by Amnesty International, Patrick Kibaalya, a primary school headmaster in Jinja, was arrested by soldiers on 20 February in Jinja, and then "disappeared". It was later learned that he had been taken to Katabi military barracks in Entebbe and tortured so severely that he died two days later.

Amnesty International was also investigating allegations of illegal detentions and torture by officials of the National Security Agency, an intelligence unit, and by officers of the Special Force, a para-military police unit.

Amnesty International expressed concern about the continued

detention without trial of several people who were arrested in 1981 and 1982. They included Ben Etiang, a Democratic Party supporter and businessperson in Tororo, and Silver Tibihika, an army lieutenant. Amnesty International repeated its calls for thorough investigations into the "disappearance" of several people arrested by the army in 1981, including Beatrice Kemigisha, a Makerere University lecturer, and Constantin Kabazaire, a former magistrate. The government continued to deny that they had been arrested. In March, Amnesty International received some information from the Minister of Internal Affairs concerning prisoners about whom it had inquired in 1982, but its request for clarification in a number of cases, and further investigations into "disappearances" received no response.

In January 200 detainees were released from Luzira Upper Prison. They were believed to have included some political detainees as well as some of the 60 or more former soldiers of ex-President Amin's army who had been detained without trial since 1979. In October the government announced the release of 2,100 prisoners in an amnesty to mark the 20th anniversary of Uganda's independence. The government did not disclose details of those released, most of whom were apparently convicted criminal prisoners, although some had been detained under the Public Order and Security Act and had been the subject of inquiries by Amnesty International. At the end of 1983 several hundred detainees were still believed to be held in Luzira Upper Prison.

Amnesty International received allegations of torture throughout 1983 of detainees held in military custody. The allegations were made by detainees who survived and were later released, detainees' relatives, and others. Detainees interrogated in Nile Mansions military offices were reportedly stripped naked and severely beaten with sticks and gun butts, and given little or no food for days at a time. Particularly severe torture reportedly occurred at Makindye and Kireka barracks. Detainees in Makindye barracks were said to be subjected to beatings and assaults with bayonets, some being shot in the limbs. Many allegedly died as a result of torture, starvation or being shot. Torture methods reported in Kireka barracks included burning sensitive parts of the body, beatings and shootings. Reports of torture were also received in respect of military detention centres in other parts of the country, for example in Bombo, Tororo and Mpigi. People held at local administrative centres in Luwero and Mpigi districts were also reportedly tortured. Amnesty International inquired about a number of such cases in 1983 but received no replies from the authorities.

Prison conditions for those held in military custody after interrogation were also said to be harsh. Detainees were held incommunicado in dirty, overcrowded cells. They were given very little food and were denied medical treatment.

Prison conditions for political detainees held in civil custody by the police or prison service – including those held in Luzira Upper Prison – were believed to be much better in comparison.

Numerous reports were received of the arbitrary and illegal killing of civilians by military personnel, both in areas of military activity against the guerrillas and in urban and rural areas outside any area of armed conflict. The government maintained that it investigated any cases of abuse of power by soldiers but few soldiers were known to have been charged with offences of violence against civilians. In one case, a soldier was charged with the murder of an opposition member of parliament, Africano Ssembattya, on 2 October, but the circumstances of the incident were not known to Amnesty International and the trial had not started by the end of the year. Deaths of non-combatant civilians allegedly at the hands of the military were rarely investigated by the police and no inquests were known to have been held in such cases.

Political killings by opposition guerrilla organizations were also reported. Allegations that specific killings were committed either by government or by anti-government forces were generally difficult to corroborate. The absence of detailed accounts of the incidents from official sources or eye-witnesses, as well as the high level of insecurity in the areas where the killings occurred, contributed to the difficulties Amnesty International faced in seeking to attribute responsibility for the killings.

In Kikyusa village in Bulemezi county in Luwero district, up to 100 people were killed in a "displaced persons" camp at the end of May. The government blamed the killings on opposition guerrillas wearing army uniform, but other sources alleged that the perpetrators were in fact government soldiers. Despite international concern about this incident, no independent inquiry was known to have been initiated by the government. In August a government spokesperson admitted in parliament that the killing of 30 people in Ssonde and Jinja villages in Mukono District on 18 March by men in army uniform had been carried out by soldiers, although the government had earlier blamed the killings on guerrilla opponents. He stated that the killings were a "mistake" but Amnesty International has no knowledge of any further investigation into the incident or of any action taken against those responsible. In September, over 60 people arrested in Mpigi West district and held in Mpigi prison were reportedly taken out by soldiers and killed nearby. The government did not reply to Amnesty International's inquiries about the incident.

Amnesty International received information that some 23 prisoners were awaiting execution in Luzira Upper Prison in March. They were all reported to have been convicted of murder and armed robbery and sentenced to death since 1979. It was not known how many death sentences were imposed in 1983 or whether any executions were carried out.

Upper Volta

Amnesty International was concerned about the detention and restriction under house arrest without trial of civilians and military officers who had occupied prominent political positions.

There was considerable political instability in Upper Volta in 1983, including several major and occasionally bloody changes in the country's leadership. Until mid-May, power was shared by the President of the *Conseil du salut du peuple* (CSP), People's Salvation Council, Major Jean-Baptiste Ouedraogo, and by the Prime Minister, Captain Thomas Sankara. During this period, nearly 25 former senior officials of the administration of General Sangoule Lamizana, which was overthrown by a military coup in November 1980, remained under house arrest while an official commission investigated their cases to determine whether they should be charged with various economic offences. Most of these cases, including those of the former President and of the former Prime Minister Joseph Conombo, were taken up for investigation by Amnesty International. After taking power from the *Comité militaire de redressement pour le progrès national* (CMRPN), the Military Committee of Recovery for National Progress, in November 1982, the CSP had announced its intention to charge and bring to trial some of the former senior officials of the Lamizana administration. Their trial was due to take place before a special court established under the CMRPN, which was composed mainly of military officers and non-jurists. Amnesty International welcomed the new government's assurance that the detainees would be brought to trial but expressed concern that the court had been given powers to try them for crimes which were made punishable under retroactive legislation and that no appeal would be permitted to a higher court. However, in late March, Prime Minister Sankara gave assurances that his administration was taking steps to alleviate these concerns.

On 19 March, Joseph Ouedraogo, a former President of the National Assembly, and three others including a former government minister and a former ambassador, were detained in the capital, Ouagadougou. The authorities accused them of attempting to "destabilize" the government, by allegedly organizing a "campaign of intoxication" against it and by allegedly mobilizing the country's merchants against its policies. Joseph Ouedraogo and at least one other detainee were taken to the remote town of Dori and held there. Subsequently, Amnesty International asked the authorities for information about the legal basis of these detentions and reminded them of the detainees' internationally-recognized right to a prompt and fair trial. However, the organization received no reply.

On 17 May, Prime Minister Sankara and the Secretary General of the CSP Secretariat, Major Jean-Baptise Lingani, were arrested on the orders of President Ouedraogo, who accused them of "irresponsible and demagogic activities". Following demonstrations against these arrests in Ouagadougou several days later, six people were detained including the Minister of Youth and Sport, Ibrahima Kone, and Soumane Toure, the Secretary General of the *Confédération syndicale voltaïque* (CSV), Trade Union Confederation of Upper Volta.

On 27 May, President Ouedraogo announced an amnesty for all political prisoners including the Prime Minister and seven others who were arrested in May. Most of the 25 former senior officials of the Lamizana administration were reportedly released from house arrest, as were several senior officers who had served in the CMRPN administration and who had been placed under house arrest in November 1982. Joseph Ouedraogo and the three other individuals who were arrested in March were also released. In early June, however, President Ouedraogo announced that former Prime Minister Sankara and Jean-Baptiste Lingani had been rearrested and placed under house arrest for their own security. Ten days later, the President was obliged to release them following an open challenge to his decision to place them under house arrest by paratroop units supporting the former Prime Minister.

On 5 August, President Ouedraogo was overthrown in a coup and arrested. He was replaced as head of government by former Prime Minister Sankara. The latter promptly announced the dissolution of the CSP and the formation of the *Conseil national de la révolution* (CNR), National Council of the Revolution. Several people were reportedly killed during or shortly after the coup, including the army Chief of Staff, Colonel Some Yorian, and Major Fidele Guebre. According to official sources, they were shot and killed while attempting to escape from custody. Ten days after the coup, President Sankara announced restrictions on the freedom of movement of nine former senior officials, including former President Lamizana, former Prime Minister Conombo and former President of the National Assembly Joseph Ouedraogo. On 11 October, the authorities announced that 13 former officials, including these nine, were being put under strict house arrest in their home villages, because the authorities had allegedly discovered that they were involved in "major plots" against the government. In mid-November, these 13 individuals were reportedly taken into custody and detained, probably in Ouagadougou. Amnesty International appealed to the authorities to clarify the legal basis of these detentions and the status of former officials who had apparently been amnestied or cleared of all charges during the administration of former President Ouedraogo.

In October, the CNR announced the formation of Revolutionary People's Tribunals, which were given jurisdiction to try cases of a political nature, those involving state security, cases of embezzlement of public funds and all cases involving offences by state officials. The tribunals were to comprise 18 judges, three of whom were to be magistrates, the rest being soldiers and ordinary civilians. Defendants appearing before the court were not to be assisted by defence counsel and no prosecutors were to be present to set out the case for the State. There was to be no appeal against conviction or sentence.

In late December 1983, the authorities announced that the Revolutionary People's Tribunals would hold their first hearings in January 1984 when former President Lamizana would face charges of embezzlement and wasting state funds.

Zaire

Amnesty International was concerned about the imprisonment of prisoners of conscience and the detention without trial of suspected opponents of the government. Some political detainees were reported to have been tortured or severely beaten while in custody. There were also allegations of torture of criminal suspects, a number of whom were reportedly killed or deliberately starved to death at one police station in Kinshasa. Amnesty International was also concerned about reports of grossly inadequate prison conditions and by the use of the death penalty.

Some 60 political prisoners whose cases were known to Amnesty International at the beginning of the year were released in May under the terms of an amnesty granted by President Mobutu Sese Seko. However, by the end of 1983 more than 100 people were known to have been imprisoned or restricted for political reasons, including many of those freed in May. The total number of political prisoners being held was unclear.

In March Amnesty International published a briefing titled *Political Imprisonment in Zaire*. This described in detail the detention without trial of suspected political opponents of the government and referred particularly to detentions which had occurred in Kivu region. It also reported the cases of prisoners of conscience who were sentenced to 15-year prison terms in May 1982 after an unfair trial at which they had been accused of trying to form a new political party, known as the *Union pour la démocratie et le progrès social* (UDPS), Union for Democracy and Social Progress. This attempt was considered by the authorities to be unconstitutional and illegal as under the terms of the constitution Zaire is a one-party state ruled by the *Mouvement populaire de la révolution* (MPR), People's Movement for the Revolution.

Many suspected supporters of the UDPS were still being detained without charge or trial at the beginning of 1983 and had been adopted as prisoners of conscience by Amnesty International. Most of them had been arrested between July and November 1982 and were being held at the Kinshasa headquarters of the Kinshasa national security service, the *Centre national de recherches et d'investigations* (CNRI), National Research and Investigation Centre, which in November was merged with the service responsible for Zaire's external security to form a new agency, the *Agence nationale de documentation* (AND), National Documentation Agency. In May the government granted an amnesty to all those known by Amnesty International to be detained as suspected UDPS supporters. The authorities informed Amnesty International that only some 17 prisoners who had been convicted of offences against the security of the state would benefit from the amnesty, but it later became clear that many other political prisoners had also been released. They included untried political detainees and Mbwaya Mupompa, a woman who had been sentenced to three years' imprisonment in April 1982 for entering the country with allegedly subversive documents. Four former soldiers, the only prisoners remaining of some 70 who were convicted in March 1978 in connection with an alleged plot to kill President Mobutu, were also freed.

Following the May releases, Amnesty International continued to appeal for the release of one person who was still imprisoned and was believed to be a prisoner of conscience.

A number of those released in May were regarded by the authorities as the leaders of the UDPS. They were known in Zaire as the "Group of 13" and included 11 former members of the national assembly, known as People's Commissioners; a former government minister, Kibassa Maliba; and a businessperson, Birindwa ci Birkashirwa. People suspected of helping any of the 13 in their political activities were arrested on a number of occasions. At the beginning of August, for example, a printer who had supplied them with visiting cards was arrested and was apparently kept in custody for the rest of the year. In mid-August, several members of the group were themselves briefly detained and subjected to severe beatings. Their arrest occurred after they had met a visiting delegation from the United States House of Representatives at Kinshasa's Intercontinental Hotel. They delivered a memorandum to the visiting delegation which apparently contained criticisms of the political situation in Zaire. After the meeting, they were cheered by a crowd of UDPS supporters outside the hotel. The security forces intervened and arrested Kibassa Maliba, four former People's Commissioners who belonged to the "Group of 13" and some 50 other UDPS supporters. They were held for a few hours, reportedly subjected to severe beatings and then released. However, one other UDPS supporter, Bossassi-Epole Bolya Kodya, who was arrested at the same time was not released, but was instead held at the CNRI headquarters in Kinshasa for several months and eventually sent into internal banishment to a town in Equateur region. He was not charged with having committed a specific offence. He had previously been detained on several occasions since July 1981 and was President of the *Ligue zaïroise pour la défense du Citoyen par la défense des droits de l'homme* (LDDH), Zairian League for the Defence of the Citizen by the Defence of Human Rights. He was adopted by Amnesty International as a prisoner of conscience.

During August arrests of suspected UDPS supporters also took place elsewhere, particularly in Mbuji-Mayi, the capital of Kasaï Oriental region, where more than 100 people were reportedly arrested. Although most were believed to have been released uncharged after a few weeks in detention, some were allegedly tortured and eventually transferred to Kinshasa, where they remained in the custody of the AND at the end of the year. They included a former People's Commissioner, Mukoka Mwena Kavulu, and Dinanga Mukunze, a businessperson who had headed South Kasaï's military forces when the area tried to secede in 1960.

Between August and November, other suspected UDPS supporters were arrested and either detained without charge or trial, or sent into internal banishment. In mid-November, Kibassa Maliba, Birindwa ci Birkashirwa and seven former People's Commissioners were sent into internal banishment under the terms of administrative banishment orders. The orders specified that they were to be restricted to isolated villages in their regions of origin, along with their wives and children, who were also named in the orders. Similar banishment orders were also served on others suspected of helping to organize the UDPS, including Professor Lihau Ebua, a former Supreme Court judge who had been consulted by the UDPS leaders early in 1982 about ways of forming a new political party in Zaire without breaking the law. Amnesty International considered them all to be prisoners of conscience.

Despite these events, President Mobutu was reported at the end of November to have told a foreign journalist that there were no prisoners of conscience in Zaire and that in Zaire people were not arrested for political reasons.

Further arrests occurred in December. Four sons of one of the banished People's Commissioners, Ngalula Mpandanjila, were detained in Kinshasa on 4 December, apparently because they were suspected of contacting foreign journalists about their father's case. In the village in Kasaï Oriental region where Ngalula Mpandanjila himself was restricted, the village chief was reportedly arrested for failing to stop other villagers from talking with the former People's Commissioner. Elsewhere in the region, more than 20 people were known to hve been arrested and detained at the AND headquarters in Mbuji-Mayi because they were suspected of supporting the UDPS.

Other suspected government opponents were also arrested in November and December. In Uvira, Kivu region, a school teacher was arrested in November, reportedly accused of having been in contact with Zairian opposition leaders living outside the country. He was allegedly tortured and later transferred to the AND headquarters in Bukavu, where he was kept in custody uncharged. In December a number of school teachers were arrested in Kisangani, the capital of Haut Zaire region, and several "relegated" to remote villages after they were accused by the AND of instigating a strike by school teachers for higher salaries.

There were renewed allegations of torture. Many concerned suspected criminals, though it was also reported that suspected UDPS supporters detained in Kasaï Oriental region in August and December had been tortured. In February there were reports that a man named Mvuezolo, who had been arrested as a suspected thief, had died as a result of torture inflicted while he was held at Maluku, north of Kinshasa, in the custody of the *gendarmerie*. Two other prisoners suspected of theft were reportedly tortured at the same time. Mvuezolo was alleged to have been kicked by guards, cut with a machete and subjected to electric shocks.

Following Mvuezolo's death, some of his colleagues at the firm where he worked demonstrated in protest and 14 of them were arrested. On the night of 4 February soldiers carried out a search operation in Maluku, breaking into houses and arresting almost 90 people. Most such detainees were apparently released after paying bribes or unofficial "fines". No official action is known to have been taken against the *gendarmes* involved in the torture.

Allegations of the torture of suspected criminals, apparently as a means of obtaining "confessions", were also received from Kinshasa. There was also strong reason to believe that certain criminal suspects held at a police station in Kinshasa's Lingwala district, under the authority of the *Brigade spéciale de recherches et de surveillance* (BSRS), Special Research and Surveillance Brigade, a branch of the *gendarmerie*, were deliberately killed, many of them being starved to death. Deaths were reported at this police station in early 1983 and again at the end of the year. In January 10 prisoners reportedly died there, including two who had been receiving hospital treatment but who were allegedly dragged from their beds and taken to the BSRS centre to be killed. By the end of the year more than 50 prisoners were reported to have been killed. The names of some of the victims were known to Amnesty International.

Despite repeated appeals to the authorities by Amnesty International and by other organizations, no effective measures are known to have been taken to prevent such killings, nor to prevent the death of other prisoners. Such deaths became frequent at Kinshasa's Makala and N'Dolo prisons in late 1983, with most of those who died reportedly having suffered from malnutrition.

Amnesty International learned that a number of death sentences were imposed by courts and confirmed upon appeal but did not know how many, if any, executions were carried out during the year.

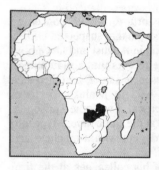

Zambia

Amnesty International was concerned about the detention without trial of alleged political opponents of the government, some of whom were taken up for adoption or investigation as prisoners of conscience. The organization was also concerned about allegations of cruel, inhuman and degrading treatment of certain prisoners under sentence of death and by reports of the death in custody in December of two criminal suspects. At least 30 people were reportedly sentenced to death during the year. Of these, seven were convicted of treason and the remainder were either convicted of murder or armed robbery with violence.

The authorities continued to use the Preservation of Public Security Regulations to authorize the detention without trial of people alleged to constitute a threat to public security. They included people suspected of opposing the government and others arrested as a result of their alleged association with Adamson Mushala, whom the government claimed was trained as a guerrilla fighter by South African forces in Namibia and was responsible for various acts of banditry in North Western Province until his death in 1982. In November 1983, an alleged former associate of Mushala appealed to the Lusaka High Court to order his release after he had spent more than six years in detention without trial.

However, no ruling on his case was known to have been made by the end of the year.

Amnesty International continued to press for the release of Nkaka Chisanga Puta, a lawyer who was adopted as a prisoner of conscience following his arrest in July 1981. The government alleged that he had conspired with others to secure the escape from prison of several people then awaiting trial on treason charges, one of whom, Valentine Musakanya, was a legal client and relation. However, no formal charges had been laid against Nkaka Chisanga Puta and he had not been brought to trial by the end of 1983, by which time he had been in detention for more than two years.

Several other people detained since 1981 in connection with the alleged escape plot also remained in custody throughout the year. However, Geoffrey Haamaundu, a lawyer whose case had been taken up for investigation by Amnesty International, was released uncharged after almost two years in detention.

Judgment in the long-running trial of Valentine Musakanya and seven others accused of treason was given on 20 January. All eight defendants were convicted and seven of them were sentenced to death. They included Valentine Musakanya, a former Governor of the Bank of Zambia, and Edward Shamwana, a lawyer and former High Court Commissioner. Four of those sentenced to death were refugees from Zaire. The eighth defendant received a 10-year sentence. All the defendants had been charged in connection with an alleged conspiracy to overthrow the government and kidnap President Kaunda in October 1980. The main evidence against them was given by former Air Force Commander Major-General Christopher Kabwe, who was originally one of those charged with treason but who was released after he agreed to testify as a state witness. The defendants lodged an appeal against their convictions and sentences but these had not been heard by the end of the year.

Amnesty International issued an international appeal to seek clemency on behalf of these prisoners and called on President Kaunda to commute their sentences should they be confirmed on appeal.

Following their conviction, the prisoners sentenced to death in January were moved to Kabwe Maximum Security Prison. In May, six of them took legal action against the prison authorities alleging that they had been subjected to cruel, inhuman and degrading treatment. They alleged that they had been denied proper medical treatment, subjected to solitary confinement in breach of prison regulations and denied the same access to visitors and newspapers as permitted to other prisoners. The court action was opposed by the state and had not been concluded by the end of 1983. However, in November it was reported that the six prisoners had decided to initiate legal proceedings against three named prison officers who, they alleged, had placed them in leg-irons in May, thereby contravening the Prisons Act. A magistrate ruled that the prison officers had a case to answer and adjourned the hearing until 1984.

Two criminal suspects, who were held for questioning about an armed robbery which took place at the end of November and which resulted in the deaths of a civilian and a police officer, reportedly died in police custody at Ndola. Alfred Mailoni had apparently jumped to his death from an upper floor window while being questioned by three police officers on 3 December. The next day, another suspect, Cornelius Musopelo, was found dead in his cell at Ndola police station. A police investigation into the deaths was ordered and the circumstances in which they occurred had not been disclosed by the end of the year.

Amnesty International remained concerned about the use of the death penalty. In addition to the seven prisoners sentenced to death for treason, at least 23 other people convicted of criminal offences were reported to have been sentenced to death during the year. A number were convicted of murder but approximately half were sentenced to death after being convicted of armed robbery with violence.

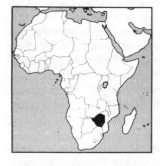

Zimbabwe

Amnesty International was concerned about the detention without trial of alleged political opponents of the government under emergency powers authorizing indefinite imprisonment at the government's discretion. There were substantial allegations of torture of political detainees and many people taken into military custody during counter-insurgency operations, particularly in Matabeleland North Province, were tortured and ill-treated. At least several hundred other people, including children, were extrajudicially executed in the same area, mostly by soldiers of the army's Fifth Brigade. Amnesty International was also concerned about the continued use of the death penalty.

The government faced armed opposition from so-called "dissidents" who allegedly included former guerrilla fighters belonging to the Zimbabwe People's Revolutionary Army (ZIPRA) and other insurgents who were said by the authorities to have received military training in South Africa. At the beginning of the year several civilians were killed and government installations were sabotaged by "dissidents" active in

Matabeleland North Province. In late January, the government imposed a curfew throughout much of the province and deployed the army's Fifth Brigade, which was subsequently accused of large scale atrocities against the civilian population, several hundred of whom sought refuge in Botswana.

The state of emergency, which has been in force continuously since 1965 and which had been reimposed at six-monthly intervals since independence in 1980, was further renewed in January and July. The government equipped itself with new powers under the emergency regulations to provide, among other things, for the prosecution and imprisonment of journalists who report, without government authorization, on security force activities in designated areas and for the arrest and imprisonment of people suspected of vagrancy. In March, however, emergency powers introduced in 1982 to give government ministers and members of the security forces immunity from prosecution for any acts which they might commit "in good faith" for the preservation of national security were amended following criticism of their provisions. The Attorney General was empowered to bring criminal prosecutions in certain circumstances, but the amending regulations did not permit private prosecutions and stipulated that the government should not be liable for damages even in respect of prosecutions brought by the Attorney General.

As a result of the maintenance of the state of emergency, the police and security forces continued to exercise wide powers of arbitrary arrest and detention without trial. Many of those arrested were supporters of the Zimbabwe African People's Union (ZAPU), the second largest party in parliament, or its former military wing ZIPRA. The ZAPU leader, Joshua Nkomo, was dismissed from the government in 1982 following the discovery of arms caches on property owned by the party but several other ZAPU members retained posts in the government and remained in office in 1983. In March, Joshua Nkomo left the country, apparently in fear of his life, and sought temporary refuge abroad following a raid on his home in Bulawayo in which security forces shot one of his employees. His wife, daughter and lawyer were all briefly detained; John Ndhlovu, his daughter's husband, was also arrested and was detained without trial for several months before being released uncharged.

The security force operation in Bulawayo in early March in which Joshua Nkomo's home was raided reportedly resulted in the arrest of several hundred people. Those detained included Sidney Malunga, a ZAPU member of parliament, who a government minister had earlier accused of membership of a secret ZAPU war council linked to the "dissidents". He was held until early April and then released uncharged. No evidence to link him with the "dissidents" was produced. Following his arrest, Amnesty International issued an international appeal on his behalf. He had previously been adopted as a prisoner of conscience by the organization when he was detained without trial for several years in the 1970s.

Another ZAPU member of parliament and former prisoner of conscience, Vote Moyo, remained in custody throughout the year. He had been arrested in June 1982 allegedly in connection with an incident in which shots were fired at the home of Prime Minister Robert Mugabe. He was charged and remanded in custody but the charges against him were dropped before he could be brought to trial and he was then served with an indefinite administrative detention order by the Minister of Home Affairs. In October, the High Court ordered his release because his detention had not been considered within one month by a Review Tribunal, but the government then imposed a new detention order and he was still being held at the end of 1983.

On 31 October, Bishop Abel Muzorewa, a former Prime Minister and the leader of the United African National Council party was also arrested under security legislation shortly after returning from a visit to Israel. The government said that he was suspected of subversive activities but no charges had been brought against him by the end of the year. He went on hunger-strike to protest against his detention but gave it up after relatives expressed fears for his health. Amnesty International issued an international appeal on his behalf and called on the government to bring him to trial or release him without delay.

On several occasions, ministerial detention orders of unlimited duration were imposed on defendants acquitted after political trials. In April, Lookout Masuku and Dumiso Dabengwa, who had both formerly held leading positions in ZAPU, and four others who stood trial with them, were detained indefinitely after the High Court acquitted them of treason and other offences. They had all been arrested in early 1982. They were still held at the end of 1983. In November, the High Court declared their detention invalid and ordered their release because their detention had not been subject to review within 30 days, but the Appeal Court subsequently overruled this decision on the grounds that the government was not responsible for the Review Tribunal's delays.

In August, six air force officers were also detained immediately after their acquittal in court. They had been charged with sabotage following the destruction of several aircraft at the main Thornhill air base in July 1982. Their redetention after a trial in which they gave detailed testimony of their torture under interrogation caused international protest and Amnesty International appealed for their release. Three of the detainees were freed after two weeks but John Cox, Barrington Lloyd and Neville Weir were held until 22 December when they were released on the recommendation of the Review Tribunal, which had apparently given priority to hearing their cases.

In Matabeleland North Province, many hundreds of people were believed to have been taken into police or military custody following renewed "dissident" activity and the imposition of a curfew in January. Large numbers of civilians suspected of holding anti-government views or of supporting the "dissidents" were reportedly rounded up and held in detention camps at Tsholotsho, Lupane and Nkayi. Another camp, reportedly administered by the Fifth Brigade, was said to have been established at Cewali in the Dandanda area north of Lupane. Many of those held in such camps were apparently held without legal sanction and there were many allegations of torture and ill-treatment. The government did not admit the existence of such camps and disclosed no information about their inmates, many of whom may have been released after a time but some of whom apparently remained unaccounted for at the end of the year. In May, Amnesty International representatives visiting Zimbabwe submitted to the Deputy Prime Minister a list of the names of 16 people whose cases appeared typical, and requested information about the reasons and legal basis for their imprisonment. The Deputy Prime Minister undertook to inquire into their cases but the government had not provided Amnesty International with any information about them by the end of the year.

There were substantial allegations of torture made during the air force officers' trial which ended in August. Five of the six defendants testified that they had been tortured during interrogation in 1982, in some cases with electric shocks, and the sixth alleged that he had been threatened with torture. There was also evidence that they had been denied their legal right to access to lawyers, had been subjected to solitary confinement and, in at least one case, had been held in leg-irons. Police denials that torture was used were contradicted by medical evidence and were not accepted by the trial judge, who ruled inadmissible "confessions" extracted from the defendants under duress and acquitted all six accused. Further allegations of torture were made later in the year by several alleged ZAPU members charged with an attack on the Prime Minister's residence in mid-1982.

Most torture allegations, however, related to incidents in Matabeleland North Province, particularly following the deployment there of the Fifth Brigade. In late January and February, members of parliament representing Matabeleland North Province, journalists who had visited the area and local church leaders alleged that the Fifth Brigade had embarked on a reign of terror against the local population as part of its operations against the "dissidents". They alleged that many civilians were being killed and that large numbers of people had been detained and assaulted. In March, Zimbabwe's Catholic bishops repeated these allegations and stated that hundreds of innocent people had been killed or maimed by the security forces. Prime Minister Robert Mugabe responded by denouncing the Catholic bishops and denying that the army was responsible for large scale atrocities. In September, the Minister of State for Defence announced that a commission of inquiry had been appointed in June comprising three lawyers and a former army commander but by late October it had still not begun to take evidence.

In February and March, Amnesty International called for urgent measures to be taken in Matabeleland North Province to prevent further killings and torture, for the establishment of an impartial inquiry and for the withdrawal of indemnity provisions granting immunity to the security forces. With regard to detainees, Amnesty International urged the government to publish their names, disclose their places of imprisonment, allow them access to relatives and legal counsel, and ensure that they would be released without delay if no criminal charges were to be brought against them.

The two Amnesty International representatives who visited Zimbabwe in May to inquire into developments at first-hand received information confirming widespread detentions and the use of torture. They also interviewed individuals, including one child, who alleged that they had been beaten or shot and wounded by soldiers and received convincing evidence that significant numbers of extrajudicial executions had been committed by government security forces in Matabeleland North Province.

Amnesty International continued to be concerned about the use of the death penalty. Six executions reportedly took place during the year: in April, two French nationals were hanged for murder and in December four other prisoners convicted of murder were executed. A number of other people were sentenced to death during the year, mostly for murder, but had not been executed by the end of 1983.

The Americas

Argentina

Amnesty International continued to work on behalf of thousands of individuals who "disappeared" following the military coup of March 1976. Despite increasing pressure in Argentina to resolve this problem, the outgoing military government of General Reynaldo Bignone took steps to prevent those responsible being brought to justice, by passing the Law of National Pacification, an amnesty law, which would have had the effect of granting complete immunity from prosecution to all members of the police and security forces for past human rights violations. On 29 October 1983 the state of siege was suspended, elections took place and on 10 December 1983 the government of President Raúl Alfonsín was sworn in. One of the new government's first measures, welcomed by Amnesty International, was to present a draft law to Congress abrogating the Law of National Pacification, which was unanimously approved on 27 December 1983. The new government also established, before the end of the year, a National Commission on Disappeared People to conduct a full inquiry into cases of "disappearance".

Amnesty International expressed concern to the government of General Reynaldo Bignone about the continuing use of the state of siege provisions to hold those detained at the disposal of the National Executive Power (PEN detainees) without charge or trial, either in prison or in restricted liberty. Amnesty International investigated the cases of more than 100 such people who were convicted by military courts in proceedings which did not appear to conform to international standards for a fair trial.

Throughout the year Amnesty International continued to receive reports of the harassment, beating and short-term abduction of journalists, human rights workers and trade unionists by groups allegedly linked to the military police or security forces. Two men abducted in May 1983 were believed to have been the victims of extrajudicial executions.

On 28 April 1983 the government published its *Final Document of the Military Junta On the War Against Subversion and Terrorism* which stated that all those who had "disappeared" during the previous eight years should be considered dead for judicial and administrative purposes. The government stressed that there would be no further disclosures about the consequences of the "war against subversion". Although the government admitted that there had been excesses, it stated that "the actions of the members of the Armed Forces in the conduct of the war were in the line of duty". In a letter to President Bignone on 11 May 1983 Amnesty International renewed its request for the government to give a "full public accounting of all those persons who 'disappeared' after arrest" and called upon the authorities to refrain from adopting measures which could impede inquiries into these "disappearances".

On 23 September 1983 the *junta* published an amnesty law, known as the Law of National Pacification. The law pardoned certain crimes committed with a political motive or purpose including kidnapping, torture and murder; it suspended criminal proceedings related to these offences and blocked all further investigations into "disappearances".

In a letter to President Bignone Amnesty International criticized the amnesty law on the grounds that it made it practically impossible to determine what had happened to the "disappeared" detainees, that it could encourage further human rights violations by giving the perpetrators of past crimes a sense of immunity, and that it prevented the perpetrators of the "disappearances" from being brought to trial. The Law of National Pacification was abrogated by the government of President Raúl Alfonsín on 27 December 1983.

The continuing official silence on the problem of "disappeared" people was in marked contrast to the steady stream of evidence being published in the Argentine press. In March 1983 an exiled former officer of the Argentine Federal Police, Rodolfo Peregrino Fernández, made a number of serious public allegations against members of the Argentine police, military and security forces. He alleged that the High Command of the Armed Forces had received secret daily bulletins from the State Intelligence Agency, SIDE, listing all operations carried out by special anti-subversive units, including abductions. He claimed that he had witnessed the torture in a secret camp in Buenos Aires of Lucía Cullen de Nell, a young woman who "disappeared" in June 1976.

Under Argentina's legal system, private parties can initiate criminal prosecutions. This mechanism has been used by human rights groups over the past few years in attempts to discover what happened to "disappeared" prisoners. Such actions have been hampered by the failure of the executive to provide judges with the information necessary to conduct investigations. The judiciary were also often unwilling to challenge the government's refusal to cooperate. The work of the courts was further obstructed by the fact that the Armed Forces High Command would not allow officers to testify before the courts, claiming that questions of national security were involved.

On 9 August 1983, lawyers filed a collective *habeas corpus* petition on behalf of the relatives of 23 individuals who were abducted between 1976 and 1978 and allegedly detained at the *Escuela de Mecánica de la Armada* (ESMA), Navy Mechanics School, a secret detention centre. The first judge handling the case took no action and the armed forces had still not responded to the *habeas corpus* petition a month later.

On 10 February 1983 the *Centro de Estudios Legales y Sociales* (CELS), Centre for Legal and Social Studies, an Argentine human rights group, filed their second complaint alleging that illegal trials had taken place at the judicial morgue in Buenos Aires and that officials there had failed to conduct official investigations into violent deaths. One of the cases cited was that of Norberto Gómez, a 27-year-old doctor who was abducted from his home in November 1976 (see *Amnesty International Report 1983*). His body was brought to the morgue in March 1977, a death certificate was issued and he was secretly buried in an unmarked grave. On 22 June 1983 the Supreme Court dismissed the complaint, absolving court officials of acting improperly despite the fact that in none of the cases had they notified the families of the deaths, nor had they investigated the causes of violent deaths as required by law.

Unmarked graves continued to be discovered in cemeteries throughout Argentina: in 1983, 1,186 bodies were exhumed. Many of the bodies, although in a late stage of decomposition, showed signs of having been shot at close range and mutilated, possibly as a means of preventing identification. In a number of cases in which formal identification was possible it was established that the bodies were those of people who had been listed as "disappeared". The remains of a 17-year-old Uruguayan exile, Adriana Gatti Casal, who was seven months' pregnant when she "disappeared" in 1977, were located in La Chacarita cemetery, Buenos Aires, and formally identified in August 1983.

At the beginning of 1983 Amnesty International estimated that there were approximately 200 PEN detainees, many of whom had been in detention for over seven years without trial. Approximately 50 whom Amnesty International considered to be prisoners of conscience were released in April 1983, including Dr Jorge Mario Domingo Marca, on whose behalf the organization had campaigned after the government had ignored a ruling by the courts in December 1982 that his continued detention under the state of siege was unconstitutional. On 29 October 1983 all the remaining PEN detainees were unconditionally freed following the lifting of the state of siege.

Amnesty International appealed on behalf of a number of PEN detainees whose state of health gave the organization cause for concern. One such prisoner, Martín Abdón Jaime González, who had completed a six-year sentence in 1981 but who had remained in detention under the provisions of the state of siege, was reported in June 1983 to be suffering from ulcerative colitis. He was released in October 1983.

By the end of 1983 Amnesty International knew of about 130 political prisoners in Argentina, all of whom had been sentenced by civilian Federal courts or by military courts. The organization believed that a number of them might be prisoners of conscience. In a message to the President-elect Dr Raúl Alfonsín Amnesty International called on the new government to consider releasing the remaining political prisoners.

On 19 May 1983 Amnesty International called on the government to conduct an independent and public investigation into the killing of two people who were abducted in Rosario, Santa Fe Province, on 14 May 1983. One of the dead men, Osvaldo Cambiaso, was adopted by Amnesty International as a prisoner of conscience in 1979. He had been released in 1982.

The two men had reportedly been abducted from a bar by heavily armed men who had forced the pair into an unmarked pick-up van and driven off. According to the police the men had been shot and killed in a car on 14 May 1983 while trying to escape a police patrol in Lima, outside Buenos Aires. However, a *habeas corpus* petition filed immediately after the abduction by the Cambiaso family was rejected on 17 May 1983 on the grounds of a lack of information – the day on which the police in Buenos Aires issued their statement. Investigations into the abduction and killing of the two men were conducted by judges in Rosario and Buenos Aires.

An autopsy performed on the body of Osvaldo Cambiaso established that he had been shot at close range and that he had been tortured. Relatives of Eduardo Pereira Rossi were not allowed to examine his body, which was handed over in a sealed coffin for burial in the presence of armed officials. In Rosario the judge investigating the alleged abduction declared himself incompetent after he and witnesses had received death threats. In June 1983 the judge in San Nicolás, Buenos Aires, charged three police officers with homicide and ordered that they be held in preventive detention. In October 1983 the criminal proceedings were dropped, the case was closed for lack of evidence and all three were released.

The search for children reported as missing following the abduction of their parents made some progress during the year. In June 1983, 9-year-old Tamara Ana María Arze, the daughter of a former prisoner of conscience, Rosemary Riveros, was traced. She had been missing for seven years. Since 1979, 12 missing children have been found. In August 1983 Amnesty International expressed concern about an attack on the staff and premises of *El Porteño*, a magazine which had published an article about missing children. The editor, his family and a journalist working for the magazine reportedly received death threats. A number of other journalists covering human rights topics were also the victims of death threats and short-term abductions.

In March 1983 Amnesty International submitted material to the United Nations related to "disappearances", torture and prolonged detention without trial. In May 1983 Amnesty International sent material on the "disappearance" of 347 European and non-Argentine Latin American citizens in Argentina to the Sixth Inter-Parliamentary Conference in Brussels between the European Parliament and the Latin American Parliament.

Bolivia

Amnesty International was concerned about reports of torture and ill-treatment by military personnel of members of rural communities and prisoners held in incommunicado detention. The *Comisión Nacional de Investigación de Desaparecidos*, Bolivian Commission of Inquiry into "disappearances", which was established on 28 October 1982, continued to investigate the "disappearances" which had occurred since 1970. On 11 August 1983 the Bolivian Government renewed the mandate of the commission "until the cases within its competence have been fully clarified".

On 14 February 1983, following an investigation by the commission at the main cemetery in La Paz, 14 bodies which had been buried in a secret grave were discovered. The bodies were those of 10 Bolivians, three Argentines and one Chilean who "disappeared" during 1971 and 1972. Examination of their remains indicated that all had been tortured. The remains of other victims were located throughout the year. On 14 April 1983 a body, believed to be that of Juan Carlos Flores Bedregal, was discovered in a secret grave in Río Seco, La Paz. In 1980 Amnesty International had appealed on his behalf after he had "disappeared" following the coup of 17 July 1980. On 13 May 1980 the body of René Sánchez Chalco, a trade union leader who was detained and allegedly tortured during the government of General Luis García Meza, was discovered in the main cemetery in La Paz. He allegedly died after an unsuccessful operation and was then secretly buried under a false name.

On 25 February 1983 the Minister of the Interior told journalists that 15 people had been detained in connection with the activities of paramilitary groups which had been implicated in "disappearances", extrajudicial executions and other human rights violations. Individuals in this group had reportedly been charged with involvement in the killing of Father Luís Espinal, a Jesuit priest and editor of the newspaper Aquí in March 1980, and of Marcelo Quiroga Santa Cruz, a leader of the Partido Socialista No. 1, Socialist Party 1, who was killed after being detained in the raid on the Central Obrera Boliviana (COB), Bolivian Trade Union Confederation in July 1980 (see Amnesty International Report 1980, 1981).

Amnesty International was concerned about the apparent lack of progress in judicial investigations related to "disappearances". Three members of the Armed Forces and one civilian indicted at the beginning of 1983 in connection with the arrest and subsequent "disappearance" of Renato Ticona Estrada, who was detained in Oruro with his brother in July 1980, had not even made initial statements to the judge by the end of 1983.

In November 1983 Amnesty International learned of the arrest in October of five Bolivians and two Chileans in the town of Luribay, La Paz Department, by army personnel. After their arrest they were reportedly taken to the barracks in Patacamay where they were briefly held before being transferred to the San Jorge military police barracks in La Paz. For 42 days their detention was not acknowledged and they were held incommunicado. During this period they were reportedly tortured in the headquarters of the Army Command and were allegedly forced to sign false statements. All the prisoners were still in detention at the end of 1983, three of them reportedly being held in isolation in small unhygienic cells.

The initial statements by government officials regarding the reason for the arrests, the specific legislation under which the prisoners had been charged and whether they would face civilian or military legal proceedings were contradictory. The Minister of National Defence, Manuel Cárdenas Mallo, informed Amnesty International members in November 1983 that the prisoners were being held under military jurisdiction in connection with alleged offences under Articles 221 and 222 of the Military Penal Code relating to the possession of arms.

On 16 December 1983 the prisoners were brought for the first time before the *Tribunal Permanente de las Fuerzas Armadas*, Permanent Court of the Armed Forces. Amnesty International was concerned that the procedures being applied might not conform to internationally recognized standards for a fair trial and that they might not comply with provisions of the Bolivian Civil Code of Penal Procedures.

Brazil

Amnesty International continued to work on behalf of six prisoners of conscience, all of whom were priests or journalists sentenced under the *Lei de Segurança Nacional* (LSN), National Security Law, for peacefully exercising their right to freedom of opinion and expression. LSN proceedings take place before military courts and are often protracted. In some cases defendants were kept in pre-trial detention for long periods and were denied access to their lawyers. In December 1983, following amendments to the LSN, all but one of the six prisoners of conscience were released. The organization also received disturbing reports of the arbitrary killing of peasant union officials and Indian leaders in rural areas.

In October 1983 Amnesty International sent an observer to attend the second appeal of two French priests, Fathers François Gouriou and Aristide Camio, and 13 peasants before the *Superior Tribunal Militar* (STM), Superior Military Tribunal, in Brasilia. The 15 were arrested in August 1981 after the peasants had allegedly ambushed a government patrol and killed one man.

Amnesty International had sent observers to all the earlier stages of the legal proceedings. In June 1982 Father Gouriou and Father Camio were sentenced to prison terms of 10 and 15 years respectively. In December 1981 their sentences were slightly reduced on appeal. The peasants received sentences of between eight and nine years' imprisonment. In a second appeal in October 1983 the STM upheld the conviction and the sentences. After the hearing Amnesty International cabled President João Figueiredo urging the immediate and unconditional release of the two priests on the grounds that they had been imprisoned for their conscientiously held beliefs and for carrying out their pastoral obligations. Amnesty International was concerned about a number of irregularities in the police investigation and about allegations that the testimony in which some of the peasants had incriminated the priests was obtained under duress. In December 1983 both the priests and the peasants benefited from amendments to the LSN which considerably reduced the penalties for their crimes, and all were released after their sentences were reduced. At the end of the year the priests announced that they intended to make a final appeal before the Supreme Federal Tribunal in an attempt to have their conviction overturned.

In November 1983 Amnesty International appealed on behalf of the prisoner of conscience Juvêncio Mazzarollo, when he went on a hunger-strike for two weeks to protest against an increase in his prison sentence. In September 1982 Juvêncio Mazzarollo, a journalist, was given a two-year prison sentence under the LSN for writing articles critical of the government. A year later the court of appeal, the STM, ruled that, as he had a previous conviction, his prison sentence should be increased from two to four years. In December 1983 he was the only remaining LSN prisoner being detained.

In December 1983 the Brazilian Congress approved amendments to the LSN which reduced both the number of offences and their penalties. The new law defined violations of national security more narrowly and reduced the number of crimes from 40 to 22. Cases involving the abuse of press freedom and the defamation of government officials would no longer be tried under the LSN but would be heard in civil courts.

The new law also modified court procedures and reduced the severity of prison sentences. The period of pre-trial detention was reduced from 30 to 15 days, and the amount of time a detainee could be held incommunicado was reduced from eight to five days. However, the Communist Party of Brazil remained prohibited under the amended LSN.

Amnesty International continued to be alarmed by reports of the arbitrary killing of members of the rural trade union movement. Fifteen peasants linked to the movement were reportedly killed with the alleged acquiescence of local authorities during the year. On 12 August 1983 the trade unionist, Margarida María Alves, was murdered in her home in Alagoa Grande, Paraíba, by a gunman allegedly employed by a local factory owner. Following this killing a 44-year-old lawyer, Tereza Braga, who worked closely with Margarida María Alves in the *Sindicato de Trabalhadores Rurais*, Union of Rural Workers, began to receive death threats and her home was subsequently bombed by a group calling itself the *Falange Patriótica*, Patriotic Phalange, though she was not injured.

Amnesty International was concerned about allegations that these crimes were not subject to prompt and effective criminal investigation by either the state or federal authorities.

Amnesty International also received reports of the killing of leaders of the indigenous population in Brazil. During 1983, 11 Indian leaders were killed and in only one of these cases, that of the murder in March 1983 of the Pataxó Hã-Hã-Hai chief, Edísio, was a criminal prosecution instituted. Amnesty International appealed for an investigation following the killing on 25 November 1983 of Marçal de Souza, a Guaraní Indian leader, while he was working alone at a health post in Campestre in the municipality of Antonio João in Mato Grosso do Sul. Before his death Marçal de Souza was allegedly threatened in order to make him exert his influence to relocate a neighbouring village of Kaiowá Indians. Amnesty International was concerned about the apparent inaction on the part of the authorities responsible for investigating these crimes and bringing those responsible to justice.

Canada

Amnesty International was concerned about allegations that prisoners convicted of common crimes had been subjected to torture or ill-treatment after a prison riot.

An Amnesty International mission visited Canada in April 1983 to investigate allegations that prisoners in Archambault Prison, Quebec, had been ill-treated following a riot in the prison in July 1982. The riot, in which three prison guards and two prisoners died, was reportedly triggered off by an abortive escape attempt by two prisoners who had taken several guards hostage.

The Canadian authorities granted Amnesty International access to prison employees, prisoners and records. The mission received sworn statements about torture and ill-treatment from 17 prisoners and interviewed six of them. They also interviewed prisoners' families, lawyers and prison officials.

The most serious allegations concerned the treatment of prisoners placed in the prison's segregation unit and included reports of beatings, the spraying of tear-gas directly into prisoners' mouths, keeping prisoners naked in their cells for periods varying from a few days to three weeks; depriving inmates of sleep and adulterating their food. Three prisoners were said to have been "choked" by having wet towels wrapped tightly around their heads.

In June Amnesty International submitted a memorandum to the Canadian Government calling for a full, impartial and independent inquiry into the allegations and urging that the results of such an inquiry be made public. The mission found that there existed at least "reasonable ground to believe" that torture or other cruel, inhuman or degrading treatment had occurred in the prison during the relevant period, and that the government had an international obligation under the terms of the United Nations Declaration on Torture to undertake such an inquiry.

In August the government announced that it had asked the Correctional Investigator of Canada to conduct an inquiry into the allegations contained in Amnesty International's memorandum. In November the government informed Amnesty International that the Correctional Investigator was still working on his report. The results of the inquiry were not known by the end of the year.

During the mission one of Amnesty International's delegates also attended a court hearing, on 12 April, in the case of Jean Claude Bernheim, Director of the *Office des droits des detenu(e)s* (ODD), Office of Prisoners' Rights, on a charge of contempt of court. The charge, which carried a sentence of up to 5 years' imprisonment on conviction, arose from a press conference given by the ODD in January to publicize a report on the allegations of ill-treatment at Archambault. At the time of the press conference 10 prisoners at Archambault were about to stand trial on charges of murdering the prison guards killed during the riot. The indictment against Jean Claude Bernheim alleged that comments he had made at the press conference about the police investigation into the killings and the treatment of the accused inmates could be capable of illegally influencing the jury at this trial. Canadian Television, Radio Canada and four newspapers who reported the press conference were also charged with contempt of court. A hearing on the merits of the case was adjourned. An Amnesty International observer attended a further hearing in May but this was also adjourned. The proceedings were dropped before Amnesty International was able to assess whether the charges constituted a violation of the right to freedom of expression under international law and whether, if imprisoned, the defendant could therefore be considered to be a prisoner of conscience.

Chile

Amnesty International was concerned about the arbitrary detention of thousands of people in connection with public protests; the large number of allegations of torture and other ill-treatment of people detained by all branches of the security forces; the banishment without trial of 127 people; the imprisonment of prisoners of conscience; the continuing enforcement of emergency legislation affecting the right to due process of law and the right of protection against arbitrary arrest; and the death of political opponents of the government in disturbing circumstances. No significant progress was made by the authorities in clarifying the fate of some 650 people documented to have "disappeared" since 1973.

Human rights violations took place against a background of growing public opposition to the policies of the government led by General Augusto Pinochet and violence – including the killing of several members of the security forces – attributed to opposition groups. The opposition organized public protests, and new political groupings were formed, although political parties remained banned by law. Trade unions called for strikes. The government reacted to these expressions of public protest by making widespread arrests.

Public rallies were broken up violently by the security forces. Fifty-eight people were killed and hundreds injured by indiscriminate gunfire by members of the armed forces, uniformed police and civilians, who appeared to be operating with the full cooperation of the uniformed police. Many of those killed were bystanders, including a number of children. Some of them were shot dead inside their own homes. Most of those killed were living in shanty towns, whose residents were held responsible by the authorities for the more active protests, and where the repression of the protests was most severe. Households where the banging of saucepans (used as a form of non-violent protest) could be heard were said to have been particularly at risk.

Several thousand people were reportedly detained during the year in the course of mass arrests carried out during political protests. Some 700 others were reportedly detained individually. Most of these detainees were released after a few hours or days of detention, either unconditionally or on bail pending trial, usually on charges under the Law of Internal State Security or the Arms Control Law.

Amnesty International was concerned about a number of cases in which the security forces allegedly fabricated evidence to secure the conviction of political detainees. Eye-witnesses described how agents of the *Central Nacional de Informaciones* (CNI), secret police, planted arms and explosives before arresting political opponents who were later charged with offences under the Arms Control Law. Amnesty International adopted several such people as prisoners of conscience, including Javier Ruiz Vera, a leader of the *Comisión de Derechos Juveniles de Valparaiso*, Valparaíso Commission for the Rights of Young People, who spent more than six months in prison on charges of arms possession, which Amnesty International believed to be based both on evidence fabricated by the CNI and a confession extracted under torture. He was released on bail on 4 October.

The use of torture and other forms of ill-treatment was reportedly widespread. According to the *Comisión Chilena de Derechos Humanos*, Chilean Commission of Human Rights, 432 individual complaints were filed in the courts. According to hundreds of testimonies examined by Amnesty International, all branches of the security forces were involved, *Carabineros* (uniformed police), *Investigaciones* (plain-clothes police), the CNI and the army. The methods used included severe beatings, the application of electricity to sensitive parts of the body, and mock executions. In many cases torture and ill-treatment took place in the street and in police vehicles. Individuals were reportedly made to run barefoot and sometimes naked in the street, occasionally on broken glass. They were said to have been made to extinguish fires with bare feet and hands. Medical reports consistent with such claims were available in a number of cases.

Amnesty International issued many appeals throughout the year urging the government to ensure the humane treatment of prisoners and to investigate thoroughly the hundreds of complaints of torture and ill-treatment. In May the organization published its report *Chile: Evidence of Torture*, containing the findings and recommendations of an Amnesty International mission to Chile the previous year. The report had been sent in advance to the Chilean Government, which returned it to the organization without comment.

On 25 November, the government announced that it would introduce a law making public the location of all secret detention centres. By the end of the year, however, no such law had been introduced. The announcement was made as a result of mounting public protest following the suicide on 10 November of Sebastián Acevedo, whose son and daughter were being held in a secret CNI detention centre in Concepción. Both alleged afterwards that they had been tortured.

Prior to the government's announcement, there had been two unprecedented court actions concerning the CNI. In the first, a judge from Viña del Mar went to a secret CNI detention centre following a complaint lodged in the courts by relatives and confirmed that 11 students arrested by the CNI were being held there. After their release, all 11 alleged that they had been tortured while being held there. On 22 November the Santiago Appeals Court, when dealing with the case of an individual threatened with arrest by the CNI, ruled that Decree Law 1878, by which the CNI was created in 1977, does not give it the power to arrest people, and that, according to the 1981 constitution, individuals could be held only in public places or prisons.

Amnesty International was concerned that, in spite of these rulings, the CNI continued to arrest, hold and torture detainees in secret detention centres.

Throughout the year there was growing public concern in Chile about torture. In January 1983, the *Comisión Nacional Contra la Tortura*, National Commission Against Torture, was formed by members of various sections of Chilean society. In 1983 the Commission published the testimonies of those allegedly tortured, and made frequent statements protesting against the continuing torture of detainees. In mid-December, the Catholic Bishops' Conference announced that "torturers and their accomplices, and those in a position to prevent torture who do not do so, will be excommunicated", and they called for urgent and wide-ranging reforms to be made in the CNI. The Chilean Medical Association announced in June that it was investigating allegations that several of its members had participated in torture sessions.

On 11 September the government, by means of Decree 1043, renewed the State of Danger of Disturbance to Internal Peace, which had been renewed regularly every six months since the constitution came into force in March 1981. As a result, and in accordance with Interim Provision 24 of the 1981 constitution, President Augusto Pinochet continued to exercise the power to hold people incommunicado in detention for up to 20 days without charge, and to banish them to remote parts of the country for three months without trial or right of judicial appeal. The government simultaneously announced that the state of emergency would not be renewed. The State of Danger of Disturbance to Internal Peace continued to be in force. The lifting of the state of emergency only resulted in the lifting of curfew restrictions.

Under Interim Provision 24, 127 people were banished for three months to remote villages, more than double the number who had been banished in 1982. They included a number of trade unionists, peasant leaders, students, shanty town dwellers and many suspected of encouraging the public protests.

In June, eight trade unionists were banished, among them Héctor Solís Saavedra, President of the *Confederación de Trabajadores de la Construcción*, Confederation of Construction Workers, in the Santiago area; Valentín Osorno Badilla, leader of the Youth Section of the above;

and José Oróstica Palma, a leading member of the *Confederación Campesina "El Surco"*, a peasant trade union. They were reportedly tortured by CNI agents before being banished. Medical professionals allegedly carried out medical examinations of the victims before and after torture took place. The three leaders and others who were arrested at the time submitted formal complaints of torture to the courts.

Amnesty International was concerned that the government continued to apply Decree 3655, whereby crimes committed against government officials or members of the armed forces in their official capacity are dealt with by military war tribunals, even in peacetime. On 15 November the government announced that a *Consejo de Guerra*, Military War Tribunal, would be held on 25 November to try five people accused of the murder on 30 August of General Carol Urzua, Santiago's Military Governor. The *Fiscal Militar*, Military Prosecutor, investigating the case, requested the death penalty for three of the accused, who were reportedly tortured during interrogation, and five-year sentences for the other two. Amnesty International appealed to the government to transfer the trial to a civil tribunal, expressed concern about the request for the death penalty, and stated its view that the legal proceedings in military war tribunals did not provide an effective guarantee of a fair trial.

The war tribunal did not take place on the scheduled date because the Supreme Court ordered the military to suspend proceedings in order that a motion filed by the defence be examined. This motion submitted that the war tribunal would violate the constitutional rights of the accused. As of the end of the year the Supreme Court had not announced its decision on the question.

Amnesty International continued to be concerned about a number of cases where the authorities alleged that individuals were killed in armed confrontations with security forces or in accidents, although the evidence suggested that they may have been extrajudicially executed.

At the beginning of November, the *Intendente de la 8ª Región*, Military Governor of the 8th Region, announced in Concepción that Victor Hugo Huerta Beiza, aged 52, had died following an armed confrontation with the security forces. However, according to a formal complaint submitted to the courts by his wife, he had been detained by armed civilians several hours before the alleged confrontation took place, his body bore marks of torture, and his arm had been broken. She also stated that her husband had been followed by men in plain clothes in a taxi whose number plate was noted on the day of his death.

Amnesty International continued to monitor legal developments in investigations into the fate of some 650 documented cases of prisoners who "disappeared" between 1973 and 1977. The organization was seriously concerned that official investigations into most of these cases had either been closed or were virtually paralysed in the courts. Relatives of the "disappeared" continued to be arrested, mostly during demonstrations protesting at the failure of the government to clarify the whereabouts of the victims.

Amnesty International appealed for the immediate release of María Cecilia Rodríguez Araya, a member of the *Agrupación de Familiares de Detenidos-Desaparecidos*, Association of Relatives of the "Disappeared". She was arrested at Santiago airport on 2 February as she was about to travel to an international meeting on the "disappeared" in Madrid. She was charged with possessing anti-government propaganda and eventually sentenced to 41 days' imprisonment, the amount of time she had already spent in preventive detention before her release on bail.

In December the United Nations (UN) General Assembly adopted a resolution on the human rights situation in Chile by a recorded vote of 89 in favour to 17 against, with 18 abstentions. The resolution, *inter alia*, reiterated its appeal to the Chilean authorities to respect the right of people to life and physical integrity and to put an end to intimidation and persecution, arbitrary detentions and imprisonment in secret places, and torture and other ill-treatment, which have resulted in unexplained deaths.

During the year Amnesty International made information on human rights abuses in Chile available to the UN Special Rapporteur on the Situation of Human Rights in Chile and the UN Special Rapporteur on Summary or Arbitrary Executions, the Inter-American Commission on Human Rights and other intergovernmental and non-governmental organizations.

Colombia

Amnesty International was concerned about extrajudicial executions which appeared to be carried out as a matter of policy by some sectors of the Colombian army. Further concerns included the reported "disappearance" of at least 80 prisoners in 1983; reports of systematic torture by the police and army, sometimes in conjunction with extrajudicial execution, and the detention – generally for relatively short periods – of leaders of peasant and Indian organizations in the course of land disputes. About 300 prisoners detained for alleged involvement in guerrilla activities faced trial in civilian courts at the end of 1983. No prisoners of conscience were adopted by Amnesty International. The organization was also concerned about cases of execution-style killings of kidnap victims held captive by Colombia's several guerrilla organizations.

Amnesty International welcomed measures by Attorney General Carlos Jiménez Gómez and civilian criminal court judges to investigate "death squad" killings attributed to police and army forces, to identify publicly those adjudged responsible and to call for their prosecution. Amnesty International received specific information on over 300 extrajudicial executions in 1983, attributed to regular forces of the Colombian army and National Police, and civilian irregular forces enlisted by rural army and police garrisons as counter-guerrilla auxiliaries, including security personnel employed by private landowners or business figures placed at the disposition of police and army units. The true number of extrajudicial executions was believed to be considerably higher.

On 3 February Amnesty International wrote to the Attorney General requesting information on the progress of an inquiry reported to have begun the previous year into killings attributed by army representatives to a "death squad" called *Muerte a Secuestradores* ("MAS"), "Death to Kidnappers". The letter expressed concern about evidence that sectors of the army and National Police had been responsible for "disappearances" and the killing of suspected opponents of the government which they had ascribed to "MAS", and that the number of such killings had greatly increased in 1982. The letter cited information on a number of cases of multiple killings reported in the Magdalena Medio region and referred to the published testimony of three civilians accused of murder in San Vicente Chucuri, Santander department, who said that they had received military training, arms, payment and orders from Fifth Brigade army officers to carry out killings as members of an army counter-guerrilla force.

The preliminary findings of the Attorney General's investigation were made public later in February. The findings confirmed that police and army personnel – including Fifth Brigade officers – had been involved in killings ascribed to "MAS", and stated that "MAS" did not exist as an organization but as a "state of mind" among some sectors of the security services. On 20 February a communique was published by the *Ministerio Público*, Public Ministry, signed by its head, the Attorney General and by seven criminal court judges identifying by name 163 people considered to merit prosecution for "death squad" actions.

The communique named 59 members of the armed forces on active duty, including commanders, deputy commanders and other top army officers of the principal garrisons in the Magdalena Medio region. They included officers of the Bárbula Battalion (Puerto Boyacá, Boyaca); the

Bomboná Battalion (Puerto Berrío, Antioquia); Operational Command No. 10 (Cimitarra, Santander); Germán Olano Air Base (Puerto Salgar, Cundinamarca); and the Patriotas Battalion (Honda, Tolima department).

Although civilian criminal courts subsequently opened proceedings against individuals named in the *Ministerio Público*'s communique, few of the civilians named, and to the knowledge of Amnesty International, none of the police and military personnel were detained or brought to trial. The Minister of War, General Fernando Landazábal, rejected the report out of hand, refusing to release active duty personnel for trial by civilian courts, and declaring that every member of the armed forces would contribute one day's salary to a fund for the defence of those accused.

In June Colombia's *Tribunal Disciplinario*, the high court that rules on conflicts of jurisdiction between civil and military courts ruled that the trials of Lieutenant Colonel Velandia Hurtado, commander of the Patriotas Battalion, and of other army personnel accused of "death squad" activities could take place only under the jurisdiction of the military courts, since their actions were not performed in a private capacity but as members of the military institution. Amnesty International was unaware of any military court subsequently having investigated or tried personnel accused of "death squad" activities.

Investigations by civilian courts and public prosecutors of crimes attributed to police or army personnel in the course of 1983 were also obstructed by death threats. Amnesty International sought information on the investigation of the "death squad" killing of the public prosecutor of Antioquia Domingo Cuello, on 27 September, after he accused National Police intelligence officers of tying the student Luis Fernando Giraldo to a lamp-post in Medellin and exploding him with dynamite on 20 August. Dr Cuello was killed after publicly rejecting the statement by National Police Director General Colonel Reinaldo Martínez which had claimed that Giraldo was a member of the guerrilla group *Ejército de Liberación Nacional* (ELN), National Liberation Army, that he had been released from custody prior to his death, and that police had not been involved in the killing. In November 1983 a Medellin court issued detention orders against the head of National Police intelligence (Section F-2) and two police lieutenants for the murder of Giraldo; the three were not detained, however, but transferred by the police to other cities. The judge who issued the orders subsequently received threats in the name of a "death squad" and left the country. The family of the murdered student and their lawyer also fled after a series of death threats. Amnesty International was unaware of any progress being made in the two murder investigations.

The number of reported extrajudicial executions in the Magdalena

Medio region increased dramatically following the creation of a XIVth Army Brigade based at the Bomboná Battalion headquarters in Puerto Berrío in April 1983, and the launching of a counter-insurgency campaign against the *Fuerzas Armadas Revolucionarias de Colombia* (FARC), Colombian Revolutionary Armed Forces, a guerrilla group operating in the area. During the first six months of 1983 Colombian human rights organizations reported 380 execution-style "death squad" killings by regular and paramilitary auxiliary forces in the region, a total which they estimated rose to about 800 by December. Most of the victims whose cases were known to Amnesty International were peasant farmers who had moved into the area since the 1950s and had cleared small plots of unoccupied land. Many such farmers increasingly came into conflict over land titles with the owners of large and expanding cattle ranches. The owners and administrators of such ranches have in recent years been the principal targets of guerrilla violence, particularly kidnappings. Military representatives have labelled peasant farmers remaining in areas of FARC activity as "communists" and guerrilla sympathizers.

In some isolated areas in the Magdalena Medio, as well as the Arauca and Caqueta regions army counter-insurgency operations served to drive suspect peasant populations from their rural communities because of the threat of mass "death squad" killings. The most widely reported incident provoking the flight *en masse* of a rural population in which mass extrajudicial executions were documented occurred in the Segovia and Remedios areas of Antioquia in August. At least 22 people were reportedly killed and survivors attributed the killings to army officers of the Bomboná Battalion's Segovia Base, which had been implicated in "death squad" activity months before by the *Ministerio Público*. In August, parish priests appealed to the Minister of War, General Landazábal, for an inquiry into army involvement in the killings, noting that victims included peasants associated with *Ligas Campesinas*, Peasant Leagues, labour organizations of farm workers, and in some cases their children. General Landazábal responded with a televised statement denying army involvement in the killings, and accusing the priests of being in the pay of the FARC. The Attorney General, in contrast, ordered an investigation which found evidence that the killings had been ordered by the commander of the Segovia Base Captain Jorge Valbuena Barriga. By the end of 1983, however, the army had apparently not permitted Captain Valbuena to appear before a civilian court, nor had it removed him from active service. It had also failed to initiate either military investigations or trial proceedings with respect to the case.

Extrajudicial executions reported outside the Magdalena Medio area followed a similar pattern, being attributed by the army and police to "death squads" operating outside their control, or being said to have occurred in the course of armed clashes between guerrilla groups and the army. In some cases killings by men in plain clothes who identified themselves in the presence of witnesses as members of "MAS" were subsequently said by the army to have occurred when the victims attacked regular army units. As in the Magdalena Medio, the principal victims of extrajudicial executions were peasant farmers, particularly those organized into peasant leagues or unions, or active in civic organizations such as the *Juntas de Acción Comunal*, Juntas of Communal Action, or *Comités de Planeación y Desarrollo*, Committees of Planning and Development, which were organized at the community level in many rural areas. Elected members of local government belonging to legal left-wing political parties have also been special targets of death threats or extrajudicial execution. Amnesty International appealed for an investigation into the reported killing by personnel of the Bomboná Battalion in Puerto Berrio of four of that city's elected councillors between July 1982 and May 1983. Other victims of extrajudicial execution or recipients of death threats included teachers, members of rural human rights committees, and leaders of urban squatters' organizations.

As a result of a November 1982 amnesty law most of the country's estimated 500 political prisoners at that time were released. Provision was made for the vocational training of ex-prisoners and an estimated 1,500 former guerrillas who had requested amnesty and a return to civilian life. At least 39 former guerrillas who accepted the amnesty, however, were reported to have been the victim of political killings and 12 were reported as "disappeared" by the end of 1983. This situation of insecurity was cited by guerrilla leaders as a reason for many guerrillas refusing to lay down their arms and for at least 50 amnestied members of the M-19 guerrilla group reportedly requesting political asylum abroad. Amnesty International appealed for an inquiry into the killing of Luis Bernal on 29 November. The killing was carried out within hours of his having registered and applied for the benefits of the amnesty. Amnesty International received testimonies from other former guerrillas who had accepted the terms of the amnesty, but on returning home had been informed by police or army officers that they would be killed if they did not agree to join the army's civilian counter-guerrilla forces.

Amnesty International launched appeals with respect to a number of reported "disappearances". Some of the results of an investigation undertaken by the *Ministerio Público* into 230 cases of "disappearances" reported over several years were made public. One "disappeared" person, Gustavo Albeiro Muñoz, a student at the University of Antioquia, was confirmed by the Attorney General's office to have been detained by an army patrol on 26 May 1982. The investigators cited confidential records kept at army headquarters in Bogotá which proved that the detention had occurred and that it had been routinely reported to headquarters by the arresting authority. The military had, however, consistently denied to the student's parents that he had ever been detained, and had presented written denials to that effect to a civilian court pursuing a writ of *habeas corpus* on his behalf. The *Ministerio Público*'s investigation confirmed that his body had been found in a small village some five weeks after his arrest, and that he had died in army custody. Despite the publication of these findings, no proceedings were known to have been initiated against the army officers responsible and the family of Gustavo Albeiro Muñoz was reportedly refused the right to recover the body.

Amnesty International wrote to the authorities in February regarding evidence that a group of political prisoners detained in December 1982 and held in secret detention at the army's intelligence headquarters in Bogotá, the *Brigada de Institutos Militares* (BIM), Military Institutes Brigade, had been tortured, and had received death threats in the name of "MAS". The prisoners included Froilán Rivera, and other leaders of the peasant organization *Asociación Nacional de Usuarios Campesinos* (ANUC), National Association of Peasants, and its associated political party. Amnesty International said that it had assessed reports of medical examinations carried out on the prisoners after they left the BIM, and had found that they recorded injuries consistent with the specific allegations of torture. In October the civilian court hearing a charge of kidnapping against these prisoners ordered charges to be dropped and they were released; 12 of the co-accused in the case fled the country as a result of having received death threats.

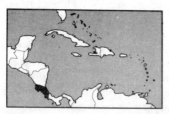

Costa Rica

Amnesty International continued to follow the cases of some 40 people held without trial on politically related charges for periods exceeding those permitted by Costa Rican law (see *Amnesty International Report 1983*). A number of such persons were brought to trial during the year, including members of an alleged clandestine group called *"La Familia"*, The Family, some of whom had been detained since 1981 without trial, and seven foreigners who were arrested in early 1982. Some of the detainees were acquitted, but several others were sentenced to prison terms of up to 12 years on charges of terrorism. The foreigners who were sentenced were then deported on the grounds that the acts of which they had been convicted were not directed at Costa Rica.

During the year, the Costa Rican press reported that allegations of ill-treatment made by these and other political detainees had not been satisfactorily resolved. Amnesty International had repeatedly called for full independent investigations into these allegations. However, proceedings against officers of the *Organismo de Investigación Judicial* (OIJ), the special police investigation unit of the Costa Rican judiciary, who had been accused of responsibility for such ill-treatment, had been closed in 1982 on the grounds that the evidence given by prisoners was contradictory.

In June 1983, the Inter-American Commission on Human Rights (IACHR) of the Organization of American States (OAS) resolved to close the case of Viviana Gallardo and others, which had originally been presented to the Inter-American Court of the OAS by the Government of Costa Rica in October 1981. Viviana Gallardo, a political detainee, had been shot and killed in her cell at Civil Guard headquarters in June 1981 and her two cell-mates, also detained on political charges, had been wounded in the same incident. Amnesty International had called on the government to institute a full and independent inquiry into the matter and to bring those responsible to justice. The government itself had asked the Inter-American Court to determine whether there had been a violation of those human rights protected under the American Convention on Human Rights; the Court had passed the matter to the IACHR on procedural grounds. The Commission decided to shelve the case in June 1983 on the grounds that the Government of Costa Rica had applied the full force of domestic law in investigating the matter and sentencing Civil Guard José Manuel Bolaños Quesada to 18 years' imprisonment for the act.

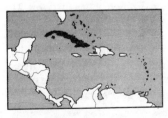

Cuba

Amnesty International's main concerns were the continued detention of long-term political prisoners after their sentences had expired, the conditions in which long-term political prisoners were held, and reports of the imposition of the death penalty.

Amnesty International continued to be concerned about the government's practice of not releasing long-term political prisoners who had completed their sentences. During 1983, 30 long-term political prisoners who had been held under such circumstances (see *Amnesty International Report 1983*) were released. One such prisoner, Raúl del Valle Vilardel reportedly spent 17 months in prison after his original 20-year sentence expired in November 1981. However, eight of the political prisoners referred to in the *Amnesty International Report 1983* were believed to be still in detention at the end of August 1983. Amnesty International also received information that at least 11 other long-term political prisoners, whose sentences expired during the course of 1983, had not been released by the end of the year. The organization expressed its concern to the government about the apparently arbitrary prolongation of these prisoners' sentences. Several of them had already spent 20 years in detention.

Amnesty International remained concerned about reports that a number of political prisoners in the maximum security wing of Boniato Prison in eastern Cuba had been denied visits from their families, correspondence rights, and open-air recreation and exercise periods since March 1981. There were also unconfirmed reports that two prisoners, Silvino Rodríguez Barrientos and Guillermo Casasús Toledo, had been ill-treated by security police when they were removed from their cells in Boniato Prison for questioning.

A number of individual arrests in 1983 were said to have been politically motivated, but Amnesty International was unable to estimate the number of political prisoners being held in the country. Difficulties in obtaining information regarding the circumstances of individual arrests were compounded by the government's refusal to respond to the organization's inquiries about human rights issues and it was often difficult to establish whether the cases fell within the organization's mandate.

Amnesty International took up the case of one person whom it believed to be a prisoner of conscience. Dr Ricardo Bofill Pagés, who was known for his dissident political views, was arrested on 24 September in Havana. Amnesty International believed his arrest was provoked by a meeting he held with two French journalists on 21 September. Since being released in April 1982 after a previous sentence, Dr Bofill had been awaiting permission to join his wife who lived in the United States. She claimed that Dr Bofill had repeatedly been denied permission to emigrate. No official explanation was given as to the reasons for his arrest, the charges against him, or the date of his trial by the end of 1983. Friends had reportedly not been allowed to visit him.

Reports of the imposition of death sentences continued to reach the organization. On 4 February it sent a cable to Vice-President Carlos Rafael Rodríguez expressing concern over death sentences reportedly given in January to five people: Ezequiel Díaz Rodríguez, José Luis

Díaz Romero, Carlos García Díaz, Benito García Olivera and Angel Donato Martínez García. Amnesty International stressed that its appeal was based on the organization's unconditional opposition to the death penalty. In the absence of a reply from the government, and in the light of growing public concern over the fate of the five prisoners, the organization launched international appeals on behalf of the five individuals on 15 March. At the beginning of May, Vice-President Rodríguez and Roberto Veiga, the *Secretario General de la Confederación de Trabajadores de Cuba*, Secretary General of the Cuban Workers' Confederation, stated that none of the five prisoners had been sentenced to death and denied earlier allegations that the sentences had been passed on account of their trade union activities. According to Roberto Veiga, they had received heavy sentences for their involvement in criminal activities, such as the burning of crops and factories, together with 33 others.

Although Amnesty International was unable to clarify the events which led to the arrests, the organization received reports that on 9 April 1983 the *Tribunal Supremo Popular*, People's Supreme Court, commuted the death sentences passed on the five by a lower court to 30 years' imprisonment.

The organization investigated allegations concerning other prisoners that a number of executions had taken place, but was unable to confirm them by the end of the year.

On 13 May 1983 Amnesty International sent a cable to the authorities requesting information on the reported arrest of the lawyers Aramís Taboada, Francisco Moura, Israel Tamayo and Rubén Armenteros Fraga, and of a judge, Nicasio Hernández de Armas. According to unconfirmed reports they were arrested for their role in publicizing the death sentences reportedly passed in January on the five people mentioned above. No reply was received from the Cuban authorities either to the cable or to further formal requests made by Amnesty International for information. In July, a Ministry of Foreign Affairs representative declared that a group of lawyers had been arrested for "violating the constitution". No further information reached Amnesty International concerning these cases and the organization was continuing to investigate them at the end of 1983.

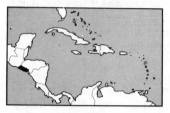

El Salvador

Amnesty International remained gravely concerned about the continued involvement of all branches of the security and military forces in a systematic and widespread program of torture, mutilation, "disappearance", and the individual and mass extrajudicial execution of men, women and children from all sectors of Salvadorian society. Paramilitary civilian defence squads which operated under military supervision as well as so-called "death squads" were also consistently named as having been responsible for such abuses. Amnesty International was also concerned that several hundred detainees arrested under the terms of Decree 507 of December 1980 remained in untried detention, some of them for over three years.

Victims of human rights violations were killed outright or were abducted and held incommunicado in police stations, army barracks or secret detention centres, where they were frequently subjected to torture and ill-treatment. While some were eventually released or were transferred to official prisons, thousands have "disappeared" over the past five years. Despite repeated requests by Amnesty International the government consistently failed to initiate any inquiries to identify those responsible for such abuses and to bring them to justice.

In many cases, officials blamed abuses on right-wing paramilitary groups — the so-called "death squads" — which the government maintained were operating outside official control. Amnesty International believed, however, that the "death squads" consisted in most cases of security agents or members of the armed forces operating in plain clothes but acting under superior orders. According to information made public in 1983 by Salvadorian sources and United States Embassy officials, names, personal details, and sometimes photographs of those selected for kidnapping and murder were passed to army officers who then assembled "death squads" from active and reserve members of the security forces and the army.

Such human rights abuses occurred in the context of a continuing civil conflict and Amnesty International received allegations that opposition forces were also carrying out individual execution-style killings. Amnesty International, as a matter of principle, condemns the torture or execution of prisoners by anyone, including opposition groups. On the basis of its collection and analysis of information concerning thousands of individual cases, including data collected by an Amnesty International delegation which visited El Salvador in July 1983, Amnesty International concluded that the majority of the reported abuses were inflicted on non-combatant civilians by forces under the authorities' control.

Amnesty International's July delegation to El Salvador included a prominent Spanish jurist, a forensic pathologist from the United States and a member of the organization's International Secretariat. It investigated how data on individual violent deaths was recorded and whether the relevant evidence was being pursued by official, medical, police and legal institutions. It concluded that the apparently deliberate failure to investigate violent deaths where security or military force responsibility was indicated, suggested that the authorities themselves lay behind the widespread killings.

A number of human rights groups continued their attempts to collect data on extrajudicial executions. Amnesty International continued to appeal to the government to investigate the cases of members of such groups who had themselves suffered arbitrary arrest or torture or who had "disappeared" or been killed in circumstances suggesting extrajudicial execution in recent years, in an apparent effort to halt their work. One such case was that of América Fernanda Perdomo, the Public Relations Secretary of the *Comisión de Derechos Humanos de El Salvador* (CDHES), the non-governmental Salvadorian Human Rights Commission, who "disappeared" following her arrest in San Salvador in August 1982.

In March 1983, Marianella García Villas, the President of the CDHES, was killed in disputed circumstances. She had previously been arrested twice; the second time she was reportedly badly beaten. She left the country in 1981 after being named by the *Comité de Prensa de las Fuerzas Armadas* (COPREFA), Armed Forces Press Committee, as a "traitor to the country", on a list widely interpreted as constituting a death threat to those named. She was killed when she returned to El Salvador reportedly to collect human rights data which she reportedly intended to submit to the United Nations Commission on Human Rights. Amnesty International called on the authorities to initiate an official investigation and to permit journalists and others to initiate independent inquiries. Instead, COPREFA issued a series of confused and contradictory accounts concerning her death.

A forensic pathologist who was a member of Amnesty International's delegation examined photographs of Marianella García Villas' body. He found that the available evidence was not sufficient to make a definitive finding as to the likely cause of death, nor did it constitute proof that she had been tortured, although this possibility could not be excluded. The delegation also concluded that the available evidence did not support the government's claim that she died while participating in or leading guerrilla actions. Amnesty International was concerned that the government's failure to carry out an adequate post-mortem examination meant that no definitive conclusion could be drawn as to how she had died.

Amnesty International's delegation to El Salvador also met the *Comisión de Derechos Humanos* (CDH), the (governmental) Human Rights Commission, which was established in December 1982 and charged with the protection, assurance and promotion of respect for human rights in El Salvador. The delegation welcomed the Commission's statement that it had located 91 of the 514 people reported to it as missing by relatives between January 1983, when it began operations, and mid-June. However, Amnesty International was disturbed that the Commission did not intend to investigate the many thousands of reported abuses which had occurred before it began operating, or to act on "disappearances" other than those reported to it by relatives. The Commission also did not plan to publicize abuses reported to it, or take steps to bring the perpetrators to justice.

However, Amnesty International welcomed the Commission's statement that it had undertaken an investigation of the reported extrajudicial execution of 18 unarmed Indian peasants by the Salvadorian army on 22 February 1983. The Commission submitted its findings to the President of El Salvador, Alvaro Magaña, but they were not made public and Amnesty International was unaware of any subsequent disciplinary action being taken against either the troops or the officer named as responsible for the raid. In June, Fermín García Guardado, a witness to the raid and the father of one of the victims, was himself arrested by the National Police. Amnesty International received no further information as to his whereabouts or the state of any proceedings against him during 1983. The organization believed that he was arrested because he testified about the 22 February army killings, and called for his immediate release.

Several hundred detainees remained in detention under the terms of Decree 507 of December 1980 at the end of 1983. Decree 507 had substantially revised the administration of justice in El Salvador with the establishment of military courts with jurisdiction over a range of offences including crimes against security and the state. Several hundred more people were detained under its provisions during 1983, despite the lifting in December 1983 of the March 1980 state of siege. Amnesty International repeatedly expressed to the authorities its concern that Decree 507 created a judicial framework, including a 15-day period of incommunicado detention, which facilitated human rights abuses including "disappearance" and torture.

In October 1983, an Amnesty International doctor and a forensic pathologist examined a teachers' trade union leader, Rafael Carias Flores, who was arrested in February 1981, and held without trial under the terms of Decree 507 until his release in April 1983. They concluded that clinical evidence indicated that liquid or gel had caused a "distribution of injuries not consistent with accidental or self-mutilation". Carias stated he had been tortured with sulphuric acid and in a number of other ways while being interrogated at an army barracks at the *Centro de Instrucción de Telecomunicaciones de la Fuerza Armada* (CITFA), the Armed Forces Telecommunications Centre, and later at National Guard headquarters, before his arrest was acknowledged after he was fortuitously seen in secret detention by representatives of the International Committee of the Red Cross (ICRC).

In July, Amnesty International called on the Salvadorian authorities to investigate the death in custody of Nelson Renderos. Renderos was detained under the terms of Decree 507 by two men in plain clothes on 31 May 1983, and his father was asked to pick up his body at a San Salvador funeral home on 1 June. The National Police stated that he had died when "the rope with which he was trying to hang himself in the National Police cells had broken". The police doctor's report stated that he had died of a broken neck, but a subsequent independent examiner found other wounds, including fractures of the fingers of both hands and fractures of both arms. Amnesty International considered that these injuries, and a number of other discrepancies and incongruities in the police doctor's findings, suggested that Renderos had died as a result of torture while undergoing interrogation at National Guard headquarters.

Other detainees held under Decree 507 during 1983 included people perceived to be in opposition to the government and their relatives, as well as those resident in or attempting to flee areas where armed conflict was taking place. Information collected by Amnesty International and others indicated that teachers, trade unionists, human rights workers and those assisting with relief and medical assistance to displaced persons were particularly at risk.

Amnesty International welcomed the release of a reported 533 prisoners under a partial amnesty established for 60 days by Decree 210 of May 1983. They included a number of prisoners whose cases Amnesty International had been investigating. The organization was concerned that detainees were not represented in the proceedings which determined whether they were to benefit from Decree 210, and that those not freed had no right of appeal. Many of those released sought exile abroad, fearing extrajudicial execution if they remained in El Salvador.

Amnesty International was also concerned that some 200 people who appeared to have been eligible for release under the new amnesty provisions remain in untried custody. Among them were a number of trade union leaders of the *Sindicato de Trabajadores de Empresa Comisión Ejecutiva Hidroeléctrica del Río Lempa* (STECEL), Union of Electricity Workers at the Río Lempa power station, whose cases

Amnesty International had been following since their arrest in August 1980, following a 24-hour strike. The military authorities had stated that the detained STECEL leaders were to be tried before a military tribunal for violating emergency legislation Decree 296 of June 1980 which had prohibited strikes or the collective abandonment of posts by officials and employees of the state and its agencies. To Amnesty International's knowledge, however, no such trials ever took place, and they remained in detention despite repeated appeals from the organization that they be brought to trial or released.

Throughout 1983 Amnesty International raised its human rights concerns in El Salvador with regional organizations and other international bodies including the United Nations (UN) Working Group on Disappearances. In its September 1983 annual report, the Inter-American Commission on Human Rights of the Organization of American States reiterated its concern regarding the continuing high number of extrajudicial executions and "disappearances" which continued to be carried out by the security forces and paramilitary groups operating with apparent government support.

Following a fresh visit to the country in September 1983, the UN Commission on Human Rights Special Representative cited an "alarming number of political murders of civilians committed by the armed forces, the security forces, or the extreme right-wing paramilitary 'death squads' ", whose activities had "ominously increased of late". The representative also stated that the capacity of the Salvadorian judicial system to investigate and punish grave violations of human rights was "notoriously unsatisfactory". The representative also expressed concern about the violation of minimum humanitarian norms in combat situations, calling attention to grave violations of the Geneva Conventions on the Protection of Victims of War of 12 August 1949, including indiscriminate attacks on civilians by the army. In December 1983, the UN General Assembly responded to the Special Representative's report with a resolution expressing its "deep concern about the continued and unbridled violations of human rights" in El Salvador and strongly urged the Salvadorian Government to "ensure that human rights and fundamental freedom were fully respected by all its agencies including the security forces".

In 1983 Amnesty International continued to express its concerns to relevant officials in the United States concerning the possible direct effect which military assistance could have on the human rights situation in El Salvador. The US President Ronald Reagan certified that El Salvador had satisfied the criteria related to human rights required by the US Congress in order that US military assistance to that country could be continued. Amnesty International subsequently made public its assessment that it had observed no noticeable improvement in the human rights situation in El Salvador.

Grenada

Amnesty International's main concern during the first part of the year was the continued detention without charge or trial of suspected opponents of the People's Revolutionary Government (PRG) (formed when the New Jewel Movement (NJM) led by Maurice Bishop came to power in March 1979). Subsequently, Amnesty International was concerned about the reported extrajudicial execution of Prime Minister Maurice Bishop and five other leading members of the PRG by members of the armed forces on 19 October, in a coup allegedly organized by a left-wing faction in the NJM. The PRG was dissolved and a Revolutionary Military Council (RMC), led by Hudson Austin, Commander in Chief of the People's Revolutionary Army (PRA), briefly assumed control of the government. The RMC was overthrown after troops from the United States assisted by forces from Barbados, Jamaica, Dominica, Antigua, St Lucia and St Vincent invaded Grenada on 25 October. All detainees held under the PRG were released from prison shortly after the invasion. Amnesty International subsequently expressed concern regarding the grounds for the detention of former supporters of the NJM by US troops, and their treatment in custody. Amnesty International also raised its concern about the detention without charge of former members of the RMC and others with the interim civilian government which was appointed in November.

In November and December 1982 some 60 political detainees had been released, including all but 35 of the cases then under investigation by Amnesty International. On 18 March 1983 the organization wrote to Prime Minister Maurice Bishop, enclosing the names of more than 100 people allegedly detained as of November 1982, whose release it had been unable to confirm and asking whether any of them remained in preventive detention. No reply was received from the government, but during the year Amnesty International investigated the cases of 97 people it believed to be detained without charge under People's Law No. 8. This provided for the preventive detention of people suspected of "intending to take action ... likely to endanger public safety". Some detainees had been held for more than three years under the law and

Amnesty International appealed for all such prisoners to be brought before a court or released, in accordance with Grenada's obligations under international law. Fourteen political detainees were released by the PRG in September. All remaining prisoners held in preventive detention by the PRG were released on 26-27 October following the US-led invasion.

In its March 1983 letter to the Prime Minister, Amnesty International also expressed concern about death sentences passed on four people convicted in November 1982 of causing death by explosives. Although the crime of murder carries a mandatory death penalty under Grenada common law, Amnesty International said that the retroactive application of the Terrorism (Prevention) Law in these cases, providing for trial by special procedures not in force at the time the crime was committed, appeared to be incompatible with Article 4(2) of the American Convention on Human Rights, to which Grenada is a party. This states that death sentences may be imposed only "... in accordance with a law establishing such punishment, enacted prior to the commission of the crime". Amnesty International urged that no executions take place in Grenada and that the death sentences be commuted. On 28 December, following the US-led invasion, the four defendants were given an unconditional pardon and released from prison by the Governor-General.

On 13 October Maurice Bishop was removed from office and placed under house arrest by the army, reportedly after a power-sharing dispute within the central committee of the NJM. On 19 October he was freed by several thousand supporters, who accompanied him to Fort Rupert military headquarters. Accounts of what happened subsequently varied. However, later that evening the military authorities announced that Maurice Bishop, former government ministers Unison Whiteman, Jacqueline Creft and Norris Bain and trade union leaders Fitzroy Bain and Vincent Noel had been killed during an exchange of gunfire inside the fort. Later reports indicated that all six were summarily executed by members of the PRA shortly after they had entered the fort.

The authorities also announced that 17 people had been killed outside Fort Rupert barracks on 19 October. Later reports stated that at least 100 people had been killed, either by the army firing into the crowd or by jumping in panic over a cliff outside the walls of Fort Rupert.

On 20 October the military authorities announced that a 16-member RMC had assumed full legislative and executive powers and that the PRG had been dissolved. A 24-hour curfew was declared.

In a telex message dated 21 October to General Hudson Austin, Commanding Officer of the PRA and leader of the RMC, Amnesty International expressed deep concern about the alleged summary execution of Prime Minister Maurice Bishop and the five people named above and requested that an independent and impartial inquiry be held into the circumstances of the deaths and that the results be made public.

Amnesty International also appealed on behalf of others arrested by the PRA during the events leading to the killing of Maurice Bishop, urging that they be given full protection under international law regarding the right to life, humane treatment and due process of law. They included Kendrick Radix, former Minister of Justice and a supporter of Maurice Bishop; George Louison, former Minister of Agriculture, Cooperatives and Social Affairs, and Alister Hughes, a freelance journalist, all of whom were released from Richmond Hill Prison, a few days after the US-led military occupation of Grenada which began on 25 October.

More than 600 Cuban nationals and over 1,000 Grenadians were subsequently detained by US and Caribbean troops. Most of the Cubans were reportedly employed as civilian construction workers by the PRG and were captured during the first two days of the occupation. They were evacuated to Cuba during November. The Grenadians, who were held for varying periods for screening and interrogation by US troops during the three weeks following the invasion, included civilians as well as former members of the PRA, People's Militia and RMC. They included Bernard Coard, deputy leader of the PRG; his wife, Phyllis Coard, a minister in the PRG; Selwyn Strachan, former Minister of Mobilization in the PRG, and General Hudson Austin. The latter four, who were alleged to have been involved in the October coup, were held aboard two US aircraft carriers for nine days before being transferred to Richmond Hill Prison on 6 November.

On 4 November Amnesty International sent a telex message to the US President, calling for full adherence by US forces to internationally accepted standards embodied in the Universal Declaration of Human Rights. Amnesty International asked in particular about the grounds and justification for the imprisonment of those in US forces' custody and their treatment.

The appeal was sent after Amnesty International had received allegations that among those detained were former members or supporters of the NJM who had no apparent involvement in the killing of Maurice Bishop and others on 19 October. Amnesty International also received reports that some detainees had been threatened or otherwise ill-treated after arrest.

Unconfirmed reports later received by Amnesty International indicated that Bernard and Phyllis Coard had been subjected to degrading treatment after their arrest by US troops and were made to roll through dung and ant-hills while bound. Bernard Coard was also allegedly held for a total of nine days in steel cages in the holds of two US aircraft carriers where the noise from the engine room was constant and deafening. Photographs showed Bernard Coard, Hudson Austin and other Grenadians stripped to the waist, manacled and blindfold while in the occupying forces' custody.

On 17 November Amnesty International again wrote to the US President expressing concern about reports that members of the PRA and others held for questioning by US military forces had, until 15 November, been held for periods of up to three days in wooden crates near Point Salines airport. The organization referred in its telex to reports that the crates, known as "isolation facilities", had been fully exposed to the heat of the sun, with little ventilation and no facilities for water and personal hygiene. Amnesty International said it considered detention in such conditions to constitute "cruel, inhuman or degrading treatment" in violation of internationally accepted standards for the treatment of prisoners.

On 2 December the US authorities replied, stating that no one had been held under interrogation in the crates for more than 24 hours and that "those undergoing questioning had free access to mess [eating] and latrine [comfort] facilities".

On 15 November the Governor-General, Sir Paul Scoon, who assumed authority for the civil government of Grenada after 25 October, vested full legal and political powers in an interim civilian administration, composed of a nine-member Advisory Council appointed by the Governor-General. The new administration was expected to run the government until elections were held the following year.

On the same date, a Preventive Detention Ordinance (PDO) came into effect giving the Advisory Council the power to detain without charge any person who appeared to it likely to act in a manner adverse to the interests of public safety, order or defence. An Advisory Tribunal was established under the ordinance to consider and make non-binding recommendations to the council with respect to any objections to a detention order; this was to review the cases of detainees within one month of their detention and thereafter every six months.

By 16 November the US forces had released or handed into Grenadian custody all remaining detainees held for interrogation at Point Salines camp. By mid-December all but 300 US military personnel had withdrawn from the island. A Caribbean Peacekeeping Force of some 450 police and military personnel from the six Caribbean countries who had also participated in the invasion remained on the island. The Preventive Detention Ordinance of 15 November gave the remaining US and Caribbean Peacekeeping Forces the power to arrest and search any persons "acting, or . . . likely to act in a manner adverse to public safety, order or defence" and to detain them for up to 72 hours.

On 18 November the Advisory Council informed Amnesty International that 47 "security detainees" were being held at Richmond Hill

Prison under the PDO of 15 November. Amnesty International had written to the Council urging it to ensure that all those in custody be treated in accordance with Grenada's obligations under international law and that all those in detention were promptly charged and brought before a court or released.

The Governor-General announced on 9 December that an investigation was being carried out into those responsible for the 19 October coup and related killings, and that charges would be brought against people being held in preventive detention, where appropriate. By the end of 1983 some 40 people were still being held without charge in Richmond Hill Prison. They included Bernard and Phyllis Coard, Hudson Austin, several former members of the PRG and most of the 16-member RMC. At the end of 1983 Amnesty International was investigating an allegation that three former members of the RMC had been beaten during November by members of the Barbados police force during interrogation at a fort near the prison. Amnesty International was also investigating allegations that detainees had been denied access to legal counsel, despite provisions for this under the constitution.

Guatemala

Amnesty International was concerned that the regular security and military forces, as well as paramilitary groups acting under government orders or with official complicity, continued to be responsible for massive human rights violations including large-scale torture, "disappearances" and extrajudicial executions. Victims included individual leaders of public opinion such as clergy, teachers and students at the *Universidad de San Carlos* (USAC), University of San Carlos, lawyers, doctors, trade unionists, journalists and community workers, as well as peasants and Indians and the urban poor.

During the government of General Efraín Ríos Montt (March 1982-August 1983), Amnesty International was also concerned about the promulgation of emergency legislation including a state of siege and Decree 46-82 of July 1982, which established Special Military Tribunals empowered to pass the death penalty for a wide range of political and politically-related offences after summary proceedings, which Amnesty International considered fell far short of international standards for fair trial. Amnesty International was particularly concerned about reports that several of the 15 people executed between September

1982 and March 1983 under its provisions had been convicted solely on the basis of information extracted under torture while held in unacknowledged detention. They had reportedly not been present or legally represented during the proceedings which convicted them.

Initially, the government of General Ríos Montt had restructured several of the security units most commonly cited as responsible for "disappearances" and extrajudicial execution but testimony from former members of the security agencies in question indicated that their personnel and operating methods remained essentially the same.

Following a pattern established by previous governments, the Ríos Montt government blamed torture, "disappearances" and individual execution-style killings in the cities on extremist groups of the left and right-wing "death squads" which they maintained were outside official control. Amnesty International, as a matter of principle, condemns the torture or execution of prisoners by anyone, including opposition groups. The organization concluded that most such abuses were carried out under superior orders by regular and reservist military or security agents acting either in uniform or in plain clothes.

Over a period of two decades, incumbent Guatemalan governments claimed that many victims died in confrontations between the security forces and guerrilla groups or had been killed or made to "disappear" by the armed opposition. Amnesty International did receive reports of individual execution-style killings being carried out in rural areas by opposition groups. The organization believed, however, that the Guatemalan military and official civilian defence squads acting under military supervision were responsible for the large-scale extrajudicial execution of non-combatant civilians in the countryside.

Amnesty International wrote to the then President Ríos Montt on 28 April 1983 calling on the authorities to investigate specific abuses which had allegedly occurred since the Ríos Montt administration came to power. These included the reported extrajudicial execution of more than 300 Indian villagers by the Guatemalan army at Agua Fría, Rabinal, Alta Verapaz, on 13 September 1982 and the unresolved "disappearance" of Graciela Morales Herrera who was abducted with her three children on 11 September 1982 from her home in Guatemala City by men in plain clothes who were believed to be members of the security forces.

Amnesty International also appealed for information concerning Yolanda Urízar de Aguilar, who "disappeared" after she was abducted on 25 March 1983 in southern Guatemala by a group of men in civilian clothes, who were believed to be members of the security forces. Urízar had returned to Guatemala following an amnesty declared by General Ríos Montt in March 1983, which permitted political opponents of the administration to return freely to the country. The organization also reiterated its disappointment at General Ríos Montt's failure to carry out promises made when he first came to office, according to which structures were to be established to investigate thousands of unresolved past "disappearances", including the "disappearance" of 25 trade unionists from the *Central Nacional de Trabajadores* (CNT), Guatemalan Workers Congress, after they were arrested in June 1980 at CNT headquarters in Guatemala City by plainclothes and uniformed members of the National Police.

Although it repeatedly claimed that it was open to investigation from human rights monitoring groups, the Ríos Montt administration never replied to Amnesty International's communications, nor did it address the substance of the organization's concerns.

Following the military overthrow of the Ríos Montt government in August 1983, the Minister of Defence General Oscar Humberto Mejía Víctores was named as Guatemalan Chief of State and announced his intention to lift emergency regulations imposed by President Ríos Montt and to abolish the Special Military Tribunals.

However, Amnesty International continued to receive reports of human rights violations including a notable increase in "death squad"-style "disappearances" and extrajudicial executions in Guatemalan cities. By the end of September, the Guatemalan press had itself reported more than 80 such "disappearances".

Those who "disappeared" included catechists, staff and students at USAC, as well as people working on rural education programs funded by the US Agency for International Development (AID) who "disappeared" in October 1983 after being arrested in Guatemala City by men in plain clothes. In November, the authorities announced that the partially charred bodies of three AID workers had been recovered from a burnt-out car. Local police and firefighters maintained that they had died when their car crashed into a cliff and burst into flames. However, eye-witnesses said the car had been pushed to the cliff, soaked with gasoline and set alight. Colleagues said that the victims could not drive. The government in announcing their deaths implied that documents found in the car had provided evidence that the victims had been involved in "suspicious" activities.

Many others who reportedly "disappeared" after General Mejía Víctores came to power remained missing despite repeated appeals on their behalf by Amnesty International and other organizations. They included the agronomist Jorge Alberto Rosal Paz, who was abducted by armed men on 12 August 1983 on the road between Zacapa and Teculután.

While there were fewer reports at the end of the year of the large-scale "disappearance" and extrajudicial execution of non-combatant civilians in the countryside then under military control, reported abuses increased in departments still in contention such as San Marcos and Alta Verapaz. In December 1983, Amnesty International called on the new administration to conduct immediate investigations into reported killings by the army; in one such case the army allegedly killed 32 people, including 14 children, on 8 August 1983 at a displaced persons camp between Cuxpemech and Peñas Blancas in Alta Verapaz.

Amnesty International also expressed its concern about reports received in November, according to which large numbers of non-combatant Kekchi Indian peasants were then in danger of extrajudicial execution at the hands of the Guatemalan military in the Chamá mountain region in Alta Verapaz. Amnesty International was unable to confirm the reports but was concerned about them in the light of previous extrajudicial executions of Indians in rural areas by the security forces.

Finally, Amnesty International's December letter expressed the organization's disappointment that the new administration had not made any attempt to establish responsibility for past "disappearances" and extrajudicial executions. In the one case known to Amnesty International in recent years where military personnel were detained in connection with abuses committed against civilians, the commander of the unit allegedly responsible for the arrest and extrajudicial execution in February 1983 of AID-employee Patricio Ortiz Maldonado and three others was subsequently released in August 1983 by the new administration. General Mejía Víctores announced that he had been absolved because there was no evidence linking him with the killings. Other sources stated that he was released because junior officers threatened a rebellion if the commander was punished for having carried out orders to eliminate Ortiz which had come directly from central military headquarters in Guatemala City.

Amnesty International's December letter to Chief of State Mejía Víctores welcomed the abolition by the new administration of the Special Military Tribunals, but expressed the view that their proceedings had been so arbitrary and had so violated generally agreed standards for fair trials that all such cases should be re-tried before regular courts. The letter also expressed concern that the whereabouts and state of proceedings against many of those originally arrested under Decree 46-82 had not been made known by the Mejía Víctores administration. Amnesty International received reports that some missing 46-82 detainees might have been held in secret detention in Guatemala City, and that others faced the danger of secret execution.

A letter allegedly smuggled out of the *Centro de Orientación Femenina*, Women's Readaptation Centre, by an acknowledged 46-82 detainee detailed the cases of three women whom the writer said had originally been arrested under Decree 46-82 but had subsequently "disappeared". Two of the missing women were arrested along with the acknowledged detainee in November 1982. One was her sister. General Ríos Montt had publicly announced the committal of the second woman to the Special Military Tribunals for trial. Ileana del Rosario Castillo, the third woman, was reportedly seen by the letter writer in custody in November 1982 at the *Escuela Politécnica*, Military School.

Amnesty International asked General Mejía Víctores to make public information on the whereabouts of the missing prisoners and the state of proceedings against them. It urged that representatives of international humanitarian organizations be invited to inspect the locations where such prisoners were allegedly held in order to ensure that the conditions of detention conformed to the United Nations Standard Minimum Rules for the Treatment of Prisoners.

Amnesty International also raised its human rights concerns in Guatemala under the Mejía Víctores administration during a meeting held in Brussels in September between representatives of the organization and the Guatemalan Vice-Minister of Foreign Affairs, at the latter's request. Similar discussions were held in December in New York between Amnesty International's Secretary General and the Guatemalan Ambassadors to the United Nations (UN) in Geneva and New York.

Amnesty International presented its human rights concerns in Guatemala to regional organizations and other international bodies. In October 1983, the Inter-American Commission on Human Rights (IACHR) of the Organization of American States (OAS) reported that military actions against Indian communities considered to be pro-guerrilla had resulted in "grave violations of human rights, in some cases including the destruction and sacking of entire villages and massacre of the inhabitants".

A July 1983 session of the Inter-American Court of Human Rights of the OAS considered whether Decree 46-82 was consistent with obligations undertaken by Guatemala under the American Convention on Human Rights. A Court advisory opinion subsequently found that Guatemala's reservation to Article 4 of the Convention, by which Guatemala retained the death penalty for common crimes connected to political crimes, did not release it from its obligation under Article 4.2 not to extend the death penalty to crimes for which it did not apply at the time Guatemala became a party to the Convention and only then for the most serious crimes pursuant to a final judgment rendered by a competent court.

In September, the UN Sub-Commission on the Prevention of Discrimination and the Protection of Minorities passed a resolution calling on the Guatemalan Government to refrain from the "enforced displacement of the Indian communities and their confinement in strategic hamlets, as well as massacre, scorched earth policies and forced 'disappearances' ".

In March 1983, a nominee proposed by the Chairman of the UN Commission on Human Rights to act as the commission's Special Rapporteur to inquire into the human rights situation in Guatemala was accepted by the Guatemalan Government; the Commission had first sought to make such an appointment in 1981. Following on-site investigations, the Special Rapporteur reported to the UN General Assembly in November 1983. He had been unable to verify all the allegations he had received concerning human rights violations under Generals Ríos Montt and Mejía Víctores, but had found no reason to doubt that the Guatemalan military had been responsible for at least some of the massacres attributed to it, such as the extrajudicial execution of more than 300 men, women and children at San Francisco, Nentón, Huehuetenango in July 1982. He also found it "virtually inexplicable" that the government continued to be so "completely unsuccessful" in resolving the cases of "disappeared" persons.

Amnesty International also expressed its concern on a number of occasions to the Mexican authorities and the UN High Commissioner for Refugees (UNHCR) regarding the reported abductions and extrajudicial execution of Guatemalan refugees in Mexico by Guatemalan military and paramilitary units. The organization urged that any repatriation program involving the return of Guatemalan refugees from Mexico to their country of origin should ensure the security of any returned refugees, and that individual interviews be held in collaboration with appropriate agencies such as the UNHCR, to ensure that any Guatemalan repatriated to Guatemala returned on an entirely voluntary basis.

Guyana

Amnesty International was concerned about reports that prisoners had died of malnutrition due to an inadequate prison diet.

In June the organization wrote to the Minister of Home Affairs expressing its concern about reports that inmates of two prisons were suffering serious illness caused by malnutrition and that, since August 1982, at least five prisoners had died of the same cause.

Amnesty International said that within the past 10 months it had received reports that more than 40 prisoners had been transferred from Camp Street Prison to the Georgetown Public Hospital, suffering from swelling of the feet, abdominal pain, vomiting, oedema and shortness of breath, leading to death in five cases. The signs and symptoms had been described by doctors who treated the prisoners as being those of beriberi or Thiamine Deficiency Disease. Amnesty International said that it had also been informed that large numbers of prisoners regularly suffered from the same symptoms in the prison infirmary. Prisoners in Mazaruni Prison also reportedly suffered from serious disorders caused by malnutrition and a very poor diet consisting almost exclusively of white rice and a small quantity of—often putrid—fish.

Amnesty International said that the prolonged deprivation of a minimum diet necessary for the prisoners' basic health constituted "cruel, inhuman or degrading treatment" in contravention of Article 5 of the Universal Declaration of Human Rights. Amnesty International told the government that it was aware that a serious problem of malnutrition affected some of the general population of Guyana at that time. However, the organization said that the government had a responsibility according to international standards and domestic law to ensure that people in the custody of the state received humane treatment.

Amnesty International urged the government to investigate without delay the provision of food in Camp Street and Mazaruni Prisons and to take immediate steps to ensure that the prisoners received an adequate diet. No reply from the government had been received by the end of the year.

Amnesty International subsequently learned of the deaths of two more prisoners, allegedly due to malnutrition during 1983.

Criminal proceedings against three men charged with treason were dropped in February, on the direction of the Director of Public Prosecution. The three, Tickaram, Krishenpaul Awdhan and Mahadeo

164

Shivpersaud, had been charged in 1980 (see *Amnesty International Report 1982, 1983*).

No written judgment in the case of Donald Rodney had been delivered by the end of 1983. He had been convicted in February 1982 of possession of an explosive device (see *Amnesty International Report 1983*). Donald Rodney, who had been released pending appeal, left the country during the year.

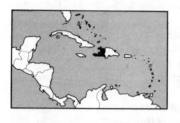

Haiti

Amnesty International was concerned about allegations of torture and other forms of ill-treatment; detention without trial, including the unacknowledged detention for prolonged periods of time of political prisoners, some of whom were prisoners of conscience; poor prison conditions; and "disappearances".

Reports of torture and ill-treatment continued to reach Amnesty International during the year. One case related to Gérard Duclerville, a lay preacher arrested on 28 December 1982 (see *Amnesty International Report 1983*), who was held in solitary confinement in the *Casernes Dessalines* military barracks, in Port-au-Prince, whom the organization considered to be a prisoner of conscience. According to reports received by Amnesty International, he was repeatedly beaten with sticks, particularly on the buttocks while tied in a position known as the "Jack". In this position the victim is trussed into a crouching position with arms hugging the legs. A pole is passed through the narrow gap between the bent knees and elbows and the pole is then placed between, for example, two desks, with the result that the victim hangs downwards. Gérard Duclerville was released without charge on 7 February 1983. His release followed appeals made on his behalf by the Catholic Church in Haiti, the *Ligue haïtienne des droits humains*, Haitian Human Rights League, and a number of international organizations including Amnesty International. The government-appointed *Commission nationale des droits de l'homme*, National Human Rights Commission, also reportedly intervened on his behalf. He is said to have needed hospital treatment, including skin grafts, as a result of the beatings. Father Gérard, as he was known, stated that during detention he was interrogated about a radio program called "*Messe du Matin*" which he broadcast daily over *Radio Cacique*. On 27 January the Haiti Bishops' Conference and the *Conférence haïtienne des religieux*, Haitian Conference of

Religious Orders, issued a pastoral letter concerning Gérard Duclerville's continuing detention, in which they stated, *inter alia*: "Today it is the turn of Gérard and those whose names we do not know, but tomorrow it will be ours, yours, mine, somebody else's. Whenever a man is being degraded and tortured, the whole human race is being degraded and tortured."

By the end of the year the government had provided no explanation for Gérard Duclerville's arbitrary detention and, to Amnesty International's knowledge, had not undertaken any official inquiry into his allegations of torture.

In addition to receiving such reports concerning political prisoners, Amnesty International also received allegations of ill-treatment inflicted by the *Volontaires de la sécurité nationale* (VSN), the political police known as the *Tontons macoutes*, and by members of the army on non-political detainees and believed that such practices were widespread. In one reported incident near Saltadère, close to the border with the Dominican Republic, several people were arrested on suspicion of smuggling rice. Two of the detainees were reportedly severely beaten: one was tied up and struck all over his body; the other was forced to lie face down on the ground and was then beaten. The former is reported to have needed hospital treatment. Despite his complaints to the authorities Amnesty International was not aware of any initiatives having been taken by the authorities to investigate the incident.

A number of prisoners of conscience were detained during the year. Most appeared to have been arrested and detained with total disregard for their constitutional and other legal rights. Arrest warrants were not presented at the time of detention and detainees were not brought before a judge within the 48 hours required by the Constitution. The detainees were, for the most part, held in unacknowledged incommunicado detention, and those released were given no explanation for their arrest and detention.

Some detainees who were later released without charge were Haitian-born individuals living abroad who had been arrested when returning to visit Haiti. Henri Lemarque, a Haitian-born United States citizen was arrested on 2 January and held in solitary confinement for 52 days in the *Casernes Dessalines*. He was said to have been questioned about his connection with groups of Haitian exiles in the United States, and about a bombing which occurred on 1 January in Haiti. He was released without explanation on 22 February.

Frank Blaise, a 70-year-old Haitian who had been living in the United States for approximately 15 years, returned to Haiti in June. He was arrested without warrant on 25 August at Petit Goâve, taken by uniformed police to the *Casernes Dessalines*, and after a superficial interrogation was taken to a dark, dirty and damp cell where he was kept in solitary confinement, dressed only in underpants, until 19 November, when he was released without any explanation. In an interview with Amnesty International, Frank Blaise described the poor conditions, deficient diet and lack of medical attention in the *Casernes Dessalines* and reported that he had been given no explanation for his arbitrary arrest.

Yves Médard, a film director known under the professional name of Rassoul Labuchin, who had lived for some years in Mexico, was arrested without warrant in Port-au-Prince on 29 August by armed civilians. He was held in solitary confinement, almost naked, in the *Casernes Dessalines* until his release in October. He was allowed to leave Haiti with his family for France, but was given no specific reason for his arrest. While in detention Yves Médard was accused by the Head of Police of having "political ambitions".

A number of other prisoners of conscience were held in arbitrary and unacknowledged detention for several months, including Jacques St. Lot and Paul Théodat, who were released in August after eight months' detention in the *Casernes Dessalines*. They were co-defendants with Sylvio Claude, President of the *Parti démocrate chrétien haïtien* (PDCH), Haitian Christian Democrat Party, in his 1982 retrial (see *Amnesty International Report 1983*). Although they had been granted full freedom by *Président-à-Vie*, President for Life, Jean-Claude Duvalier in September 1982, they had been obliged to report every three days to the authorities prior to their arrest. As a result of continuous harassment and fear of rearrest, five other co-defendants took asylum in the Mexican Embassy at the beginning of 1983, and subsequently left the country.

Oreste Léon and Nicole Dagobert, also members of the PDCH, were arrested in May and released without explanation on 24 December. Nicole Dagobert was reported to have been held naked in the *Casernes Dessalines* throughout the period of her detention. They are believed to have been arrested because of their connections with Sylvio Claude.

The harassment, detention and ill-treatment of Sylvio Claude, his family, and supporters of the PDCH, continued during the year, apparently motivated by Sylvio Claude's refusal to leave the country voluntarily, and his desire to involve his party in Haitian political life. In January one of his daughters, Marie-France, who was also Vice-President of the PDCH, sought political asylum in Venezuela, following her continual harassment by members of the VSN. In September Sylvio Claude's wife was ill-treated while detained for a few hours, and another of his daughters, Marie-Jocelyne, was held for three days in the *Casernes Dessalines*, where she said she was beaten up. Her testimony was confirmed by ex-prisoners who were interviewed by Amnesty International.

In October, Sylvio Claude was again arrested and taken to the *Casernes Dessalines*. He was reportedly severely beaten before being released in December. While detained he was said to have been threatened with death if he did not agree to leave Haiti. After his release he was kept under house arrest. Despite his poor health, occasioned by ill-treatment, fear of persecution prevented local doctors from giving him medical treatment after his release.

Amnesty International appealed for the release of Maître Dupleix Jean-Baptiste, a former judge and founder member of the *Ligue haïtienne des droits humains*, Haitian League of Human Rights, who was detained with several others in May. They were released without charge in August. All are thought to have been arrested because of their links with Sylvio Claude.

At the end of 1983, the government had still not officially acknowledged the detention of several other people suspected of political activities. No charges had been brought against them and access to them was not permitted. For example, Frantz Héraux and José Sinai had been held since March, reportedly in the *Casernes Dessalines*, in solitary confinement. Others believed to have been arrested in 1983 and to have been held in the *Casernes Dessalines* in unacknowledged detention were: Joseph Pardovany, Frid Esper, Schneider Merzier, Dominique Joseph, Joseph Lomini, Frantz Joachim and Eugène Nazon.

Amnesty International continued to press the government to bring charges or to release several political prisoners who had been in detention for several years without any legal proceedings being held. Among them were Vladimir Jeanty, Jean-Roland Denis, Jean-Claude Bastien, and Roosevelt Blaise Moise, who had all been in detention since 1981 in the *Pénitencier National*, National Penitentiary.

In 1983 Amnesty International renewed its appeals to the government to acknowledge the detention of Rock Charles Derose (also known as Jérôme Jean) and William Josma, who "disappeared" in 1981 and 1982 respectively and to disclose their whereabouts. In both cases Amnesty International received eye-witness reports that they were in detention centres, and that they had been taken by the authorities to unknown destinations. Amnesty International submitted both cases to the United Nations Working Group on Enforced or Involuntary Disappearances.

An Amnesty International delegate visited Haiti from 1 to 12 December. Before the delegate's arrival the organization had requested a meeting with the Minister of the Interior, but this was not granted. However, the delegate was able to meet the majority of the members of the National Commission of Human Rights, to whom he explained Amnesty International's concerns in Haiti. Representatives of the

168

Minister of the Interior and the Minister of the Presidency were also present at the meeting.

Amnesty International submitted a report in April on the violation of human rights in Haiti to those authorities in the United Nations dealing with work on human rights, under Economic and Social Council Resolution 728F (XVIII). This report had been presented previously to the Haitian Government, but at the time of writing no comment had been received.

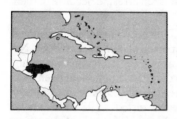

Honduras

Amnesty International continued to be concerned about arbitrary arrests and detentions; torture; "disappearances"; and the apparent extrajudicial execution of both Honduran and foreign citizens, including refugees.

The organization was also concerned that previously reported cases of "disappearances" and extrajudicial executions remained unresolved.

Amnesty International was not in a position to provide precise figures concerning the occurrence of such human rights violations in 1983, but believed that the statistics issued by human rights monitoring groups in Honduras, including the independent *Comité para la Defensa de los Derechos Humanos en Honduras* (CODEH), Committee for the Defence of Human Rights in Honduras, provided an indication of the scale on which they had occurred. The committee reported that 26 people had "disappeared", and that 24 others had died in political killings where security force or military agents were reportedly responsible. The committee recorded that 41 people were arrested for political reasons in 1983; the majority "disappeared" temporarily until they were either fortuitously located in custody or their arrests were officially acknowledged and they were consigned to court. In addition, 400 peasants were acknowledged by the governmental body, *Instituto Nacional Agrario* (INA), National Agrarian Institute, to have been arrested for short periods under the provisions of the *Ley Anti-Terrorista*, Anti-Terrorist Law, Decree 33 of May 1982, apparently because they had occupied land. Decree 33 defined a large number of acts, including the occupation of land, as subversion against the state.

Victims of human rights abuses included trade union and peasant leaders, teachers, students and politicians, as well as Salvadorian, Guatemalan and Nicaraguan refugees in the country. The abuses were reportedly carried out by uniformed members of the Honduran army and the *Fuerza de Seguridad Pública* (FUSEP), Public Security Force, by plainclothes agents of the *Dirección Nacional de Investigaciones* (DIN), National Directorate of Investigations, and by special new anti-terrorist units formed in 1982, including the *Tropas Especiales para Operaciones de Selva y Nocturnas* (TESON), Special Troops for Jungle and Night Operations, and the "*Cobras*", the *Cuerpo de Policía Anti-Subversivo*, Anti-Subversive Police Corps.

Plainclothes and uniformed security and military agents from El Salvador and Guatemala who crossed the border into Honduras, on some occasions with the tacit or overt assistance of Honduran security agents, were implicated in the detention, torture, "disappearance" and extrajudicial execution of refugees from El Salvador and Guatemala.

Amnesty International also received reports that the Honduran authorities and military officials had offered both tacit and logistical support to irregular units opposed to the current government in Nicaragua. These groups, known as the *contras* (counter-revolutionaries), operated from Honduran territory and conducted raids during 1983 which reportedly resulted in the "disappearance" and extrajudicial execution, in some cases on Honduran soil, of both Honduran and Nicaraguan non-combatant civilians, including Nicaraguan refugees in Honduras.

Such abuses have been reported since 1981 in the context of increasing armed conflict throughout Central America, but largely appeared to be directed at non-combatants who had no involvement with armed opposition groups either in Honduras or elsewhere.

Many of those arbitrarily detained in 1983 were held in incommunicado detention, for periods exceeding those permitted under Honduran law, in places not publicly recognized as detention centres where they were reportedly tortured. Some such people were eventually freed without charge, or were released under bail, but with charges pending against them. Victor Inocencio Peralta, a worker of the *Unión Nacional de Campesinos* (UNC), National Association of Peasants, was arrested in Choluteca by DIN agents on 17 October. DIN denied his arrest until he was brought to court on 31 October and accused of having collaborated with Salvadorian opposition groups and arms trafficking. He was allegedly tortured during this period in incommunicado detention. He was released on bail in December 1983.

In other cases "disappeared" people whose arrest was eventually acknowledged by DIN remained in detention without trial for periods exceeding those permissible under Honduran law. Between March and May 1983, Amnesty International repeatedly appealed for information concerning the whereabouts of Inés Consuelo Murillo Schwaderer and José González Flores, who were reportedly detained on 13 March in the city of San Pedro Sula by men believed to be plainclothes members of *Inteligencia Militar* (G-2), Military Intelligence. Relatives and local human rights groups also presented *habeas corpus* petitions on their behalf.

The local DIN headquarters repeatedly denied holding the two until 31 May 1983, when they were remanded by DIN into the custody of the *Juzgado Primero de Letras de 1° Criminal*, Criminal Court of the First Instance, in Tegucigalpa, on charges of terrorism. Both had reportedly been tortured during their period in unacknowledged incommunicado detention, and both had still not been brought to trial by the end of the year.

The detention of a number of others reportedly arrested in the course of 1983 was never acknowledged. They included members of a group which allegedly launched an armed action against the Honduran Government in the department of Olancho in September, several of whom reportedly died under torture while in military custody. Amnesty International continued inquiries on their behalf, as well as on behalf of those who "disappeared" before 1983, and whose cases remained unresolved. These included the trade union leader Fidel Martinez and the journalist Tomás Nativí, who "disappeared" following their abduction in June 1981 by armed plainclothes agents believed to be members of the security forces. Tomás Nativí had been detained by the regular security forces and badly beaten on a number of occasions prior to his eventual unresolved "disappearance".

Amnesty International also continued to appeal on behalf of Honduran and Salvadorian members of a Christian community group, who were arrested in Tegucigalpa on 22 April 1981. The forcible detention of several members of the group by agents of the DIN was witnessed by a foreign development assistance worker. Documentation, including stamped passports, was made available to Amnesty International and indicated that four children among the group, along with one of the children's grandmother, had been processed through a Honduran border post into El Salvador by Honduran officials. However, the Honduran authorities have never acknowledged that any of the detentions took place and the others remained "disappeared".

In May 1983, Amnesty International called on the Honduran authorities to institute a public and independent inquiry into the killing on 28 March 1983 of four leaders of the Honduran trade union *Sindicato de la Compañia Agricola y Ganadera de Sula* (SITRA-COAGS), Union of the Agricultural and Livestock Company of Sula, and the wounding of four other members of the same union. The incident occurred a few hours after union leaders had met a representative of the Honduran Ministry of Labour to discuss COAGS' refusal to negotiate a new collective agreement for its banana workers.

Initially, the armed forces denied that those who had shot the men were soldiers. Later, the authorities acknowledged that they were members of the army, but stated that they had acted independently, and not in their capacity as soldiers, in carrying out the shootings. Eventually, in response to repeated expressions of international concern regarding the killings, the Honduran armed forces gave public assurances that they intended to apply the "full force of the law" in determining responsibility for the incident. The Honduran press reported that the three soldiers implicated in the shootings had received a payment of US$ 2,000 to carry out the attack from executives of the company where the trade unionists worked. The soldiers in question were reportedly arrested but then escaped, reportedly with the help of the soldiers guarding them.

In response to an inquiry from the International Labour Organisation (ILO) regarding the case, the Honduran authorities stated in August 1983 that the judicial investigation was still in progress, and that its results would be made public when the secret *sumario* (indictment) stage of the inquiry had been completed. As far as Amnesty International was aware there had been no further developments by the end of 1983.

Throughout the year Amnesty International raised its concerns in Honduras with regional organizations and other international bodies, including the United Nations (UN) Working Group on Disappearances. In June, an Amnesty International telex to the UN High Commissioner for Refugees (UNHCR) asked for information concerning the situation of 10 refugees who had been removed on 17 June from the refugee camp for Guatemalans at El Tesoro by Honduran military officers, reportedly accompanied by Guatemalan paramilitary agents in Honduran uniform. During the incident, a UNHCR employee who had attempted to defend the refugees was threatened by Honduran soldiers, leading to a protest to the Honduran President from the High Commissioner. Seventeen refugees had originally been detained; seven were released the same day. In July the other 10 were allowed to resettle in Bolivia. All were reportedly beaten and tortured while in the custody of the Honduran army.

In its 1982-1983 Annual Report, issued in September 1983, the Inter-American Commission on Human Rights (IACHR) of the Organization of American States noted that it was concerned by reports of "disappearances" in Honduras. The IACHR also stated that it was concerned that detentions in Honduras were customarily followed by long periods of incommunicado detention, during which the authorities, especially the police and security agencies, responded to writs of *habeas corpus* by denying that the persons being sought were actually in custody.

Jamaica

Work for the abolition of the death penalty and against impending executions was the main focus of concern for Amnesty International during the year. Eight prisoners were hanged in 1983, bringing to 22 the number of people executed since 1980.

An Amnesty International mission visited Jamaica in November to discuss its concerns regarding the death penalty with the government. The mission met the Prime Minister, the Minister of Justice and the Governor-General.

Amnesty International was concerned about a resumption of executions in 1980, after more than four years (1976/1980) in which none had been carried out. During this period parliament had set up a committee to consider whether or not the death penalty should be abolished. In January 1979 the House of Representatives voted by a narrow majority to retain capital punishment, but recommended unanimously that the cases of all those awaiting execution – many of whom had been sentenced during the period of *de facto* suspension of executions – be reviewed. In February 1979 the Senate passed a resolution recommending that capital punishment be suspended for a further 18 months while another committee sat to examine the question in greater depth. However, executions resumed on 27 August 1980.

All of the 18 individuals executed in 1982/83 by hanging had been sentenced to death either before or during the period in which executions were held in abeyance while parliament considered the issue. In June 1982 the Judicial Committee of the Privy Council in England (which serves as the final appeal court for Jamaica) had considered final appeals in the cases of five of the prisoners executed later that year. Although the prisoners' appeals were denied on technical grounds (by a narrow majority of 3-2), the majority opinion stated that a long delay in the carrying out of the sentence for which the condemned man was in no way responsible, must be an important factor in deciding whether to exercise the prerogative of mercy (see *Amnesty International Report 1983*).

The executions were carried out despite a recommendation by the Committee on Capital Punishment and Penal Reform in December 1981 that all death sentences passed before 31 March 1981 be statutorily commuted.

During the mission Amnesty International urged the government to take immediate and positive steps towards the early abolition of the death penalty, and to commute the sentences of those awaiting execution. Amnesty International further urged that, as a minimum first step toward abolition of the death penalty, parliament or the government should consider limiting its application.

Earlier in the year, Amnesty International had appealed for clemency in the cases of Anthony Hewett and Lloyd Aitkens, who were executed on 31 May; Stafford Pine and Junior Whyte, who were executed on 28 June; and Ransford Thomas and Clive Hayles, who were executed on 19 July. Ransford Thomas had been sentenced to death in 1974, with the others having been sentenced between 1976 and 1978. In the case of Stafford Pine, a psychiatric report in June 1983 had found the prisoner to be schizophrenic and apparently insane at the time of the examination.

At the end of 1983 more than 130 prisoners were under sentence of death, some 60 of whom had been sentenced before 31 March 1981.

Mexico

Amnesty International's main concerns were the arbitrary arrest and prolonged incommunicado detention of political detainees, convictions based on confessions reportedly obtained as a result of torture and ill-treatment, and continued reports of "disappearances". The organization was also concerned about reports of the arbitrary arrest and killing of members of rural communities and indigenous groups carried out in some cases by members of official security forces, or by armed civilians, apparently acting in concert with them. Peasants involved in land disputes with rural landowners and members of peasant organizations and rural trade unions which had been established outside the official framework of the ruling *Partido Revolucionario Institucional* (PRI), the Institutional Revolutionary Party, were among those affected by these abuses.

During a visit to Mexico in November 1983 an Amnesty International representative met an official of the Ministry of Foreign Affairs and the Attorney General of the State of Sinaloa and held meetings with representatives of human rights groups and organizations working on behalf of "disappeared" persons, members of political parties and trade unions, lawyers, academic researchers and journalists.

The *Comité Nacional Pro-Defensa de Presos, Perseguidos, Desaparecidos y Exiliados Políticos* (CNPDPPDEP), the National Committee for the Defence of Prisoners, the Persecuted, Disappeared Persons and Political Exiles, continued to list more than 500 people who were still missing following arrest, mainly between 1974 and 1981. There was no public investigation into allegations that the *Brigada Blanca*, a paramilitary unit, had been responsible for many such abductions during this period (see *Amnesty International Report 1983*). In January 1983, however, the government dissolved the *División de Investigaciones de la Prevención de la Delincuencia* (DIPD), Division of Investigations for the Prevention of Delinquency, a plainclothes police unit from which, it was believed, the *Brigada Blanca* was partly recruited. Nevertheless, other police forces, in particular the state and federal judicial police and the *Dirección Federal de Seguridad*, Federal Security Bureau, continued to be cited during 1983 as responsible for politically motivated abductions. These generally resulted in periods of incommunicado detention, after which prisoners were either remanded formally into custody and charged, or released. The whereabouts of eight people reportedly abducted in this way during 1983 had still not been officially clarified by the end of the year. In six of these cases, eye-witness accounts indicated that the abductions had been carried out by the official security forces.

In December Amnesty International appealed to the Mexican authorities to acknowledge the arrest and clarify the whereabouts of five people reported to have "disappeared" following their arrest in the period between June and September. These included Candelario Campos Ramírez, a leader of a group of *colonos* (poor residents) in Ticomán, Mexico City, who was reportedly abducted on 20 August with a companion in the street by a group of men who subsequently identified themselves as members of the *Brigada Blanca*. His companion claimed after his release to have been held, blindfold for much of the time, for a period of 43 days in different places of detention, repeatedly beaten and tortured with water and electric shocks, and interrogated about his presumed political activities. No further news was received concerning the fate or whereabouts of Candelario Campos Ramírez.

During the year Amnesty International took up for investigation the cases of eight people who had "disappeared" during 1981 and 1982. Of these, Mario Jesús Alvarado Prieto, Fernando Javier Chong Santiago, María Teresa Gutiérrez Hernández, Rubén Hernández Padrón, Marco Antonio Murillo and Roque Reyes García had been teachers or students at the *Preparatoria Popular de Tacuba*, Tacuba People's School, an independent school in Mexico City which had become known for its political radicalism. Members of the school listed 16 teachers and students who, they claimed, had remained "disappeared" since January 1978 following their arrest by security forces. In September Amnesty International sent an appeal to the Attorney General of the Federal District, Señora Victoria Adato de Ibarra, asking for information concerning the whereabouts and legal situation of several of these people, but no reply was received.

In May Amnesty International addressed appeals to federal and state authorities asking for clarification of the charges against Santos García Hernández, a 22-year-old *campesino* from General Lázaro Cárdenas, in Chalma, State of Veracruz. He was arrested on 26 December 1981, when his village was raided by a detachment of soldiers who, he alleged, beat and tortured him in order to force him to confess to two murders. He was later transferred to a prison in Pachuca, in the state of Hidalgo. He was a member of the *Organización Independiente de Pueblos Unidos de las Huastecas de Veracruz, Hidalgo y San Luis Potosí*, (OIPUH), the Independent Organization of the United Peoples of the Huasteca Region of Veracruz, Hidalgo and San Luis Potosí, an independent regional peasant organization. Amnesty International was concerned that his confession might have been obtained under duress in order to justify his continued detention which was itself intended to curb his activities for OIPUH. A reply was subsequently received from the office of the Attorney General of Hidalgo stating that he had been charged with the crimes of homicide and wounding and that he had confessed on both counts. No reference was made to the requests expressed in the Amnesty International appeal that an investigation be carried out into the allegations of torture. The organization later received information indicating that Santos García Hernández' activities on behalf of poor peasants in the area had brought him into conflict with local landowners and that he had been held for 13 days incommunicado following his arrest.

In October Amnesty International wrote to the state authorities of Chiapas appealing for information concerning the legal situation of 16 peasants and agricultural workers from the region of Simojóvel in northern Chiapas, who were believed to have been detained as a result of their participation in an independent rural trade union the *Central Independiente de Obreros Agrícola y Campesinos* (CIOAC), Independent Union of Agricultural Workers and Peasants. Many of those arrested were tied agricultural workers (*peones acasillados*). The majority of the prisoners, most of whom were arrested between April and August 1983, were reported to be held awaiting trial in Cerro Hueco prison, in the state capital, Tuxtla Gutiérrez. Reports issued by CIOAC alleged that in separate incidents in April, June and July, groups of armed men, acting on the orders of local landlords and police, had carried out attacks on villages in the Simojóvel area, burning crops and houses, shooting and wounding villagers and arresting peasants, apparently as a reprisal against their trade union activities.

In its letters to the state authorities Amnesty International asked that assurances be given that each of the detainees would have access to a defence lawyer and that any allegations of torture or ill-treatment while in custody be immediately investigated.

In October, 10 of those for whom Amnesty International had appealed were released on bail (*bajo fianza*). Legal proceedings against them continued. Those released included Manuel Arreola, Victor Arreola, Luis Lara, Joaquín de Lucía and Agustín Ruiz, peasants from the village of Cabeza de Toro, in the municipality of Tonalá, Chiapas. Amnesty International had issued an urgent appeal in June on receiving a report that they had been taken prisoner on 29 May, when police reportedly opened fire on a house where a meeting to discuss land problems was taking place. As a result of the incident one peasant, Oscar Mendoza, died of gunshot wounds.

On 2 December 1982 Arturo Albores Velasco, a prisoner of conscience who was being held on a murder charge in Cerro Hueco prison, Tuxtla Gutiérrez, Chiapas, was released. Arturo Albores Velasco was arrested in May 1981 together with two Tzotzil villagers from Venustiano Carranza who remained in detention – Victórico Hernández Martínez and Agustín de la Torre. Amnesty International believed that all three had been imprisoned because of their non-violent political activities as members of an independent peasant organization, the *Coordinadora Nacional Plan de Ayala*, National Coordinating Committee of the Ayala Plan (CNPA).

In July 1983 Amnesty International sent urgent appeals on behalf of Gustavo Zarate Vargas, a 29-year-old economics teacher at the *Universidad Autónoma de Chiapas*, Autonomous University of Chiapas, following reports of his arrest on 24 July at his home in San Cristóbal de las Casas, Chiapas. He subsequently claimed that he had been arrested without a warrant, and tortured while being held incommunicado for five days. An appeal for *amparo* (similar to *habeas corpus*) was rejected by the court, and he was formally charged with possession of firearms, explosives and marihuana. He had actively participated in a movement for university reform and in support of political demands made by local peasant groups. Amnesty International was investigating his case at the end of the year.

Amnesty International was also following the case of Jesús Vicente Vásquez, a 28-year-old student of economics and former commander of the municipal police in Juchitán, Oaxaca, who was detained in the street in Mexico City on 15 December by a group of armed men in civilian clothes, believed to be members of the *Policia Judicial Federal*, Federal Judicial Police. He was a leading member of the *Coalición Obrero Campesino Estudiantil del Istmo* (COCEI), the Coalition of

Workers, Peasants and Students of the Isthmus, a regional political organization allied with the *Partido Socialista Unificado de México* (PSUM), the United Socialist Party of Mexico, a legally recognized opposition party. In March 1981 the COCEI won municipal elections in the city of Juchitán, Oaxaca, but as a result of repeated clashes between COCEI supporters and local members of the PRI opposition in Juchitán, the state legislature voted, on 3 August 1983, to depose the COCEI municipal administration. Fresh municipal elections were held on 20 November which were won by the PRI candidate in a disputed vote. More than 300 local COCEI members and supporters were reportedly detained on 12 and 13 December after they had occupied town halls to protest against the election result. After reportedly being held incommunicado on police premises in Mexico City for seven days, where he was severely beaten, Jesús Vicente Vásquez was transferred to a prison in Tehuantepec, Oaxaca, where he was remanded in custody to await trial.

The total number of prisoners of conscience in Mexico was difficult to estimate. Existing laws protected freedom of expression and political and trade union organization, but Amnesty International believed that the arrest, trial and conviction of a number of individuals on criminal charges was the result of their political, trade union or peasant activities, rather than of any criminal acts and that in such cases convictions had been obtained as a result of prolonged incommunicado detention and ill-treatment. Amnesty International was compiling information on prisoners held in remote rural areas, where lack of information had in past years presented difficulties in forming a reliable estimate of the numbers of political arrests.

Although not a party to the United Nations (UN) instruments for the protection of refugees, Mexico accepted some 40,000 Central American refugees, principally from Guatemala. In May Amnesty International appealed to the Mexican authorities to clarify the whereabouts of two Guatemalan refugees, following unconfirmed reports that they had been deported to Guatemala after their arrest in Comitán, Chiapas, at the end of March. In March and June the Secretary General of Amnesty International cabled the Mexican authorities asking for assurances that appropriate procedures would be followed to ensure that any refugees who returned to Guatemala did so on a purely voluntary basis. On 28 June the Mexican Foreign Ministry stated that the refugees' wishes would be taken into consideration as a basic condition of repatriation. Amnesty International also appealed to the Mexican authorities not to forcibly repatriate Salvadorian refugees to El Salvador.

Amnesty International submitted information to the UN Working Group on Enforced or Involuntary Disappearances during 1983. In its report published in January, the Working Group noted that the Mexican Government had given assurances that it would investigate all reports received from the relatives of the "disappeared" until the families were satisfied, but that the relatives had apparently not received the hoped for information. The report stated, nevertheless, that the Working Group did not propose to take any further action on the cases presented to it.

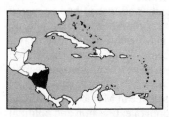

Nicaragua

Amnesty International's concerns included trials of political prisoners which fell short of internationally accepted standards; the detention of prisoners of conscience; the detention of political prisoners after their sentences had expired; and the prolonged incommunicado detention of political prisoners in the custody of the *Dirección General de Seguridad del Estado* (DGSE), Department of State Security. Amnesty International welcomed the release in a December 1983 amnesty of most of the Miskito and Sumo Indian prisoners known to the organization, some of whom it had believed were prisoners of conscience.

An estimated 2,500 prisoners – most of them former National Guards – were held as a result of having been convicted of crimes committed under the authority of the government which was overthrown in July 1979. Most of these prisoners had been convicted by *Tribunales Especiales*, Special Tribunals, set up by the new government; about 70 had been tried by ordinary courts after the disbanding of the Special Tribunals in February 1981. Amnesty International criticized trial procedures used in these cases. The organization urged that a systematic review of the cases be carried out and expressed concern that some of these prisoners were kept in custody for up to three months after their sentences had elapsed, under the provisions of a state of emergency which had been in force since March 1982.

Most of the political prisoners held in connection with crimes allegedly committed since July 1979, some of whom Amnesty International believed might be prisoners of conscience, were held under the Law for the Maintenance of Public Order and Security (or Public Order Law), which was first published in July 1979 and was applicable in 1983 in the amended form promulgated by Decree 1074 of 6 June 1982. Although arrests could be made without charge under the state of emergency, most political arrests were made on the basis of suspected offences under the Public Order Law, and prisoners were generally formally charged or released. However, many supporters of legal political parties, trade union organizations, and other bodies opposing government policies were detained for questioning for periods ranging from several hours to over one month in incommunicado detention, before being released without charge. Amnesty International believed that a pattern of harassment emerged from the detention of trade union members and other suspected opponents of the government for short periods of questioning. Many such detainees subsequently reported being threatened that they would be detained again for prolonged periods under the Public Order Law if they did not assist the security forces or resign from certain lawful organizations.

Amnesty International appealed to the authorities for clarification of the legal status of five detained members of the Urban Transport Drivers' Union (SIMOTUR); all were bus drivers for the state-owned transport system ENABUS in Managua, the capital, and were detained between 7 and 14 November. They were arrested in the context of an inter-union dispute between SIMOTUR – which is an affiliate of the Christian Democratic *Central de Trabajadores de Nicaragua*, Nica-raguan Workers' Centre, and unions affiliated with the governing party *Frente Sandinista de Liberación Nacional*, Sandinist National Libera-tion Front.

The government replied that two of the five, Orlando Mendoza and Napoleón Molina Aguilar, had been detained under Articles 1 and 2 of the Public Order Law on charges of forming part of "a terrorist network financed and directed by the C.I.A. intending to carry out Sabotage and destruction of Centers for electric power and agricultural production". Bismark Antonio García Estrada was said to have been charged with having been aware of the criminal activity of the network and having failed to report it to the authorities. Manuel Antonio Zeledon Cano and Roberto Mauricio Rosales Aviles were said to have been detained under the Public Order Law for unspecified reasons. García Estrada, Zeledon Cano and Rosales Aviles were released when charges were dropped in late December; but Amnesty International continued to investigate the basis for the charges against Mendoza and Molina.

While certain trade union activities, including strikes and stoppages, were banned under the prevailing state of emergency and punishable under the Public Order Law, Amnesty International was unaware of any trade unionists having been detained or prosecuted under these provisions. Charges were generally reported to have been based on allegations of collaboration with violent opposition groups, or involve-ment in specific acts of sabotage or terrorism within the terms of the Public Order Law. While most of the trade union members detained under the Public Order Law were apparently released after charges were dropped, some were subjected to repeated periods of short-term detention. Amnesty International issued appeals on behalf of Denis Maltes Lugo and Alejandro Arnuero, both leaders of the Stevedores' Union at the port of Corinto, who were detained on 7 November 1982; released on 15 November 1982 and 14 January 1983, respectively; and rearrested with six other stevedores on 9 June 1983 after conflicts between their union and other unions. All were at liberty by December 1983.

Leaders of political opposition parties were also arrested under the Public Order Law. Amnesty International made inquiries following the detention on 9 June of María Haydée Trana, aged 65, a leading member of the Conservative Party. She was detained for questioning, apparently without charge, after returning from a visit to Costa Rica, and was subsequently confirmed to have been released within a week of her detention. Other leaders of opposition parties who were possible prisoners of conscience remained in detention for considerable periods in 1983, sentenced with offences under the Public Order Law.

They included three leaders of the *Partido Social Cristiano*, Social Christian Party, who were detained in May and June 1982, and were the object of Amnesty International appeals. Francisco Rodríguez, the Secretary General of the party's youth branch, was detained on 2 June while distributing leaflets and subsequently held incommunicado for questioning for over a month at "El Chipote", the top-security jail at the Managua headquarters of the Department of State Security service. He was reportedly interrogated solely on political matters. He was subsequently sentenced to two years' imprisonment on a drugs charge but was released on 18 November 1983. Feliciano Polanco, a local Social Christian party leader, was detained on 14 June 1982 and sentenced to 10 years' imprisonment on charges of collaboration with armed opposition groups; his release was confirmed, however, in December 1983.

Although ordinary courts previously had jurisdiction for trials of persons accused of Public Order Law offences, a decree of April 1983 created a system of special courts, the *Tribunales Populares Anti-somocistas*, Popular Antisomocist Tribunals, to try those accused of "crimes of war and against humanity", as defined in Articles 1 and 2 of the Public Order Law. The courts consist of three magistrates: a lawyer, serving as president, and two others appointed from nominations by "popular organizations" supporting the government. Procedures in the new courts are similar to those applied in the Special Tribunals created immediately after the fall of the Somoza government. Prisoners are given two days after formal notification of the charge to prepare their defence, and a period of eight days, which may be lengthened to 12, is permitted for consideration of evidence by the court. Sentences must be delivered within a further three days. The right to defence has reportedly been severely curtailed by limitations on the time allowed for the preparation and presentation of defence arguments. Like the former Special Tribunals, the new courts include both first instance courts and appeal courts – with no further appeals possible to the ordinary courts or the Supreme Court of Justice. In 1983, 185 people were known to have been convicted by these new courts under the Public Order Law, the sentences handed down ranging from three to 30 years.

While most of the political prisoners and possible prisoners of conscience detained in 1983 were held on Public Order Law charges, some local supporters of lawful opposition groups and independent community organizations were imprisoned without trial for six months or more after being sentenced for alleged petty offences by police magistrates. Hearings in such cases occur outside the judicial process, and appeals are possible only through an administrative procedure, through the Legal Department of the National Police. One prisoner sentenced by such procedures whose case was being investigated by Amnesty International was Vicente Márquez Alemán, who was detained on 24 October 1983 after taking part in a neighbourhood meeting which was attacked and broken up by members of a pro-government political organization. Although not formally charged, he was apparently arrested for trying to defend participants in the meeting. He was taken to the Department of State Security headquarters in Managua and held in the "El Chipote" jail for 24 days. He was then sentenced by a police magistrate to six months' imprisonment, reportedly without having been present at a hearing, without having had access to a lawyer, and without having been formally informed of the precise charges against him.

Amnesty International received few specific allegations of ill-treatment of prisoners in 1983. Some detainees in isolated areas were reportedly beaten at the time of their arrest and some allegations of beatings in urban detention centres were made. However, there was evidence that allegations of ill-treatment had been investigated by the authorities, and that some members of the civil and military security services had been prosecuted. At least one case of criminal prosecution was known to be in progress in 1983, involving police personnel who were charged with ill-treating prisoners in León.

While Amnesty International welcomed government responses to allegations of the abuse of authority, it was concerned that the findings of investigations into similar abuses reported previously had not been made public. These included serious abuses alleged to have occurred in the 1981/1982 period in the Atlantic Coast area, and in particular during an offensive by Honduran-based forces along the Coco River in December 1981.

Of particular concern to Amnesty International was an incident at the Coco River hamlet Leimus on 23 December 1981, when at least seven people, and possibly many more, were reportedly killed by government forces at the time of an attack on Leimus from Honduras. Although Amnesty International was informed in 1983 that the incident was being investigated by the government-supported National Commission for the Protection and Promotion of Human Rights, and that arrests of security personnel had been carried out after the incident, no reports of the findings of the inquiry were made public, and the names of security personnel involved were not made known.

Amnesty International was also concerned about evidence, including statements to the news media by their leaders, that armed groups based in neighbouring countries regularly carried out the execution-style killing of individuals captured in Nicaragua. The victims included foreign medical personnel and members of Miskito Indian and other rural communities which refused support to such armed groups. In some cases prisoners were reportedly tortured and mutilated before being killed. Amnesty International condemns the torture and killing of individuals detained by anyone, including opposition groups.

A total of 307 Nicaraguans of Miskito and Sumo Indian origin who had been held at different times since mid-1981 under the Public Order Law, were released on 1 December as a result of an amnesty law applying "to those Nicaraguan citizens of Miskito origin, who may have committed crimes against public order and security or any other related crime from 1 December 1981 to the present." The decree granted amnesty both to people in detention and to those at liberty inside Nicaragua or abroad who may have faced charges during the period, and also applied to Nicaraguans not of Miskito origin who had been detained in connection with the conflict along the Coco River frontier with Honduras in December 1981. In a telex on 7 December Amnesty International welcomed the releases, and sought confirmation that 45 prisoners being held in the Atlantic coast port of Bluefields as of 3 December would be included in the amnesty. To Amnesty International's knowledge eight prisoners apparently qualifying for the amnesty remained in custody on the Atlantic Coast at the end of the year. Eighteen Miskito and Sumo Indian prisoners who had been held since 1982 were released in an earlier amnesty in October, including Higinio Frank López, a Sumo Indian initially sentenced to 12 years' imprisonment for allegedly collaborating with violent opposition groups. He had been the object of Amnesty International appeals as a possible prisoner of conscience.

At the end of 1983 an estimated 930 political prisoners continued to be held either awaiting trial or having been convicted under the Public Order Law. Amnesty International worked on behalf of 30 possible prisoners of conscience, 21 of whom were released in the course of the year when charges were dropped or pardons were granted.

Paraguay

Amnesty International was concerned about the arbitrary arrest, detention, torture, "disappearance" and forcible expulsion from the country of political detainees. Many of these human rights violations resulted from an abuse of the powers provided for under the state of siege which has been in force almost continuously for nearly 30 years. People detained under the state of siege are denied the right to a fair trial and due process of law and have no recourse against being detained indefinitely. Amnesty International was also concerned about the effect of two anti-subversive laws which have increasingly been used to arrest and detain people who were peacefully exercising their human rights. Amnesty International believed that there were 35 political prisoners detained in Paraguay as of December 1983, 24 of whom had been adopted by the organization as prisoners of conscience. The organization was investigating the cases of three other prisoners.

In May 1983 Amnesty International organized appeals following the arrest of more than 30 people in Asunción. Those detained included students, teachers and trade unionists and staff members of the *Banco Paraguayo de Datos* (BPD), Paraguayan Data Bank, and the owner and employees of the *Estudio Gráfico* (a printing company). The BPD is a research institution which produced regular bulletins on the political, social and economic situation in the country. By September only three of those who had originally been arrested in May remained in detention in Tacumbú Prison. They were Roberto Antonio Villalba, Enrique Goossen Martens and Desiderio Arzamendia López and were charged with violating Law 209 on Defence of Public Peace and Liberty of Persons. Law 209 prohibits a large number of activities – such as printing, storing or distributing pamphlets or publications – if the authorities deem these activities to be Marxist-inspired. Amnesty International believed that Law 209 was applied to detain these individuals for the non-violent exercise of their human rights and it adopted all three as prisoners of conscience in September 1983.

Amnesty International was concerned about numerous irregularities in the legal proceedings against those arrested in connection with the BPD. The arrests took place without an official warrant. Three of the detainees were reportedly tortured while in detention and others were allegedly threatened with violence and ill-treatment. Other detainees claimed that they had been coerced into signing statements drawn up by police lawyers. The detainees were held incommunicado until their transfer to regular detention centres, some 10 days after their arrest.

The abuse of state of siege powers to justify lengthy arbitrary detention was illustrated by the case of Guillermo Escolástico Ovando, a cavalry sergeant who had been imprisoned for 21 years. He acted as a driver for Captain Modesto Napoleón Ortigoza who is alleged to have been a political rival of President Alfredo Stroessner. The Captain and his driver were arrested in December 1962 and accused of being responsible for the death of a military cadet and involvement in a conspiracy to overthrow the President. Captain Ortigoza and Sergeant Ovando eventually received sentences of 25 years' and 15 years' imprisonment respectively. Amnesty International believed that neither received a fair trial and was concerned about reports that the evidence used against them was obtained under torture and that forensic evidence about the cause of the cadet's death conflicted with the official version of events. Sergeant Ovando remained in detention in the *Guardia de Seguridad*, a high security detention centre, under the state of siege after completing his sentence in December 1977. *Habeas corpus* petitions presented on his behalf were routinely rejected by the Supreme Court on the grounds that detentions under the state of siege are not subject to judicial scrutiny. On 17 October 1983 a new *habeas corpus* petition was filed on Sergeant Ovando's behalf alleging that the Supreme Court's attitude compounded "an absurd rule of law in which individual freedoms and guarantees are perpetually suspended". On 15 November 1983 the Supreme Court rejected the petition and in December 1983 the President of the Supreme Court, Dr Luis María Argaña, filed a law suit against Ovando's lawyers accusing them of slander.

At the end of 1983 Amnesty International was investigating the case of Alejandro Mella Latorre, a 33-year-old Chilean, who had been detained incommunicado in the *Guardia de Seguridad* for three years under the state of siege. Although the authorities alleged that he had been involved in the assassination of the former Nicaraguan President, General Anastasio Somoza, in Asunción in 1980, he was never formally charged or tried.

Amnesty International believed that legal proceedings against political detainees did not conform to internationally accepted standards for fair trials. The organization was also concerned that detainees were often denied their right to be brought promptly before a judge and to either be tried within a reasonable time or to be released. The organization expressed concern about the delay in bringing to trial a group of peasants who were arrested in March 1980 and accused of hijacking a bus in Caaguazú. Four of the detainees were adopted by Amnesty International as prisoners of conscience. The organization believed that they were detained for their alleged connection to the non-violent peasant organization, *Ligas Agrarias*. The four, Andrés Centurión, Luciano Centurión, Ramón Paiva Acosta and Eliodoro Giménez, were released in 1983. Although the case had still not come to trial, they had already been detained for longer than the maximum possible sentence. Six peasants remained in detention awaiting the judge's verdict. Under Article 154 of the Code of Criminal Procedures, the investigative stage of a trial should last only two months, but in the Caaguazú case it lasted 32 months before the judge proceeded to the final stage in November 1982. Even then the prosecution did not produce a single witness or any evidence in court relating to the charges.

Political prisoners staged a series of hunger-strikes throughout the year to protest against judicial delays and ill-treatment. Amnesty International expressed concern about the state of health of over 30 political prisoners held in the two main prisons in Asunción, many of whom were adopted prisoners of conscience, when they went on hunger-strike on 6 August 1983. The prisoners' demands, which were published in the newspaper *ABC Color*, included the release of all political prisoners, the lifting of the state of siege and the repeal of the wide ranging anti-subversive laws 209 and 294, which are used to curb freedom of expression and association. Law 294 on the "Defence of Democracy" prohibits the activity of any Marxist-inspired political group. On 24 August 1983 five of the hunger-strikers were transferred to the *Policlinico Rigoberto Caballero*, the police clinic. The hunger-strike lasted approximately two weeks and was suspended after the authorities had guaranteed that legal proceedings against the detainees would be speeded up.

In April 1983 Amnesty International wrote to the Paraguayan authorities expressing concern about the death of the political detainee Leonídas Bogado viuda de González, who was detained with her daughter and three sons in February 1982 and accused of having links with the "Chinese wing" of the illegal Paraguayan Communist Party. She died in a cancer clinic on 10 February 1983 only two days after being admitted to the clinic from the *Casa del Buen Pastor* prison where she had been held. Amnesty International was concerned that she had not been given adequate medical care during her imprisonment and that she had been prevented from receiving specialist treatment until two days before her death, in contravention of Article 22(2) of the Standard Minimum Rules for the Treatment of Prisoners. For the last four days of her life she was reportedly held incommunicado.

Nineteen individuals remained in prison charged in connection with alleged membership of the Paraguayan Communist Party. All of them were adopted by Amnesty International as prisoners of conscience.

Amnesty International continued to be concerned about reports of the torture of both political prisoners and common criminal suspects. Political arrests were often not acknowledged for several months, putting prisoners at particular risk of ill-treatment. Allegations of torture were usually denied by the Paraguayan authorities and were rarely the subject of legal action.

Under Article 59 of the Paraguayan Constitution a suspect must be brought before a judge within 48 hours of arrest and must be granted access to a lawyer. These regulations appeared to be repeatedly disregarded, with prisoners being kept incommunicado in police stations for weeks. During this period they were allegedly tortured to force them into signing incriminating statements which could form the basis for subsequent prosecutions.

On 8 August 1983 Carlos Bogarín, aged 23, was taken by three plainclothes police officers to the local police station in Puerto Presidente Stroessner. One hour after his arrest his family was informed that he had died and that his body was in a hospital morgue in Hernandarias. No official cause of death was given and the Chief of Police stated that the death had occurred during an operation carried out by members of his police force. The death of Carlos Bogarín resulted in the arrest of 10 police officers, including the Chief of Investigations. In statements to the judge a number of the accused admitted to beating the prisoner with truncheons on the orders of the Chief of Investigations. At the time of writing the judge was continuing his investigation into the death of Carlos Bogarín.

Another of the arrested suspects, Eulalio Rojas, was transferred to the police hospital in Asunción, reportedly in a serious condition. His family reported that his body was covered with wounds and bruises and that he was unable to urinate or eat as a result of blows to his stomach and kidneys.

A number of short-term detentions were reported during 1983, with journalists and students particularly at risk. In July Amnesty International intervened on behalf of Aldo Zuccolillo, the editor of *ABC Color*, who was placed in preventive detention on 15 July 1983 after publishing documents critical of the judicial system. He was released on bail after 12 days. Cristóbal Alcibiades González Delvalle, a journalist from *ABC Color* who had been subjected to several periods of short-term detention since 1979, was again arrested on 23 September 1983.

He was kept in incommunicado detention under the state of siege provisions allegedly as a result of articles he had written about the ruling Colorado Party. Amnesty International appealed to the authorities for his immediate and unconditional release. Two petitions for *habeas corpus* were filed on his behalf but were rejected by the Supreme Court. He was released on 7 December.

In a number of cases people have been arrested and then summarily expelled from the country. In June 1983 Dr Jorge Alvarenga, a general practitioner, was arrested after attending a meeting at the National University about trade unions and repression. He was allegedly tortured while in detention and was deported to Argentina a few weeks after his arrest.

In 1983 Amnesty International submitted information concerning the imprisonment and torture of members of the BPD to the Inter-American Commission on Human Rights of the Organization of American States and to the United Nations Educational Scientific and Cultural Organization. On 6 September 1983 the United Nations (UN) Sub-Commission on the Prevention of Discrimination and Protection of Minorities adopted a recommendation to the UN Commission on Human Rights inviting the Government of Paraguay to consider ending the state of siege, in order to encourage the promotion of, and respect for, human rights in the country.

Peru

Extrajudicial executions and "disappearances", which had been alleged only rarely in Peru prior to January 1983, became Amnesty International's primary concern during the year. Amnesty International continued to be concerned about torture; the prolonged detention of prisoners of conscience, most of them leaders of peasant organizations or communities; extensive delays in trials of political prisoners; and poor prison conditions. The organization was also concerned about execution-style killings and torture carried out by guerrillas of the *Sendero Luminoso* (Shining Path) movement in some mountain areas.

Emergency measures to counter the Shining Path organization included the declaration of a state of emergency in March 1982, suspending the right to *habeas corpus* and other constitutional guarantees initially in nine and later in 11 highland provinces of the departments of Ayacucho, Huancavelica and Apurimac. On 26 December 1982 a Political-Military Command based in the city of Ayacucho was established to administer political affairs in the zone and to carry out a counter-insurgency offensive. Amnesty International subsequently received reports of extrajudicial executions in the region, sometimes after torture, and of "disappearances". Such abuses were attributed to military and police forces, as well as to civilian patrols under their supervision.

Amnesty International was concerned in particular about the reported detention and killing of 16-year-old Nivardo Urbay by members of the *Guardia Civil*, Civil Guard, on 3 March in Simariba, Huanta, Department of Ayacucho, and the reported killing of two teachers of the rural school in Paras, Cangallo, Department of Ayacucho, and shopkeeper Estilo Ayala by the Civil Guard on 10 April. Although initial reports based on official sources attributed the killings to Shining Path guerrillas, international publicity surrounding the cases in September was followed by a press statement by the Interior Minister, Luis Percovich, declaring that the three had been killed on 3 April "in an armed clash with the police". However, reports received by Amnesty International indicated that the teachers, Patrocinio Quiccha and Virgilio Huarancca, Ayala and a fourth man – initially wrongly identified as the teacher Milón Gutiérrez – had been detained on 10 April when their names were read out from a list at a police road-block, and had then been summarily executed by members of the Civil Guard.

Amnesty International launched an appeal in July for an inquiry into the apparent extrajudicial execution of four members of the Pacheco family in the Andean community of Manzanayocc, Department of Huancavelíca. Félix Pacheco, a local leader of the legal left-wing party *Unión Democrática del Pueblo*, Democratic Popular Union, and the Anco District Peasant Federation, was reportedly shot in cold blood by members of the Civil Guard on 5 February. His parents, Cirilio Pacheco, 73, and Hermenegilda, 68, were subsequently detained on 11 March, by men in civilian clothes and were executed at the Manzanayocc cemetery. His brother, Teodosio Pacheco, was also detained and killed on 12 March. In September Minister Percovich stated publicly that the police intelligence service had reported that Félix Pacheco had been shot in an armed clash, and that his parents and brother had been "brought to justice" and killed by the spontaneous action of the community of Manzanayocc after they had demanded that it support Shining Path. Amnesty International subsequently received a copy of the 8 June court testimony of one of the alleged civilian participants in the killings of 11 and 12 March, Marcial Erazo Estroza. He was appointed Vice-President of the community of Manzanayocc by the regional political-military commander 10 days after the killings and testified that he and others had been instructed by army and police personnel to detain local people named as suspected supporters of Shining Path, and that after taking one prisoner to the army garrison at Pampas, he had been told "that if they capture members of Shining Path, if possible they should just kill them, because these were negative elements and enemies of the Constitutional Government".

In August Amnesty International sent a letter to President Fernando Belaunde expressing the organization's concern about evidence of torture, "disappearances" and extrajudicial executions in the emergency zone. Calling for the President to take immediate steps to investigate reported grave abuses of human rights, the organization urged that particular attention be paid to over 100 reported "disappearances" and extrajudicial executions, outlined in an accompanying memorandum. The letter condemned the reported "execution" on 3 April of 67 people in the Lucanamarca district by Shining Path, but expressed concern about evidence that a joint army, police and marine operation had carried out mass extrajudicial executions in retaliation, including a military communique which reported the killing of 69 "terrorists" in the district between 4 and 10 April. The communique did not, however, identify any of the dead and Amnesty International was unaware that any prisoners had been taken. Military communiques from the same area reported the killing on 21 May in Saccsamarca of 70 "terrorists", and 47 in neighbouring Huancasanccos on 22 May.

Although most such killings were attributed to units of the regular military and police services, information on others indicated the involvement of civilians organized into community patrols. These included the execution-style killing of eight Peruvian journalists and their guide on 26 January in the remote community of Uchuraccay, Huanta.

Amnesty International's letter also expressed concern about detention procedures in force since January that involved the temporary or prolonged "disappearance" of suspects in the emergency zone after been detained in night raids by security men in plain clothes and often hooded. Such detentions were systematically denied to have occurred. Ten cases were outlined in Amnesty International's letter.

No response was received to the letter and the document was made public on 22 September. The government then attacked the document as biased, maintaining that there was no basis to the reports of torture, "disappearance" and extrajudicial execution. National concern over reported human rights violations in the emergency zone grew, however, in late September when the Ayacucho district attorney, Dr Ricardo Pequeño, said in a televised interview that his office had acted on the cases of 160 reported "disappearances" and that the head of the

Political-Military Command had refused to respond to or assist in his inquiries. The presentation to the authorities of detailed dossiers on 78 cases of "disappeared" prisoners by the Roman Catholic *Comisión Episcopal de Acción Social* (CEAS), Episcopal Commission of Social Action, prompted a press statement by Prime Minister Fernando Schwalb declaring that the cases would be investigated. Similarly, the reported execution of 34 men, women and children in the Ayacucho hamlet of Soccos on 13 November, by members of the Civil Guard who had been insulted at an engagement party, was followed by a public commitment by the government to institute an inquiry into the incident.

Although Peruvian public opinion became aware of the gravity of the human rights situation in the emergency zone in late 1983, and some measures to investigate reported violations were promised by national officials, extrajudicial executions and "disappearances" continued to occur in the zone which remained under military administration. A Committee for the Relatives of the Disappeared was organized in Ayacucho in late 1983, comprising the families of 192 people believed to have been detained and "disappeared". By the end of the year Amnesty International held individual dossiers on 350 prisoners reported to have "disappeared" but believed the actual number of "disappearances" to be higher.

Amnesty International received detailed reports that a stadium in the city of Huanta was being used as a secret detention centre, and unconfirmed reports that "disappeared" prisoners had been held at Civil Guard, army and marine posts at the private farm Fundo Luisiana (La Mar, Ayacucho), at Canaria (Victor Fajardo, Ayacucho), at Cangallo (Cangallo, Ayacucho), at Pampas (Tayacaja, Huancavelica) and in "safe-houses" in the city of Ayacucho.

Most of Peru's political prisoners, including prisoners of conscience, were held without formal charge for investigation, or were among approximately 900 prisoners formally charged with the crime of terrorism, under Decree 046 of March 1981. The conclusions of the trials of much prisoners were subject to long delays sometimes lasting years.

Although prisoners apparently considered dangerous were immediately sent by armed forces aircraft to Lima to await trial, many community leaders, trade unionists and members of legal opposition parties charged with "terrorism" remained *depositado*, "deposited", in provincial jails, their cases being frozen.

Among prisoners of conscience charged with "terrorism" were leaders of peasant organizations who described their situation as being "between two fires", in that they were under threat from both the Civil Guard and Shining Path guerrillas. The latter have attacked those who do not fully support them, summarily executing or publicly beating and threatening uncooperative leaders of peasant communities and co-operatives and of the major national peasant organizations.

At a town meeting on 13 February members of the peasant community of Colcabamba, Huancavelica, voted to protest against arbitrary arrests and harassment by the Civil Guard, but also to reject demands by Shining Path guerrillas that the community destroy bridges and otherwise collaborate with them. On 14 February seven dead dogs hung from the bandstand in the Colcabamba plaza by Shining Path were found, together with the names of the seven principal leaders of the community written in blood with a warning that they would be executed for collaborating with the Civil Guard. Later the same day, however, two of the leaders threatened by guerrillas – Miltón Taype Campos and José Palomino García – were detained by the Civil Guard and accused of "terrorism". On 18 February the Colcabamba community president Juan Alonso Tunqui and the former president, Clemente Quispe, were detained on the same charge. Amnesty International appealed for the release of all four as prisoners of conscience; all but Clemente Quispe were released in March and April 1983; Quispe remained in detention in Huancayo, his case being frozen while awaiting consideration by a court in Lima.

Alberto Altamirano, the principal leader of the peasant community of Cocairo in Apurímac Department, was also adopted by Amnesty International as a prisoner of conscience. In February the community had protested in an open letter to President Belaunde that guerrillas had slaughtered the community's 25 milk cows, beaten some members publicly with whips, and shaved the heads of two women whom they accused of collaborating with the authorities. The Civil Guard was in its turn said to have forced residents to assemble on 31 January and to have stripped two *comuneros* (peasants working communal land) naked. They were then kicked, beaten and slashed with razor blades while being questioned about the guerrillas. Civil Guards were reported to have smeared the blood of the two prisoners (who were later released) on their own faces, apparently to terrify the assembled villagers.

About 180 prisoners charged under Decree 046, including 65 prisoners associated with the legal political parties of *Izquierda Unida*, United Left, and with traditional peasant and labour organizations, were held in two wings of Lurigancho prison in Lima. Most Decree 046 prisoners known to Amnesty International to be prisoners of conscience were transferred from El Frontón island prison, six miles from Lima's port of Callao, to Lurigancho prison in late 1982 and early 1983, except for 14 prisoners of the Cajamarca peasant community of Huayllabamba. About 100 women charged with terrorism were being held in the small women's prison of Callao.

Amnesty International worked on behalf of 48 prisoners of conscience and possible prisoners of conscience.

Amnesty International continued to express concern about conditions in Peru's prisons. Severe overcrowding was the norm, with endemic hepatitis and tuberculosis. There were virtually no medical facilities, food supplies were contaminated and water supplies were extremely limited. About 400 prisoners charged with "terrorism" were being held at El Frontón, housed in a single block, the "Blue Pavilion", which was designed in 1981 for about 150 prisoners. On 10 May two prisoners, Angel Botonero Alvarado, aged 26, and Américo Solorzano Rojas, aged 23, were shot dead there by members of the Republican Guard's special counter-insurgency unit, *Yapan Atik* – a Quechua name meaning "all powerful" – during protests at the scarcity and poor quality of food, and lack of water. In Lurigancho prison, housing almost 6,000 prisoners, a severe lack of water was also reported as well as systematic beatings and the shooting of prisoners by Republican Guard warders. Political prisoners in all the detention centres in Lima have protested against severe restrictions imposed on visits by relatives, the arbitrary suspension of such visits, and the brutal treatment of visitors.

Suriname

Amnesty International continued to call for an independent and impartial inquiry into the extrajudicial execution by the army of 13 prominent civilians and two army officers in December 1982. The organization was also concerned about the incommunicado detention of alleged opponents of the government without charge or trial and reports of ill-treatment of detainees.

In December 1982 Amnesty International had written to Lieutenant Colonel Desi Bouterse, leader of the military-controlled government, expressing its concern about the reported torture and summary execution of 15 people who were shot dead in the early hours of 9 December after being held incommunicado for 24 hours in Fort Zeelandia military headquarters. (see *Amnesty International Report 1983*). The organization called for a full inquiry into the circumstances of the deaths.

In January the government replied, stating that the reports referred to by Amnesty International did "not reflect the truth of the matter" and that "a number of persons detained for their involvement in activities to overthrow the government by violent means were killed in an unfortunate accident as a result of their attempt to escape from custody". However, Amnesty International believed that all 15 had been tortured and were then executed without legal proceedings. Eye-witnesses who subsequently identified the bodies in a city mortuary testified that the victims had severe bruising and cuts on the face, smashed jaws, broken teeth, fractured limbs, and multiple bullet entry wounds in the face, chest and abdomen.

In July Amnesty International wrote to Prime Minister Errol Alibux reiterating its appeal for the government to institute an immediate inquiry into the circumstances of the deaths and the treatment received by the deceased during their detention. Amnesty International also called for the results of such an inquiry to be made public. The Prime Minister replied to Amnesty International in September expressing regret that the complete protection of civil and political rights had not always been possible due to repeated external threats (citing four attempts since 1980 to overthrow the government). He stated the government's determination "to take firm steps towards the protection and promotion of human rights in general and the social and economic rights in particular". No official inquiry into the deaths had taken place by the end of the year.

Fifteen to 20 people were arrested on 30 January, accused of involvement in an attempted coup against the government. They included two former government ministers and Major Roy Horb, former Commander-in-Chief of the Paramaribo army garrison and second-in-command to Lieutenant Colonel Bouterse. Major Horb had resigned from the army a month before, reportedly in protest at the executions in December 1982. In a telex message to Lieutenant Colonel Bouterse dated 1 February, Amnesty International urged that full protection regarding the internationally recognized rights to life, humane treatment and due process of law be granted to those detained.

Major Horb was subsequently reported to have been found hanged in his cell in Fort Zeelandia on 3 February. Shortly after his death the government announced that an autopsy had been performed and that the cause of death had been found to be suicide by hanging. At least 10 of the people arrested were later released. Lieutenant Hardjoprajitno, one of those arrested, was tried in October on a charge of illegal possession of arms and sentenced to 16 months' imprisonment.

In December Amnesty International appealed for the humane treatment of people arrested during November and reportedly held incommunicado in military custody. On 29 November the military authorities announced that they had arrested 10 people during the previous week on suspicion of plotting a coup against the government.

However, up to 90 people, mainly from the Hindustani population, were believed to have been arrested. Some of them were then reportedly beaten while in custody. Amnesty International was further concerned about reports that, after the beginning of December, relatives and lawyers were denied access to those detained and that some detainees had been transferred from Fort Zeelandia to an unknown destination.

Amnesty International sent Lieutenant Colonel Bouterse a telex on 8 December with a list of the names of 14 people it understood to be in detention. On 14 December, in response to reports that those detained had been transferred into civilian custody, Amnesty International sent a telex to the Minister of Justice, Frank Leeflang, asking to be informed whether the people named on the list were still detained, how many people were in fact detained and where. Amnesty International asked that those detained be granted full protection by the authorities, that they be promptly charged and brought before a court or released, and that they be granted access to lawyers and relatives. Amnesty International sent a similar appeal to the Prime Minister on 20 December asking him to inform it of the names and place of detention of all persons still in custody in connection with the recent alleged coup attempt.

Amnesty International subsequently learned that seven people had appeared before a magistrate on 21 December and that the judge had ordered the release of two of those detained; their release was reportedly refused by Lieutenant Colonel Bouterse. Another two detainees were released into house arrest in early December. At the end of the year, Amnesty International was still investigating unconfirmed reports that up to 90 people arrested in connection with the alleged November coup attempt were still being detained.

United States of America

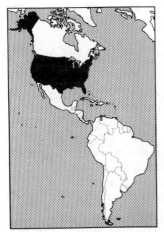

Amnesty International's major concern was an increase in the number of executions. Five prisoners were executed during the year, bringing to 11 the number of people executed since 1976. Amnesty International was also concerned about allegations of politically or racially motivated prosecutions, and by procedures which the organization believed had a possible impact on the fairness of trials in such cases.

In 1976 a 10-year moratorium on executions ended with a US Supreme Court ruling that the death penalty for murder was constitutional if imposed under certain conditions. In 1972 the Supreme Court had vacated all existing death sentences on the grounds that most state laws as then applied violated the US constitution (see *Amnesty International Report 1983*). Since then 38 states had introduced revised death penalty laws and the number of prisoners on death row had steadily risen. On 20 December 1983, 1,289 prisoners were under sentence of death, the highest figure ever recorded in the USA. By 1983, the appeals of many of those sentenced after 1972 had run out, and lawyers predicted a large increase in executions in the future.

Amnesty International appealed for clemency in the cases of the five prisoners executed during the year and in a number of other cases where prisoners were granted last minute stays of execution.

John Louis Evans, who was convicted of murder in 1977, was executed by electrocution in Alabama on 22 April 1983. According to press reports, it required three separate jolts of 1,900 volts each over a 10 minute period before he was officially pronounced dead. During the first jolt the electrode on his leg burned through and fell off and prison guards repaired it after doctors said he was not dead. During the second shock smoke and flame erupted from his left temple and leg. The third jolt was given after doctors put a stethoscope to his chest and said they were still not certain he was dead. This was the first execution in Alabama for 18 years. Amnesty International subsequently wrote to the Governor of Alabama expressing its unconditional opposition to the death penalty and pointing out that "prolonged suffering was manifestly inflicted in this case". Amnesty International also appealed to the Governor to grant a reprieve in the case of Wayne Ritter, who was scheduled to be executed on 13 May 1983 in the same chair used to electrocute John Louis Evans (Wayne Ritter was subsequently granted a stay of execution by a federal court).

Amnesty International also wrote letters of concern to the American Medical Association about the reported participation of doctors in John Louis Evans' execution.

Jimmy Lee Gray, who was convicted in 1977 of the murder of a child, was executed in the gas chamber in Mississippi on 2 September.

On 30 November Robert Sullivan was killed in the electric chair in Florida, the second execution in the state since 1976. He had been on death row since November 1973, longer than any other prisoner in the USA. Two days before the execution, Robert Sullivan had been granted a stay in order that a decision could be taken on whether to hear alleged new evidence in the case, but the US Supreme Court refused to reopen the case.

On 14 and 15 December Robert Wayne Williams and John Eldon Smith were executed by electrocution in Louisiana and Georgia respectively. These were the first executions in both states since the early 1960s.

Amnesty International had earlier appealed for clemency in the case of James Autry who was scheduled for execution by lethal injection in Texas on 5 November. Thirty minutes before this was due to be carried out, James Autry was granted a stay of execution by the US Supreme Court. Reportedly, he had already been strapped to a chair and a saline solution, which acts as a vehicle for the fatal drug, had been injected into his veins. This would have been the second execution by lethal injection in the USA. By the end of the year, 12 states had introduced this as a sole or alternative method of execution: Arkansas, Delaware, Idaho, Illinois, Montana, Nevada, New Jersey, New Mexico, North Carolina, Oklahoma, Texas, Washington.

A number of Supreme Court decisions during the year, denying appeals in death penalty cases, reduced the grounds on which future appeals could be lodged and could therefore speed up the carrying out of executions in the future. The Supreme Court further ruled (in Barefoot v Texas) on 6 July 1983 that lower federal courts could promulgate their own rules for expediting *habeas corpus* appeals on constitutional issues in death penalty cases, by summarily considering the merits of an appeal at the same time as deciding whether or not to grant a stay of execution. (Many federal courts had previously automatically granted stays of execution pending a separate hearing of the merits of an appeal.) In the same decision, the Supreme Court ruled that lower courts should apply tighter standards for considering appeals and should refuse to hear repeated or "frivolous" appeals. One of the dissenting Supreme Court judges criticized this opinion, noting that

70 per cent of capital cases decided on their merits by federal courts of appeals since 1976 had resulted in the death sentence being vacated: he stated that it would be wrong for appeals courts in the future to decide such cases under "special truncated procedures".

No prisoners were adopted as prisoners of conscience during the year but Amnesty International continued to investigate a number of cases where people charged with criminal offences alleged that the real reason for the prosecution was political or racial.

On 8 July Amnesty International sent the US Attorney General a copy of its observer's report on the trial of Eddie Carthan in October 1982 on a charge of murder (see *Amnesty International Report 1983*).

Although Eddie Carthan was acquitted of the murder charge, Amnesty International was concerned about procedures which the organization believed had a possible impact on the fairness of the trial; in particular the possible misuse by the prosecution of the "plea bargaining" process, whereby two witnesses, both of whom had confessed to actually carrying out the killings, had been offered generous incentives, including the dropping of serious criminal charges, in return for testifying against Eddie Carthan.

Amnesty International's observer also found that other charges against Eddie Carthan (of assaulting a police officer and two counts of fraud) indicated a pattern of selective prosecution, discriminatory sentencing and harassment of the accused.

Amnesty International raised these concerns with the Attorney General, referring in particular to "the prosecution's apparent misuse of the plea bargaining process which may have encouraged false testimony and which may be evidence of prosecutorial discrimination against Eddie Carthan on political and racial grounds". Amnesty International asked the Attorney General to review the various cases involving the former mayor. No reply was received by the end of the year. When Amnesty International sent its report to the Attorney General, Eddie Carthan was serving a three-year sentence for bank fraud, and prosecution on the second fraud charge was pending.

The charge of food fraud against Eddie Carthan was later dropped by the prosecution and in October 1983 a federal judge reduced the sentence on the bank fraud charge to just under nine months. He was released from prison on 13 October 1983.

On 25 July an Amnesty International observer attended part of the retrial of Johnny Harris on a capital murder charge in Bay Minette, Alabama. Johnny Harris, an inmate of Holman Prison, Alabama, had been convicted and sentenced to death in 1975 for the murder of a prison guard during a riot in the prison's segregation unit in 1974. The only death penalty statute then in force in Alabama was one providing for a mandatory death sentence if a prisoner serving a life sentence was convicted of murder. Johnny Harris, who denied involvement in the guard's killing, alleged that he had been singled out for prosecution because he was the only prisoner in the segregation unit serving a life sentence at the time of the riot; the prosecution had publicly declared a commitment to seeing that the death penalty would be imposed in this case. The conviction had been based not on evidence that Harris had actually carried out the guard's killing, but on the prosecution's claim that he had taken a leading role in the riot, an accusation which Johnny Harris also denied.

In 1981 a federal judge had quashed Johnny Harris' conviction and ordered a new trial on the basis of (possibly exculpatory) evidence from a former inmate of the prison's segregation unit, which had been withheld by the prosecution at the time of the first trial. At the retrial, which began on 18 July 1983, Johnny Harris was again convicted of first-degree murder and sentenced to death.

Amnesty International was concerned that this prosecution may have been politically motivated by the state's desire to obtain a death sentence following the 1974 riot and killing of the prison guard, and that Johnny Harris had been given a mandatory death sentence under a statute pre-dating the US Supreme Court decisions in the 1970s on the death penalty. When, during this period, the Supreme Court ruled that the death penalty was constitutional only if imposed under certain conditions, it specifically reserved consideration of the question of whether mandatory death sentence statutes could constitutionally be applied to prisoners serving life sentences. The Alabama statute under which Johnny Harris was tried therefore contained none of the procedural safeguards laid down then by the Supreme Court; these included the outlawing of mandatory death sentences under all other statutes and provision for a separate sentencing hearing in death penalty cases, in which the aggravating and mitigating factors of each case must be considered. At the end of the year Amnesty International was still investigating the case, and an appeal was pending.

On 13 September an Amnesty International observer attended an appeal in the case of Leonard Peltier before the 8th Circuit Court of Appeals, St Louis, Missouri. Leonard Peltier had been convicted in April 1977 of the murder of two agents of the Federal Bureau of Investigation (FBI) and had been sentenced to two consecutive life prison terms. The defence sought a retrial on the grounds that newly discovered documents from FBI files showed that the prosecution had suppressed exculpatory evidence at Leonard Peltier's trial. According to the defence, this included suppression of a "firing-pin" test proving that bullet casings found in one of the murdered agents' cars could not have come from the gun alleged to have been Peltier's. The defence asked the appeals court to grant a full evidentiary hearing into the motion for a retrial. The appeals court had not yet given its decision by the end of the year.

Amnesty International's concern in this case arose from allegations that Leonard Peltier had been "targetted" for prosecution because of his active membership of the American Indian Movement and that the FBI may have falsified evidence in order to secure a conviction. Amnesty International's concern was increased by the fact that the FBI had previously admitted fabricating evidence in order to secure Leonard Peltier's extradition from Canada to stand trial in 1977 (evidence which was not used to obtain a conviction at the trial).

On 10 October an Amnesty International observer attended a pre-trial hearing in Wasco County Circuit Court, Oregon, in the cases of a number of American Indians accused under state and federal laws of violating fishing regulations. They were charged with various counts of catching and selling fish at illegal times and depleting salmon stocks in the Columbia river. The defendants, some of whom had been sentenced to up to five years' imprisonment in a federal court on some of the charges, denied the charges and alleged that they had been subjected to selective and discriminatory prosecution on account of their ethnic origin, rather than for violating fishing regulations, and were being held responsible for a record low salmon run in order to protect the interests of the commercial marine fishing industry. Amnesty International was still investigating the charges at the end of the year.

Uruguay

Amnesty International was concerned about the large number of prisoners of conscience; the continuing practice of unacknowledged detention of suspected members of illegal political parties; the lack of legal guarantees for political detainees; the administrative detention of prisones who had completed their sentences; torture; and inhumane prison regimes.

In April 1983 an Amnesty International delegation visited Monte-video comprising Professor Heleno Claudio Fragoso of Brazil, Vice-President of the International Commission of Jurists, and a member of Amnesty International's International Secretariat. A member of the delegation held a meeting with the Minister of Foreign Affairs, Dr Carlos Maeso. The delegation also met representatives of non-governmental organizations, including the *Colegio de Abogados*, Uruguayan Bar Association; the *Servicio de Paz y Justicia*, Peace and Justice Service, an ecumenical human rights organization; members of political parties and trade unions and private individuals. In July, Amnesty International submitted a memorandum outlining its concerns in Uruguay to President Gregorio C. Alvarez. The memorandum called in its recommendations for the release of prisoners of conscience, the adoption of measures to prevent torture, a thorough investigation to publicly clarify the fate or whereabouts of people reported to have "disappeared" following their arrest and the repeal of the Law of State Security and Internal Order (1972) which brought civilians accused of political offences under the jurisdiction of military courts. Amnesty International also urged the government to review the regimes currently in force in military prisons, to bring these into line with the United Nations (UN) Standard Minimum Rules for the Treatment of Prisoners and to ensure that prisoners received proper medical attention and treatment.

No reply was received from the government to the memorandum, and in November the text was published in full in an Amnesty International report, *Human Rights Violations in Uruguay*. At the end of 1983 Amnesty International estimated that there were approximately 800 political prisoners in Uruguay, 670 men and 130 women. The organization was working on behalf of 279 adopted prisoners of conscience, and the cases of a further 85 prisoners were being investigated.

The release of 55 prisoners for whom Amnesty International had worked was confirmed in 1983. Rita Ibarburu de Suárez, a 68-year-old former journalist, who had suffered from a serious heart condition since her imprisonment in October 1975 and for whose release Amnesty International had consistently appealed, was released in October, having completed her eight-year sentence in full. A small number of prisoners were granted early release before their sentences had expired. These included Juan Manuel Rodríguez Bas, a university teacher of Spanish birth, who was released in January 1983, three years before the expiry of his eight-year prison sentence. In July Alberto Altesor González, a former leader of the Uruguayan railway workers' union and a member of the Uruguayan parliament, was released three months early. Amnesty International had appealed for his early release to allow him to receive post-operative care following the major heart operation he underwent in July 1982 while in prison. Rita Ibarburu de Suárez, Juan Manuel Rodríguez Bas and Alberto Altesor González had all been adopted by Amnesty International as prisoners of conscience.

Amnesty International adopted 61 prisoners of conscience during the year, of whom 28 were arrested in 1983.

At least 50 university students and other young people were detained in June. A police official stated that 25 had been charged with "subversive association" and "assistance to a subversive association", offences under the Military Penal Code which carried possible prison sentences of between three and 18 years and two and eight years respectively. The students and young people were accused of membership of the illegal *Unión de Juventudes Comunistas* (UJC), Union of Communist Youth, and were held responsible for the planning of anti-government demonstrations on 27 June 1983, the tenth anniversary of the closure of parliament by the armed forces. The UJC was the youth branch of the *Partido Comunista del Uruguay* (PCU), the Uruguayan Communist Party, which was banned by the armed forces in December 1973, along with 13 other political parties and groups. The 25 young people, who were awaiting trial by military court, were adopted by Amnesty International as prisoners of conscience.

Amnesty International continued to investigate the cases of 15 prisoners who had been kept in detention on new charges following the expiry of their prison sentences. They were accused of a political conspiracy in prison as alleged members of a political group known as the *Seispuntistas*, Six Point Group. Amnesty International believed that the new legal proceedings against them did not conform to internationally recognized standards for a fair and impartial trial. Trial proceedings were based on confessions obtained under duress while prisoners were held incommunicado for prolonged periods and trials were conducted in secret. To Amnesty International's knowledge, no evidence had been produced that the prisoners had used or advocated violence since the date of their imprisonment. Five of the prisoners were reported to have been convicted on the new charges and given fresh prison sentences ranging from seven to 10 years.

Américo Gastón Roballo, whom Amnesty International had previously listed as "disappeared", was located at the end of January 1983 in a military barracks in Montevideo (see *Amnesty International Report 1983*). The Uruguayan authorities had repeatedly denied that he had been detained. However, in notes sent to the Inter-American Commission on Human Rights, which had taken up the case, the authorities subsequently maintained that he was arrested on 20 January 1983. Amnesty International believed that he had in fact been held in unacknowledged detention for a period of more than four months, from 20 September 1982 until the end of January 1983.

No new cases of "disappearances" were reported in 1983. Amnesty International continued to work on behalf of Miguel Angel Mato Fagiani, Félix Ortiz Piazzoli and Omar Antonio Paita Cardozo, all of whom reportedly "disappeared" in 1981 and 1982. In February 1983 Amnesty International asked the authorities for confirmation of their detention and information on their whereabouts. No replies were received. However, in response to inquiries made through diplomatic channels, the authorities stated that they had not been detained and that no warrant for their arrest existed.

Amnesty International remained concerned about the continued practice of holding in administrative custody prisoners who had completed their full prison terms. Detention orders were issued in such cases by higher military authorities, without recourse to military courts, supposedly under emergency powers provided for by Article 168. 17 of the constitution.

In September and November 1983 two prisoners for whom Amnesty International had worked, Jorge Selves Lawlor and Washington Guinovart Tonelli, were released and left the country. They had been detained for approximately two and a half years and one and a half years respectively, after the expiry of their prison sentences. Both men had been held for an extended period in a military barracks in the provincial town of Florida, the *Batallón de Ingenieros de Combate No. 2* (see *Amnesty International Report 1983*.)

In an interview published after his release Jorge Selves Lawlor maintained that he had been confined to a punishment cell in Libertad prison for 125 days after the expiry of his sentence before being transferred to the military barracks, where, he said, he was held for several months in isolation in a basement cell.

Reports that suspected members of illegal political parties were tortured while being held incommunicado following their arrest continued. In June Amnesty International sent urgent appeals to the Uruguayan authorities asking for guarantees of the physical safety and integrity of the students and young people arrested that month on political charges. In July, Montevideo newspapers published a statement made by the Peace and Justice Service which alleged that many of the prisoners detained in June had been tortured while in police custody. The reported methods included electric shock torture and beatings and semi-asphyxiation by immersion in water, a technique known as the *submarino*. Several women were said to have been raped in the presence of other detainees. Amnesty International received a detailed account of the torture inflicted on one of the students, Lucia Arzuaga Gilboa, which occurred before her arrest had been officially recognized. In August Amnesty International urged an immediate and thorough investigation of these allegations. Two Catholic priests were questioned by police in connection with the public statement on torture issued by the Peace and Justice Service, but to Amnesty International's knowledge no official inquiry was undertaken into the allegations it contained. On 31 August the Peace and Justice Service was banned by government decree.

Amnesty International remained concerned about the harsh treatment of prisoners and the inadequate provision for medical attention in Uruguay's two major military prisons for political prisoners: the *Penal de Libertad*, Libertad prison, for men, and the *Penal de Punta de Rieles*, Punta de Rieles prison, for women.

During the year Amnesty International medical groups wrote to prison authorities expressing concern about reports of the serious ill-health of 11 prisoners, and urging that prompt and appropriate medical care be provided. In a number of cases, a formal reply was received from the *Oficina Central de Información sobre Personas* (OCIP), Central Office for Information on Persons, a government office which was established in 1978 to deal with inquiries and appeals received from abroad concerning political prisoners. Such replies invariably provided basic information concerning the prisoners' legal situation and general state of health, without responding to the specific concerns raised by Amnesty International, or making available any details concerning medical treatment. However, Amnesty International continued to receive reports of delays in medical attention, delays in the transfer of sick prisoners to hospital for treatment or surgery, and of an irregular supply of medicines.

In September Amnesty International organized appeals to end the inhumane treatment of nine prominent leaders of the *Movimiento de Liberación Nacional – Tupamaros* (MLN), National Liberation Movement– Tupamaros. The appeals coincided with the 10th anniversary of the transfer of the nine from Libertad prison to separate military barracks in the interior of the country, where they had been kept in solitary confinement in tiny cells without adequate nutrition, ventilation or sanitary facilities. The nine were reported to be frequently denied exercise, reading and writing materials, regular family visits, legal assistance and adequate medical attention. In June, Amnesty International issued an urgent appeal for one of them, Raúl Sendic Antonaccio, having received reports that he had been tortured on being transferred to another military barracks. In its *1983 Report on Human Rights Violations in Uruguay*, Amnesty International urged the transfer of the nine to a regular prison in accordance with the UN Standard Minimum Rules for the Treatment of Prisoners.

In 1983 Amnesty International submitted information under the UN procedure set up to examine a "Consistent pattern of gross and reliably attested violations of human rights". Amnesty International also submitted information to the UN Working Group on Enforced or Involuntary Disappearances. During the year the Human Rights Committee, established under the International Covenant on Civil and Political Rights, published its views on 12 Uruguayan cases. In all of these cases the Uruguayan Government was found responsible for violations of the Covenant, particularly of Article 7, referring to torture, Article 10, referring to the ill-treatment of prisoners, and Article 14, referring to trial procedures. Ismael Weinberger Weisz and Lilián Celiberti, two prisoners for whose immediate release the Committee had asked in decisions reached in previous years, were released in 1983. Ismael Weinberger was released in January, one year before the expiry of his eight-year prison sentence. Lilián Celiberti was released in November, a few days before completing her five-year sentence. Both had been adopted by Amnesty International as prisoners of conscience.

Asia

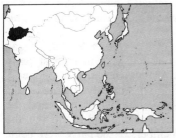

Afghanistan

Amnesty International's concerns were the imprisonment of prisoners of conscience, the detention of political prisoners without charge or trial, the torture and ill-treatment of detainees, the use of the death penalty and reported extrajudicial executions. Amnesty International was also concerned that the few trials of political prisoners it learned of appeared to fall far short of internationally recognized standards.

The continuing civil war between the government of President Babrak Karmal, supported by forces of the Soviet Union and various Islamic militia was accompanied by allegations of human rights violations on both sides. The civil war itself and the continued denial of access to the country by the Afghan Government to international humanitarian organizations and most of the world press hampered Amnesty International's collection of information and the verification of such allegations.

It was therefore difficult for Amnesty International to gauge the full extent of political detention, but the available information indicated that several thousand detainees were held in the Kabul area alone.

Amnesty International continued to be concerned about the imprisonment of several academics from the University of Kabul whose arrest was reported in the *Amnesty International Report 1983*. Although several members of this group were released, at least three – Professor Hassan Kakar, Dr Osman Rustar and Shukrullah Kohgadai – were tried *in camera* for "counter-revolutionary offences". The three men had reportedly participated in a discussion group at the University of Kabul which tried to suggest possible peaceful solutions to the civil war which has been fought in Afghanistan since the establishment of the government of President Babrak Karmal on 27 December 1979 and the intervention of the armed forces of the Soviet Union. During their trial all three defendants were reported to have pointed out that their actions had not violated in any way the Afghan constitution, known as the Fundamental Principles. The three men were reportedly denied access to a lawyer during their period of detention and at their trial. Dr Rustar received a sentence of 10 years' imprisonment, Professor Kakar was sentenced to eight years' imprisonment and Shukrullah Kohgadai was sentenced to seven years'. All three were denied any right of appeal and were adopted as prisoners of conscience by Amnesty International.

Amnesty International also investigated the case of another university teacher, the nuclear physicist Dr Mohammad Younis Akbari, who was arrested on 27 April 1983. No charges were brought against him and his place of detention was not known.

Several hundred alleged members of the *Afghan Mellat*, Afghan Social Democratic Party, a clandestine left-wing nationalist party which advocated a negotiated settlement of the civil war, were reportedly arrested between May and July 1983. To Amnesty International's knowledge none of those detained were charged or tried and the organization continued to express concern about their detention to the authorities. The cases of 35 alleged members of the party were being investigated by Amnesty International.

Most people detained in Afghanistan for political reasons are held without charge or trial. The few trials which took place were reportedly held *in camera* without the defendants being legally represented. Visits by relatives appeared to be strictly forbidden during the period when prisoners were interrogated, which in some cases lasted for up to two years. Defendants were sometimes not informed of the charges against them before appearing in court.

Amnesty International received reports that 19 alleged members of the central committee of *Sama*, a Maoist group actively opposed to the government of President Babrak Karmal, had been arrested and secretly tried in August 1982. It would appear that the accused were tried *in camera* without legal representation and with no right of appeal. Amnesty International received no response from the government as to the fate of 18 of the prisoners. However, the family of one of the accused, Engineer Zamari Sadique, was reportedly informed that he had been executed.

Throughout 1983 Amnesty International was disturbed by consistent reports of torture and ill-treatment of people taken into custody by the *Khedamat-e Atla't Dawlati, Khad* (State Information Police). Political arrests were usually said to take place at night without warrant, in many cases without the arresting officers identifying themselves. Detainees' families were generally not informed of the place of detention.

Detainees were allegedly subjected to beatings, deprivation of sleep and electric shock torture involving the use of electric shock batons or electrodes wired to a telephone. Former detainees interviewed by Amnesty International, and other reports the organization has received, indicated that the use of such torture techniques during interrogation was systematic in eight *Khad* interrogation centres in Kabul. Most ex-detainees also complained of a complete absence of medical care.

In an international news release and background paper issued on 2 November Amnesty International identified the eight interrogation centres in Kabul where torture was known to take place. The eight were: (1) *Khad* "Office Number Five", known as *Khad-i Panj*; (2) the headquarters of the *Khad* in the Shashdarak district; (3) the Internal Affairs Ministry building; (4) the Central Interrogation Office, known as the *Sedarat*; (5) the office of the military branch of the *Khad*, known as *Khad-i Nezami*; (6) and (7) two private houses near the *Sedarat* building – the Ahmad Shah Khan house and the Wasir Akbar Khan house – and (8) the *Khad* office in the Howzai Barikat district.

Those arrested and subjected to torture included not only people accused of involvement in armed resistance to the government but civil servants, doctors, teachers, students and many others seized on suspicion of non-violent opposition. In most cases torture was apparently used either to extract information or to force confessions from detainees.

In some cases detainees reportedly suffered serious physical and mental injuries as a result of their torture and ill-treatment. Several cases of detainees dying as a result of these injuries were reported to Amnesty International. The organization received reports at the end of 1983 alleging the death in detention following torture of Gholam Shah Sarshar-e Shomali, a poet and former manager of the newspaper *Anis*.

As in previous years, Amnesty International continued to be concerned about the use of the judicial death penalty and about reported extrajudicial executions. In April four men were executed following conviction for alleged terrorist offences; six more executions were officially announced in November, four of those executed being members of the ruling People's Democratic Party of Afghanistan accused of the abduction and execution of a fellow party member. Two further executions involving alleged members of an Islamic fundamentalist group were reported in December. There were allegations of unpublicized death sentences and executions but Amnesty International received neither details of these nor the names of those concerned other than that of Engineer Zamari Sadique of the *Sama* group referred to above.

Amnesty International also received reports of the execution of individuals detained by the many Islamic groups which were carrying out insurgent activities against the government of President Babrak Karmal and which effectively controlled territory, although these were rarely officially acknowledged by the groups. At the end of December 1983 an Afghan Army Captain, Mohammad Naim, was reportedly executed following a "trial" by one such group in Nangarhar province. More than 20 members of the ruling People's Democratic Party of Afghanistan were reportedly captured and later executed in November by insurgents in Herat.

Amnesty International also received occasional reports of extra-judicial executions by both government and Soviet forces. On 30 June Soviet forces were allegedly involved in the killing of 23 unarmed civilians in the village of Rauzda in Ghazni province, outside the context of combat. On several occasions Amnesty International urged the Afghan Government to establish an inquiry into such reported extrajudicial executions and, if the reports were found to be true, to charge and try responsible officials in conformity with the penal code of Afghanistan. No reply was received from the government.

Afghanistan ratified the International Covenant on Civil and Political Rights and the International Covenant on Economic, Social and Cultural Rights on 24 January 1983.

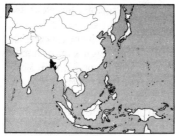

Bangladesh

Demonstrations against martial law were met by the short-term political detention of opposition party leaders, workers and students. Amnesty International also remained concerned about the trial of political prisoners by military courts applying summary procedures, allegations of torture, prison conditions, and the death penalty.

On 14 February students in Dhaka, supported by an alliance of opposition parties, demonstrated against proposed educational reforms, which would have included Arabic as one of the compulsory languages in primary education. During the demonstrations, which spread to other towns, violence occurred and at least five people were killed. On 15 February 30 leading politicians of an 18-party political alliance were arrested for holding a meeting in defiance of martial law regulations. They included Kamal Hussain, a former Foreign Minister; Sheikh Hasina Wazed, the leader of the Awami League; Mohammad Farhad, Secretary General of the Communist Party; and Rasheed Khan Menon of the Workers' Party. On 17 February the government announced that 1,331 people had been arrested and detained in connection with the February demonstrations of whom 1,021 had been released as of 18 February. The remaining 310, it said, would also be released, if not "identified as trouble makers".

On 22 February Amnesty International cabled Lieutenant General Ershad, the Chief Martial Law Administrator, expressing concern about these continued detentions, asking that all those arrested be given access to lawyers and relatives and urging the release of all those detainees against whom no charges had been brought.

On 1 March the government announced that 27 leaders of political parties, who had been held in preventive detention, were being released. On 19 March Lieutenant General Ershad ordered the release of some 200 students and members of political parties who had been arrested after the 14 February demonstrations.

An Amnesty International delegate visited Dhaka from 14 February to 2 March and discussed the February arrests with officials in the Home Ministry. The delegate was informed of the government's intentions for the early release of the detainees and discussed Amnesty International's concern about the continued use of the 1974 Special Powers Act (SPA) to detain political opponents without trial. He was informed by the government that the number detained under the SPA had been reduced since March 1982 but that, as of January 1983, over 400 political detainees and people suspected of criminal offences were being held.

Amnesty International wrote to Lieutenant General Ershad on 31 March acknowledging the government's cooperation during the delegate's visit and welcoming the reported release of political detainees, many of whom appeared to be prisoners of conscience. It requested clarification of reports in the Bangladesh press that several detainees remained imprisoned and expressed concern about allegations that several people taken into custody after 14 February had been tortured and ill-treated. Amnesty International said that detainees held in the Dhaka Army Cantonment had reportedly been kept bound in iron fetters, and that prisoners were interrogated under threat of torture. It also received reports that prisoners were being beaten, whipped, hung upside down from the ceiling and that, in some cases, electric shock torture had been used. Amnesty International named seven detainees allegedly subjected to torture or ill-treatment and asked the government to set up an independent inquiry to investigate these allegations.

Amnesty International also reiterated its long-standing concern about the detention of political prisoners under the SPA and said that it had received repeated allegations of the arbitrary arrest, torture and ill-treatment of detainees in army custody in the Chittagong Hill Tracts.

One of these reports concerned the journalist Sunil Kanti De from Rangamathi, who was arrested on 4 June 1981 and held under the provisions of the SPA until November 1981, when he was charged under Regulation 16 of the SPA and Martial Law Regulation (MLR) No. 17 with committing a "prejudicial act". During the initial period of his detention he was reportedly tortured. Amnesty International also expressed concern that civilians such as Sunil Kanti De continued to be tried before martial law courts employing summary procedures without the right of appeal. In September 1983 a Summary Martial Law Court ordered his acquittal and release subject to the approval of the Zonal Martial Law Administrator, but as of November Amnesty International was not aware whether such approval had been given.

Sunil Kanti De was one of the 14 prisoners adopted by Amnesty International in 1983 as a prisoner of conscience. Other adopted prisoners included trade unionists sentenced by military courts to several years' imprisonment for contravening martial law regulations prohibiting strikes.

Four prisoners of conscience were released during the year. Among them was Shawkat Ali, a retired army colonel and member of the Awami League, who, after his arrest on 10 May 1982, had been detained under the SPA and subsequently charged with criminal offences allegedly committed eight years earlier. He was acquitted by the Special Martial Law Court in October 1982, after which he had been held under the SPA. He was released on 8 September. Three students, arrested on 16 September 1982 and sentenced on 23 September to seven years' imprisonment for "fixing anti-state and anti-government posters", were released in July 1983.

On 7 November Amnesty International wrote to Lieutenant General Ershad welcoming these releases but presenting information about 10 others believed to have been imprisoned for holding or expressing non-violent political beliefs. They included trade unionists, labour leaders, members of political parties, a newspaper editor and a journalist imprisoned for publishing articles allegedly critical of the government. Amnesty International asked Lieutenant General Ershad to consider their early release together with that of all other individuals detained for the non-violent exercise of their human rights.

Amnesty International also expressed concern that political opponents had been tried under successive governments by military courts, both for participating in normal political activities made punishable under martial law or for allegedly committing offences punishable under the Bangladeshi penal code. The organization was concerned that procedures before military courts were summary; that those presiding at such courts were largely army personnel not required to have legal qualifications; that legal representation was not allowed before Summary

Martial Law Courts, although the accused might be assisted by a person of his or her choosing; that customary rules of evidence and procedure designed to safeguard fair trial had been changed; and that it was not possible to appeal against any order, verdict or sentence handed down by military courts. Amnesty International said that such procedures did not meet the minimum standards provided for in the International Covenant on Civil and Political Rights and urged the government to review the cases of all political prisoners who had been tried by military courts, with a view to ordering either their retrial before an ordinary court of law or their release on bail pending such a review.

In view of these concerns, Amnesty International requested that the government review the cases of six former government officials who were arrested between March and July 1982 and were reported to be in hospital because of bad health. While realizing that these men had been sentenced to long terms of imprisonment by military courts for offences including "abuse of official position", "anti-state activity" and "obtaining pecuniary advantage", Amnesty International expressed concern that normal legal safeguards had not been applied. In some cases prisoners were reportedly only informed of the charges against them on the day they were brought before the military court. In others, no record of cross-examination by the defence was kept, and there was no right of appeal. Amnesty International also expressed its concern about the reported arrest of political detainees, including 12 people, among whom were students, teachers, a former state minister and an advocate, who were arrested in May in connection with an alleged conspiracy in Jessore on 29 March. Some of them were apparently held under the SPA and one of them – a former Minister of State for Post and Shipping – had reportedly been tortured with electric shocks during his detention in Dhaka Army Cantonment. Amnesty International asked the government to order an impartial investigation into these reports and to inform the organization about the results of such an investigation and about the charges against the other prisoners.

Some 170 tribesmen in the Chittagong Hill Tracts were reportedly arrested in April and May on suspicion of being "guerrilla sympathizers", but few details about these arrests were known because the area is largely inaccessible.

The martial law ban on political activities was temporarily lifted on 14 November, only to be reimposed on 28 November. On 28 November opposition demonstrations against military rule resulted in violence during which at least four people were killed and over 600 were reportedly arrested, among them opposition leaders. Amnesty International cabled Lieutenant General Ershad on 2 December expressing its concern that among those arrested were people who had not been involved in the violence but had merely participated in demonstrations to express their political views. The organization asked the government to take immediate steps towards the release of any such prisoners.

On 11 December Lieutenant General Ershad assumed the presidency under the Proclamation Third Amendment Order 1983. On 15 December Amnesty International wrote to President Ershad welcoming the reported release of 200 political detainees who had been arrested on 28 November and requesting full details of the government's release program, in view of reported claims by opposition parties that the number of arrests as a result of the November demonstrations well exceeded the number of political prisoners – 120 – who were released in Dhaka and the 80 whom the government announced on 14 December would be released.

In the context of its concern about the conditions in which political detainees were being held in Bangladesh, Amnesty International had asked the government in its 7 November letter whether the report of the Jail Reform Committee established on 4 November 1978 and headed by Justice F.K.M.Z. Munim – which apparently submitted its final report to the government on 27 November 1980 – had been published. The report was believed to have made a number of important recommendations concerning prison conditions and Amnesty International asked to be sent a copy, and inquired whether steps had been taken to implement its recommendations. The organization had not received a reply to this and other requests by the end of the year.

Amnesty International appealed to Lieutenant General Ershad in six cases for the commutation of death sentences imposed by civilian or special military courts following convictions for murder. On 30 September Lieutenant Colonel Fazle Hussain was executed in Chittagong for his alleged involvement in the killing of President Ziaur Rahman on 3 May 1981. While Amnesty International had been informed that Lieutenant Colonel Fazle Hussain was arrested on 3 June 1981, it had no details of his subsequent trial and conviction. In its letter of 7 November, the organization recorded its concern about this execution and requested information about whether the minimum standards contained in the International Covenant on Civil and Political Rights – against the arbitrary deprivation of life and stipulating trials by competent courts with the right to seek pardon or commutation – had been applied in his case.

Brunei

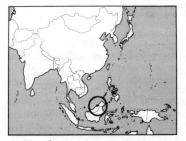

Amnesty International was concerned about the continued detention of eight people who had been held without trial for their alleged involvement in the rebellion of December 1962. Most had been held continuously since their arrest at that time under Emergency Orders issued in connection with the rebellion. Amnesty International was also concerned about the detention without trial of approximately 20 other people arrested for political reasons during the 1970s who were also being held under the Emergency Orders.

The eight detainees arrested in connection with the 1962 rebellion were regarded by Amnesty International as prisoners of conscience. Following the defeat of the rebellion, launched by the *Partai Rakyat Brunei* (PRB), Brunei People's Party, about 2,500 members of the party and its military wing, the *Tentera Nasional Kalimantan Utara* (TNKU), North Kalimantan National Army, were arrested. By the beginning of 1982, all but the eight detainees mentioned above had either been released, had escaped or had died in detention. Amnesty International believed that the eight remaining detainees, none of whom was prominent in the PRB or the TNKU, continued to be detained not for their alleged role in the 1962 rebellion but as a general deterrent to political activity in the territory. Amnesty International was also concerned that several of the detainees had reached advanced years and that their detention in virtual isolation without regular visits or correspondence was a danger to their well-being.

On 4 January 1983, Amnesty International wrote to the Sultan of Brunei expressing its concern about the situation of the detainees and appealing for their release. In September 1983, it initiated action to secure the release of the eight detainees and on 8 September 1983 submitted a statement to the United Nations Special Committee on Decolonization presenting its information on the detainees.

Burma

Amnesty International continued to receive occasional reports of arrests on political grounds and was concerned that some of those arrested were said to be held without charge or trial. There were also allegations that some of these detainees were ill-treated. Many of those arrested belonged to ethnic minority groups and lived in areas where there was armed opposition to the government. Often the information received by Amnesty International related to the period before 1983. Five people were known to have been sentenced to death during 1983.

Political detainees may be held without formal charge or trial under the 1975 Law for the Protection of the State from Subversive Elements which provides a loose and broadly formulated definition of "subversion". The authority to order arrests is vested in a committee known as the Central Body, chaired by the Minister for Home and Religious Affairs, with the members being the Ministers of Defence and Foreign Affairs. The Central Body is empowered to order detention of a suspect for renewable two-monthly periods up to a maximum of 180 days under Section 10(a) of the 1975 law, following which advance approval by the Council of Ministers must be sought. The Council of Ministers can extend the period up to three years under detention orders which are renewable at 180-day intervals (Sections 12 and 14). Detainees can appeal against the detention order, to the Council of Ministers when detention is authorized by the Central Body and to the highest judicial authority, the Council of People's Judges, when detention has already been authorized by the Council of Ministers. Amnesty International was concerned that the 1975 law made no specific provision for detainees to be informed of the grounds of arrest, or for legal representation during the appeals process.

Some detainees arrested under the anti-subversion law were reportedly held incommunicado and beaten during interrogation by personnel of the Military Intelligence Service (MIS) (also known as the Defence Services Intelligence), the main operating agency of the National Intelligence Bureau which was reported to control all intelligence and security activities. Article 159(b) of the consititution of 1974 states: "No citizen shall be placed in custody for more than 24 hours without the sanction of a competent judicial organ", but this safeguard does not apply to detainees held under the anti-subversion law.

The Government of Burma does not issue information concerning arrests and detention. Amnesty International continued to face difficulties in obtaining information on individual cases of political detention without charge or trial and about other human rights violations. Amnesty International investigated reports that political arrests occurred in Arakan and Karen states both before 1983 and during the year. In some cases detention was apparently short-term but some detainees were said to have been held for several months without formal charge or trial. Members of the Burmese Army deployed in counter-insurgency operations in Karen and Shan states were allegedly responsible for the politically motivated killing of non-combatants, but Amnesty International was unable to substantiate these allegations.

Five people were sentenced to death in Burma during 1983, the first death sentences recorded by Amnesty International since 1978. One woman, Daw Ni, and two men were sentenced to death in late October 1983 for murder. In the second case, two North Koreans, Major Zin Mo and Captain Kang Min-chul, were sentenced to death under Article 302 of the penal code for murder. They were found guilty of a bomb attack at the Aung San Mausoleum in Rangoon in October 1983 in which 21 people, including four South Korean cabinet ministers, died. On both occasions, Amnesty International appealed to President U San Yu for clemency should the death sentences be confirmed by the appellate court to which all these prisoners were entitled to appeal under Article 101 of Burma's constitution. Amnesty International also wrote to the Minister of Home and Religious Affairs, Major General Min Gaung, on 3 November 1983, noting that few death sentences have been handed down in recent years and urging that consideration be given to abolishing the death penalty for all offences or, at least as a first step, limiting the number of offences for which the death penalty may be imposed. The number of judicial executions in Burma since the country's independence in 1948 is reported to have been fewer than 10.

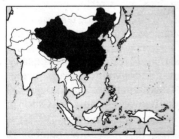

China

Amnesty International's main concerns were the large number of executions carried out during a campaign against crime; the adoption of legislation which removed vital safeguards in some capital cases; the continued imprisonment of prisoners of conscience and new arrests of people for peacefully exercising their human rights; and trials of political prisoners that fell short of internationally-accepted standards.

On 28 February 1983, Amnesty International sent a memorandum to the Government of the People's Republic of China describing its concerns in the country. It invited comments from the government but received no response. Drawing attention to some aspects of Chinese law and practice which permit the imprisonment of prisoners of conscience and other violations of fundamental human rights, Amnesty International recommended:

● the release of all prisoners of conscience;

● the revision of the provisions of the criminal law which permit the imprisonment of people solely for the peaceful exercise of fundamental rights;

● repeal of the provisions of the 1957 Decision of the State Council on the Question of Rehabilitation Through Labour under which people having dissenting views can be detained without charge or trial and subjected to compulsory labour for the purposes of "re-education-through-labour";

● that consideration be given to modifying the provisions of Article 92(2) of the Law of Criminal Procedure, to establish safeguards against unlimited detention without trial, and specific safeguards against arbitrary detention;

● that the government consider adopting measures so that any trial procedures relating to political prisoners conform to internationally established norms, including the right to public hearings and the right to be presumed innocent until proved guilty according to law; and that detailed records of the trial of any political prisoner be published;

● the introduction of procedures to ensure the effective protection of prisoners against cruel, inhuman or degrading treatment, such as the right of relatives and legal counsel to visit and communicate freely with a detainee shortly after arrest and regularly thereafter;

● that steps towards the abolition of the death penalty be taken, such as reducing the number of offences punishable by the death penalty.

A major concern in 1983 was the increased use of the death penalty. Mass executions were carried out during a nationwide campaign against crime launched in August. Amnesty International recorded over 600 executions in some 20 cities and counties between August and October, when the rate of executions was the highest since the early 1970s.

However, the organization believed that the total number of executions carried out throughout the country was far higher. Foreign correspondents in Beijing estimated the total number at over 5,000. Although the rate of executions appeared to be lower in November and

December, many continued to be carried out. Among the cases reported were those of a 27-year-old woman executed in Shaanxi province after being convicted of stealing large quantities of petrol and selling it on the black market, and a 20-year-old man executed in Guangzhou after being convicted of kicking several women in the streets.

Many were executed in groups of 15 to 40, being shot together in the same place after being paraded in public in the streets or during mass rallies. Most were reportedly unemployed people of between 18 and 40. While the majority appeared to have been convicted of murder, rape or robbery, people were also executed for a wide range of other offences, including theft, spying, organizing a secret society, corruption, embezzlement, molesting women or gang fighting.

On 28 October 1983, Amnesty International wrote to President Li Xiannian, calling for a halt to the wave of executions and expressing concern about the continuous increase in the use of the death penalty in the previous few years. The organization noted with particular concern various measures adopted on 2 September 1983 by the National People's Congress (NPC) Standing Committee to increase the number of offences punishable by the death penalty and to accelerate the procedures for trial, appeal and execution in some capital cases. One such measure introduced the death penalty for seven new categories of offence, bringing to 29 the total number of crimes for which Chinese citizens can be executed under the criminal law. Another measure removed vital safeguards in order to speed up the procedures for trial and appeal in capital cases involving homicide, rape, robbery, explosions and "other activities that seriously threaten public security". Defendants could now be brought to trial without being given a copy of the indictment in advance, and the time limit for appeals after sentencing was reduced from 10 to three days. In order to speed up the procedure for execution, it also became possible for provincial high courts to approve death sentences without referring them to the Supreme People's Court (SPC). Following the adoption of these measures, a man named Chen Guangsen was reportedly executed in Guangzhou on 12 September 1983 only eight days after the alleged offence.

Amnesty International said that the speed with which trials and executions were being carried out under this legislation did not allow for the procedural safeguards against the death penalty to which the United Nations General Assembly had drawn attention several times and pointed out that the increased use of the death penalty contradicted the aim of rehabilitation acknowledged in Chinese law.

Amnesty International's information concerning prisoners of conscience often remained incomplete since no official information on prisoners was published and the authorities usually did not reply to Amnesty International's inquiries. The organization believed that the prisoners of conscience of whom it was aware represented only a fraction of the total number of those detained.

Amnesty International continued to appeal for the release of Wei Jingsheng, an electrician and former editor of an unofficial journal who was reported to have been held in solitary confinement at Beijing Prison No. 1 since 1979. In 1983 it was reported that he was being allowed out of his cell for exercise only once a month and was still being prevented from meeting other prisoners, working or receiving visits from his family. Amnesty International was particularly concerned about the length of time he had spent in solitary confinement and its effect on his health.

Other prisoners of conscience of concern to Amnesty International included the 83-year-old former Bishop of Shanghai, Gong Pinmei, who had been imprisoned in Shanghai for nearly 30 years, and at least 10 other elderly Roman Catholic priests from Shanghai who were arrested for the second time in 1981. Most were in their 60s or 70s and had previously served lengthy terms of imprisonment. Four of them were reportedly tried in early 1983. Father Vincent Zhu Hongsheng, aged 68, and Father Joseph Chen Yuntang, aged 75, were tried in mid-March and sentenced to 15 years' and 11 years' imprisonment respectively for "counter-revolutionary" offences. No official information about the trial was released but information received by Amnesty International indicated that the trial was not held openly. About 100 people were officially invited to attend, but not relatives of the defendants. According to sources in Shanghai, the charges against the priests referred only to their contacts with foreigners, their continued allegiance to the Vatican and their independent religious activities.

Two other priests, Father Stanislaus Shen Baishun and Father Stephen Chen Caijun, were reportedly tried on similar charges in February or early March 1983. Father Shen Baishun, aged 79, was sentenced to 10 years' imprisonment and Father Chen Caijun, aged 65, to two and a half years' imprisonment. Again, no details of the trial were officially released. Father Shen Baishun was reportedly transferred to a prison hospital in Shanghai after the trial for treatment for a heart condition. Another Catholic priest, Father Francis Zhu Shude, aged 69, was tried in Chao Xian, Anhui province, sentenced to 10 years' imprisonment with a further three years' deprivation of civil rights on 10 June 1983 and subsequently died in detention in December of natural causes.

In December 1983 foreign press reports alleged that 90 religious leaders had been arrested throughout China in 1983, but they gave no details about the people concerned. However, the Bishop of Baoding, Monsignor Fan Xueyan, aged 76, and his Vicar-General, Monsignor Huo Binzhang, aged 70, were later reported to have been tried on charges of "maintaining links with the Vatican" and each sentenced to 10 years' imprisonment. Both had reportedly been under house arrest for over a year before being taken into custody and tried; and both had been imprisoned previously.

Numerous arrests were carried out during the campaign against crime launched in August 1983 and a simultaneous movement of "rectification" within the Chinese Communist Party aimed at "weeding out" people officially considered to be extremists from either the left or right. Whereas most of those arrested were believed to have been charged with ordinary criminal offences, others appeared to have been detained for purely political reasons. Yan Heitou, a former official from Hebei province, was reportedly rearrested in November 1983 after his release from prison for making contact with his former "leftist comrades". According to the *Hebei Daily*, cited by *Agence France-Presse* in Beijing on 18 December 1983, he was sent to prison for seven years in 1976 for taking part in the "Gang of Four's" attempt to seize power. His release sparked off celebrations, the *Hebei Daily* said, and within a month dozens of his former comrades came to see him and expressed disenchantment with the current situation. In another case, Xu Guangcheng, a former official in a Shanghai corporation, was reportedly arrested in autumn 1983 for organizing sit-in protests against his expulsion in 1982 from the Chinese Communist Party, following the discovery of a diary in which he had written "reactionary words and sentences to vent his dissatisfaction with the party organization and to attempt to reverse the verdict and stage a comeback".

Amnesty International was also concerned about the arrest of Tibetans reportedly detained since August 1983 for meeting foreign journalists or Tibetan exiles visiting their homeland. One of them, Kalsang Tsering, a monk aged 20, had been interviewed by journalists at Drepung Monastery at the beginning of August 1983 and was reportedly arrested on 26 August 1983. Amnesty International continued to investigate the cases of other Tibetans reported to have been arrested in the previous three years for political or religious reasons in the Autonomous Region of Tibet.

The series of political trials which had started in 1982 continued during 1983. Most of the trials reported by the Chinese news media concerned people described as "followers" of the "Gang of Four" or of Lin Biao – the former Defence Minister who disappeared in 1971 after an alleged attempted coup. In June 1983, the SPC stated in its report to the NPC that "the historical task of trying the Jiang Qing and Lin Biao cliques had been fulfilled". With respect to many of the cases reported in 1983, articles published in the official Chinese press after the arrest of the defendants several years previously clearly indicated that they were presumed guilty before their trials. Although the official press did not usually publish details of trial procedures it often detailed the accusations brought against the defendants. Some were accused of having used violence, but others appeared to have been charged with political offences not involving the use of violence.

Some of those tried during the year had been adopted by Amnesty International as prisoners of conscience. In one case, Liu Shanqing, a resident of Hong Kong, was tried in Guangzhou on 7 February 1983, and sentenced to 10 years' imprisonment plus three years' deprivation of political rights for "counter-revolutionary" offences. Amnesty International believed that Liu Shanqing was detained for exercising his right to freedom of opinion and association. He was arrested in December 1981 in Guangzhou, a few days after leaving Hong Kong for the PRC in order to see the families of two imprisoned dissidents. Despite numerous inquiries, his family and friends in Hong Kong were not informed in advance of his trial. However, in a letter dated 10 August 1983 to the Students' Union of the Chinese University of Hong Kong, which had campaigned for Liu's release, the Guangzhou Intermediate People's Court claimed that Liu Shanqing had been brought to a public trial, and gave details of the verdict.

Amnesty International learned of the release of several prisoners of conscience during the year. They included Ren Wanding, one of the founders of a group called the "Chinese Human Rights Alliance", who had been detained without trial in Beijing since April 1979, and Chen Lu, a 37-year-old technician and member of the same group, who was also arrested in 1979.

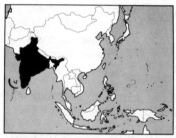

India

Amnesty International remained concerned about the use of preventive detention legislation to detain political opponents of the government, and widespread reports that people arrested had been tortured and ill-treated by the police. It continued to receive occasional reports of deaths in custody and of extrajudicial killings in staged "encounters" with the police. Judicial executions, which had been temporarily suspended, were resumed in October.

During February 1983, widespread communal violence occurred in the state of Assam where an estimated 3,500 people, mainly Bengali-speaking immigrants, were killed by Assamese (many of whom had been campaigning for the repatriation of Bengali Muslims who had entered the state). Demands for political autonomy throughout the year in the Punjab were increasingly marked by violence attributed to Sikh extremist groups. Amnesty International sought to ensure the observance of specific human rights by governments by addressing itself to official measures taken in these and other Indian states which had resulted in the detention of political opponents who had participated in apparently non-violent political activities under preventive detention legislation – especially the provisions of the 1980 National Security Act (NSA) and the 1981 Essential Services Maintenance Act and, in Jammu and Kashmir the Public Security Act (PSA).

The practice of preventive detention was reportedly widespread although no statistics for the number of detainees held were published during the year. Those detained included student leaders in Assam; trade union leaders in Bombay; tribal leaders in Bihar, reportedly for trying to organize meetings; political leaders in the Punjab for peacefully expressing their views in favour of greater autonomy in the province; and political workers in Bihar who were campaigning for minimum wages but were allegedly "Naxalite extremists". In Jammu and Kashmir several members of the Congress (I) Party and of Islamic fundamentalist parties were detained. The NSA allows detention without trial for a maximum period of 12 months for the broadly defined purposes of "the security of the state . . . the maintenance of public order . . . or the maintenance of supplies essential to the community". On 11 March, the Union Home Minister is reported to have directed senior police "to fully utilize the National Security Act while dealing with activities which . . . threaten the security of the state".

On 28 December 1983 Amnesty International wrote to the Prime Minister expressing concern that since its promulgation in 1980 the NSA had been used to detain hundreds of non-violent opponents of the government, despite earlier public assurances that there was no question of using it to "curb political dissent or trade union action". Amnesty International cited the examples of two leaders of the Sikh autonomist party *Akali Dal*, Jagdev Singh Talwandi and Sukhjinder Singh, and of the newspaper editor, Bharpur Singh Balbir, who were detained under the NSA's provisions after being arrested on 3 October 1983 "for their inflammatory speeches and writings", despite the fact that they had apparently only engaged in peaceful political activities. (Jagdev Singh Talwandi remained in detention at the end of 1983 whereas the latter two were released within two weeks of their arrest after their detention orders had been quashed by an advisory board set up under the act's provisions.)

Amnesty International said that it recognized that most cases of preventive detention were short-term but that it also knew of a few cases where the maximum period of 12 months' detention had been ordered. The Supreme Court as well as High Courts of the various states occasionally ordered the release of detainees on the grounds that existing legal safeguards had not been observed. Kamlahar Prasad Chaturvedi from Madhya Pradesh was released by the Supreme Court on the grounds that the "detaining authority had taken into account stale and old incidents while issuing the order". Such court decisions confirmed that detention practices under the NSA did not always conform to the safeguards provided in Indian law and that cases of arbitrary arrest and detention continued to occur. They also underline the importance of independent judicial review of detention.

Amnesty International also expressed concern about reports in the Indian press that the release of *Akali Dal* leaders by the State Advisory Board in November had caused the Home Ministry to consider removing the supervisory powers of the courts over the use of the Act. The organization reiterated its appeal to the government to repeal all preventive detention laws in India and to introduce further safeguards against arbitrary arrest and detention by, for example, considering bringing into force Section 3 of the 44th Consitutional Amendment, already enacted by Parliament in 1978 but so far not implemented. Among other provisions, it would have restricted the maximum period of detention without obtaining the opinion of an advisory board from three to two months.

Amnesty International also wrote to the Chief Minister of Jammu and Kashmir on 26 October to inquire about an estimated 50 people arrested in late August and early September following several violent incidents. Reports suggested that members of the *Jamat-e-Tulba*, (People's League) and the *Muhaz-i-Azadi* (Liberation Front), had been indiscriminately arrested, without necessarily being connected with the violence. The reply from the Chief Minister on 20 December 1983 was not specific and failed to give details about individuals named by Amnesty International, all of whom remained in detention without trial at the end of the year.

On 1 August the Supreme Court ordered the Bihar Government to release and pay a large sum of money in compensation to Rudal Sah, who had been illegally detained for 14 years after his acquittal by a sessions court in 1968. It also ordered that compensation be paid to Ramachandra of Baluji village, who was released on 3 December 1981 after being held for 30 years without trial. Amnesty International was concerned that delays in being brought to trial were also experienced by political prisoners.

Amnesty International remained concerned about widespread reports that criminal suspects and some political detainees had been tortured or ill-treated while being held in police stations. People held in army custody or in prisons were also reportedly tortured and ill-treated. Members of the tribal or of the "Untouchable" communities were reportedly most at risk. Police in Bihar arrested five members of the *Adivasi* (tribal) community on 1 June who had reportedly complained about unemployment in the Singhbhum district. They were reportedly tied to a police car, dragged along for 200 metres and subsequently hung upside down by the police in the village market square and flogged. The leader of the five, Vedar Nag Munga, is said to have died on the spot. Amnesty International received reports of torture from many Indian states. The alleged methods included: beatings while hanging prisoners upside down; denying prisoners food and sleep; rolling heavy iron rods over prisoners' upper legs and knees; and the occasional use of electric shock torture in the states of Uttar Pradesh and Rajasthan. On 20 November the Supreme Court ordered a judicial inquiry into reports that prisoners in a New Delhi jail were subjected to sexual assaults. However, such judicial inquiries are rarely held.

In its letter of 28 December 1983 Amnesty International expressed concern that existing laws and machinery to deal with complaints about torture and ill-treatment by the police had been ineffective. The organization described in detail 10 cases of deaths in police custody reported during 1983, including the case of Krishna Kumar Rajan, who died in a Bombay hospital on 9 August 1983 within 24 hours of his release from police custody where he had been seriously beaten.

Amnesty International continued to receive reports that alleged members of the Communist Party of India (Marxist-Leninist) ("Naxalites") and criminal suspects were taken into custody and subsequently tortured and killed by the police. Official reports stated they were killed in "encounters" with law-enforcement officials. The Supreme Court heard writ petitions during 1983 concerning a number of political activists alleged to have been deliberately killed by the police in "encounters" in Tamil Nadu, Andhra Pradesh, and Uttar Pradesh. Amnesty International raised with the government five such "encounters" which reportedly occurred between November 1980 and January 1982 in Tamil Nadu, Andhra Pradesh, Uttar Pradesh and Maharashtra. The organization received a reply in October summarizing the findings of an inquiry held into the death of one of the five, Peddi Shankar. According to the government he was killed during an exchange of fire between the police and a "Naxalite" group. However, Amnesty International received a detailed report from a civil liberties group which found that no "encounter" had taken place and that Peddi Shankar had been shot in the back by a police guard. In its 28 December letter to the Prime Minister, Amnesty International welcomed the fact that an investigation had been held, but stated that only the publication of a full report detailing the nature of the inquiry held, its methods of investigation and the evidence relied on in support of its conclusions, would allay the suspicion that Peddi Shankar had been shot dead in cold blood by the police. Amnesty International also reiterated its appeal for a full independent inquiry by a judicial authority into all cases of "encounter" killings where there was reason to believe the police had killed people after taking them into custody, and urged the government to consider establishing an independent judicial mechanism before which complaints of such extrajudicial killings could be considered from the entire country. Amnesty International also expressed concern that laws which conferred broadly defined powers to shoot to kill appeared to facilitate the illegal and arbitrary killing of political opponents in a number of Indian states. The organization referred to: the Disturbed Areas Act of Andhra Pradesh; the Armed Forces (Assam and Manipur) Special Powers Act; the Punjab Disturbed Areas Act; the Chandigarh Disturbed Areas Act; and the Armed Forces (Punjab and Chandigarh) Special Powers Act which were enacted following the imposition of presidential rule in Punjab on 6 October 1983 and a declaration on 7 October 1983 that Punjab and Chandigarh were "disturbed areas".

Amnesty International continued to be concerned about the reported execution of people sentenced to death, although some steps towards abolition of the death penalty were taken. On 7 April the Supreme Court declared unconstitutional Section 303 of the Indian penal code which prescribed a mandatory death sentence for people serving sentences of life imprisonment for murder. The Supreme Court commuted several death penalties in 1983, in one case on the grounds that a very lengthy delay in execution was an important reason for commuting the death sentence. Some individuals sentenced to death have been awaiting execution for periods of nine to 11 years. As of 22 April 1983, 21 petitions for mercy were pending with the President, which the Home Ministry stated would be dealt with shortly.

During May and June the Supreme Court stayed the execution of a number of prisoners who had challenged hanging as a cruel and unconstitutional punishment. However, on 23 September the Supreme Court upheld hanging as constitutional and on 9 October executions were resumed, with at least two executions subsequently taking place. Amnesty International asked the government to take steps towards the abolition of the death penalty and to commute the sentences of all prisoners under sentence of death to life imprisonment.

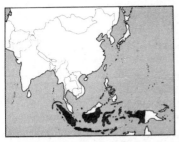

Indonesia and East Timor

Amnesty International was concerned about the persistent use of extralegal methods by the security forces, which resulted in extrajudicial executions; the illegal detention of people without charge or trial on political grounds; torture; and "disappearances". Several thousand alleged members of criminal gangs were victims of a campaign of extrajudicial killings in which there was considerable evidence of official complicity. As in previous years targets of extralegal practices also included people suspected of supporting secessionist movements in Irian Jaya and Aceh, people suspected of resisting the Indonesian occupation of East Timor, and Muslims suspected of trying to establish an Islamic state. Amnesty International was also concerned that political detainees who had been arrested in connection with the alleged coup of September 1965 continued to serve lengthy prison terms imposed in many cases after trials which failed to meet international standards. The organization was also concerned about the lack of uniformity in the application of policy regarding the sentencing of and the granting of remission and parole to these prisoners; the imposition and carrying out of the death penalty; and the continuing detention for long periods of prisoners held under sentence of death.

There was strong evidence that an officially sanctioned nationwide anti-crime campaign of extrajudicial killings had taken the lives of approximately 4,000 suspected criminals by the end of the year. These killings were carried out without any judicial process to determine the guilt of the victims, who were frequently reported to have been in the custody of the authorities when they were killed. Official comment indicated approval of and acknowledgement of responsibility for the killings. The Minister of Justice, Lieutenant General Ali Said, described the killings as "surgical operations to save the life of the patient". The former Minister of Information, Lieutenant General Ali Murtopo, admitted in July that the killings were being done "in accordance with the regulations of the Ministry of Defence and Security". The many similarities in the circumstances of the killings, the choice of the victims, and the simultaneous outbreak of the killings in provinces throughout Indonesia also pointed to an officially sanctioned campaign. The killings were reportedly being carried out by squads from the army paratroop special unit, *Kopassandha*, working with lists of suspected criminals supplied from police files. From 29 July 1983, Amnesty

International issued repeated appeals to the Indonesian Government to stop the killings. Criticism of the campaign by politicians and human rights organizations within Indonesia and international representations had not persuaded the authorities to halt the campaign, which was still continuing at the end of the year.

Amnesty International was concerned about the continued detention of approximately 300 so-called "A Category" prisoners, who had been arrested and tried in connection with the alleged communist coup of September 1965, many of whom may have been prisoners of conscience. Amnesty International took up for investigation a further 46 of these prisoners during the year, most of them detained in Balikpapan, East Kalimantan and Pamekasan, Madura. The organization was concerned that they may have not received a fair trial and that many were receiving unequal treatment with regard to implementation of rules relating to sentencing, remission and parole.

An instruction issued in November 1978 enabled "A Category" prisoners to have the period of pre-trial detention deducted from their sentences, and in November 1979 they were made eligible for remission and parole on the same terms as ordinary criminal prisoners. During the year Amnesty International learned of the release of some "A Category" prisoners who had benefited from remission, parole or deduction of pre-trial detention from sentence. One prisoner of conscience, Ismail Bakri, was released in August 1983. He had been arrested in June 1967 and had received a life sentence in September 1973. Five years later, his sentence had been commuted to 20 years' dated from the time of his arrest and he subsequently received remission. Three women prisoners, Sudjinah, Ubed Djubaedah and Ratna Djuwita, were released from Tanggerang prison near Jakarta, also in August 1983. Ubed Djubaedah had been sentenced to 14 years' imprisonment in September 1974, with no deduction of pre-trial detention, but was eligible for release on parole after receiving remission. However "A Category" prisoners were not treated uniformly. Sundari Abdurachman, whose case was being investigated by Amnesty International, was a former member of parliament who had been arrested in October 1968 and sentenced to life imprisonment in October 1976. Her sentence was commuted to 20 years in August 1982, as permitted by the remission decree, but her eight years of pre-trial detention were not deducted. "A Category" prisoners faced other administrative problems. Where prosecutors or convicted prisoners had appealed against a verdict, sentences sometimes did not begin to run until the prison commander was formally notified of the decision of the appeals court. Release could be further delayed by the failure of the authorities to issue release papers. On 30 December 1983, Amnesty International wrote to President Suharto pointing out some of these difficulties and urging him to review these cases and to consider taking steps to ensure the consistent application of existing guidelines on sentencing, remission and parole.

The same letter also urged that the procedural safeguards of the *Kitab Undang-Undang Hukum Acara Pidana* (KUHAP), Code of Criminal Procedure, enacted on 31 December 1981, be extended to cover people charged with offences which had been specifically excluded from the protection of the code, including the offences of subversion with which people arrested in connection with 1965 events had been charged. The letter pointed out that such exclusions had been described by the code itself as temporary and that, with the two-year transition period for introduction of the code due to end on 31 December 1983, it might be an appropriate time to consider extending the KUHAP to offences so far excluded.

People detained for political reasons did not generally enjoy the legal protection available to criminal prisoners under the new code. The code provided for pre-trial judicial investigation; maximum periods for detention without charge or trial; compensation for wrongful detention or conviction; and access to legal assistance, including during interrogation. In August/November, for example, approximately 25 people, most of them students and civil servants, were arrested without warrant in Jayapura, Irian Jaya, by members of *Kopassandha* for allegedly having links with the *Organisasi Papua Merdeka* (OPM), Free Papua Organization, and at least some of them were held incommunicado in an unauthorized place of detention. Once charged, political detainees often experienced long periods of imprisonment without trial. Six women, who had been arrested in August 1980 for allegedly having hoisted the Papuan flag and whose cases were being investigated by Amnesty International (see *Amnesty International Report 1982*), were finally tried and sentenced in July 1983. Amnesty International continued to investigate the cases of 10 Muslims arrested in Central Java in 1978/79, of whom six were still awaiting trial at the end of 1983. They were reportedly held for allegedly having supported the aims of the so-called *Kommando Jihad* to establish an Islamic state through armed insurrection. Several of them had reportedly been tortured immediately after arrest and one was reported to have been tried without having had access to a defence lawyer. On 4 November 1983 Amnesty International appealed on behalf of 13 individuals who were reported to have been tortured after arrest during the previous four months in Aceh, North Sumatra, on suspicion of having supported the secessionist National Liberation Front of Aceh-Sumatra (NLFAS).

Amnesty International was concerned about new reports of serious human rights violations in East Timor, including the "disappearance" and extrajudicial killing of non-combatants and the torture and ill-treatment of people taken into the custody of Indonesian forces. Amnesty International was also concerned about the arrest and detention without trial of people held on suspicion of opposition to the Indonesian occupation. Since the Indonesian invasion of East Timor in December 1975 Amnesty International had received reports indicating that Indonesian forces there had persistently resorted to torture and the arbitrary killing of non-combatants. In July, Amnesty International received a copy of manuals issued to Indonesian troops in East Timor which indicated that such practices were officially condoned. The manuals contained guidelines condoning the use of torture in certain circumstances during interrogation and the issuing of threats to the lives of people undergoing interrogation to ensure their cooperation. After taking steps to establish the authenticity of the manuals Amnesty International issued a news release on 20 July 1983 disclosing their existence. Amnesty International wrote to President Suharto the same day, expressing its concern that the instructions contained in the manuals and the practices which were their foreseeable consequence violated international human rights standards prohibiting torture in all circumstances. The letter stated: "Rather than comply with these standards, these military instructions, while describing the use of force and threats during interrogation as something generally to be avoided, explicitly allow for the possibility of torture and provide guidelines to prevent its exposure." On 2 September 1983, Amnesty International delivered a statement in New York to the United Nations Fourth Committee on Decolonization in which it presented a review of its concerns in East Timor since the invasion in December 1975. The statement also expressed Amnesty International's concern about reports that a new military offensive had recently been launched, since in the past the torture, killing and "disappearance" of non-combatants had been associated with increased military activity. Amnesty International subsequently learned of the arrest in connection with the offensive of several hundred people in the areas of Dili, Baucau and Viqueque. Amnesty International was unable to confirm reports that individuals arrested since the August offensive had subsequently been sent to Atauro, an island off mainland East Timor which the Indonesian authorities have used since 1980 to detain people held without charge or trial, and to regional military headquarters in Bali. On 21 September 1983, Amnesty International appealed on behalf of seven named people and others who had reportedly been arrested and might have been sent to Atauro and Bali but whose precise circumstances were not known.

Amnesty International also received reports of several separate incidents involving the killing of non-combatants. One such report alleged that as many as 200 people in the village of Kraras, Viqueque, had been killed by Indonesian troops reportedly in reprisal for the killing of 16 Indonesian soldiers on 8 August 1983.

Amnesty International was concerned that a number of people were imprisoned under sentence of death in Indonesia. They included as many as 50 prisoners who had been sentenced in connection with the alleged 1965 coup and had been detained for many years. Amnesty International appealed to President Suharto on 25 August 1983 to commute the sentences of two of these prisoners, Mohammed Munir and Ruslam Wijayasastra, after learning that their appeals had been rejected by the Supreme Court. It has not been the government's practice to execute prisoners sentenced to death in connection with the alleged 1965 coup and Amnesty International urged the government to commute their sentences so that they could become eligible for eventual release. On 25 April 1983, the organization sent a telegram to President Suharto expressing its grave concern about the execution earlier in April of Imran bin Muhamad Zein, who had been sentenced to death for his role in the March 1981 hijacking of an Indonesian aircraft flying to Bangkok and an attack on a police station. Three of Imran's followers were also under sentence of death, one of them being sentenced in April 1983. Amnesty International learned of others being sentenced to death for non-political crimes such as premeditated murder. On 8 March 1983, in Langsa, Aceh, two Taiwanese citizens became the first people to be sentenced to death in Indonesian courts for drug trafficking. In July, the Minister for Social Affairs stated that it was the government's intention to impose the death penalty regularly for drug trafficking.

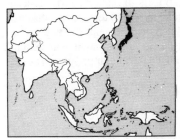

Japan

Amnesty International continued to urge the authorities to commute all death sentences and to abolish the death penalty.

An Amnesty International mission visited Japan from 21 February to 3 March 1983 to convey the organization's concerns about the death penalty, to gather information, and to seek Japanese views on its abolition. The Amnesty International delegates met senior officials of the Ministry of Justice, including officials involved in the preparation of a bill for the revision of the penal code. They also met senior officials of the Supreme Court Secretariat, chairpersons and members of the Committees on Justice of both Houses of the *Diet* (parliament), senior officials of the Japan Federation of Bar

Associations and of the Japanese Council on Crime and Delinquency as well as religious leaders and others concerned about the use of the death penalty.

On 31 May 1983, Amnesty International sent a memorandum to the Government of Japan containing the delegates' findings and recommending that no further executions be carried out and that the death penalty be abolished for all offences. There was no official response to the memorandum.

Amnesty International's concern that the death penalty is irreversible and can be inflicted on the innocent was highlighted by the retrials in several capital cases. On 15 July 1983, a court found Sakae Menda, who had been sentenced to death in March 1950, not guilty of the crime for which he had been convicted at that time. He was released after more than 33 years under sentence of death during which time he had applied for retrial six times before his application was accepted. The retrial of Shigeyoshi Taniguchi, sentenced in 1952 for murder, continued. The first court hearing in the retrial of Yukio Saito, granted in December 1979, took place in July 1983. Yukio Saito had been convicted of murder and arson in October 1957.

In 1983, four death sentences were confirmed by high courts and five imposed by district courts. One of the latter became final when the prisoner waived his right of appeal. One death sentence was commuted by a high court. In another case, the Supreme Court reversed a high court decision to commute a death sentence. Amnesty International learned that one prisoner was executed on 29 November 1983.

According to information available to Amnesty International, there were more than 60 prisoners under sentence of death at the end of 1983, including 15 who had exhausted all appeals to higher courts. During their visit the Amnesty International delegates tried to confirm details of individuals believed to be under sentence of death, but the authorities refused to verify the information on the grounds that it was official policy not to disclose to the public whether a particular prisoner was still alive or had been executed.

Kampuchea

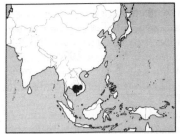

Amnesty International's main concern was the reported detention without trial by the authorities of the People's Republic of Kampuchea (PRK) of people they suspected of opposing their policies or of supporting groups engaged in armed resistance against them. The civil war between the Government of the PRK and the Coalition Government of Democratic Kampuchea (CGDK), which controlled some areas of the country, made it difficult for Amnesty International to substantiate reports of human rights violations or to obtain detailed information from areas controlled by either side.

In July 1983 refugees arriving at camps near the western border reported that widespread arrests had taken place in the army and administration of the Government of the PRK and among the peasants of people suspected of association with the Khmer People's National Liberation Front (KPNLF), one of the three groups constituting the CGDK. Starting in April 1983, 300 people were reportedly arrested in the western provinces of Siem Reap, Oddar Meanchey and Battambang. Among them were said to be Chan Seng, the Governor of Siem Reap province; Keo Ha, his former deputy; as well as military officers, teachers and village cadres. In early August 1983 the PRK authorities officially denied the reports of the arrests. Villagers were reportedly arrested during the year for protesting against arrests, military conscription and forced relocation. Further arrests of government officials were reported in October and December 1983 in Kampor and Kompong Cham provinces. Amnesty International had no information on the reasons for these arrests.

Refugees from western provinces also reported the arrest, ill-treatment and torture in June 1983 of villagers by Vietnamese soldiers present in the country who suspected them of helping the armed operations of the KPNLF.

Amnesty International was unable to estimate the number of people detained on political grounds or to obtain information on individual cases in order to establish whether those involved were prisoners of conscience. Among the individual cases it investigated was that of Mao Ayauth, a former television and radio producer who was working in the government's information service and was reportedly detained in 1981. Amnesty International learned of the release at the end of 1982 of Nam Bunnaraya, director of the orchestra of the Kampuchean radio, after 18 months' detention without charge or trial.

Most political detainees were believed to be detained without charge or trial. One trial was reported to have taken place before the Phnom Penh People's Court on 6 and 7 December 1983. Ten people who had joined the PRK administration after apparently being former officials of the Democratic Kampuchea (DK) administration of 1975 to 1979, were tried and convicted of actively helping the *Khmers rouges* armed forces in Prey Veng and Phnom Penh. Details regarding the trial and its procedures were not available.

Amnesty International was concerned about reports that some of the prisoners held in the *Prison Centrale*, Central Prison, in Phnom Penh were kept in fetters and in unlit cells, especially during their period of interrogation.

Detention for "re-education" purposes without charge or trial appeared to be widespread. On several occasions, local authorities announced that, in accordance with the government's policy of clemency towards "misled people", detainees were being allowed to return to their families after attending political courses and pledging support to the government. In the first half of 1983, over 600 "misled people" were reportedly released in Khompong Thom province. There were reports of the long-term detention for "re-education" purposes of "hard core" former cadres of the DK administration. In June 1983, the authorities confirmed that more than 100 were being detained in a camp in Takeo, some having been held for up to three years.

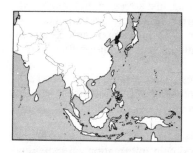

Korea (Democratic People's Republic of)

Amnesty International's work on the Democratic People's Republic of Korea (DPRK), North Korea, continued to be seriously impaired by the absence of any official information during the year concerning any arrests, trials, or death sentences. Nor was any information on these subjects published in the international press.

Amnesty International continued to investigate reports that four prominent political figures, Pak Kum-chol, Kim Chang-bong, Ryu Chang-shik and Li Yong-mu, have been detained for several years (see *Amnesty International Report 1983*). Continued inquiries to the DPRK government about their reported detention failed to elicit any response.

There was no reply to a letter which Amnesty International sent in December 1982 outlining its concerns in the DPRK.

In June 1983 it was reported in the Japanese press that 1,090 people had been "purged" between January and April for opposing the growing political power of Kim Chong-il, son of President Kim Il-sung. It was thought that some of these people may have been detained.

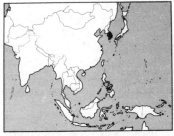

Korea (Republic of)

Amnesty International remained concerned about the detention of prisoners of conscience, reports of torture and unfair trials and the use of the death penalty. Amnesty International was also concerned about widespread arrests of students and the use of short-term detention without charge and house arrest against students and other critics of the government. Several long-term prisoners of conscience, some detained since 1971, remained in detention. Some 306 political prisoners, including 73 adopted by Amnesty International as prisoners of conscience, were released in presidential amnesties in August and December. Torture reportedly continued to take place and confessions said to have been obtained under torture were allegedly used as prosecution evidence. Death sentences were imposed for criminal offences and legislation was passed to provide the death penalty for some economic crimes. The President commuted three death sentences in political cases.

Students arrested for holding anti-government demonstrations or distributing anti-government leaflets continued to constitute the majority of prisoners of conscience. Most demonstrations were peaceful, although the police often used tear-gas to break them up and scuffles took place while participants were being arrested. More than 300 students were arrested during the year and prosecuted under the Law on Assemblies and Demonstrations (LAD) which prohibits gatherings "feared to trigger social unrest". Those who were tried before the end of 1983 were sentenced to between one and three years' imprisonment. More than 200 students were released under presidential amnesties on 12 August 1983 and 23 December 1983. Many had nearly completed their sentences. In announcing the 23 December amnesty, the authorities said that students still detained would be released if they "repented".

In February 1983, 19 students were detained for up to three weeks in Seoul and questioned about documents analyzing South Korean society which they had allegedly prepared. One student, Chung Chin-tae, was subsequently charged with anti-state activities under the National Security Law (NSL) and sentenced to three years' imprisonment. Amnesty International considered him to be a prisoner of conscience.

Several well-known political or religious personalities were put under house arrest or detained, some without warrant, for short periods for expressing their non-violent political views. The Reverend Koh Young-keun was detained on 25 February 1983 for delivering a sermon entitled "Let us Establish Justice", in which he questioned the legitimacy of the government and criticized the death sentences imposed on Moon Pu-shik and Kim Hyong-jang in the Pusan arson case (see below). Charges brought against him on 1 March were later dropped and he was released on 7 April 1983. Several people were reportedly taken into custody and threatened with arrest on charges relating to distribution of copies of his sermon.

On 16 May 1983, Kim Young-sam, a former leader of the banned opposition New Democratic Party (NDP) who had been held under house arrest since June 1982, gave a press interview in which he called for the release of people imprisoned for criticizing the government. Two days later, he went on hunger-strike to demand the restoration of democracy in the Republic of Korea (South Korea). On 25 May 1983, the police forcibly removed him from his home to hospital where he was placed in solitary confinement. Ten former members of the NDP, several members of the Human Rights Committee of the Korea National Council of Churches and other leading dissidents, including the Reverend Moon Ik-kwan, Quaker leader Ham Sok-hon, Dr Lee Moon-young, lawyer Hong Nam-soon and former National Assembly member Yeh Choon-ho, all previously adopted by Amnesty International as prisoners of conscience, were placed under house arrest for expressing support for Kim's demands. All were released from house arrest by mid-June 1983.

At the end of August 1983, up to 500 teachers and university students were reportedly detained without warrant for periods ranging from several days to several weeks and interrogated by the police about their involvement with workers' night schools sponsored by local churches. They were reportedly forced to state, allegedly under torture, that their activities were aimed at building a socialist society. Kim Han-jo was held for three weeks in September 1983 at the National Police Headquarters in Seoul. She was interrogated about her previous work with night schools and her involvement in a research project directed by the Christian Institute for the Study of Justice and Development which examined the presentation of the issue of Korean unification in government textbooks. Eight other school-teachers involved in the project were detained from mid-December to 30 December 1983. On 30 and 31 December, four others connected with the project were detained: Kang Man-kil, a former Professor at Korea University in Seoul; Lee Yoang-hee, a former Professor at Hanyang University in Seoul; and the Director and a member of staff of the institute – the Reverend Cho Seung-hyuk and Lee Mi-kyung. They were said to face charges under the NSL of supporting the Democratic People's Republic of Korea (North Korea). Both Professor Lee and the Reverend Cho had previously been adopted by Amnesty International as prisoners of conscience.

Amnesty International also continued to investigate the detention of Kim Hyong-jang in connection with an arson attack on the United States Cultural Centre in Pusan in March 1982. The organization believed that he may have been imprisoned for his political views and that the charge that he had incited people to commit arson was false. He reportedly claimed that his confession admitting the charges, which was used as evidence at his trial, had been obtained under torture. Kim Hyong-jang and another defendant, Moon Pu-shik, were sentenced to death in August 1982. Amnesty International appealed for the commutation of the sentences. On 15 March 1983 President Chun Doo-hwan commuted the sentences to life imprisonment.

Amnesty International continued to appeal for the immediate and unconditional release of the prisoners of conscience Soh Sung and his brother Soh Joon-shik, who were arrested in 1971 reportedly because of their involvement in student demonstrations during the presidential elections. Soh Sung was sentenced to life imprisonment. Soh Joon-shik's seven-year term of imprisonment expired in May 1978. His appeal against his continued detention under the Public Security Law was rejected by the Seoul High Court on 30 May 1983. Among the other long-term prisoners of concern to Amnesty International was Dr Lee Sung-hee, one of 17 members of the National Council for the Defence of Democracy, an informal opposition group, arrested in March 1974 and sentenced to life imprisonment for espionage. Amnesty International continued to investigate his case as it was concerned that Dr Lee may have been wrongly convicted and imprisoned for his non-violent political opinions.

Amnesty International continued to appeal for the release of prisoners convicted under the NSL of being members of an anti-state organization, *Aram-hoe*, and of plotting rebellion. They were arrested in August 1981 and claimed at their trial that they had been tortured into signing false confessions. They were later acquitted by an appellate court on the grounds of insufficient prosecution evidence, but in October 1982 the Supreme Court overruled the appellate court's decision and returned the case for retrial. On 21 June 1983 the Seoul High Court sentenced them to between 18 months' and 10 years' imprisonment. Amnesty International believed that the charges brought against them were false and that they had been imprisoned for their non-violent political beliefs.

Another case of continuing concern to Amnesty International was that of eight teachers at Kunsan Number One High School and a former teacher working for a broadcasting company in Kunsan who were detained in November 1982 on charges under the NSL of forming an "anti-state" organization, the "Five Pines Society", in April 1982. At their trial they admitted that they held views critical of the government, but denied that they had supported communist ideology or praised North Korea. They also claimed in court that they had been tortured and threatened with death during interrogation to force them to sign false confessions. Chongju District Court sentenced them to terms of between one and four years' imprisonment, suspended for six of the defendants. In July 1983, the Kwangju High Court reversed the decision and imposed sentences of between one and seven years' imprisonment on all of the defendants.

Nine officials of the Wuongpoong Textile Company union were sentenced by the Seoul District Court in April and May 1983 to terms of imprisonment ranging from 10 to 18 months. They had been arrested in November 1982 under the LAD for protesting against the violent harassment of union members by other company employees. Amnesty International considered them to be prisoners of conscience. All were released in the August 1983 amnesty.

Other prisoners of conscience released in the 12 August presidential amnesty were two trade unionists at Korea Control Data; Father Choi Ki-sik, arrested in the Pusan arson case; 10 students and workers arrested in the Kwangminsa case; seven defendants from the Pusan Good Books Association (*Purim*) case; three defendants in the Hanul Bible Study Group case; and Lee Jae-oh, arrested in the South Korean National Liberation Front (SKNLF) case. Among those released in the 23 December amnesty were students arrested for participating in campus demonstrations and others convicted of violations of the NSL, including defendants from the SKNLF, *Purim* (see *Amnesty International Report 1983*) and *Aram-hoe* cases. In the August 1983 amnesty, Lee Tae-bok had his life sentence commuted to 20 years', and Park Ki-rae's death sentence, imposed in 1974, was commuted to life imprisonment.

Torture reportedly continued to be used against people suspected of both political and ordinary criminal offences. After the death in March 1983 of Kim Kun-jo from brain injuries caused by beatings during interrogation by police, the National Police Headquarters in Seoul issued a statement in which it said it regretted the incident and would take measures to prevent further police brutality. The Director of the National Police resigned, taking responsibility for not having prevented the incident. The Minister of Home Affairs, Roh Tae-woo, ordered the police to conduct a full investigation and a police officer was subsequently sentenced to seven years' imprisonment for fatally injuring Kim Kun-jo. In mid-April, the Minister of Home Affairs told the National Assembly that the government would "mete out stern punishment against police officers who resort to violence during investigations". In December 1983 the National Assembly passed an amendment to the Law on Weighted Penalty for Special Crimes which would provide for a maximum term of life imprisonment for law enforcement officials convicted of torturing and killing criminal suspects. The authorities did not reply to requests by Amnesty International for claims of torture made in several political cases to be independently investigated.

In spite of measures taken to remedy the shortage of medical staff in prisons and the discretionary power of prison directors to transfer prisoners to hospital when necessary, several prisoners of conscience reportedly received inadequate medical care. Many of them were said to be suffering from the effects of torture or were ill as a result of their conditions of detention. Choi Sok-jin, sentenced to life imprisonment in the SKNLF case of 1979, was admitted to a hospital in early February 1983 with a kidney infection. He was returned to prison four days later. Amnesty International continued to receive reports that he was sick and not receiving adequate medical care (see *Amnesty International Report 1983*).

Amnesty International learned of several death sentences imposed or upheld for criminal charges and appealed to the authorities to commute all death sentences.

The organization was concerned that the National Assembly passed bills in mid-December 1983 to provide the death penalty for economic crimes such as fraud and embezzlement, thereby increasing the number of offences punishable by the death penalty.

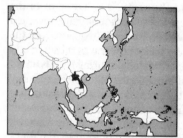

Laos

Amnesty International's main concern remained the continued detention in "re-education" camps of large numbers of people detained without trial since 1975 for their political activities or positions under the former government, and the lack of legal safeguards for people detained on political grounds. The number of detainees held in "re-education" camps was difficult to estimate due to releases and the closure of some camps since 1981. According to some sources, there were still between 1,000 and 3,000 people detained in various camps throughout the country. Eight years after the establishment of the Lao People's Democratic Republic, the country still had no published constitution or legislation. It was reported however that the drafting of a constitution was nearing completion and that some provisional regulations for arrest and trial had been disseminated to local authorities in October 1978. The texts of these regulations were not available to Amnesty International.

Detainees in "re-education" camps included former civil and military officials and professional people from the former administration who were sent to such camps after the change of government which marked the end of the "neutralist" coalition in Laos in 1975. The highest-ranking civil servants and military officers were sent to camps in the northeast of Laos, particularly Houa Phan province, but camps were also established in Phong Saly, Xiengkhouang, Savannakhet and several other provinces.

A large number of releases from such camps took place in 1980 and 1981, with those released usually being allowed to return to their original place of residence. Since then, however, few unconditional releases appear to have taken place, although some detainees with professional skills were offered assignments on work sites away from the camps and others were encouraged to settle with their families in the area where they had previously been detained. Many camps are said to have been closed down as a result of such "releases on the spot". There was evidence, however, that many people were still detained in camps or subjected to such restrictions and control that their lives were hardly different from those of detainees.

One new camp for detainees was reportedly being built in Houa Phan province in 1983 to replace two camps established in the province since 1975/76 (camps 05 and 06). This followed the transfer of the administration of these camps from the military to the civilian authorities of Viengsay town. The new camp was said to be between

Samneua and Viengsay and to have held about about 800 people in the summer of 1983. Camp 05 was reported to have been closed after it had burned down. The detainees were then transferred to Viengsay town or nearby work sites, working in part on building the new camp.

Amnesty International continued to work on behalf of about 50 political detainees who were adopted as prisoners of conscience or whose cases were being investigated. They included Samlith Ratsaphong, a former Director General in the Ministry of Education from 1973 to 1975, who had been detained in Houa Phan province since August 1975 and was last reported to be held at Camp 05. Tenh Teso, the former Director of the Royal Institute of Law and Administration, who had been detained since the end of 1975, was among those reportedly still held in the Viengsay area, as was Phao Southy, a former Director of the Department of War Veterans in the Ministry of the Interior who had been detained since August 1975. Phao Southy, aged 55, was reported to suffer from kidney trouble and malnutrition.

Amnesty International continued to receive reports concerning detainees in poor health due to the cumulative effect of several years in detention without proper medical care, while receiving an inadequate diet and being subjected to hard manual work. It appealed in particular on behalf of Colonel Kynone, a military engineer aged 45, who was reported to be suffering from malaria, diabetes and heart disease. Detained for "re-education" since 1975, he was first held in a camp in the northeast and was later transferred to a construction site in the same area, but still worked under restrictions.

Despite such reports concerning the health of individual detainees, conditions in "re-education" camps were generally reported to have improved, particularly in respect of receiving mail, parcels and visits from relatives. Some detainees were allowed to correspond with relatives abroad and receive parcels from them for the first time in many years, and facilities were granted for family visits. In the Samneua area, for example, detainees receiving visits from their wives would reportedly be given a room where they could stay together during the visit. Some detainees who were considered to have a "good" attitude and were trusted by the camp administration were reportedly given some freedom of movement, being allowed to leave the camp and go on their own to surrounding areas or villages.

Several new cases came to Amnesty International's attention during 1983. They included that of Phouphet Phommachanh, a 40-year-old major in the Royal Lao Army who was arrested in August 1975 in Vientiane and sent to a "re-education" camp in Houa Phan province. Originally from Savannakhet, Phouphet Phommachanh had joined the army at the age of 18 and was appointed secretary to the Commander in Chief of the Armed Forces in Vientiane in 1971. He was still holding this post in 1975. He was last reported to have been assigned to a construction brigade in Viengxay.

Amnesty International was also concerned about the case of Tiao Souk Bouavong, a former parliamentarian and Vice-President of the National Assembly, whom it had adopted as a prisoner of conscience. He was reportedly arrested at his home in Vientiane in October 1975 and accused of plotting a coup against the new government. He was then aged 71 and reportedly nearly paralysed with rheumatism. He was never formally charged or tried. Following his arrest, he was sent to Samkhe prison, near Vientiane, where he was apparently held for several years. In 1983 he was reported to be detained in Houa Phan province and to be in poor health.

Among others arrested later was Souvat Boulom, a former Secretary General to the National Assembly in Vientiane between 1964 and 1974, who was arrested in 1979. According to information received by Amnesty International, he retired from his position in the National Assembly in 1974 and went to farm family land near Vientiane. His arrest in 1979 is said to have been part of a group of arrests concerning people from the Sam Neua area. He was not charged with any offence and was simply sent to a "re-education" camp in the northeast where he was still reportedly being held in late 1983.

Amnesty International learned of a few individual releases during the year. In one case, a seriously ill detainee who had been transferred to Vientiane for medical treatment was subsequently allowed to stay there. It was also reported that groups of low-ranking functionaries were released locally and asked to settle in villages where they had previously been detained but no specific information was available to Amnesty International about such releases or on the closure of camps outside Houa Phan province.

A group of about 50 government officials was reported to have been arrested in Vientiane in early 1983 and accused of anti-party activities and corruption. They included the Deputy Minister for Construction, Sengkham Phinit, and the Vice-Chairman of the National Committee for Social Welfare and War Veterans, Thongvanh Phanrajsavong, who was previously Director of the Irrigation Department in the Agriculture Ministry. Some of those arrested were reportedly placed under house arrest or sent to "re-education" seminars. As of late 1983, they were not known to have been formally charged or tried.

Malaysia

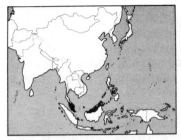

Amnesty International's main concerns remained the continued detention without trial of over 200 political detainees under the Internal Security Act (ISA) 1960, and the imposition and carrying out of the death penalty.

According to official figures, the releases of political detainees which started in 1981 appear to have continued in early 1983. However, little information reached Amnesty International about individual releases during 1983 and most of the releases it heard of concerned detainees who had been freed in 1982.

Amnesty International continued corresponding with the government regarding a proposed visit of an Amnesty International delegation to Malaysia to discuss the organization's concerns with the authorities. However, the visit was cancelled after Amnesty International had been asked on several occasions by the government to postpone it and had then been informed that the government officials it had requested to see would not be available to meet the delegation.

In mid-March 1983, the Deputy Minister of Home Affairs stated in the Malaysian Parliament that there were still 266 ISA detainees. The ISA allows for the detention without charge or trial for renewable two-year periods of people whom the government considers a threat to national security. He also said that the cases of all the remaining detainees "would be reviewed by the Advisory Board from time to time". The Advisory Board, which is responsible to the Prime Minister's office, makes periodic reviews of detainees' cases and presents recommendations to the Minister of Home Affairs for decision on release or continued detention. The reviews, however, are based mainly on the results of interrogations carried out by Special Branch officers to assess the detainees' behaviour and in particular whether they admit to the accusations against them. In several cases known to Amnesty International, detainees were transferred from detention camps to undisclosed police lock-ups or "rehabilitation" centres to be subjected to such interrogations. Detainees in "rehabilitation" centres were reportedly held in solitary confinement and were usually denied exercise or books. Those held for long periods were occasionally taken blindfold to police stations for visits by relatives. The length of time spent in the centres appeared to vary from several days to several weeks or months. Some were subsequently released—often without explanation —while others were sent back to their detention camps. Among detainees reported to have been transferred to "rehabilitation" centres was Ng Teo Huan, a former shopkeeper aged 36 who had been detained without trial since 1972. He was reported in early 1983 to have been transferred from Batu Gajah detention camp to an unknown "rehabilitation" centre. Another detainee, Wong Yong Huat, was reported to have been sent to police interrogation centres three times in 1982 and early 1983 before being transferred to the Taiping detention camp in Perak.

Amnesty International continued to work on behalf of over 20 adopted prisoners of conscience or people whose cases were being investigated. During the year, it learned of the release of several of these detainees. Among those reported to be still detained in 1983 was Lim Mai Kim, a factory worker from Malacca who was arrested in Singapore in 1974 and reportedly sent to Malaysia in 1975 where she was held without trial under the ISA in Taiping detention camp. Another ISA detainee, Chin Ah Kau, was officially reported to be still detained because of "his insistence to pursue" his past "communist activities". Such official acknowledgement and justification of the continued detention of a detainee was rare. The authorities did not usually answer Amnesty International's inquiries about individual cases and the organization's information about prisoners remained incomplete. Amnesty International was particularly concerned about the cases of several detainees whose fate remained unknown despite numerous inquiries to the authorities. They included two women: Chan Wai Sin, who was reported to have been continuously held in police stations since her arrest in 1979 and was last heard of in 1982 when she was transferred to a "rehabilitation" centre; and Liew Yet Hua, a widow aged over 60 who was arrested in 1977, detained in the Taiping detention camp and was last reported to be in poor health, suffering from rheumatism and anaemia. Amnesty International's continued inquiries about her detention had been unanswered since 1979.

All political detainees held in the Batu Gajah detention camp, one of the two such camps used since the 1960s for political detainees, were reportedly transferred elsewhere in February or March 1983. The camp remained open for other categories of prisoner. Those transferred were sent either to the Taiping detention camp or to police lock-ups and "rehabilitation" centres throughout the country. As of April 1983, some 160 political detainees were reported to be held in the Taiping camp and over 100 were believed to be detained in unspecified locations, in police lock-ups or "rehabilitation" centres. Amnesty International was concerned about the large numbers detained in such undisclosed places of detention, apparently for interrogation purposes. Conditions in the Taiping camp were reported to be poor, with detainees being confined to extremely hot and poorly ventilated cells for about 20 hours a day.

Amnesty International learned in 1983 of the release of several prisoners of conscience, most of whom had been freed during the second half of 1982. They included Ng Wei Siong, a former secretary of the Labour Party and town councillor who had been detained since 1967. Amnesty International was concerned that most released detainees were served with restriction orders prohibiting them from political or trade union activities, from travelling without permission and sometimes from choosing their area of residence. The restrictions usually also included a curfew and an obligation to report regularly to the local police station. In some cases the restrictions were increased several months after release.

The use of the death penalty remained a major concern in 1983. Fourteen people were executed in 1983 and 19 were sentenced to death on various charges. Most of those executed had been convicted of the illegal possession of firearms under the ISA, Section 59 of which provides a mandatory death penalty for this offence. According to information available to Amnesty International, 39 people were executed for offences under the ISA between 1980 and December 1983, 10 of them in 1983. In late 1983 the cases of 32 people sentenced to death under the ISA were still pending. People charged under the ISA were usually tried under special trial procedures known as the Essential (Security Cases) (Amendment) Regulations, which restrict the rights of defendants. One of those executed for illegal possession of firearms, Lim Kwang Yeow, had been arrested in 1977 and was detained for two years before being charged under the ISA reportedly for possessing one bullet and two bullet cases.

Twenty-four of the people executed in Malaysia between 1975 and December 1983 had been convicted of drug offences. One of them was executed in 1983 and six others were sentenced to death on such charges during the year. In mid-April 1983, the Malaysian Parliament adopted amendments to the Dangerous Drugs Act, 1952, making the death penalty mandatory for possession of a certain quantity of drugs and lowering the amount for which the death penalty can be imposed.

Three of those executed in 1983 were convicted of murder and 11 others were sentenced to death on such charges. They included a former government minister and member of the Malaysian Parliament, Datuk Mokhtar Hashim, who was convicted of murdering a "political rival" and sentenced to death in March 1983. His appeal to the Federal Court was rejected on 23 July 1983 but he later appealed for clemency to the King. His case was still pending in December 1983.

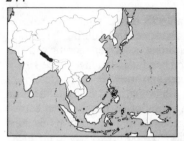

Nepal

Although over 50 political detainees held under the Public Security Act (PSA) were released in 1983, Amnesty International continued to be concerned about the arrest and imprisonment of opponents of the government, often for short periods, and in many cases without charge or trial.

On 18 July 1983 the Minister of Home Affairs, Padma Sundar Lawati, announced in the *Rastriya Panchayat* (National Assembly) that the new government under Prime Minister Lokendra Bahadur Chand had decided to release political detainees held under the PSA, which allows preventive detention under renewable nine-month detention orders up to a maximum of three years without judicial review. Amnesty International wrote to Prime Minister Chand welcoming the announcement of the release of detainees and requesting details of those concerned. The government announced on 20 July 1983 that 28 detainees had been released. A further 20 detainees were released on 30 August 1983. No confirmation was given by the government that all detainees held under the PSA had finally been released and Amnesty International was concerned that some prisoners held under the PSA remained in detention beyond August 1983.

Detentions on political grounds, often of a short-term nature, occurred regularly during the year. Political activity is severely restricted under Nepal's "partyless" *panchayat* system of government. The Organizations Control Act prohibits political parties or advocacy of support for the party system. Political prisoners, some of whom may have been prisoners of conscience, were held under the provisions of this act as well as under the PSA for participating in meetings of political parties, in particular the Nepali Congress Party (NCP), or for possessing or circulating pamphlets critical of government policies. Approximately 400 students belonging to the Nepal Students Federation, an affiliate of the NCP, were arrested between 26 and 30 September 1983 when planning to hold their national convention. One hundred and ninety-three were released on 4 October 1983 and all the others were reportedly freed by 7 October.

Workers and labour activists were also detained for protesting about working conditions. Thirty-four labour leaders of the Balaju Industrial Estate in Kathmandu were arrested in late March 1983, six of whom remained in detention until late October 1983. Eight people, including one trade union leader, Sikandar Bux, were arrested on 19 May 1983 and detained for one month after attempting to hold a demonstration.

Nepal's press laws forbid publication of any news or comments directed against the Nepalese monarch or other members of the Royal Family. Amnesty International was investigating the case of Ramchandra Humagain, editor and publisher of the weekly *Nepal Bhooni*, who was sentenced to one year's imprisonment by a Kathmandu court in June 1983, having been found guilty of publishing remarks disrespectful of King Birendra.

Amnesty International also received reports that Christians in some parts of Nepal had been arrested, accused either of proselytizing or of having changed religion, both of which may be deemed offences under Nepal's constitution. Some of these detainees were reportedly released on bail, while others were freed without formal charges being brought. The local authorities appeared to exercise considerable latitude in determining arrests and prosecution. Amnesty International wrote to the government on 12 October 1983, making reference to internationally-established standards pertaining to religious freedom, and urging it to ensure that citizens of religious beliefs other than Hinduism had their rights peacefully to practice and teach their faith protected.

The total number of prisoners of conscience in Nepal was difficult to estimate because imprisonment was often short-term. Some arrests took place in remote areas of the country which also made it difficult to obtain detailed information.

Nepal has abolished the death penalty for ordinary criminal offences, retaining it only under legislation covering attacks on the Royal Family, certain anti-state acts (for example, treason and insurrection) and some military offences.

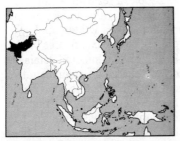

Pakistan

Amnesty International remained concerned about the widespread arrest and imprisonment of prisoners of conscience. Prisoners charged with political offences, including the non-violent expression of opinions, continued to be tried by military courts applying summary procedures. Amnesty International also received reports that dozens of political prisoners had been detained for over two years without formal charges being filed. The organization continued to receive reports of the torture of some political prisoners and several detainees suspected of criminal offences reportedly died in police custody as a result of torture. A large number of death sentences were imposed, often by special military courts from which there is no judicial right of appeal, and many executions took place. There was a sharp increase in the number of prisoners who were sentenced to be flogged. Sentences of amputation continued to be imposed and political detainees were reportedly held in bar shackles for long periods. Amnesty International was also concerned about the possible expulsion of refugees to territories where their life or freedom would be threatened (*refoulement*).

Martial law entered its seventh year on 5 July 1983. Under martial law regulations, political parties are proscribed and all political and trade union activities are banned. President Zia-ul-Haq announced on 12 August 1983 that provincial and national elections, postponed indefinitely under martial law, would be held by March 1985, when martial law would be ended. The Movement for the Restoration of Democracy (MRD), an alliance of several major opposition parties, launched a campaign of "civil disobedience" on 14 August to press demands for an immediate return to democratic government under the suspended parliamentary constitution. Political demonstrations were held in defiance of martial law regulations. Opposition politicians, party workers, lawyers and students were among those arrested in connection with these protests.

MRD activity found greatest support in Sind province, where some demonstrations resulted in the death of law-enforcement personnel and demonstrators and damage to property. Over 60 deaths of law enforcement personnel and demonstrators were officially acknowledged to have occurred by late September, while opposition sources claimed that there were more than twice that number of civilian deaths alone. Several thousand people were arrested. By the end of the year, the government had released some 3,000 people. President Zia-ul-Haq announced in December that those prisoners held without trial who had "courted" arrest could be released on submitting a written apology.

Although Amnesty International did not have exact figures on the number of detainees held at the end of 1983 several hundred detainees were known to be held without formal charge in administrative detention, including most prominent opposition politicians. These detainees had either been arrested before the opposition campaign began or were held for "courting" arrest during demonstrations or had been arrested by police from their homes at different times. Other detainees arrested in the course of demonstrations were brought to trial before Summary Military Courts, before which there is no right to legal representation and no right of appeal. In some cases, trials reportedly took place so soon after arrest that the detainees were not informed of the charges against them and had no chance to defend themselves. Some were charged with criminal acts such as assault and damage to property. Charges against other detainees were purely political, for example raising anti-government slogans and delivering speeches "with a view to creating dissatisfaction among the people". The majority of those tried were sentenced to one year's imprisonment and in many cases sentences of flogging were imposed. Some political prisoners were known to have been flogged although Amnesty International was unable to verify that all sentences of flogging were implemented. Amnesty International wrote to President Zia-ul-Haq on 20 September, expressing concern that among the large number of people arrested in the previous four weeks were many whom Amnesty International believed could be prisoners of conscience, arrested for participation in non-violent political activities. The organization urged that all such prisoners be promptly released if there was no evidence of their involvement in criminal acts such as assault or damage to property. Amnesty International also reiterated its grave concern about the large number of prisoners sentenced to be flogged, having already sent urgent appeals a month earlier requesting the President's intervention to stop the implementation of sentences of flogging.

Amnesty International was also concerned that some detainees arrested in connection with the MRD's campaign were reportedly transferred from regular places of detention and held incommunicado during interrogation by military and police security personnel. Several detainees were said to have been taken from Karachi Central Jail to the Baldia Interrogation Centre where they were held for several days and reportedly beaten. Amnesty International cabled President Zia-ul-Haq on 8 December to express concern about the absence of legal safeguards for detainees, citing the case of Sardar Shaukat Ali, Secretary General of the *Mazdoor Kissan* (Workers' and Peasants') Party, who was reportedly held incommunicado in Lahore Fort from 12 October.

Lawyers were also detained during 1983 for protesting about the continuation of martial law. During October over 100 lawyers were detained in Punjab and Sind provinces while organizing and subsequently participating in a National Coordination Committee (NCC) of Lawyers' day of protest on 19 October. Those arrested included Abdul Hafeez Lakho, President of the Karachi Bar Association (KBA), and two former secretaries of the KBA, Farooq H. Naek and Rasheed Razvi. A case was filed against them and seven other Karachi lawyers under Martial Law Regulations (MLR) Nos. 13 and 33 banning political activity and criticism of the armed forces. No trial proceedings had begun by the end of 1983 and all but one of these lawyers remained in detention in Karachi Central Jail. Amnesty International launched appeals on their behalf, concerned that they were being detained for the peaceful expression of their views, and urged that all charges against them be dropped.

Although some prisoners of conscience held without trial were released during the year, including Zamin Shah and Abdus Saleem in April and Irshad Rao in July 1983 (see *Amnesty International Report 1983*), several long-term prisoners of conscience continued to be held in administrative detention. Two political party leaders, Air Marshal (Retd.) Asghar Khan of *Tehrik-i-Istiqlal* (TI) and Nawabzada Nasrullah Khan of the Pakistan Democratic Party (PDP) had both been held for over two years under house arrest. With only a brief interval, Asghar Khan had been detained under martial law without charge or trial for a total of over four years. Rasul Baksh Palejo, who was due for release on completion of a one-year prison sentence in October 1980, continued to be held under Martial Law Order No. 78, under which individuals can be held indefinitely without being informed of the grounds for their arrest. Amnesty International appealed to the authorities in October 1983 urging his release and that he be given immediate medical treatment, having received persistent reports that his health had seriously deteriorated. He was finally transferred to hospital in Lahore in late November, where he remained in detention.

Political detainees other than those arrested in connection with MRD protests were brought to trial before military courts. Amnesty International was concerned that the conduct of these trials did not conform to internationally accepted standards. Three university lecturers who had been adopted by Amnesty International as prisoners of conscience, Tariq Ahsan, Mohammad Saleem and Jamil Omar, were tried by Special Military Court No. 52, Rawalpindi, between February and April 1983, over 14 months after their arrest. They were charged with sedition and possession of subversive documents, material which the court did not make public. The court's verdict was not handed down until several months after the completion of trial proceedings. In November Tariq Ahsan was sentenced to two years' imprisonment, Mohammad Saleem to three years' and Jamil Omar to seven years' in addition to large fines. Prisoners tried before special military courts are permitted no judicial review of their sentences.

Many political detainees were reportedly held for periods of over two years without formal charge or trial. On 8 November 1983, Amnesty International wrote to President Zia-ul-Haq raising the cases of some 82 political prisoners reportedly held in these circumstances, the majority being held in Haripur Jail, North West Frontier province. Nineteen members of the Pakistan People's Party (PPP) were held in Rawalpindi District Jail, most having been arrested in early 1981. They were held under sections of the Pakistan penal code relating to murder and conspiracy, and MLR No. 13 which bans criticism of the armed forces. No specific charges were brought against them. Amnesty International sought clarification as to the eligibility of all these detainees for bail under Section 497 of the Code of Criminal Procedure, as amended in December 1979. On 26 December 1983, it was announced that Section 497 had been further amended to exclude certain categories of offenders including "a hardened, desperate or dangerous criminal".

As of December 1983, Amnesty International was working for the release of 53 prisoners of conscience and investigating the cases of 33 possible prisoners of conscience.

Amnesty International received reports that some political prisoners continued to be tortured while held incommunicado during interrogation. They reportedly included students and political party workers, especially members of the PPP and people accused of involvement with the so-called *Al-Zulfikar* organization, which the authorities alleged was responsible for violent activities. Torture reportedly took place in Lahore Fort, as well as other interrogation centres. In addition, between September and December 1983, the Pakistan press reported the death in police custody of at least seven detainees arrested on criminal charges. In all seven cases there were complaints alleging that death resulted from torture and investigations were reported to have been undertaken. Amnesty International wrote to the Minister of the Interior Mahmoud A. Haroon on 12 December 1983 welcoming reports that official investigations were being conducted into allegations of police torture and ill-treatment. Amnesty International further noted the trial by Special Military Court in April 1983 of nine people accused of torturing a prisoner to death in police custody in 1979. In keeping with its unconditional opposition to the death penalty, however, the organization regretted that three police officers convicted of the offence were sentenced to death and executed in November 1983.

Amnesty International remained concerned about the high number of death sentences and executions in 1983. Many death sentences were handed down by special military courts from which there is no judicial right of appeal. Although those sentenced to death may apply to the President for clemency, Amnesty International knew of no instance during 1983 when such clemency was granted. No official statistics were published for the total number of executions. It was reported in March 1983 that 1,350 prisoners in Punjab province alone were under sentence of death.

In addition to prisoners convicted during protests by the MRD, many hundreds of other prisoners were sentenced to be flogged during the year for a wide range of offences. Amnesty International cabled President Zia-ul-Haq on 19 April expressing concern about reports of mass floggings in Karachi Central Jail between 15 and 18 April. It was reported that 216 men convicted of participation in sectarian rioting had been sentenced to be flogged. Amnesty International was unable to verify whether all sentences of flogging were implemented.

Two men were sentenced to amputation of the hand and foot for theft in December 1983 and the Federal *Shari'a* (Islamic) Court, to which appeals are addressed, confirmed a sentence of amputation in June. Amnesty International appealed to President Zia-ul-Haq to ensure that these sentences were not implemented. President Zia-ul-Haq stated publicly in October 1983 that no amputations had ever taken place in Pakistan.

Amnesty International received disturbing reports that both criminal and political detainees were kept in bar shackles for extended periods, contrary to provisions of the United Nations Standard Minimum Rules for the Treatment of Prisoners. Two half-inch thick rods of steel, approximately three feet in length, were said to be fastened at the waist with iron chains and at the ankles with clasps of iron, making it impossible to bend the legs.

On 6 May 1983, Amnesty International cabled President Zia-ul-Haq concerning reports that a number of Iranian nationals faced possible *refoulement*. Amnesty International urged the government to initiate procedures to prevent the *refoulement* of any Iranian who may be deemed a refugee. Amnesty International received no subsequent information to indicate that the individuals in question had been returned to Iran.

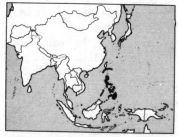

The Philippines

Amnesty International was concerned that the pattern of serious human rights violations established in earlier years showed no sign of changing. The organization received frequent reports of the torture and ill-treatment of detainees, often while undergoing interrogation in incommunicado detention, "disappearances" and extrajudicial executions. The government continued to be reluctant to investigate these practices and to punish those responsible. Amnesty International was also concerned about the use of emergency powers to detain people without trial frequently for long periods, some of whom Amnesty International believed were prisoners of conscience. The organization continued to be concerned about the imposition of death sentences and the detention for long periods of people who were awaiting the outcome of appeals against death sentences.

Many of these concerns had been presented to the government in the *Report of an Amnesty International Mission to the Republic of the Philippines November 1981* published in September 1982. In March 1983, the government replied to the mission report in a letter signed by the Deputy Minister of Defence. The government's reply questioned Amnesty International's motives, presented alternative versions of the cases recorded by Amnesty International and rejected most of the recommendations outright. In a letter to the government dated 22 November 1983 Amnesty International responded by reiterating that the purpose of the mission had been to investigate the discrepancy between reports received by the organization over several years indicating serious violations of human rights and the government's stated commitment to upholding those rights. The reply also summarized the findings of the mission, questioned the standards of the investigations previously undertaken by the government into the cases presented by Amnesty International and stressed the need for urgent measures to be taken in view of the evidence that serious violations of human rights had continued in the year following publication. Concern was expressed about the apparent official tolerance of human rights violations, evidenced by: new legislation tending further to erode respect for fundamental rights; official statements apparently justifying the failure to adhere to constitutional safeguards on grounds of national security; and by the government's continuing failure to initiate impartial investigations into human rights abuses and to take disciplinary action where appropriate.

Amnesty International continued to receive reports of the arrest and subsequent incommunicado detention of people accused of subversive political activity. These arrests were usually validated by Presidential Commitment Orders (PCOs) issued under the emergency powers retained by President Marcos after the lifting of martial law in 1981. PCOs issued on the sole authority of the President without recourse to the judiciary were the subject of much domestic controversy, particularly after the Supreme Court, in its decision in Garcia-Padilla v Enrile in April 1983, appeared to abdicate its right to inquire into such actions by the executive in times of emergency. On 5 August 1983 the government announced the abolition of the PCO and its replacement by the Preventive Detention Action (PDA). The scope of the legislation introducing the PDA was almost identical to that of the PCO as PDAs can also be issued by the President without reference to the judiciary.

Following arrest, detainees were frequently reported to have been held in unauthorized places of detention known as "safehouses" and to have been ill-treated and tortured while undergoing interrogation. Lay church leader Carl Gaspar "disappeared" following arrest by an intelligence unit and detention on the basis of a PCO issued some days later. The authorities denied any knowledge of his whereabouts, despite repeated attempts by friends and relatives to locate him. In fact, for three days after his arrest, he was detained in a "safehouse", then being flown to Manila where he was held incommunicado for a further 12 days at the headquarters of Military Intelligence Group 15 at Bago Bantay, Quezon City. Carl Gaspar alleged that during this period of incommunicado detention he had been held in solitary confinement in a small unlit cell and had been kept blindfold and handcuffed to his bed for part of the time.

Amnesty International also received reports involving the "disappearance" of people believed to have been taken into the custody of government agents but who never reappeared.

On 8 June 1983, Amnesty International appealed to the government to investigate the reported "disappearance" of Yolanda Gordula, who was last seen leaving the house of friends in Caloocan City, Metromanila, with Dr Jose Escandor on the evening of 30 March 1983. At 3 am on 31 March, Dr Escandor was reportedly shot dead by troops of the Metromanila Philippines Constabulary (METROCOM). Efforts by her family to locate Yolanda Gordula in detention centres in Manila and elsewhere were unsuccessful. In its appeal, Amnesty International presented evidence suggesting that Yolanda Gordula had been taken into the custody of the authorities.

Amnesty International received frequent reports of serious human rights violations directed against civilians in areas where units of the Armed Forces of the Philippines were engaged in operations against insurgent groups. One such report concerned an operation from 4 to 6 May 1983 in *barrios* (villages) in Tubo, Abra, during which a Philippine Constabulary (PC) unit allegedly ill-treated members of the local Tinggian tribal minority and killed three people on 6 May, including a pregnant woman and her child, in the *barrio* of Be-ew. On 5 July Amnesty International appealed to the authorities to investigate the incident and asked for information about steps taken by the government to prevent the recurrence of such abuses. In December, an inquiry ordered by the Minister of National Defense found 12 soldiers who were involved in the operation guilty of perpetrating abuses but not responsible for the three deaths.

Amnesty International issued a similar appeal for an investigation into the reported killing of four men and the torture of others following the arrest of 16 people on 17 August 1983 in Libungan, North Cotabato, by military personnel of Regional Commands XI and XII. Four of the men had been arrested and transferred to the custody of the provincial commander for Davao del Sur in Bansalan, where they were reportedly killed. Subsequent press reports stated that the four had been killed in an encounter with armed forces personnel, but Amnesty International believed that they may have been bound and in the custody of military personnel at the time they died and appealed on 16 December 1983 for an impartial investigation into the four deaths.

Amnesty International continued to be disturbed by the failure of the Philippines Government to conduct impartial investigations into alleged human rights violations and to prosecute and punish those implicated even in cases where the allegations were well-attested and widely publicized. The assassination at Manila International Airport on 21 August of the opposition leader Benigno Aquino as he returned to the Philippines from exile in the United States and the government's subsequent decision to set up a commission to investigate the killing prompted Amnesty International to issue a statement on 6 October 1983 setting out criteria for a satisfactory investigation. These included: that those entrusted with the inquiry should be chosen for their recognized impartiality, independence and competence; that the investigative body should have the power to ensure the cooperation of witnesses and to obtain all information necessary to its inquiry; and that the methods, evidence, findings and conclusions of the investigative body should be made public.

On 10 October 1983, members of the first commission of inquiry into the Aquino assassination resigned in the face of widespread public doubts about their independence. A second commission of inquiry requested the Chief of Staff of the armed forces to discontinue a separate investigation being conducted by the armed forces on the grounds that witnesses might be discouraged from testifying before the official inquiry as a result of intimidation by the military investigators. At the end of the year the official inquiry was still proceeding. Members of the Aquino family claimed that a number of witnesses who had evidence which would rebut the official version of the assassination were afraid to testify for fear of reprisals.

The alleged perpetrators of one widely publicized case of extra-judicial execution were tried in 1983. The case involved Macli-ing Dulag, a tribal chief of the Kalingas in northern Luzon, who had led his people's opposition to government plans for a dam project in Kalinga territory. Macli-ing Dulag was shot dead in his home on 24 April 1980. In August 1980 on the basis of the findings of an official inquiry, the Minister of National Defence had ordered the arrest and detention of four soldiers pending the filing of murder charges before a military court. Amnesty International had noted in its mission report of September 1982 that no progress had been reported in the case. On 9 June 1983 the court martial of two of the four soldiers named in the report of the official inquiry began and although there were reported irregularities in the proceedings, including the alleged intimidation of prosecution witnesses, the two soldiers were each sentenced to 14 years' imprisonment on 29 November 1983.

Amnesty International was also concerned about the judiciary's lack of promptness in resolving cases of people charged with political offences. In the Karagatan-Andrea arms smuggling case, People of the Philippines v. Jose Maria Sison et al. (see *Amnesty International Report 1980*), trial proceedings continued throughout the year, having begun in November 1978. The cases of two of the defendants – Fidel Agcaoili, arrested in May 1974, and Saturnino Ocampo, arrested in January 1976 – were being investigated by Amnesty International.

Another detainee whose case Amnesty International was investigating was Baltazar Pinguel, who was held in Camp Bagong Diwa, Bicutan, Metromanila. Baltazar Pinguel had been arrested with 21 others in May 1980 and charged with subversion before a military tribunal in September 1980. In January 1981, soon after the lifting of martial law, the case was formally transferred to a civil court. However, no hearings in the case were held after January 1981. Baltazar Pinguel was the only one of the defendants still in detention at the end of 1983.

Amnesty International learned of several cases of detainees who, despite court orders for their release, continued to be detained on the basis of PCOs or PDAs. However, a number of detainees whose cases had been taken up by the organization were released. They included Sixto Carlos Jr., who had been arrested on 24 April 1979, and was released on 4 November 1983 after subversion charges against him were dismissed and Felix Olalia, one of about 50 trade unionists arrested in August/September 1982 (see *Amnesty International Report 1983*), who was transferred from detention camp and placed under house arrest on 1 May 1983. Aquilino Pimentel, a leading opposition figure arrested in April 1983, was transferred from detention in Cebu City to house arrest in Cagayan de Oro City in July 1983. Six of the prisoners of conscience held in Tagum, Davao del Norte, were released during the year (see *Amnesty International Report 1983*). Amnesty International issued an appeal in October 1983 on behalf of another member of this group of detainees, Purificacion Trinidad, urging that she be given proper medical treatment after learning that she was in poor health. After receiving medical treatment, she was released into the care of the Bishop of Tagum in November 1983. Her husband, Rolieto Trinidad, was the only member of the group to remain in detention at the end of the year.

Amnesty International believed that more than 800 people were under sentence of death, most of them being held in the National Penitentiary, Muntinlupa. Most of those under sentence of death had been awaiting review of their sentences for several years, including some who had been convicted in the 1950s. Executions in the Philippines are rare, and none were reported during 1983. However, Amnesty International continued to receive reports of death sentences being imposed for murder and drug smuggling.

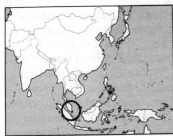

Singapore

Amnesty International was concerned about the powers of preventive detention exercised by the Singapore Government under the Internal Security Act (ISA) whereby individuals were held without trial because of their alleged political beliefs or activities. Although one prisoner of conscience who had been detained for 13 years without trial under the ISA was released in August 1983, Amnesty International continued to appeal for the unconditional release of the only other known long-term ISA detainee, held without trial since 1966 and adopted by the organization as a prisoner of conscience. Amnesty International was also concerned about the case of a prisoner charged under Section 27(1) of the ISA governing "possession of subversive documents". Two people were executed during 1983 and four others sentenced to death. The organization continued to be concerned about the use of caning as a judicial punishment.

Section 8(1)(a) of the ISA empowers the Minister of Home Affairs to issue renewable detention orders of two years' duration on grounds of national security. There is no judicial review of these detention orders.

The government has justified its use of long-term preventive detention by reference to the alleged security threat posed in particular by the illegal Communist Party of Malaya (CPM), claiming that all remaining detainees have some connection with the CPM. The government has repeatedly stated that detainees may be released by signing a statement publicly abjuring future support for the CPM or its affiliated organizations, or the forcible overthrow of the government. Alternatively, the government has said that detainees can be released if they agree to live in permanent exile.

In spite of the government's insistence on these conditions several ISA detainees released during 1981 and 1982 were not required to make such undertakings. Neither were they forced into exile, although restrictions on movement, association and employment were imposed on them. Amnesty International had no details about the circumstances of the release of the one long-term prisoner of conscience, Chng Min Oh, who was freed in August 1983 after 13 years in preventive detention.

The number of detainees held under the ISA decreased from an estimated 20 people in late 1981 to nine officially acknowledged detainees as of September 1982. The authorities reportedly acknowledged holding only one ISA detainee at the end of the year, eight detainees (including Chng Min Oh) having been freed during the year. Amnesty International continued to appeal for the unconditional release of Chia Thye Poh, imprisoned since 1966. He was formerly a member of parliament for the *Barisan Sosialis*, Socialist Front, editor of the party's newspaper and assistant lecturer at Nanyang University.

In addition to providing for preventive detention, the ISA also permits the trial of people accused of "possession of subversive documents" (Section 27(1)). Trials of political prisoners have rarely taken place in Singapore and only two trials are known to have been conducted under the act. The first occurred in February 1982 (see *Amnesty International Report 1983*) and the second in November 1983, when Tan Chu Boon, a tropical fish breeder, was sentenced to one year's imprisonment. He was found guilty on two charges: having under his control a tombstone carrying an inscription which, the judge ruled, tended to advocate acts prejudicial to the security of Singapore, and having in his possession a document bearing the same words as those inscribed on the tombstone. The tombstone had marked the grave of Tan Chu Boon's brother, Tan Chay Wa, a member of the Malaysian National Liberation Front (MNLF), an organization affiliated to the CPM, who was executed in Malaysia in January 1983 for a firearms offence. The tombstone described Tan Chay Wa as a "martyr" and a patriot. Amnesty International did not consider that Tan Chu Boon's actions demonstrated personal adherence to the political views ascribed to his brother and considered that they therefore did not amount to incitement to overthrow the government. Tan Chu Boon filed an appeal against the court's decision.

Amnesty International expressed deep regret following the executions in Chiangi Prison of two men convicted of drug trafficking offences. Anwar Ali Khan was hanged on 4 March 1983 and Lim Chuan Keam on 21 October 1983. A total of 14 prisoners were reported to have been executed for drug trafficking offences since the Misuse of Drugs Act was amended in 1975 to provide a mandatory death sentence for trafficking in certain quantities of specified drugs. The only occasion when a mandatory death sentence imposed for drug trafficking offences was commuted was in February 1983, when the death sentence passed on Siti Aminah Jaffar, co-accused in the case against Anwar Ali Khan was commuted to life imprisonment by President Devan Nair. Amnesty International had initiated urgent appeals on behalf of both prisoners. Four death sentences were imposed by the High Court during 1983, three for murder and one for a drug trafficking offence. At least eight prisoners were reported to be under sentence of death at the end of the year.

In 1973, caning was made mandatory for about 30 offences, in most cases in addition to a term of imprisonment. The law specified the minimum number of strokes that should be imposed by the courts. Sentences of between five and 15 strokes are generally handed down, although habitual criminals may receive up to 40 strokes. Caning as administered by the authorities in Singapore is said to split the skin and may leave scars. Women, children and men over 50 are exempt from the punishment, except children convicted of armed robbery who may receive a maximum of 10 strokes. Amnesty International believed that dozens of prisoners were sentenced to caning during 1983.

Sri Lanka

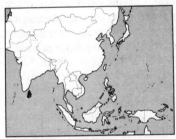

Amnesty International remained concerned about the use of the Prevention of Terrorism Act (PTA) and the Emergency Regulations to detain members of the Tamil minority and of opposition parties without trial, sometimes incommunicado, and about continuing allegations of torture of detainees held under the PTA. A major concern was the killing of randomly selected Tamil civilians by members of the armed forces and the killing in prison of a large number of Tamil detainees held under the PTA.

The year was marked by increased political tension resulting from demands for a separate state by the Tamil minority, accompanied by acts of violence on the part of Tamil extremist groups, members of the security forces and the majority Sinhalese population. A state of emergency was reimposed on 18 May 1983 for the stated purpose of preventing violence during parliamentary by-elections and remained in force throughout the year.

On 6 July 1983, Amnesty International published the *Report of an Amnesty International Mission to Sri Lanka, 31 January – 9 February 1982*. The report, describing events until May 1983, concluded that political suspects held under the PTA were frequently held incommunicado, sometimes for more than eight months, and that they had been tortured both in army camps and by the police. Methods of torture reportedly included hanging victims upside down from hooks, beating them with metal bars, driving needles under finger-nails and applying chili powder to sensitive parts of the body. When the report was published Amnesty International said that it had continued to receive reports that detainees were being ill-treated, that relatives were being denied information about their whereabouts and that lawyers were being prevented from meeting them for weeks after arrest. The mission also collected evidence that three Tamils had been abducted and killed by the security forces, apparently in retaliation for the killing of two police officers on 3/4 June 1981 and that two other Tamils had been abducted, shot and left for dead, and that apparently no measures had been taken against those responsible – despite verdicts of homicide having been given by the magistrate in all cases. The report made 12 detailed recommendations which included: informing detainees of the grounds for arrest; disclosing the place of detention to relatives and allowing immediate and regular access to lawyers; establishing an independent machinery to investigate complaints of torture; and restoring the normal rules of evidence, according to which statements made solely to the police while in custody and not made before a magistrate are inadmissible in court. Amnesty International sent the report to President J. R. Jayewardene on 7 February 1983 with a request to meet the President, offering to publish the government's comments. On 6 April the government informed Amnesty International that it was not possible to discuss the report.

The government issued a nine-point statement on the day of the report's publication denying in general terms that the human rights violations described had taken place, although stating that some people had been held incommunicado. Amnesty International wrote to President Jayewardene on 19 July to express its grave concern about the government's response. On 22 July the Sri Lanka High Commission in London released a more comprehensive statement on the report, Amnesty International's response to which was described in an *Amnesty International Statement updating its human rights concerns in Sri Lanka, July – September 1983* (see below).

On 23 July 1983, 13 soldiers were killed near Thinevely, Jaffna, reportedly by a group of Tamil extremists. Violence directed against the Tamil minority started immediately in Colombo, subsequently spreading throughout the country, several hundred Tamils being killed by Sinhalese groups. During the following few days Amnesty International received renewed reports that unarmed members of the Tamil minority were being killed at random by the security forces in the north, apparently in retaliation for the killing of their own men; that Tamil detainees, held under the PTA, were being killed in a Colombo prison and that members of left-wing opposition parties were being arrested under the Emergency Regulations.

Amnesty International cabled the President on 26 and 28 July saying that it was deeply disturbed by reports of killings by the army, giving details of 16 such killings and urging the government to order an independent investigation into the killings and to bring those responsible to justice. Amnesty International said its concern about these killings was compounded by the government's failure to take legal action against any members of the security forces responsible for earlier killings and the continued existence of Emergency Regulation 15A, promulgated on 3 June, which allows the security forces to dispose of corpses in secret and without inquest procedures.

On 6 August the government admitted that 20 people had been killed by the armed forces "on the rampage". In late August, the government put the figure at 37, and in a statement of 9 November 1983 by the Sri Lanka High Commission in London the government acknowledged 51 killings, a figure which tallied with the number reported to Amnesty International in July. Inquest proceedings were reportedly held in only one of these cases. By the end of 1983, Amnesty International was not aware of a full independent investigation having been instituted into these killings or of any legal action having been taken against responsible officials although statements were given to the police by relatives in many cases. Six more killings by the security forces of Tamil civilians reportedly occurred in four separate incidents on 31 August, in early September, on 30 September and on 18 November 1983. Amnesty International cabled the President on 12 October 1983 expressing its deep concern about the reported killing of four Tamils in September. Two of the corpses were reportedly cremated by the security forces after official permission had been obtained. Amnesty International repeated its call to the President to take immediate steps to halt further killings, to order independent investigations into the four deaths and to rescind Emergency Regulation 15A. Despite deep concern expressed about Emergency Regulation 15A by Amnesty International, by members of the Human Rights Committee which monitored compliance with the International Covenant on Civil and Political Rights in the course of considering Sri Lanka's report in October/November 1983, and by other international organizations, the provisions of the regulation remained in force throughout the year.

Amnesty International was also gravely concerned about the killing of a total of 53 Tamil political prisoners detained or convicted under the PTA on 25 and 27 July in Welikada Prison. According to official reports Sinhalese inmates were responsible for the attack but several reports received by Amnesty International alleged the complicity of some prison personnel. On 26 and 28 July the organization cabled the President urging the government to take immediate measures to protect the lives and safety of detainees. While welcoming the fact that the government followed normal proceedings in setting up a magisterial inquiry the day after the killings, Amnesty International urged that a comprehensive independent inquiry be instituted into the killings, with publication of its findings in full. The magistrate held a one-day inquiry into each of the two incidents, finding that Tamil detainees had been killed by Sinhalese inmates and directing the police to conduct further investigations since prison officials had been unable to identify any of those responsible for the killings.

In an *Amnesty International Statement updating its human rights concerns in Sri Lanka, July – September 1983*, presented to the government on 15 September and subsequently published, Amnesty International described its concerns about the July army killings and the Welikada prison killings, as well as the government's decision to arrest, under emergency regulations, several dozen members of, or alleged sympathizers with, three left-wing opposition parties, the *Janata Vimukhti Peramuna*, the *Nava Sama Samaja* Party and the Communist Party, which were banned on 30 July 1983 for their alleged involvement in the July violence. Amnesty International cabled the President on 3 August 1983 urging that the government publish the names and places of detention of those held and to consider their early release if no specific charges had been brought. Some of the detainees were reportedly being held in incommunicado detention without trial for weeks after arrest under the provisions of Emergency Regulation 17, which allows for the indefinite detention of those whom the government believes may act in a manner "prejudicial to national security".

The organization urged that they be allowed access to lawyers and friends on a regular basis. On 9 November 1983 the government informed Amnesty International that it had arrested 42 people under the provisions of Emergency Regulation 17, of whom 16 had been released. On 29 December 1983 Amnesty International wrote to the Secretary to the Ministry of Defence welcoming the release of some detainees. Those released included four members of the Communist Party and a 60-year-old lawyer, Prins Gunasekera, whom Amnesty International had adopted as a prisoner of conscience. The organization also asked whether the remaining detainees would also be released given the fact that they had been held for nearly five months without trial and no evidence had apparently been produced concerning their alleged involvement in the July events.

Arrests under the PTA continued to be reported throughout the year, with 170 people being arrested under its provisions between

261

October and December from Batticaloa, Vavuniya, Trincomalee and Jaffna. On 29 December 1983 Amnesty International wrote to the Minister of Internal Security expressing concern that people continued to be arrested and held without trial under the PTA, and specifically inquiring about the 170 reported arrests, of which it provided details concerning 75 cases. In view of previous evidence of the torture of people arrested under the PTA, Amnesty International asked for official assurances that responsible officials be directed to ensure that none of the detainees were subjected to torture or ill-treatment, that relatives and lawyers were granted immediate and regular access to detainees and that detainees be granted all rights normally accorded to other prisoners.

In a number of cases reported to Amnesty International during the year people arrested under the PTA were said to have been tortured following which several allegedly died while in army custody. One such case was that of K. Navaratnarajah, a young farmer from Trincomalee, who was arrested under the PTA on 27 March and died in Gurunagar army camp on 10 April, reportedly as a result of torture by the army. At the end of a judicial inquiry into his death, the magistrate returned a verdict of homicide and 25 external wounds and 10 internal injuries were described in a medical report. However, inquest proceedings were not held in the case of the other three people who reportedly died during the year after having been tortured while held in the custody of the security forces.

Although the death penalty remains on the statute books, no executions are known to have taken place since the United National Party government took office in 1977.

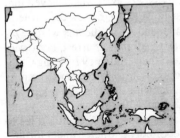

Taiwan

Amnesty International continued to appeal during 1983 for the release of some 40 prisoners of conscience and was investigating the cases of some 70 other political prisoners who had been detained for several years. Thirteen other prisoners of conscience were released on parole during the year. Amnesty International investigated nine reported arrests on political grounds and one report of torture. It was also concerned about the execution of convicted criminals and the handing down of death sentences.

Among the prisoners of conscience on whose behalf Amnesty International appealed were 17 who had been sentenced to life imprisonment in 1950 on charges of pro-communist activities. After years of inquiry, the organization could find no evidence that they had used or advocated violence. Seven were released on humanitarian grounds in February and March 1983. Ten others remained in detention although in mid-October 1983 press reports quoted Minister of Defence Soong Chang-chih as saying that a review of their cases initiated in October 1982 was progressing and that some of them would soon be released.

On 4 October 1983 another prisoner of conscience, Lin Wen-chen, the former Dean of the Women's Bible School in Taipei, who had been detained since January 1980, was granted parole on medical grounds. Amnesty International had been concerned about her rapidly deteriorating health. Also in October, five other prisoners of conscience were released on parole between two and four months before their sentences had expired. They were Yang Chin-chu, a writer, Chang Fu-chung and Chen Chung-hsin, journalists, and two former employees of the banned opposition magazine *Formosa*, Yu Ah-hsing and Chiu Chui-chen. They had been arrested after the Kaohsiung Incident in December 1979 (see *Amnesty International Report 1981*).

There were no indications that the government was reviewing the cases of other prisoners of conscience or of prisoners convicted of sedition after trials that Amnesty International believed fell short of internationally accepted standards. One prisoner of conscience, Pai Ya-tsan, an opposition politician,was sentenced to life imprisonment in November 1975 for circulating an election leaflet with questions to the Prime Minister on politically sensitive topics. Amnesty International continued to appeal for the release of Yen Ming-sheng, an opposition candidate in the 1975 parliamentary elections, and Yang Chin-hai, his campaign manager and a businessperson. It was believed that the immediate reason for their arrest in May 1976 was their role in the preparation of a conference of independent politicians which was intended to establish an opposition party. After their arrest, both were held incommunicado for two months. At their trial in 1976 Yang Chin-hai testified that he had been tortured in order to force him to confess that he had been planning terrorist activities. Yang Chin-hai was sentenced to life imprisonment and Yen Ming-sheng to 12 years' imprisonment. The principal evidence produced by the authorities to support the charges was confessions reportedly extracted under torture. Amnesty International adopted both men as prisoners of conscience.

Although the constitution guarantees the right to freedom of expression, several writers and journalists remained in detention for their writings. Among them was Lin Cheng ting. Amnesty International believed that his arrest in 1957 was the result of an editorial he wrote criticizing the way the government and the United States Embassy handled a mob attack on the embassy which followed the killing of a Chinese by a US soldier, and the organization adopted him as a prisoner of conscience. Another prisoner of conscience, Huang Hua, was serving his third sentence for sedition and was in his mid-40s. In October 1976 he was sentenced to 10 years' imprisonment for articles he contributed to the *Taiwan Political Review*.

Among the cases being investigated by Amnesty International were those of some 10 people who were serving terms of three years' "reformatory education" (detention during which political "re-education" is administered) for allegedly producing pro-communist propaganda. One of them was Lee Ta-chuan, a retired soldier. He was reportedly charged with gambling, but Amnesty International believed that he may have been arrested for circulating petitions to President Chiang Ching-kuo calling for negotiations with the People's Republic of China (PRC) and for complaining about police brutality.

Although Amnesty International received several reports of the detention of political prisoners under the Law for the Punishment of Police Offences, it had details in only one case. Article 28 of this law allows the police to send "a person who habitually commits police offences . . . to a suitable place for correction . . .". Police offences include "disseminating rumours sufficient to affect public peace". Wang Ching-hsiung, a lecturer at the College of Chinese Culture, was convicted of producing pro-communist propaganda in the early 1970s. He completed his sentence in 1980 but remained in detention under Article 28 reportedly because he refused to change his political views. Amnesty International adopted him as a prisoner of conscience.

Amnesty International was concerned that many prisoners of conscience were reported to be in ill-health and to be receiving inadequate medical treatment, in spite of assurances from the authorities to the organization that adequate medical facilities were available within the prisons and that provision was made for medical examinations or treatment outside prison where necessary.

Amnesty International investigated nine arrests which took place during the year. Yang Huan-hsi was arrested on 5 January 1983 and charged with having written to friends who held official posts in the PRC, suggesting initiatives for the reunification of China by the PRC. On 9 February 1983, the Taiwan Garrison Command (TGC) announced that he had been sentenced to three years' "reformatory education" but he was conditionally released in view of his age and poor health. In another case, Maeda Mitsue, a Japanese citizen, Professor Lu Hsiu-yi, Dean of the Political Science Department of the College of Chinese Culture, and Ko Szu-pin were arrested on 3 and 8 January 1983 and accused of working for an organization based in Japan which, the prosecution said, advocated the formal independence of Taiwan, to be achieved through a violent revolution backed by the PRC. Amnesty International urged the authorities to allow them immediate access to lawyers of their choice and asked that they be humanely treated. They were held incommunicado until 25 February 1983 when the prosecution recommended lenient sentences on the grounds that they had cooperated and repented during their interrogation. Their trial before a military court was believed to have taken place in late February but no details were available. They were sentenced to three years' "reformatory education", suspended, except in the case of Lu Hsiu-yi.

Amnesty International was concerned about the case of Chang Ming-chuan, who was arrested in March 1982 and sentenced to death for murder and robbery. He appealed against his conviction, claiming that he had been tortured into making a false confession as well as pointing out discrepancies in the prosecution evidence. In early 1983 the Supreme Court sent the case back for review to the Taiwan High Court on the grounds of unsatisfactory evidence. The High Court reimposed the sentence and, following another appeal, the Supreme Court on 15 December 1983 again returned the case to the High Court for review. It was not known whether the authorities conducted an independent inquiry into the claim of torture.

Amnesty International also continued to urge the authorities to set up independent inquiries into all previous claims of torture made by prisoners still detained. In early 1983 the government said that all such complaints had been "carefully investigated without any concrete finding of torture or other ill-treatment". The reply did not indicate the nature of the investigations, the participants involved or the methods used.

On 5 August 1983 Amnesty International wrote to President Chiang Ching-kuo to express concern about the execution in July 1983 of 10 people convicted of ordinary criminal offences. Two more executions of criminal convicts took place in September and December. Twenty-seven people were reportedly sentenced to death for criminal offences during the year. One prisoner under sentence of death was acquitted and released in February 1983.

Thailand

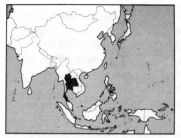

Amnesty International was concerned about the use of legislation outlawing criticism of the Thai Royal Family to prosecute opponents of the government, the trial of civilians for political offences in military courts employing judicial procedures which did not meet internationally accepted standards, and the imposition of the death penalty. In 1983, for the first time in several years, Amnesty International adopted two prisoners of conscience in Thailand.

In recent years Amnesty International has known of very few people being imprisoned in Thailand on account of the non-violent expression of their political or other beliefs. The organization was therefore concerned about the arrest on 27 April 1983 and subsequent trial of political activist Anant Senakhan for *lèse majesté*, the crime of defaming, insulting or threatening the Thai Royal Family set out in Article 112 of the Thai penal code. He was found guilty of contravening Article 112 at a trial on 17 August 1983 before a military tribunal and was sentenced to three years' imprisonment. He was a reportedly outspoken opponent of a senior military figure, and was apparently arrested for openly criticizing alleged political involvement by the Queen. In December he was sentenced to a further three years' imprisonment after being tried on a second count of *lèse majesté*, again before a military tribunal.

Following legislation enacted after the October 1976 coup by the ruling National Administrative Reform Council (NARC) and still in force for charges of *lèse majesté*, defendants are tried by martial law courts composed of civilian judges. According to information received by Amnesty International, Anant Senakhan was denied the right to call witnesses on his own behalf and his trial was held *in camera*. There is no right of appeal from the ruling of a martial law court in Thailand. Amnesty International adopted Anant Senakhan as a prisoner of conscience.

Amnesty International was also concerned about the arrest on 3 July of Saman Kongsuphol, a campaigner for civilian democracy, also on a charge of *lèse majesté*. Saman Kongsuphol, the alleged publisher of a reportedly critical history of the Thai monarchy, was held incommunicado for six days and refused bail following his arrest. On 30 December he was sentenced to eight years' imprisonment by a martial law court. He was subsequently adopted by Amnesty International as a prisoner of conscience.

Other crimes tried by martial law courts are offences against the internal and external security of the state and offences against public order. Offences under the Anti-Communist Activities Act, whereby a suspected "communist" may be held for up to 480 days without a warrant, are tried by "special military tribunals" composed entirely of military officers. Amnesty International was concerned that the rights of defence of civilians tried before martial law courts and "special military tribunals" on political charges appeared to be seriously impaired and to fall far short of the relevant international standards.

In a letter addressed in December 1983 to Prime Minister Prem Tinsulanond, Amnesty International expressed concern that people tried by military courts appeared to be restricted in their rights of defence and denied the right of appeal guaranteed by the Universal Declaration of Human Rights and the International Covenant on Civil and Political Rights. It urged Prime Minister Prem to recommend that Anant Senakhan be pardoned by King Bhumibhol and asked for charges against Saman Kongsuphol to be dropped.

Amnesty International welcomed reports that the Thai Government had sponsored a parliamentary draft bill that would extend legal safeguards for suspects held in police custody. In particular, the organization noted that the new legislation would, if enacted, guarantee the right to private consultation with a lawyer at the time of arrest, the right to receive visits and medical treatment and the right to appeal against refusal of temporary release on bail. Amnesty International believes that such guarantees can greatly increase a detainee's protection from possible ill-treatment in custody.

Amnesty International also continued to be concerned about the imposition of the death penalty in Thailand and appealed on behalf of a number of sentenced criminals during 1983. The organization learned of at least 25 death sentences being passed (including three on police officers), 16 death sentences being commuted to life imprisonment, 12 death sentences being upheld by the Appeal Court (including 11 on police officers) and one death sentence being upheld by the Supreme Court. (A person condemned to death by the Thai Criminal Court may appeal to the Appeal Court, the Supreme Court and then to the King for clemency.) In August 1983 Amnesty International launched an urgent appeal for clemency on behalf of Chirawat Khienpanya, a former student leader accused of complicity in the murder of a policeman in 1978 and sentenced to death in July. As the murder occurred while Thailand was under martial law, Chirawat Khienpanya was tried by a military tribunal and therefore was unable to have his case reviewed by a higher court. He appealed for clemency to King Bhumibhol, and at the time of writing Amnesty International was awaiting the outcome of the appeal.

Official figures on executions have rarely been released in Thailand, but Amnesty International noted one report claiming that five people had been executed in 1982. No figure was available for 1983. Executions take place in Bangkok's Bang Khwang Prison, and a press report in March 1983 discussing the prison's recent acquisition of two West German-made machine-guns to be used for carrying out death sentences noted that 16 people were awaiting execution, having exhausted all appeal procedures. In May 1983 it was reported that 121 people were under sentence of death in the country.

Finally, Amnesty International was concerned to learn in 1983 of the reported "disappearance" of a Vietnamese refugee from Sikhiu refugee camp. Four witnesses claimed to have seen the refugee, Le van Hai, taken out of the camp by armed Thai guards after being interviewed by the deputy commander of the centre on 12 September 1982.

In its December 1983 letter to the Prime Minister, Amnesty International called on the Thai Government to investigate the "disappearance" fully and to make the results of the inquiry public.

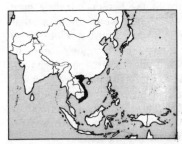

Viet Nam

Amnesty International continued to be concerned about the long-term detention without trial of thousands of members of the former South Vietnamese Government in "re-education" camps. It was also concerned about other categories of political prisoner in Viet Nam whom the organization had adopted as prisoners of conscience. The absence of adequate legal safeguards to protect detainees in pre-trial detention and the use of the death penalty remained other Amnesty International concerns in Viet Nam.

In a submission to the Vietnamese Government in April 1983, Amnesty International pointed out that the majority of detainees in "re-education" camps had been detained without charge or trial for more than eight years. The organization urged the government to abolish detention without trial for "re-education" and to investigate the cases of untried detainees in order either to charge and try them or to release them promptly.

Those detained in "re-education" camps were held under a decree of the former Democratic Republic of Viet Nam (North Viet Nam), Resolution No. 49 NQ/TVQH of 1961, which permits indefinite detention without trial for "obstinate counter-revolutionary elements" and "all professional scoundrels".

Amnesty International considered the continued detention for "re-education" of several thousand people merely because of their position under various governments of the Republic of Viet Nam (South Viet Nam) and the automatic assumption by the Vietnamese Government that all those so detained were guilty of "serious crimes against the people" to be inconsistent with international legal standards. In particular, Amnesty International believed these practices to be incompatible with the provisions of the International Covenant on Civil and Political Rights, to which Viet Nam became a party in September 1982, relating to arbitrary detention, the right to fair trial and the right to be presumed innocent until proved guilty. Such detention may also violate the important legal principle of non-retroactive penalization, because detaines are held on the basis of legislation enacted after the reunification of the country.

In an interview with a correspondent of the *Far Eastern Economic Review* in April 1983, Phan Hien, the Minister of Justice, stated that there were some 10,000 prisoners remaining in "re-education" camps. He also stated that the Council of State had sent delegations to check conditions in the "re-education" camps in 1982 to ensure they were satisfactory and to review individual cases. There were indications that such checks became more regular in 1983 and that the Vietnamese Government was considering closing many "re-education" camps to allow released prisoners to return to their homes, where local organizations would be responsible for them. In the interview cited above Justice Minister Phan Hien indicated that this system of "re-education in place" would first be tried on criminal detainees to gauge its effectiveness before being applied in political cases. However, there was no subsequent evidence that this policy was being enacted.

The criteria the authorities used to evaluate the degree of "re-education" attained by a prisoner and whether he or she might be released were difficult to assess. In many cases the prisoner's state of health and behaviour during detention were apparently considered. Small groups of prisoners seemed to be released regularly to celebrate important dates in the Vietnamese calendar. While Amnesty International knows of generals and other former senior military officers having been released, many junior officers, often involved only in administration before 1975, remained in detention.

Information on a number of individuals held for "re-education" since 1975 indicated that they had had no responsibility for the conduct of combat during the war and indeed, in some instances, that they had opposed the policies of former South Vietnamese President Nguyen van Thieu: Dr Truong van Quynh, aged 62, a former hospital director in Saigon, and the writer and literary critic Ly Dai Nguyen, a member of the opposition to President Thieu, had both been detained for more than eight years without charge or trial and were adopted by Amnesty International as prisoners of conscience.

Amnesty International continued to receive reports that many detainees in "re-education" camps were suffering from serious illnesses including malaria, tuberculosis, heart ailments and malnutritional disorders. Amnesty International has had a long-standing concern about the detention of old or seriously sick prisoners in "re-education" camps where medical facilities tend on the whole to be inadequate. Among the cases known to Amnesty International was that of Do Trong Hue, a former army colonel and lecturer, detained in the Ha Son Binh "re-education" camp and suffering from advanced tuberculosis, beri-beri and a fractured collarbone. Dr Ly Trung Dung, a medical doctor and former member of parliament was also in markedly poor health, suffering from a serious leg injury sustained in the 1950s. Both detainees had been imprisoned for more than eight years and were adopted by Amnesty International as prisoners of conscience.

In December 1983 Amnesty International learned of the death in November of Vo van Hai, who was aged 64 and a former aide to ex-President Ngo Dinh Diem from 1954 to 1963. He was being held in Camp 1870, Xuan Phuoc, Phu Khanh province, suffered from a kidney complaint and a weak heart and had been detained since January 1977 without charge or trial. In December 1982 Amnesty International had written to Prime Minister Pham van Dong appealing for Vo van Hai's early release in view of his ill-health, citing Article 7 of Provisional Revolutionary Government Policy Statement 02/CS/76 which stipulated that detainees in "re-education" camps who were old or seriously ill would be released with the guarantee of their families.

In addition to the large number of people detained when the former South Vietnamese Government collapsed in 1975, many others were subsequently detained on political grounds without trial, including a number of intellectuals arrested in the late 1970s whom Amnesty International adopted as prisoners of conscience. Among them were the well-known artist and writer Nguyen Hai Chi (alias Choe), the writer Nguyen Sy Te and the lawyer and former student leader Nguyen Huu Giao. Giao was one of the authors and signatories of the "Declaration of Disinherited Vietnamese on Human Rights" and had been detained since 1977 in the Xuan Phuoc "re-education" camp. Other writers, including some from northern Viet Nam, were also detained in recent years. Poet Bui Hoang Cam, for example, a former Communist Party member and battalion commander in the Viet Minh, was arrested in August 1982 and accused of having "cultural relations with foreigners" after having allegedly attempted to send a collection of his verse, banned since 1958, out of the country. He was not formally charged or tried.

Throughout 1983 Amnesty International appealed to the

government on behalf of several lay Roman Catholics and priests whom it believed to be detained for their conscientiously held beliefs. Among those reportedly detained were Monsignor Nguyen van Thuan, whom members of an Amnesty International mission to Viet Nam had met near Hanoi in December 1979 and who had previously been detained without charge or trial between 1976 and 1978. Another priest whom Amnesty International adopted as a prisoner of conscience was Father Tran van Khoa, who had been a missionary and social worker with members of the ethnic minority in central Viet Nam before his arrest in May 1975.

Four Roman Catholic priests, including the senior Jesuit in the country, were among seven people sentenced to between three years' and life imprisonment in June after they had been convicted of "plotting to overthrow the government and disseminating counter-revolutionary propaganda". All seven men, detained for two and a half years before their trial, were adopted by Amnesty International as prisoners of conscience. Six others, including three Jesuits and a Dominican priest, were released after the trial with suspended sentences or an official warning. The trial lasted only three days and was seriously prejudiced beforehand when several press commentaries denounced the detained men as "reactionaries" and "counter-revolutionaries". The leader of the Jesuit community in Viet Nam, Father Nguyen Cong Doan, received a 12-year prison sentence. Others sentenced were Nguyen van Hien, Father Le Thanh Que, Father Do Quang Chinh, Hoang Kim Khanh, Brother Pham Huu Lai and Truong van Tuyen.

On a number of occasions in 1983 Amnesty International appealed to the authorities to commute death sentences imposed by the courts. In April the organization appealed on behalf of Phan van Khoi, Hoang Tung and Mac van Vy, three men who had been found guilty of subversion and whose execution it feared was imminent. In July Amnesty International appealed on behalf of another man convicted of "counter-revolutionary activity", Nguyen Huu Cau. The following month two other men, Nguyen Huan Huynh and Chuon Bin Tan, were sentenced to death for subversion.

Executions have rarely been announced by the Vietnamese authorities in recent years. However it was officially admitted in June 1983 that four men had been executed on 31 May in Ho Chi Minh City. Two had been convicted of murder and two of plotting against the state. The two men found guilty of subversion, Nguyen van Hoang and Tran Quang Man, had been sentenced to life imprisonment in November 1981 but as a result of a prosecution appeal had later received death sentences.

Europe

Albania

Amnesty International was concerned about the imprisonment of prisoners of conscience, the lack of legal safeguards for people arrested and tried for political offences; allegations of ill-treatment of detainees, and harsh prison conditions. Several former senior government officials were alleged to have been executed.

In November 1982 the First Secretary of the Albanian Party of Labour, Enver Hoxha, announced the arrest of Fecor Shehu, Minister of the Interior until 1982, and of a "group of plotters" linked with him. In 1983 sources outside Albania claimed that Fecor Shehu had been executed together with Kadri Hazbiu, former Defence Minister, and two other senior officials. Fiqrete Shehu, the wife of Mehmet Shehu – a former Prime Minister officially said to have committed suicide in December 1981 – was alleged to have been sentenced to 25 years' imprisonment, as were a former Foreign Minister, Nesti Nase, and a former mayor of Durres. Two sons of Mehmet Shehu were also said to have been imprisoned. Albanian diplomatic representatives in Vienna reportedly declined to comment on these allegations but confirmed that legal proceedings against "traitors" had taken place.

During the year Amnesty International received information about a number of people said to have been imprisoned in previous years as a result of having non-violently exercised their basic human rights. Many such prisoners were reportedly charged under Article 55 of the criminal code with "anti-state agitation and propaganda". This article makes "Fascist, anti-democratic, religious, war-mongering or anti-socialist agitation and propaganda, as well as the preparation, dissemination or the possession for dissemination of literature of a content liable to weaken or undermine the state of the dictatorship of the proletariat" an offence punishable by three to 10 years' imprisonment. If this offence is committed in time of war or has "especially grave consequences" the penalty is 10 to 25 years' imprisonment or death.

In June an Albanian refugee who had fled to Yugoslavia reportedly stated that a man from his village had been sentenced to 10 years' imprisonment for "anti-state agitation and propaganda" after he had listened to Radio Pristina (the radio station of the capital of Kosovo province in Yugoslavia). In another case, a former prisoner stated that he had been arrested in 1978 and sentenced to four years' imprisonment on charges of "anti-state agitation and propaganda" after he had expressed criticism of the authorities to foreign tourists.

Three members of Albania's Greek minority who fled to Greece in 1983 after having been amnestied in November 1982 described how they had been arrested and sentenced for expressing pro-Greek sentiments. Two received eight-year prison sentences, the third a six-year sentence. In a sworn statement made in Athens in November, one of them gave the names of over 100 members of the Greek minority whom he claimed were serving sentences for political offences in Ballsh prison camp.

Other reports indicated that prisoners were serving prison sentences of up to 25 years for having exercised their right to freedom of expression or for having attempted to leave the country without official permission. Freedom of movement is severely limited by the authorities and Article 127 of the criminal code punishes "illegal border crossing" with up to five years' imprisonment. In some circumstances, this offence may be treated as "treason" and carries a penalty of 10 to 25 years' imprisonment or death under Article 47(11).

In 1967 Albania was officially proclaimed an atheist state; all places of worship were closed. Religious officials of the Muslim, Orthodox and Roman Catholic faiths were prohibited from carrying out religious duties and many were persecuted. In November 1983 the Vatican condemned religious persecution in Albania and claimed that by 1981 seven bishops, 64 diocesan priests, 33 Franciscans, 14 Jesuits, 10 seminarists and eight nuns had died in prison, and that two priests had been executed for baptising children. Among other cases referred to by emigre religious sources was that of the Roman Catholic priest, Fran Mark Gjoni, who was said to have been sentenced to 12 years' imprisonment in 1977 after it had been discovered that he possessed Bibles. However, an article in the official Albanian press in October denied that religious believers had been persecuted and said that religious faith had been opposed with arguments. It quoted a saying by Enver Hoxha that "to believe or not to believe is each person's right", but did not assert that the public practice of religious belief was permitted.

No official figures for the number of political prisoners were published and Amnesty International believed that it had details of only a fraction of the total number. Between 2,500 and 3,000 political prisoners were believed to have been held in Ballsh and Spac camps prior to an amnesty in November 1982. According to one former prisoner there were also some 300 political prisoners detained in Burrel prison in 1982. Political prisoners were also reported to have been held in Tirane. Young people and women convicted of political offences served their sentences together with ordinary criminal prisoners in prison camps in Lezhe and Kosove (Elbasan district), respectively.

Amnesty International does not know how many political prisoners benefited from the amnesty of November 1982, but according to one unofficial source some 360 prisoners were released from Spac – almost a third of the total of those held there. However, Amnesty International received allegations that the arrest of senior government officials referred to above was accompanied by further arrests of their presumed supporters.

In addition to imprisonment, the criminal code provides for a supplementary penalty of banishment or internment for up to five years. This penalty may also be imposed administratively, without trial and for unspecified periods, on both those people considered by the authorities to represent a danger to the country's social system and on "members of the family of fugitives living inside or outside the state". Amnesty International learned of a number of such cases during the year.

Amnesty International continued to be concerned about the lack of legal safeguards for people accused of political offences. Reports about trial procedures relating to recent years indicated that political detainees had been held for up to six months in solitary confinement without access to lawyers or relatives and that officials conducting investigations had frequently beaten suspects to obtain confessions. In June 1983 the People's Assembly introduced legislative changes which were described as strengthening the socialist legal order. Under these amendments the investigation of crimes, which had previously been the responsibility of a department of the Ministry of Internal Affairs, was entrusted to an Investigation Office under the direct control of the People's Assembly and the Presidium of the People's Assembly. Amnesty International was unable to evaluate how investigation proceedings had been affected by this change.

Reports of political trials in recent years indicated that most defendants were not allowed defence counsel and were obliged to conduct their own defence. Former prisoners held in Spac, Ballsh and Burrel described conditions there as harsh, with poor food, hygiene and medical care, and the conditions under which prisoners mine copper and pyrite in Spac as often dangerous.

Bulgaria

Amnesty International was concerned about the imprisonment of prisoners of conscience; and also about two cases in which people were allegedly confined in a psychiatric hospital for political rather than medical reasons. The organization learned of two executions and the imposition of two death sentences.

The criminal code contains a number of articles under which a person may be imprisoned for having non-violently attempted to exercise the rights to freedom of movement and freedom of expression. The constitution does not guarantee the right to freedom of movement and citizens who seek to emigrate are rarely permitted to do so by the authorities. Those who seek to leave the country without official permission may be punished, under Article 279, with up to five years' imprisonment, or up to six years' imprisonment if the offence is repeated.

People who express views which are not officially approved of or who possess literature containing such views may be imprisoned for up to five years for "anti-state agitation and propaganda".

Amnesty International adopted a recently graduated high-school student, Kiril Spasov, as a prisoner of conscience. He was reportedly sentenced to three years' imprisonment on charges brought under Articles 279 and 108 after having been convicted by a Sofia court in September of having made preparations, together with a friend, to leave the country without official authorization. He was also reportedly convicted of possessing tape-recordings of foreign radio broadcasts and leaflets which the court considered to be "anti-state propaganda".

Amnesty International sought to investigate allegations that Aleksander Nikolov, the editor of an army newspaper, had been forcibly confined in the psychiatric section of a military hospital in early October after expressing criticism of the country's political leaders at a meeting of the newspaper's correspondents. Amnesty International also received reports that Volodya Nakov, aged 29, from Sofia had been confined for over a week in July in a psychiatric hospital after informing foreign embassies of his wish to emigrate. He was subsequently alleged to have been threatened with prosecution on charges under Article 108 of "slandering the state" if he continued to contact those embassies.

Amnesty International continued to seek information from the Bulgarian authorities about a number of political prisoners whose cases it was investigating. These included Asen Andonov, aged 38, who was sentenced to eight years' imprisonment in 1973 for leaving the country without official permission while doing military service. In 1975 he received a further sentence, making a combined sentence of 14 years and six months. He was convicted of having founded, while detained in Pazardzhik prison, a group which aimed to undermine the authority of the state "by kidnapping and taking the life of state and party officials". Amnesty International sought further information from the authorities about the grounds for the latter charges, but received no reply.

Amnesty International also continued to seek details of the charges and of the current legal status of Jumer Ilanski and Mr Bunzev, two Pomaks (Bulgarians of Muslim faith) who were sentenced to 15 and 20 years' imprisonment respectively in 1973 after they had taken part in protests against an official ruling requiring Pomaks to change their Muslim names to Bulgarian ones.

Information about human rights violations in Bulgaria was severely restricted by official censorship and Amnesty International believed that it learned of only a small proportion of the total number of prisoners of conscience. According to estimates by former political prisoners there were approximately 250 political prisoners detained in Stara Zagora prison – where most political prisoners were held – at the beginning of the 1980s. Many of them were reportedly people convicted of having attempted to leave the country without permission. People convicted of this offence were also held in Sofia Central Prison. In addition, 20 to 30 political prisoners were reported to be held at that time in Pazardzhik prison, where recidivists are generally sent. Amnesty International did not receive any information indicating that the above figures had substantially changed by 1983, nor that prison conditions, described as poor – and particularly harsh in Pazardzhik – had improved.

Amnesty International learned of two executions and of two death sentences, in all four cases for murder. It was reported on 24 October that Stoiko Iliev Getov had been executed and on 5 November that Mustafa Yustenov Mustafov had been executed. It was reported in February that Todor Tsvetanov Ivanov had been sentenced to death and in December that Maria Hristova Georgieva was appealing to the Supreme Court against a death sentence imposed on her.

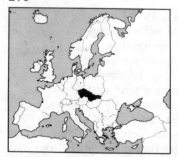

Czechoslovakia

Amnesty International's main concerns were the continuing detention of prisoners of conscience, the ill-treatment of some prisoners of conscience, and the use of the death penalty. At the end of 1983, Amnesty International had 23 cases under adoption or investigation, but believed that the total number of prisoners of conscience was higher.

People continued to be imprisoned for the non-violent exercise of their right to freedom of expression and information under broadly formulated articles of the penal code. They included Dr Jaromir Savrda, a 50-year-old writer and signatory of Charter 77, who was arrested on 24 September 1982 following the confiscation of Charter 77 materials and *samizdat* (unofficial and uncensored) literature during a search of his home. On 3 March 1983, he was sentenced by the District Court in Ostrava to 25 months' imprisonment in the second (stricter) prison category for "incitement" under Article 100 of the penal code. The court found him guilty of collecting, reproducing and disseminating unofficial "anti-state" texts. Among the incriminating materials was a poem by Alexander Tvardovsky which had been published in Czechoslovakia as well as in the Soviet Union and which he had borrowed from a public library. Jaromir Savrda was reportedly seriously ill and according to prison doctors required surgery which could not be performed in any of the prison health institutions. Nonetheless, the court which considered an appeal that his sentence be waived or interrupted concluded on 23 June that he did not require surgical treatment outside the prison health-care system and that surgical intervention was not urgent. Jaromir Savrda had served a two-and-a-half-year prison sentence for a similar offence in 1978/81 (see *Amnesty International Report 1980*).

Dr Ladislav Lis, a 57-year-old Charter 77 signatory and a member of the unofficial human rights group VONS, the Committee for the Defence of the Unjustly Persecuted, was arrested on 5 January 1983, after having his home in Northern Bohemia searched, on charges of "incitement" and "theft of socialist property". The latter charge, referring to two bags of corn collected in a field after the harvest, was subsequently dropped. In May 1983, he went on nine days' hunger-strike in protest against his imprisonment and against his wife not being allowed to visit him. On 21 July, the District Court in Ceska Lipa sentenced him under Article 100 to 14 months' imprisonment, followed by three years' protective surveillance. The main charges against him were that he had disseminated texts of an "inciting nature", that he showed several people copies of letters he had written in June 1982 to the authorities asking for protection for his children, whose lives were threatened by anonymous people, and that he had written a letter to western peace movements. Ladislav Lis had been detained, without trial, from May to December 1979 on charges of "subversion" (see *Amnesty International Report 1980*) and repeatedly between 1980 and 1982.

Jiri Wolf, a 32-year-old worker and Charter 77 signatory was remanded in custody on 17 May on charges of "subversion". He was accused of giving information about prison conditions in the CSSR to the Austrian Embassy in Prague and of writing articles of an "anti-state" nature which were published in emigre journals abroad. At the trial on 5 and 6 October, the Prague Municipal Court ordered a psychiatric examination of the accused and adjourned the hearing. On 21 December, Jiri Wolf was sentenced to six years' imprisonment for "subversion in collusion with a foreign power" (Article 98, Sections 1 and 2a) and for "endangering state secrets" (Article 173, Section 3). He had served three and a half years in prison in 1978/81 (see *Amnesty International Reports 1979, 1981*). He was again arrested for 48 hours on 2 February 1982 during a police action against a group of young people who produced and distributed leaflets denouncing the imposition of martial law in Poland and calling for solidarity with Polish workers.

People engaged in unofficial religious activities continued to be arrested throughout the year, in most cases for "obstructing the state supervision of the churches and religious bodies" (Article 178). On 27 March and on subsequent days, the State Security Police searched the houses of some 250 clerical and lay members of the Franciscan Order in many parts of the country, confiscating religious literature, typewriters, money and religious objects. All those whose homes were searched were reportedly interrogated and some were detained for up to 48 hours. Some 20 people were remanded in custody on suspicion of "obstructing the state supervision of churches and religious bodies". Three Franciscan laymen from Slovakia, Peter Rucka, Anton Smid and Jaroslav Brazda, were the last to be released, without trial, on 15 July. Two Franciscan priests, Frantisek Pometlo and Josef Mazanec, were brought to trial on 13 July before the Plzen Municipal Court charged with circulating an unlicensed religious publication, with admitting a novice into their religious order and with celebrating mass in the presence of other priests. They were sentenced under Article 178 to six months' and eight months' imprisonment respectively. However, they were released three days later. An appeal hearing took place on 30 September. The Regional Court in Plzen upheld the sentences, which had been suspended.

Three prominent Jehovah's Witnesses, engineers Frantisek Risler, Zdenek Taborsky and Jiri Kubik, were sentenced on 21 July by the court in Usti nad Labem to 13 months' imprisonment each for engaging in religious activities and thereby infringing Article 178 of the penal code. The sect is not recognized by the state.

On 23 September, the District Court in Sumperk convicted two Catholics, Jiri Snajdr, a mining technician, and Jan Mokry, a worker, of meeting their families and friends in private houses, of reading the Scriptures, meditating and praying and singing religious songs without state consent, and gave them suspended prison sentences of 10 and 12 months respectively under Article 178.

Amnesty International learned that several Pentecostalists were awaiting trial under Article 178. Rudolf Bubik, head of the sect, and two other members, Josef Wojnar and Jan Kotajny, were sentenced on 21 December 1982 by the District Court in Karvina to one year's imprisonment each, suspended for two years, for organizing religious meetings without state consent. Rudolf Bubik appealed against this judgement and his appeal was pending.

Amnesty International received reports of the ill-treatment of some prisoners of conscience. Jaroslav Javorsky, who was serving a 13-year sentence in the strictest prison category in Valdice Prison, and who was seriously ill, went on hunger-strike on 17 February to protest against the lack of medical attention. Before ending the hunger-strike he was reportedly beaten and placed in an underground cell without water.

Jiri Gruntorad, serving a four-year prison sentence in Minkovice Prison (see *Amnesty International Report 1982*), was reported to have been harassed by the prison administration and subjected to frequent administrative punishments including solitary confinement and reduced food rations. On 17 March, he was reportedly beaten by a prison guard and, after complaining, was placed in solitary confinement for six days until traces of his injuries disappeared. On 7 April, he was charged with "making a false accusation".

At least five people were sentenced to death and three were executed in 1983. These figures mark an increase over recent years. Two people who were executed in April had originally been given 25-year prison terms, but had had their sentences changed by the appeal court to the death penalty.

Federal Republic of Germany

Amnesty International's main concerns were the imprisonment of conscientious objectors to military service and the prosecution of people in violation of their right to freedom of expression. The organization also called for an investigation into the procedures followed with respect to the case of a Turkish refugee who committed suicide during proceedings following an extradition request by the Turkish government.

Amnesty International appealed on behalf of six people convicted for their refusal on conscientious grounds to perform military service. Among them was Thomas Hansen (see *Amnesty International Reports 1982, 1983*), whose rejected application for conscientious objector status was based on moral and political considerations. He was sentenced to six months' imprisonment on 7 October 1981 for his refusal to obey, which was increased to 10 months without probation on appeal. He did not begin serving his sentence until 21 April 1983, following the rejection of several appeals.

Amnesty International also intervened on behalf of Hubert Kappelhof, who was sentenced to eight months' imprisonment on 24 March 1982 on charges of "desertion" and "insubordination" after the rejection of his application for conscientious objector status on moral and political grounds. This sentence was reduced to six months at his appeal hearing on 20 December 1982 by the *Landgericht* (regional court) of Münster. A further appeal was rejected by the *Oberlandesgericht* (regional supreme court) of Hamm on 30 March 1983 and he began serving his sentence on 17 June. Meanwhile, the Public Prosecutor drew up an indictment against Hubert Kappelhof on the same charges, because of his absence from the army between 18 March and 6 October 1982 (he was officially released from the army on 17 January 1983). His second trial took place on 28 June and he was sentenced to nine months' imprisonment, increased to one year without probation by the *Landgericht* of Münster on 12 and 20 October. Hubert Kappelhof appealed against this decision but the appeal had not been heard by the end of 1983.

Amnesty International remained concerned about what it regards as an excessively wide interpretation of the offence of "making propaganda for a terrorist association" (Article 129a of the criminal code), which makes punishable the expression of certain views considered to be beneficial to such organizations, including views considered to "gain sympathy" for them. According to a line of reasoning adopted by many prosecuting and judicial authorities, criminal culpability for this offence depends not so much on what is said, printed or otherwise disseminated, as on what those who (allegedly) expressed themselves supposedly sought to achieve. These authorities seek to establish their "real aims" by investigating the persons' political beliefs, their personal connections, and books, leaflets and letters in their possession.

Amnesty International sent an observer to the trial, in September/ October 1983, of three people who with seven others had been charged under Article 129a with having sprayed slogans on motorway signs in support of the demand by prisoners of the avowedly violent Red Army Fraction (RAF) to be detained together in groups. The spraying had taken place in April 1981 at a time when a large number of prisoners from the RAF (including the husband of one of the accused) had been on hunger-strike in support of this demand (see *Amnesty International Report 1982*). The period of pre-trial detention lasted some 10 weeks and was served under the same maximum security conditions that the accused had expressed concern about. Both the judge responsible for ordering pre-trial detention and the prosecutor in his indictment argued that although the slogans tried to create the impression that the accused were only motivated by humanitarian concern about prison conditions, their "real" aim had been to support a terrorist association, the RAF.

The trial court in Stuttgart rejected this reasoning on the basis that under the rule of law the determining factor for criminal culpability under Article 129a could never be found solely in the aim of the perpetrator. Since the texts of the slogans did not indicate any aims other than an improvement in prison conditions, any such aims could not be attributed to the accused, who were therefore acquitted of having made "propaganda for a terrorist association" and only fined for damaging property. The prosecutor subsequently appealed to the highest Federal Court. At the end of 1983 this appeal was still pending.

On 31 August in a telex message to Minister of Justice Hans Engelhard, Amnesty International called on the government to investigate the procedures followed in the case of Kemal Altun, a Turkish citizen who had sought asylum in the FRG and who had jumped to his death from a sixth-floor window in a West Berlin court building on 30 August. On 6 June 1983 Kemal Altun had been recognized as a refugee by the *Bundesamt*, Recognition Board, of Zirndorf which stated that he should be afforded asylum, a decision which was subsequently challenged by the *Bundesbeauftragter*, the Representative of the Minister of the Interior within the asylum proceedings.

Following Kemal Altun's application to the FRG Government for asylum, the Turkish authorities had asked for him to be extradited, alleging that he had hidden weapons used in the murder in 1980 of a right-wing politician, Gun Sazak. They had dropped earlier charges that he had been directly involved in the murder.

Amnesty International had previously appealed to the Government of the FRG not to authorize the extradition because Amnesty International believed that Kemal Altun faced the serious possibility of being tortured were he to be returned to Turkey.

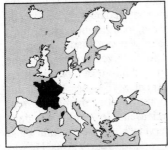

France

Amnesty International's major concern in 1983 was the imprisonment of prisoners of conscience who had refused to conform to the national service law. The prosecution of conscientious objectors continued despite major alterations in both the structure of the law and provisions for military and alternative civil service. The reimprisonment of objectors who had already served prison sentences continued.

On 1 January 1983 the military courts, *Tribunaux permanents des forces armées* (TPFA), Permanent Tribunals of the Armed Forces, which had tried conscientious objectors were abolished and replaced by civilian courts.

Amnesty International requested repeatedly for the introduction of less restrictive legislation concerning conscientious objectors. On 23 May, while the Parliamentary Commission was studying a draft bill, Amnesty International wrote to the Minister of Justice, stating that the grounds on which conscientious objectors could claim the right to do civil instead of military service should be less restricted and that this service should be outside the "war machine" and not of punitive length. An amnesty was requested for all prisoners sentenced under the existing laws.

The new law modifying military service (Loi 83-605 of 8 July 1983) was welcomed by Amnesty International insofar as it contained greater flexibility in granting conscientious objector status and an improvement in the type of alternative civil service objectors were allowed to perform. However, the duration of alternative service remained 24 months, which is double that of the period of military service. Amnesty International believed this to be punitive and continued to adopt as prisoners of conscience objectors to both military and civil service (commonly known as total objectors).

Amnesty International worked on the cases of twelve conscientious objectors. The trial of one conscientious objector, Michel Fache, took place on 14 April, before the reform of the law came into effect. He was sentenced to 18 months' imprisonment for refusal to carry out alternative service because of its restricted nature. On 24 October the Rouen appeal court reduced the sentence to a three months' suspended sentence, although Michel Fache remained liable for military service.

In another case Robert Loncar was sentenced to one year's imprisonment on 23 March 1983 by the new civilian court in Paris for "refusal to obey". He had informed the authorities that although he did not oppose wearing military uniform or carrying out non-armed military service, he refused to bear arms on philosophical and religious grounds. His request for recognition as a conscientious objector was not made within the permitted time limit because he claimed not to have been aware of the existence of legal provisions for the recognition of conscientious objectors. After four months' imprisonment at Fresnes he had his sentence reduced on appeal to eight months' imprisonment with four months' remission of sentence and was released. However, a few days later he was again called up for military service. He presented himself at the barracks and stated that he once again refused to carry arms. He was then reimprisoned. He was put on trial at Versailles on 11 October and sentenced to one year's imprisonment, which he was serving at the end of 1983.

The case of Michel Springaux, a pacifist and total objector, well illustrated Amnesty International's concern over the reimprisonment of conscientious objectors. He refused to perform military service, was amnestied in April 1982, but remained liable for military service. On 15 February 1983 he presented himself at the barracks and was imprisoned at Dijon on 18 February. Sentenced on 13 April to four months' imprisonment, three of which were suspended, he was rearrested by the army as soon as he left the courtroom and ordered to put on military uniform. When he refused he was again imprisoned. On 6 July he was put on trial and sentenced to eight months' imprisonment. On 19 October he was released but yet again rearrested by the army and charged with the same offence.

German Democratic Republic

Amnesty International continued to be concerned about the imprisonment of people for the non-violent exercise of human rights, in particular the right to freedom of expression and the right to leave one's country. During the year, the organization worked on behalf of over 200 such prisoners of conscience or likely prisoners of conscience, but believed the total number to be much higher.

The secrecy surrounding political imprisonment made it difficult to establish the total number of prisoners of conscience. Once arrested, they are unable to communicate the reasons for their arrest to their families in letters or visits. Trials in such cases are held *in camera*, with even close relatives being excluded in nearly all instances known to Amnesty International. Prisoners' relatives or friends risk arrest and harassment if they pass information out of the country.

The GDR authorities deny the existence of political imprisonment, but certain articles of the penal code directly restrict the non-violent exercise of human rights and individuals are regularly tried and convicted under them. Basic human rights, with the exception of the right to leave one's country, are included in the Constitution but limitations are set on the exercise of such rights. In referring to the right to freedom of expression the official Commentary to the Constitution states that there is a "constitutional duty to oppose . . . the spreading of anti-socialist ideology which is practised in the name of 'freedom', 'democracy' or 'humanity' . . . Obviously, expressions of opinion of an insulting or slanderous nature do not enjoy the protection of the Constitution either . . .". The penal code itself proscribes a somewhat wider range of activity. In addition to forbidding the discrediting of "social conditions" (under Article 106 – "incitement hostile to the State") or distributing writings which are "liable to disturb the socialist way of life or bring the State or public order into contempt" (under Article 220 – "public vilification"), it places severe restrictions on sending information out of the country. Article 99 ("treasonable passing on of information") proscribes sending information to "foreign organizations . . . and their helpers" if it is "to the disadvantage of the interests" of the GDR. The law explicitly concerns information which is not classified as "secret" and the Commentary to the law makes it clear that people may be prosecuted even where the information was accurate.

These laws continue to be applied, in the majority of cases known to Amnesty International, not to people who had expressed anti-socialist or even critical views, but to would-be emigrants who persisted in trying to obtain exit visas. Many contacted foreign organizations in the hope that support or publicity would improve their chances of emigration and were convicted under Article 99 of the penal code, the "information" passed on apparently being copies of their applications for exit visas, photographs, and descriptions of the authorities' reactions to these applications. Typical of these prisoners was Horst Lorbeer, a steel-worker, who was arrested in the autumn of 1982 and sentenced on 19 January 1983 to three years' imprisonment under Article 99 after information about his efforts to obtain permission for himself and his family to emigrate had been publicized in foreign news media.

Article 99 was also applied to detain people who sent information about unofficial peace activities out of the country. These included Ulrike Poppe and Bärbel Bohley who had been involved in a number of peace initiatives organised by women and were arrested on 12 December. Ulrike Poppe had, among other things, organized a non-state nursery for parents who did not wish their children to be subjected to military propaganda. Information about these initiatives was passed on to a visiting journalist from New Zealand who was also briefly detained under Article 99. The article was also applied to a group of people in Jena, following publicity in the foreign news media about an attempt to hold a silent peace demonstration on 24 December 1982 and about activities in support of some imprisoned friends, including Roland Jahn whose case is described below. The group were arrested in the second half of January but released again on 25 February, without having been brought to trial.

Amnesty International attempted to send a delegate to the trial of Roland Jahn, whom it had adopted as a prisoner of conscience. However, the delegate was effectively denied a visa to the country. Roland Jahn, who had been arrested after riding a bicycle through Jena bearing a small Polish flag with the words "Solidarity with the Polish people", was sentenced on 17 January to one year and ten months' imprisonment for "public vilification" (Article 220 of the penal code) and "misuse of state symbols" (Article 222 of the penal code). On 25 February he was released together with those arrested in January. A few months later members of the group were given permission to leave the country at short notice. Roland Jahn, who did not wish to leave, was locked on board a train bound for the Federal Republic of Germany (FRG).

As in previous years, a number of would-be emigrants who tried in various ways to persuade local authorities to grant them exit visas were prosecuted for "impeding the activity of public bodies" under Article

214 of the penal code. Among these was a group in Jena who had applied unsuccessfully for exit visas and subsequently gathered silently for an hour in a circle outside the government offices responsible for handling their applications on Saturday mornings during July and August. They wore white to underline the non-violent nature of their demonstration and became known as the "White Circle". After a series of such demonstrations, a number of them were arrested at the end of August, six of them being charged and later sentenced to prison terms under Article 214. Amnesty International received reports of similar gatherings of would-be emigrants in other towns, some of whom were also arrested and convicted under Article 214.

During the year, Amnesty International called on the GDR to change laws under which people were imprisoned for the peaceful exercise of their right to freedom of expression and to release prisoners currently held under these laws, stating that such laws were incompatible with the GDR's international commitment to respect the right to freedom of expression, as spelt out in Article 19 of the International Covenant on Civil and Political Rights. The organization further expressed its concern about the regular practice of holding trials *in camera* contrary to Article 14 of the Covenant.

Amnesty International received no direct response from the GDR authorities and GDR embassies refused to meet delegates from the organization. In response to other inquiries a few GDR embassies denied the existence of political imprisonment in the GDR.

Amnesty International also adopted as prisoners of conscience those imprisoned for attempting to leave the country without permission, a crime under Article 213 of the penal code. Amnesty International considered that their imprisonment violated Article 12 of the International Covenant on Civil and Political Rights, which sets out the right to leave one's country. A typical case was that of Roger Stoof, a craftsman, who was arrested in Czechoslovakia while trying to cross the border to the FRG (GDR citizens may travel to Czechoslovakia without visas). He was returned to the GDR by the Czechoslovak authorities and subsequently sentenced to 18 months' imprisonment under Article 213.

Amnesty International also worked for the release of conscientious objectors to military service. The GDR makes some provision for those who object "for religious or similar reasons" to armed military service by allowing them to work in "construction units" on the construction of military installations and similar tasks. However, as there is no alternative service outside the country's military and defence system, Amnesty International adopted as prisoners of conscience those imprisoned for refusing for reasons of conscience to do either armed or unarmed service. Reports were received for the first time during the year of the imprisonment of conscripts who had applied for and had been refused the option of service in the "construction units".

In April 1983, Amnesty International submitted the cases of 14 prisoners of conscience in the GDR to the United Nations under the procedure for monitoring human rights violations set up under ECOSOC (Economic and Social Council) Resolution 728F.

As in previous years, prisoners were released to the FRG before completing their sentences in return for payment by the FRG Government. Press reports indicated that over 1,000 were released in this way during 1983. Amnesty International believed that the majority of these were prisoners of conscience. While welcoming these releases, Amnesty International sought to remind the GDR Government of its obligations in international law to release prisoners of conscience without conditions.

Greece

Amnesty International's main concerns were the continued imprisonment of Jehovah's Witnesses for refusing on conscientious grounds to perform military service and allegations that people charged with criminal offences had been tortured. During the year Amnesty International worked for the release of approximately 15 conscientious objectors, but was informed that the total number of imprisoned conscientious objectors was approximately 200 at any given time. However, no details were available about most of these prisoners.

On 21 January Amnesty International informed the Minister of Justice George Mangakis of reports that a Polish national imprisoned in Thessaloniki Prison had been in the prison hospital for more than three months as a result of having been tortured. Amnesty International asked for an investigation into the allegation and to be informed of the findings. No reply was received.

Further allegations of torture in police stations and prisons in various parts of Greece were made by both foreigners and Greeks imprisoned on criminal charges.

Hungary

Amnesty International was concerned about the imprisonment of conscientious objectors to military service and about the short-term arrest and harassment of people, some of them pacifists, who exercised their right to non-violent freedom of expression. The organization learned from unofficial sources of several political trials and was concerned about the reported restriction of public access to the courtroom in each case. Amnesty International was also concerned about four executions.

According to the Procurator General there were fewer offences against the state in 1983 than in the previous year when there were 57 such cases. It was thought that most of these offences in previous years had been related to people charged with "incitement". Under Article 148 of the criminal code people who incite hatred of Hungary's constitutional order or allies, or national, racial or religious hatred, may be imprisoned for one to five years. If the offence is committed before a "large public", or as a member of a group, the punishment is two to eight years' imprisonment. Balasz Benda, an 18-year-old high-school student, was reportedly tried by a court in Szeged on 2 May on charges under Article 148 of "incitement" carried out before a "large public". He was reportedly accused of having posted up bills in several places in Szeged in March demanding freedom of the press, freedom of conscience, speech and assembly, an independent peace movement, Hungary's political and economic independence, the withdrawal of foreign troops from Hungary and the unification of Transylvania (part of present-day Romania) with Hungary. The presiding judge reportedly refused members of the public entry to the courtroom. The trial was held *in camera*. Balasz Benda was found guilty, but received a sentence below the prescribed minimum: he was sentenced to six months' imprisonment suspended for two years.

Amnesty International was concerned about an increase in the harassment and short-term arrest of people for non-violently exercising their right to freedom of expression. Most of those involved were editors or publishers of unofficial publications. In January police briefly detained Janos Kis, Gyorgy Petri, Miklos Haraszti and Ferenc Koszeg, who were members of the editorial board of an unofficial magazine. In February they were fined for unauthorized publishing. In March police were reported to have raided several apartments in Budapest and detained six people overnight on charges of unauthorized publishing and distribution of unofficial literature. By May up to 100 people had reportedly been interrogated by police in connection with unofficial publishing acivities.

In late September Gabor Demszky, aged 31, the founder of the independent publishing house *AB*, was stopped by police close to his home while driving his car. He had previously been detained and questioned by police a number of times about his connection with *AB* and other dissident activities and had also been fined for unauthorized publishing. On this occasion, the two police officers reportedly searched his car and took a bag which contained a letter. Gabor Demszky was said to have protested and to have tried to recover the letter. In the course of an altercation which followed he was tear-gassed and beaten, resulting in his confinement in hospital for four days with concussion and bruises. In October he was charged with assaulting police officers, under Article 229 of the criminal code. Pending trial he remained at liberty. At his trial on 21 December police reportedly admitted beating the accused, but stated that Gabor Demszky had struggled with them and had kicked one of them. They themselves reportedly did not claim to have suffered serious injury. Gabor Demszky denied the charges against him, but was found guilty and sentenced to six months' imprisonment suspended for three years. Court officials restricted access to the trial and an observer sent by Amnesty International was not permitted to attend court proceedings, thus preventing the organization from making a proper assessment of the evidence in the case. It noted, however, that the accused had a history of being harassed by the authorities in connection with his exercise of the right to freedom of expression.

Military service is compulsory in Hungary and the law does not provide for alternative civilian service outside the military system for those who refuse conscription for reasons of conscience. People who refuse conscription may be punished under Article 336 of the criminal code with up to five years' imprisonment (five to 15 years in time of war). Since 1977, however, members of several numerically small Christian sects, including the Nazarenes, have been allowed to do unarmed military service. According to one unofficial report, in mid-1983 there were some 130 conscientious objectors serving sentences in Baracska prison (where conscientious objectors are generally sent), nearly all of whom were Jehovah's Witnesses. Amnesty International did not have details of these cases, but adopted five Roman Catholic conscientious objectors, three of whom were sentenced and imprisoned in 1983 under Article 336. Janos Magyar, Laszlo Mohos and Laszlo Habos received sentences of between 30 and 34 months' imprisonment for refusing conscription on grounds of conscience. Janos Magyar and Laszlo Mohos, both members of pacifist Roman Catholic communities from Szekesfehervar, were arrested in early 1983.

There were also reports that other pacifists, members of an unofficial "Peace Group for Dialogue", had been briefly detained. In July it was reported that 15 peace activists from Western Europe had been arrested and expelled from the country and that 20 Hungarian citizens, members of the Dialogue group, had been detained by police but released after questioning. At the end of July the group announced that it had decided to dissolve itself because of harassment by the authorities.

In November 1983 Amnesty International appealed for the release of Kurt Krimmel, a citizen of the Federal Republic of Germany who was arrested on 24 September after he had attempted to smuggle his sister-in-law's child from Hungary into Austria. The mother, a citizen of the German Democratic Republic, had crossed from Hungary into Austria several days before without official authorization. Following his arrest Kurt Krimmel was allegedly held for 40 days in solitary confinement and his health was reportedly poor. His trial began on 15 December but was adjourned until 29 December so that he could receive a medical examination. At the hearing on 29 December the court ordered his release on condition that he leave the country immediately.

Amnesty International learned of four executions and of the imposition of two death sentences; in all cases those accused had been convicted of murder. The executions of Laszlo Tibor Bencsik and of Mihaly Nyiri were reported on 4 January and 13 July respectively. Amnesty International had previously appealed to the Presidential Council to commute their death sentences after it had learned that these had been confirmed by the Supreme Court. It was also reported that Kalman Orsos and Jozsef Kondics were executed on 15 July and 2 December respectively.

Ireland

Amnesty International continued to be concerned about the case of Eamonn ("Nicky") Kelly, a member of the Irish Republican Socialist Party who was arrested in 1976 and subsequently convicted of participating in an armed robbery and sentenced to 12 years' imprisonment.

After sending observers to court hearings in the case in 1980 and 1982, Amnesty International wrote to the Minister of Justice in

November and December 1982 to express concern about the standards applied in the case regarding the acceptance of confessions in evidence in the face of complaints that they had been made after physical ill-treatment and prolonged, exhaustive questioning (see *Amnesty International Report 1983*).

The office of the Minister of Justice replied in February 1983 that in the absence of new evidence it would not interfere in the decisions taken by the courts in the case.

In May 1983 an Amnesty International delegate went to Ireland to gather further information on the case. On 19 May Amnesty International asked the Minister of Justice for a meeting to discuss the case. The Minister's office replied that the Minister would not meet an Amnesty International delegation.

In June Amnesty International sent a detailed letter to the government outlining its concerns. Amnesty International expressed appreciation for the position of respect for the courts enunciated by the government, but said that doubts remained about the fairness of Mr Kelly's conviction. Amnesty International urged the government to take remedial action. The organization subsequently published its letter to the government.

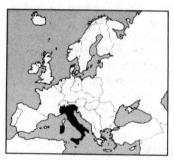

Italy

The excessive length of judicial proceedings involving political prisoners remained a principal concern of Amnesty International. Allegations of torture and ill-treatment of detainees reported in 1982 were the subject of judicial investigations and in one case police officers were sentenced to suspended prison terms following legal proceedings. Amnesty International continued to work for the release of imprisoned conscientious objectors.

The trial known as "7 April" was of special concern to Amnesty International. (See *Amnesty International Reports 1980, 1981, 1982* and *1983*). The majority of the defendants had been in custody since 1979. Amnesty International had sent observers to the trial on three occasions since it opened on 7 June 1982 and the trial continued at the end of 1983. In February 1983 Dr Kurt Meier of the Zurich Bar visited Rome as an Amnesty International delegate to discuss the progress of the trial with interested parties.

In a review of its concerns in Italy, published in April 1983, Amnesty International criticized judicial provisions regarding the length of preventive detention (*carcerazione preventiva*). Cases which carry prison sentences of 20 years or more on conviction may lead to defendants spending a total of 10 years and eight months in prison before a final verdict is reached on the case.

The situation regarding preventive detention came under mounting criticism in Italian legal circles in 1983. The Minister of Justice, Mino Martinazzoli, acknowledged that the length of time defendants spent awaiting trial was "excessive". The practice of filing multiple charges in political cases in order to ensure "the maximum permissible period of preventive detention" was criticized by Giuliano Vassalli, the President of the Justice Commission of the Senate.

Amnesty International was aware that the government was attempting to reduce the maximum length of preventive detention. A draft bill proposed by the government and approved by the Council of Ministers on 4 October 1983 would cut the maximum length of preventive detention by one third (to eight years). However, Amnesty International believed that even if the current government bill were to become law preventive detention in Italy would still be extremely long, and its concern about the situation of those prisoners being held in long-term detention would be unchanged, since the draft bill referred only to cases which may arise in the future.

Amnesty International noted with concern that some courts used their powers under emergency legislation to increase the already excessive length of preventive detention. One detainee, Giustino Cortiana, had his request for provisional liberty rejected by the Court of Assizes in Rome, even though the judicial limit of two years and eight months pending sentencing in the trial of first instance had expired. Giustino Cortiana had originally been charged with being a member of the Red Brigades, a left-wing armed group. He was acquitted of this charge by an appeal court in Milan in March 1983, but was charged in the meantime with membership of an armed band in connection with the "7 April" case. He was due to be granted provisional liberty once the judicial time limit for this charge had expired. However, in November 1983 the Court of Assizes in Rome rejected Giustino Cortiana's request, on the basis of Article 112 of the penal code. This allows for an extension of the normal time limit if the number of persons alleged to have been involved in a crime is five or more. This in turn implies he could be held for five years and four months, pending sentencing in the trial of the first instance.

Amnesty International became increasingly concerned that long-term detention was being further lengthened in some cases by the alteration of charges, or by the bringing of new ones by judges in other parts of the country, while judicial proceedings were already underway.

On 21 June 1983 several defendants in the "7 April" trial in Rome, including Luciano Ferrari-Bravo and Emilio Vesce, were issued with fresh warrants by the Deputy State Prosecutor for Padua, Dr Pietro Calogero, in connection with possession of arms between 1971 and 1979 (Article 21 of Law No. 110 of 18 April 1975). An *Amnesty International Newsletter* article published in August 1983 said that "The bringing of a new charge at this stage — apparently unsupported by new evidence against defendants who are already on trial in connection with charges relating to an armed band — will permit a further extension of up to four years' preventive detention on this separate charge. Some of the arms in question were the subject of a separate trial of different defendants in July 1980."

In this case, the investigating judge, Dr Palombarini, ordered that the defendants be released in October 1983, on the grounds that the new charge should be subsumed under the original armed band charge, for which the judicial time limit had already expired.

In 1982 there had been a sharp increase in the number of allegations of torture and other forms of ill-treatment of detainees in relation to arrests made at the time of the kidnapping of NATO Chief-of-Staff, Brigadier-General James Lee Dozier (see *Amnesty International Report 1983*). Judicial inquiries were set up into these allegations in Rome, Padua, Venice, Viterbo and Verona shortly after the General's release in January 1982.

In July 1983, four police officers on trial in Padua as a result of these investigations were found guilty of abusing their authority while interrogating a member of the Red Brigades, Cesare Di Lenardo, by beating him, tying him to a table and forcing him to drink large quantities of water. The officers were sentenced to suspended prison terms of one year to 14 months. A fifth officer was not put on trial because he was elected a parliamentary deputy in the June 1983 elections and thus benefitted from immunity.

In November 1983 the Venice tribunal investigating similar torture allegations — including some made by other police officers — decided to end its inquiry on the grounds of a lack of sufficient evidence. As regards the inquiries in other cities, Amnesty International was unaware of any findings being made public by the end of the year.

Amnesty International received no new allegations of ill-treatment of detainees during 1983.

There was a decline in the number of conscientious objectors to military service adopted as prisoners of conscience by Amnesty International. As a result of the 1981 reform of the Military Code, which introduced an appeal structure, conscientious objectors were generally released from prison pending appeal. They may also be released prior to being sentenced in order to make new requests to perform alternative, civilian, service. In the case of Franco Fornasari, a pacifist song-writer, his application for alternative civilian service was turned down by the Ministry of Defence, reportedly because his general behaviour was "manifestly in contrast with the moral principles" required of conscientious objectors. The local *carabinieri* had opposed Franco Fornasari's request for alternative service stating, among other things, that although of "normal moral conduct" he had a "poor public reputation", had taken part in unauthorized demonstrations, and had been involved in the left-wing Italian Workers' Autonomy movement, an allegation he strenuously denied. He was arrested on 11 December 1982 but released nine days later from the military prison of Forte Boccea to allow him to make a second request for alternative service.

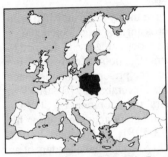

Poland

Amnesty International was concerned about the imprisonment of large numbers of prisoners of conscience, allegations of ill-treatment of political prisoners and the use of the death penalty.

According to official figures, on 4 January 1983 about 1,000 people, most of whom Amnesty International believed to be prisoners of conscience were still in prison and an additional 500 people were held awaiting trial for politically motivated offences.

On 21 July, the day before martial law was officially lifted, the *Sejm* (parliament) passed an amnesty law affecting 21,571 people, including 3,666 political offenders, of whom 2,123 had been imprisoned. Under the terms of the amnesty law, men over 21 who had received sentences of over three years' imprisonment had their sentences reduced by a half, and all men under 21 at the time of the offence were released, as were all women regardless of age, and all men over 21 sentenced to up to three years' imprisonment. In most cases those benefiting from it were liable to serve the remainder of their sentence in addition to a new penalty if they committed another similar offence before 31 December 1985.

By 22 July 1983, 687 individuals had already been unconditionally pardoned under a special "speeded up" procedure introduced after martial law was suspended in December 1982. Another 122 applications had been turned down by the State Council's Clemency Commission, because these concerned detainees "who had performed leading roles in organizing activities banned under martial law, had used terror, intimidation, or had criminal records" or who were said to have shown a hostile attitude in prison. Among those released from prison by 20 August were prisoners of conscience adopted by Amnesty International such as Zofia Romaszewska, who was sentenced to five years' imprisonment in February 1983 for activities in connection with the underground radio *Solidarnosc* (Solidarity), and Ewa Kubasiewicz, who was sentenced in 1982 to 10 years' imprisonment for violating martial law regulations, later reduced in a retrial to three years suspended.

Among those also released were individuals who had been arrested but not yet tried and sentenced, including the press spokesperson of the banned independent trade union Solidarity, Janusz Onyszkiewicz, and Solidarity adviser, Bronislaw Geremek, and Zbigniew Belz and Andrzej Sóbieraj, local Solidarity leaders.

At least 20 people were not eligible for amnesty since they had been sentenced for attempted illegal border crossings or were convicted or accused of political offences of the most serious category, ie deemed to be against the "Fundamental Political and Economic Interests of the Polish People's Republic". They included the prisoners of conscience Edmund Baluka, a former leader of the December 1970 strikes in Szczecin who was sentenced to five years' imprisonment on 30 June 1983 on charges relating to his alleged anti-state activities during his stay outside Poland in the period 1973/1981; and Robert Leszek Moczulski, Tadeusz Stanski and Romuald Szeremietiew, leaders of an unofficial opposition group called the Confederation of an Independent Poland (KPN), who were sentenced to five years' imprisonment in October 1982.

Eleven people awaiting trial were also excluded from the general provisions of the amnesty law: four members of the *Komitet Obrony Robotnikow* (KOR), the Committee for the Defence of Workers, Jacek Kuron, Adam Michnik, Henryk Wujec and Zbigniew Romaszewski (the latter already sentenced at an earlier trial), and seven leading Solidarity officials, Jan Rulewski, Seweryn Jaworski, Karol Modzelewski, Grzegorz Palka, Andrzej Rozplochowski, Andrzej Gwiazda and Marian Jurczyk. At the end of 1983 both groups were facing charges of "preparing, in agreement with others, activities aiming to overthrow the Polish socio-political system by force". Their trials were announced several times as imminent, but had not taken place by the end of 1983.

The security forces continued to arrest large numbers of people during demonstrations in cities throughout the country. According to official statements, about 1000 people were arrested in 15 Polish provinces during demonstrations in May, most of whom were reportedly released after several hours and were fined. Numerous arrests were also reported during the Pope's visit to Nowa Huta on 22 June and during demonstrations on 31 August, the third anniversary of the birth of Solidarity

At least 60 individuals were detained in December during demonstrations commemorating the workers killed during street protests along the Baltic Coast in December 1970.

Arrests were also reported of people involved in the underground structures of Solidarity. The number of such arrests increased greatly during December. According to official reports in the Polish media, more than 250 arrests took place in Wroclaw (55), Szczecin (44), Gdansk (36) and other parts of the country. In Warsaw, Kielce and Bydgoszcz, 13 members of the All-Polish Committee for Farmers' Resistance (OKOR) were detained, including two of its leaders, Jozef Teliga and Wienczyslaw Nowacki.

In nearly all these cases the accused were charged with continuing trade union activities, anti-state activities, disseminating and printing of illegal publications, activities connected with the underground radio *Solidarnosc* or calling for illegal gatherings (mostly under Articles 271 and 278 of the criminal code).

Hundreds of others, including trade union activists and defence lawyers of human rights and trade union activists were detained for periods of up to 48 hours. On 27 December Wladyslaw Sidorowicz, a doctor, was detained for 48 hours because he refused to hand over to the police the file of Krystyna Frasyniuk, the wife of the prisoner of conscience Wladyslaw Frasyniuk. In some cases, people were repeatedly detained for short periods and subsequently released without having been charged. Lech Walesa, the chairperson of Solidarity, was detained in this way on several occasions.

Political trials continued to take place throughout 1983 but the number reported in the media declined and the list of crimes subject to summary proceedings was reduced when martial law was suspended in December 1982.

A number of lawyers encountered increasing difficulties while trying to represent the interests of charged Solidarity activists, including Stanislaw Afenda who was reportedly suspended from carrying out his legal functions in July, and Piotr Andrzejewski,who was suspended from his professional duties by the Supreme Court on 14 December for "contempt of court" at a trial in 1982.

On 22 July, when martial law was formally lifted, a number of features of martial law were permanently or provisionally incorporated into the constitution and other legislation. A new law on the Ministry of Internal affairs was passed by the *Sejm* on 14 July, whereby people who are considered a risk for state security and public order could be taken into preventive detention without the orders or agreement of a prosecutor or judge.

Some of the amendments to the criminal code that became law on 29 July were further reaching than the corresponding martial law decree regulations of 1981. A paragraph was added to Article 282a allowing people to be sentenced to up to three years' imprisonment for organizing or leading a protest meeting. In a clear reference to organizations like Solidarity, membership of organizations that had been banned or refused legal status also became punishable by up to three years' imprisonment (amendment of Article 278, paragraph 1).

The jurisdiction of the Military Courts was reduced but one extension promulgated under martial law remained in force permanently – that concerning offences against the fundamental interests of the Polish People's Republic (Article 565, paragraph 2 of the Criminal Procedures Code).

Amnesty International received a number of reports that prisoners had been subjected to cruel, inhuman and degrading treatment. Wladyslaw Frasyniuk was reportedly beaten while held in Leczyca Prison in August. Nine political prisoners in Barczewo Prison reportedly wrote to the Polish Council of State in December stating that they would go on hunger-strike to protest against their ill-treatment. They were subsequently reported to have been subjected to beatings, sprayed with cold water and forced to undress in cold cells. The prisoners involved were the three KPN leaders mentioned above and six Solidarity and trade union leaders, P. Bednarz, A. Slowik, J. Kropiwnicki, P. Kosmowski, E. Baluka and W. Frasyniuk, again. Complaints and protests about prison conditions and ill-treatment allegedly often resulted in disciplinary punishments such as the "hard bed", the "tiger cell" (cage) or the *kabryna* (punishment cell). Such allegations were frequently made with respect to Braniewo, Strzelin and Hrubieszow prisons, where a number of hunger-strikes reportedly took place to protest against bad prison conditions. At the end of the year about 20 Solidarity activists were on a hunger-strike in Strzelin Prison to protest against rotten food, lack of basic medical care, insufficient contact with families, unhygienic conditions and to demand political prisoner status. Some of them had reportedly been forcibly fed.

Amnesty International received frequent reports that members or supporters of Solidarity had been beaten about the head, body and legs with rubber truncheons, kicked, punched or forced to run the gauntlet of truncheon blows between a double row of police.

Most of these allegations concerned ill-treatment at the time of arrest, during transport in militia vehicles and above all while in custody at militia headquarters.

Seweryn Jaworski, a Solidarity leader awaiting trial in Rakowiecka Remand Prison in Warsaw, was reportedly beaten by guards several times in May and kept in isolation for wearing a badge with the national colours of Poland. He was reportedly punched in the abdomen and in the neck and threatened "he would not leave here alive". At least five of a group of 11 miners from Lubin who had been charged with "terrorist activities" in 1982 reportedly complained at their trial in November that plastic bags had been put over their heads until they nearly suffocated and that they were beaten on the soles of their feet.

Eleven people reportedly died in unexplained circumstances during or shortly after periods in police custody. Most of them had been Solidarity activists. In at least one case, that of the 19-year-old high school student, Grzegorz Przemyk, allegations that the death was caused by police ill-treatment were supported by affidavits of the findings of the prosecutor's office. He was reportedly arrested on 12 May in Warsaw and taken to a police station in Jezuicka Street. He died in Solec Hospital two days later from severe injuries to the spleen and liver. On 16 May the prosecutor of Warsaw Srodmiescie (inner town) opened an investigation into his case. On 23 December formal indictments were issued against two civic militia members, two members of the ambulance service and two doctors. No date for the trial had been set by the end of the year.

During 1983 nine death sentences were passed, seven for murder. A diplomat who defected and an academic were both sentenced to death *in absentia* on charges of high treason and espionage respectively. In addition, one death sentence passed in 1982 was upheld by Lodz Provincial Court. The Polish press reported that Waldemar Krakos was executed on 10 October. He had originally been sentenced to 25 years' imprisonment for a murder committed in January. The Procurator General and the Minister of Justice appealed against the sentence. The Supreme Court subsequently sentenced him to death and his appeal for clemency was turned down by the State Council. The executions of Tadeusz Wencel and Julian Koltan took place on 8 July and 12 December respectively, the latter having been sentenced to death in 1982 for murder and attempted murder.

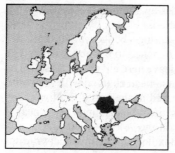

Romania

Amnesty International was concerned about the imprisonment of prisoners of conscience, most of them would-be emigrants. In several cases where Amnesty International had details of trial proceedings relating to political charges, defendants were not accorded fair trials. The organization received allegations of the ill-treatment, following arrest, of people held on political charges. Prison conditions were described as harsh. Amnesty International was also concerned about the imposition of 12 death sentences.

Amnesty International continued to receive reports of people who had been harassed by the authorities or imprisoned for having applied to emigrate or for having attempted to leave the country without official authorization after this had been refused or delayed. Ilie Savu, aged 32, a mechanic from Bucharest, and Paul Barolescu were adopted as prisoners of conscience by Amnesty International after being sentenced to two and one-and-a-half years' imprisonment respectively by the municipal court of Bucharest Sector II in September on charges of "fraudulent crossing of the frontier". This is an offence punishable under Article 245 of the criminal code with up to three years' imprisonment. They were reportedly arrested by Yugoslav border guards after they had dived into the Danube from a Romanian excursion boat and had swum to the Yugoslav bank. After serving a 25-day prison sentence in Yugoslavia they were reportedly returned to Romania. Ilie Savu was reportedly not allowed to see his lawyer or his parents during investigation proceedings; his lawyer was permitted to see his court dossier only two days before the trial. In a similar case, Alex Pop, a 26-year-old Pentecostalist from Timisoara, was sentenced to three years' imprisonment. He had been arrested and returned to Romania by the Yugoslav authorities after crossing the Yugoslav border.

Amnesty International appealed to the authorities for the release of Constantin Buica, an artist aged 27, and Vicentiu Boambes, a technician aged 26, who were arrested in Bucharest between 15 and 19 August after they had gone on hunger-strike in protest against the refusal of the authorities to grant them permission to leave Romania. They were allegedly beaten by police after being taken into custody.

Individuals continued to be imprisoned for the non-violent exercise of their human rights on charges of "parasitical" or "anarchic conduct" under decree 153/1970, which provides for summary trial without the right to legal defence and prescribes sentences of up to six months' imprisonment or "corrective labour without deprivation of liberty". Amnesty International continued to receive reports of the harassment and arrest of religious believers, in most cases members of Protestant evangelical sects, and adopted four Baptists from Caransebes and Timisoara as prisoners of conscience. The four, Dinu Virgil Gadea, Corneliu Refec, Ovidiu Podborschi and Petru Marianec, were members of an unofficial "Organization Committee of the Young Baptists Union" who had sent a petition to Church representatives in March, asking them to press for the re-establishment of the Young Baptists Union which had been dissolved by the authorities in 1950. This petition reportedly stated that such an organization would enable young Baptists to take a united stand against various forms of state repression against religious believers, such as discrimination in education and employment, house-searches and interrogation by police, and in the case of believers found distributing religious literature, arrest, ill-treatment and imprisonment. Shortly afterwards they and three other signatories of the petition were reportedly detained by the police for questioning and threatened with imprisonment if they persisted in their demands. On 10 August they were among a group of Baptists who were arrested after they had held a public demonstration in which they carried posters calling on the government to cease the harassment of believers and enter into a dialogue with them. They were released but re-arrested on 15 August and tried and sentenced the same day under decree 153/1970 in Caransebes. They were sentenced to four months' imprisonment, increased on appeal to six months.

Amnesty International continued to appeal to the Romanian authorities for the release of the prisoner of conscience Father Calciu-Dumitreasa, aged 57, a Romanian Orthodox priest, serving a 10-year sentence imposed in 1979 (see *Amnesty International Report 1980*). It also appealed for the release of two men from Radauti imprisoned under Article 166 of the criminal code, which makes "propaganda against the socialist state" an offence punishable by between five and 15 years' imprisonment. The two men were Petru Cazacu and Dragos Oloieru (see *Amnesty International Report 1983*). Petru Cazacu was sentenced to six years' imprisonment in February 1982 (later reduced to three and a half years on appeal) for writing letters complaining about alleged corruption among local officials.

Amnesty International sought details of charges brought against two ethnic Hungarians from Miercurea-Ciuc, Laszlo Buzas, an economist, and Erno Borbely, a high-school teacher, who were reportedly arrested in November 1982. Their arrest appeared to be connected with the arrest of at least 10 other ethnic Hungarians at that time, which followed the publication of a memorandum in an unofficial Hungarian-language journal produced in Romania. The memorandum was addressed to participants of the Madrid meeting of the Conference on Security and Cooperation in Europe and claimed that the Hungarian minority was the object of an official policy of assimilation. Although most of those arrested were released after a few days, Laszlo Buzas and Erno Borbely were said to have been sentenced to prison sentences of up to eight years by a military court in 1983.

Amnesty International received allegations in 1983 that several ethnic Hungarians who had been arrested in November 1982 had been beaten while being held in police custody. Among these was Karoly Toth. Police allegedly beat his head against a wall and beat him over the back with truncheons.

Prison conditions were reported to be harsh, with poor food, hygiene and medical care. Prisoners were allegedly sometimes denied the right to visits by relatives.

Amnesty International was also concerned about the use of the death penalty. At least 12 death sentences were reported in the Romanian press, whereas Amnesty International did not learn of any such reports the previous year. Although there were grounds for believing that death sentences had been imposed in 1982 which were not reported in the press, the available information suggested that in 1983 there was an increase both in the number of death sentences handed down and in the number of offences for which this penalty was imposed. Six of the 12 reported death sentences were for murder; the remainder were for economic offences which did not involve loss of life; in April Ion Zangorescu was sentenced to death for stealing pork from a meat factory; in November death sentences imposed on Aurelian Pircalabescu and Viorel Boceanu for "robbery to the detriment of public property with particularly serious consequences" were confirmed by the Supreme Court; and in December a military court in Tirgoviste sentenced Vasile Boiangiu, Teodor Manciulea and Ilea Florea to death for undermining the national economy by stealing and selling meat "to the serious detriment of public property". Amnesty International did not know if any death sentences were carried out but was concerned that the imposition of the death penalty for economic offences appeared to reflect a change in sentencing policy. In April 1979 a Romanian representative informed the Human Rights Committee that in the past 15 years the death penalty had not been applied in a single case involving an offence against state property, and that under new legislation being drafted at that time the death penalty would be applied exclusively as an exceptional measure and as an alternative in cases of homicide, treason, espionage and aerial piracy having particularly serious consequences.

Spain

The torture and ill-treatment of detainees, principally people detained under anti-terrorist laws, continued to be Amnesty International's main concern. Prolonged incommunicado detention, which Amnesty International considered to facilitate torture, was still allowed and new procedural laws on legal assistance, which came into effect at the end of the year, continued to restrict severely detainees' right of access to legal counsel. Police officers were found guilty of torturing and ill-treating detainees in a few significant court cases but the majority of accusations made against the police failed to reach a hearing. Amnesty International sent observers to two trials involving freedom of expression and numerous prosecutions were pending of individuals accused of criticizing the state or its institutions.

In 1983, 691 people, mostly in the Basque country, were detained under anti-terrorist laws, many of them for alleged links with *Euskadi Ta Askatasuna* (ETA), Basque Homeland and Liberty, the armed Basque group allegedly responsible for many of the 43 politically motivated killings recorded during the year. Many of them were subsequently released without charge.

Detainees can be held under the anti-terrorist laws for up to 10 days in incommunicado detention with no access to legal assistance following which they must be released or produced in court. Under the Ministry of the Interior's rules, officially authorised doctors are supposed to examine all such detainees to ensure that torture or ill-treatment does not occur. Provincial court judges also have the power to investigate the conditions under which detainees are held, but Amnesty International believed these safeguards were insufficient to protect the well-being of those detainees held incommunicado and denied legal assistance during the crucial preliminary stages of police interrogation. Two cases in particular illustrated the inadequacies of the system.

Joaquín Olano Balda, a 25-year-old mechanic from Lasarte (Provincia de Guipúzcoa), was arrested by the Civil Guard at dawn on 29 July and held incommunicado under the anti-terrorist law in the *Guardia Civil*, Civil Guard, station in San Sebastián. The duty judge ordered the official doctor to examine the detainee after receiving a private complaint that screams and cries, accompanied by loud radio music, were coming from the building where he was held. Following the examination he was admitted on 30 July to the Red Cross Hospital in San Sebastián, under guard and still incommunicado.

The official medical report remained confidential at the end of 1983 but the report of the doctor at the Red Cross Hospital recorded that he was suffering from concussion, cuts on the head, multiple grazes and bruises (ecchymoses) on the back, abdomen and arms. A statement issued by the police on 30 July claimed that he had been injured following an attempt to escape and as a consequence of efforts to restrain him.

He was permitted to see a lawyer while in hospital only when Civil Guards were present in his bedroom. He made a judicial declaration that he had been tortured and on 11 August he was discharged from hospital and taken to Martutene prison in San Sebastián. He alleged that he was beaten on the head with a telephone book, hit on the body, given electric shocks, and that he was partially asphyxiated with water and plastic bags. He subsequently alleged that he had been beaten again by Civil Guards in the van during the transfer from hospital to prison. His lawyer noted the existence of new marks on his back.

On 14 August, Joaquin Olano was admitted to the Provincial Hospital of Guipúcoa for medical examinations and tests. On 18 August he was transferred back to Martutene prison, where he remained at the end of the year, not having been formally charged.

José María Olarra, the Assistant Mayor of the town of Villabona (Provincia de Guipúzcoa), was arrested by the Civil Guard on 26 October with his two brothers and two other people, all of whom were examined by the official doctor on the day of their detention. The doctor certified that none of them claimed to have been ill-treated and that there were no visible signs of such treatment. In the meantime the Civil Guard unit had received permission from the Minister of the Interior to hold the five detainees in extended incommunicado detention on suspicion of having links with ETA. The National Court, which is judicially responsible for such detainees, gave its formal assent to this two days later.

According to José María Olarra's subsequent statement, ill-treatment began as soon as the doctor had left on 26 October. He alleged that the leader of a group of eight or 10 men in plain clothes kicked him in the testicles and that he was then indiscriminately punched and slapped on the head and body by the others. He described how he was subsequently secured to a device which allowed his head to be submerged in filthy water and also how he was partially asphyxiated with plastic bags.

José María Olarra's brothers were freed on 29 October and the emergency service of the local hospital certified that they had been bruised on the chest, abdomen and back. José María Olarra was hooded and taken by road with other detainees to Madrid where he was released on bail by the National Court on 2 November. An official doctor examined him for a second time a week after his arrest and certified the existence of 10cm long abrasions on his chest, as well as bruising on his back and groin and grazing on the arms.

The Civil Guard refused Olarra's lawyer and a notary access to him throughout the entire period of his detention. The three brothers made a formal judicial declaration of torture and ill-treatment and, after investigation, two members of the Civil Guard were detained. They were released unconditionally on 2 December by order of the Provincial Court, but the inquiry was reportedly still being pursued at the end of 1983.

Amnesty International was concerned about certain features of a new law severely restricting the right to legal assistance of detainees held incommunicado under the anti-terrorist law, which came into force on 28 December 1983. Under the new law detainees are unable to inform relatives that they have been detained, lawyers are not freely chosen and have no right to interview the detainee, even after the "investigation" (*la practica de la diligencia*).

Formal denunciations of torture or ill-treatment to the court have rarely been successful in achieving a hearing, but in 1983 there were two important cases.

On 29 March the Provincial Court in Bilbao found two police officers guilty of torturing and threatening Dr Xavier Onaindia, a detainee held in 1979 under the anti-terrorist law. He was released without charge after nine days incommunicado detention during which time he was reportedly beaten, deprived of sleep and tortured with electric shocks. The officers were sentenced to 10 months' imprisonment and 10 years' special suspension of duties.

Two police officers in Madrid were acquitted in December of responsibility for inflicting the burns and bruises revealed by the autopsy on the body of José Arregui, who had died in police custody after nine days of incommunicado detention in February 1981. The court held that the responsibility of the two officers was not proven. The police had submitted a list of 72 people who had come into contact with the deceased. The state prosecutor appealed against the judgment, but the result of this appeal was not known at the end of 1983.

Amnesty International continued to be concerned about the prosecution of people for the non-violent exercise of the right to freedom of expression.

In October 1983 Amnesty International sent Maître David Lachat of the Geneva Bar to observe the trial in the Supreme Court of Miguel Castells de Arteche, a prominent Basque lawyer and former Senator in the Spanish parliament. He was charged with having insulted the government by writing an article, published in July 1979, which concluded that the government and its forces must lie behind the killing of Basque dissidents. He was sentenced to one year's imprisonment which was the subject of an appeal before the Constitutional Tribunal. The prosecution had requested a sentence of six years and one day.

Amnesty International sent Dr Hans Rau of the Max Planck Institute in Hamburg to observe the trials in November 1983 before the Supreme Court in Madrid of 16 parliamentary members and town councillors who were in the Basque coalition party *Herri Batasuna*. They had been charged with insulting the King as head of state and raising public disorder by singing the Basque nationalist anthem during the King's visit to the Basque parliament in Guernica. (See *Amnesty International Report 1983*).

Amnesty International was concerned about the prosecution for insulting the King and causing public disorder and the possible restriction of the right of *Herri Batasuna* members to express freely their political views, irrespective of protocol.

The accused were acquitted of insulting the King and found guilty of public disorder and sentenced to three months' imprisonment and a 20,000 pesetas' fine in 15 cases and five months' imprisonment and a 50,000 pesetas' fine in one case. The results of appeals against these sentences were not known at the end of 1983.

Switzerland

Amnesty International was concerned about the imprisonment of conscientious objectors and the lack of any alternative civilian service.

Alternative service was the subject of increasing public discussion pending a new referendum, scheduled for February 1984. The referendum proposal, put forward by an independent group of citizens, advocates the establishment of an alternative period of civilian service one and a half times longer than the period of military service.

An affirmative referendum result would require a change to the Swiss Constitution. Article 81 of the military penal code would continue to apply in the interim. Under Article 81 all conscientious objectors are sentenced to terms of imprisonment, even in cases where the military tribunal recognizes a "severe conflict of conscience" on religious or ethical grounds. If the objection to military service is considered to be primarily political, a longer term of imprisonment is imposed.

In 1983 Amnesty International worked for the release of 10 conscientious objectors, who had been sentenced to terms of imprisonment of between five and 15 months. Some sentences were reduced on appeal. Under Article 36 of the military penal code all defendants were subsequently excluded from service in the army.

On 15 December 1982 Josef Egloff, an architect, was sentenced to 15 months' imprisonment by a military tribunal at Lucerne for refusing to perform military service. The court's decision was based primarily on what it considered to be serious inconsistencies in the defendant's attitude to non-violence and it stated that Josef Egloff's refusal showed an attitude of "clear rebellion against the state". The sentence was reduced on appeal to eight months by a military court at Aarau on 8 March 1983. Josef Egloff maintained that the first court had misconstrued his arguments concerning non-violence; the appeal court found the length of the original sentence "inappropriate".

Olivier Maulini, a pacifist, was sentenced to eight months' imprisonment on 16 December 1982 for refusing to perform military service, and began his prison sentence at Bellechasse on 21 June 1983. He stated that he would have been willing to carry out an alternative civilian service had it existed, but objected on ethical grounds to military service.

Although the tribunal at Aigle accepted the moral basis of his beliefs it concluded that Olivier Maulini had not been able to prove that he was the victim of a serious conflict of conscience and his sentence was therefore not reduced.

Martin Karlen was given a relatively short sentence of five months' imprisonment by a military court at Berne, which found that "his way of life accords with his high ethical and religious convictions". Martin Karlen began his sentence on 28 February at the prison of Realta in Cazis.

In December 1983 Amnesty International was investigating the case of Simeon Jakob, a former primary school teacher who was sentenced to 10 months' imprisonment by a military court at Lucerne on 9 November 1983. At his trial he stated that he had become increasingly uneasy about the nature of the military training he had originally agreed to and that he had become a member of an agricultural collective, influenced by ideas of non-violence. At the end of the year Simeon Jakob was appealing to have his sentence reduced.

Turkey

Amnesty International continued to be concerned about the imprisonment of large numbers of prisoners of conscience; widespread and systematic torture and ill-treatment of political prisoners; and the imposition and use of the death penalty. The organization was also concerned that Iranian political refugees were returned to Iran from Turkey.

According to official figures, on 30 June 1983 there were 21,046 political prisoners held in military prisons, but after the ratification of sentences by the Military Court of Cassation political prisoners are transferred to civil prisons and no figure was available for the number of political prisoners in civil prisons. Amnesty International knew of several hundred prisoners who had been charged or convicted on account of their non-violent political or religious beliefs or activities, but believed that the actual number might be much higher.

Following elections in November 1983, civilian government was restored to Turkey, but martial law continued to be in force throughout the country and political offences continued to be tried in martial law courts.

Most prisoners of conscience known to Amnesty International were charged or convicted under Articles 141 and 142 of the Turkish penal code which respectively prohibit "membership of an illegal organization" and "making communist propaganda". These articles were generally used to imprison left-wing political activists, as well as journalists, publishers, writers, translators and academics. Hundreds of alleged members of the illegal Turkish Communist Party, were imprisoned for offences under Articles 141 and 142, as well as members of parties which were legal before they were banned after the September 1980 military coup, such as the Turkish Workers' Party (TIP), the Turkish Socialist Workers' Party (TSIP) and the Turkish Workers' and Peasants' Party (TIKP). Members of TÖB-DER, the teachers' association, and of the Progressive Women's Association (IKD) were also imprisoned under these articles.

On 14 November in Istanbul 23 leading members of the Turkish Peace Association were convicted of offences under Article 141 and received five or eight year prison sentences, to be followed by periods of internal exile (see *Amnesty International Report 1983*). Initially taken into custody in February 1982, most of them were released in December 1982 while their trial continued, but all those present in court when the verdict was announced were immediately reimprisoned.

Among those sentenced to eight years' imprisonment were Mahmut Dikerdem, a former Turkish ambassador; Reha Isvan, former Deputy Head of the Istanbul Department of Education; Erdal Atabek, President of the Turkish Medical Association; Ali Sirmen, a journalist, and Metin Özek, a Professor of Psychiatry. Those sentenced to five years' imprisonment included Orhan Apaydin, former President of the Istanbul Bar Association, and Melih Tümer, former Dean of the Istanbul Academy of Political Sciences.

Amnesty International learned of the prosecution of many writers, publishers, translators and journalists under Article 142. Many remained free pending the completion of legal proceedings, but a number of those convicted received lengthy prison sentences, including Recep Marasli, the director and editor in charge of Komal Publishing House in Istanbul, which specialized in the history of the Kurdish ethnic minority in Turkey. He was already serving a four-year sentence passed in July 1982 for publishing a book on Kurdish issues when, in January and May 1983, he received two further sentences of 12 years' and three years' imprisonment because of other publications variously alleged to have weakened national feelings, made separatist propaganda, and to have insulted the Grand National Assembly, the security forces and the "moral personality" of the government. Among the works brought out by Komal Publishing House were those of Dr Ismail Beşikçi, a sociologist serving a 10-year sentence passed in March 1982 (see *Amnesty International Reports 1982, 1983*).

Some of the numerous trials of Kurds were concluded during the year. Many were charged with violent offences, but among those charged under Articles 125, 171 and 173 of the penal code with separatist activities were some who were not accused of involvement in violence and were adopted by Amnesty International as prisoners of conscience. They included Mehdi Zana, former Mayor of Diyarbakir, who was sentenced to 24 years' imprisonment on 26 October 1983. An Amnesty International mission visited Diyarbakir in April 1983 to observe the trials of various groups of Kurdish activists, all charged with separatist activities, eventually being admitted to the trial of members of the Labour Party of Kurdistan (KIP), after initially being denied access to any trial in Diyarbakir.

The trial of leaders, officials and advisers of the Confederation of Progressive Trade Unions (DISK), which started in December 1981, continued throughout the year. Some defendants, including Ahmet Isvan, the former Mayor of Istanbul, were released, but were still on trial, while new defendants were added to the trial. At the end of 1983 the total number of defendants was 85, of whom 40 were still in prison. All the defendants with one exception were charged under Article 146 of the Turkish penal code, 74 under paragraph 1, which carries the death penalty, the remainder under paragraph 3, which provides for a prison sentence of not less than 15 years (see *Amnesty International Report 1983*). The 817-page DISK indictment did not state explicitly that the defendants committed or advocated acts of violence and they were not charged with any specific violent acts. Amnesty International believed all the DISK defendants to be prisoners of conscience.

Leading members of the National Salvation Party, a legal political party before the 1980 coup, were sentenced in February 1983 to terms of between two and four years' imprisonment under Article 163 of the penal code for intending to adapt "the basic social, economic, political or judicial orders of the State to religious principles and beliefs". At the end of 1983 they were still free pending the outcome of appeals. Throughout the year the Turkish media carried frequent reports of the detention and in some cases the trial of members of various religious sects, also charged under Article 163. On 6 May Ankara radio reported the conclusion of the trial in Antalya of 115 officials of religious philanthropic associations, charged under Article 163. Forty-six were sentenced to two years' imprisonment, eight to one year's imprisonment and 11 to six months' imprisonment.

All political offences were tried by martial law courts. Most lawyers acting in political cases continued to have insufficient access to their clients and were unable to have private consultations with them. Some were also reportedly put under pressure by having criminal charges brought against them. In April 1983 seven lawyers in Istanbul were brought to trial, charged with having damaged the reputation of the state abroad by providing information about conditions in Metris Military Prison. They were acquitted in September after expert testimony had established that they had not personally signed the document in question.

Amnesty International continued to be concerned about the length of time – 45 days – a person might be detained incommunicado before being brought before a court to be charged or released. Most allegations of torture received by Amnesty International related to this period. In many cases families were reportedly unable to discover the whereabouts of detainees.

Amnesty International continued to receive allegations that prisoners charged with political offences had been tortured and that in some cases death had resulted. In December 1982 Amnesty International was informed that Mustafa Hayrullahoglu, who had been detained in October or November 1982, had been tortured and was in a critical state of health. On 9 December Amnesty International asked the Turkish Ambassador in London, Rahmi Gümrükçüoglu, for information about Mustafa Hayrullahoglu's whereabouts and state of health and called for an investigation into the torture allegations. No reply was received, so on 5 January 1983 Amnesty International asked the Turkish Foreign Minister, Ilter Türkmen, for the same information. No reply was received. On 5 April 1983 Amnesty International learned that Mustafa Hayrullahoglu was dead. After months of trying to discover his whereabouts his family finally learned that he had been buried in Kasimpasa cemetery in Istanbul. They subsequently received two letters from the authorities. The Martial Law Prosecutor for Istanbul stated that Mustafa Hayrullahoglu had been detained on 21 October 1982 and had committed suicide on 26 October. The Public Prosecutor for Istanbul stated that he had been detained on 5 November 1982, had become sick on 16 November and had died on the way to hospital. On 11 May 1983 Amnesty International wrote again to the Turkish Ambassador asking to be informed if any investigation had taken place into Mustafa Hayrullahoglu's death. No reply was received.

In July 1983 Amnesty International received reports that approximately 2,000 prisoners in Metris, Sultanahmet, Sagmalcilar and Kabakoz prisons in Istanbul were on hunger-strike in protest against prison conditions, executions, torture and restrictions on access to lawyers. During the hunger-strike, which lasted for a month, an Amnesty International delegate visited Istanbul to seek information about the treatment and condition of the prisoners.

Throughout the year Amnesty International received frequent allegations that Kurdish prisoners in Diyarbakir and Erzurum Military Prisons were being subjected to torture. Among them were Halil Aksoy, whose brother Metin had died as a result of torture in October 1980, Mümtaz Kotan, Ruşen Arslan, Mehdi Zana, Paşa Uzun, Nurettin Baysut and Salih Altindag. At a court hearing in Erzurum on 2 November Nurettin Baysut appeared with his head bandaged, allegedly because of wounds caused by torture, and Salih Altindag took off his clothes and showed marks he alleged to have been the result of torture. The two men stated that torture in Erzurum Military Prison consisted of savage beating, *falaka* (beating of the soles of the feet) and being hit with sand bags. They demanded that their testimony be recorded in the minutes of the hearing.

In September 1983 a hunger-strike by political prisoners took place in Diyarbakir Military Prison in protest against torture, bad prison conditions and restrictions on access to lawyers. On 8 September Amnesty International expressed concern to President Kenan Evren and the Martial Law Commander of Diyarbakir, General Kaya Yazgan, about reports that prisoners on hunger-strike had been tortured.

There were 24 executions in 1983, bringing to 48 the number of people executed since the September 1980 coup (prior to which no executions had taken place since 1972). Amnesty International did not know the total number of people awaiting execution at the end of 1983, but believed it to be between 250 and 300. The organization appealed throughout the year to the authorities for a halt to executions and for the abolition of the death penalty.

In November 1983 approximately 60 Iranian refugees in Turkey were forcibly returned to Iran by the Turkish authorities. Amnesty International expressed concern about these *refoulements* to President Kenan Evren and pointed out that at least some of the refugees were in danger of imprisonment, torture or even execution in Iran because of their alleged political opposition to the Iranian Government.

On 6 December 1983 the European Commission on Human Rights declared admissible the inter-state complaints filed against Turkey by Denmark, France, the Netherlands, Norway and Sweden. The applicant-governments had alleged that during the period 12 September 1980 to 1 July 1982 Turkey had violated the following provisions of the European Convention on Human Rights: Article 3 (prohibition of torture); Article 5 (liberty and security of person); Article 6 (right to fair trial); Article 9 (freedom of conscience); Article 10 (freedom of expression); and Article 11 (freedom of assembly and association). The applicant-governments alleged that torture and inhuman or degrading treatment of detainees was a widespread and systematic practice and that the measures taken by the Turkish Government to combat such treatment were not sufficient. The Commission in its decision on admissibility found that there was *prima facie* evidence of a "repetition of acts" of torture and ill-treatment of prisoners. It noted the large number of complaints which had been addressed to the Turkish authorities between June 1981 and July 1982 and concluded that the efforts of the government to prevent violations of Article 3 on a considerable scale had apparently not been sufficient. This seemed to indicate "that there was tolerance, at the level of direct superiors of those immediately responsible for the acts involved, of such violations".

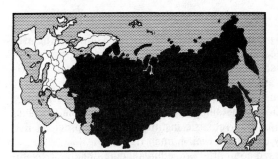

Union of Soviet Socialist Republics

Amnesty International was concerned about the continued imprisonment of large numbers of prisoners of conscience, including the detention of people in psychiatric hospitals for peacefully exercising their human rights. Reports were received of the ill-treatment of prisoners of conscience in prisons, corrective labour colonies and psychiatric hospitals. Amnesty International worked on behalf of approximately 400 people known or thought likely to be prisoners of conscience, but believed the actual number of prisoners of conscience to be much higher. Amnesty International learned of 24 death sentences and eight executions.

In September a new law was introduced which prescribes terms of up to five years' imprisonment for prisoners convicted of "wilfully disobeying" the administration of their prison or corrective labour colony. In December Amnesty International expressed its concern at the introduction of Article 188-3 into the Russian Penal Code, pointing out that the terms of the law are open to arbitrary interpretation and that prisoners have limited opportunities for legal defence. Since January Amnesty International learned of 12 prisoners of conscience being given additional sentences while serving their original sentences. All these prisoners were already serving their terms in corrective labour colonies for criminal prisoners. The organization feared that they had been convicted in trials which fell short of internationally-agreed standards of fairness, many having been tried *in camera* within the penal institutions themselves. It was not known whether they had had access to the legal counsel of their choice. Amnesty International was concerned that Article 188-3 makes prisoners of conscience increasingly vulnerable to wrongful reimprisonment.

Amnesty International was also concerned that the right of prisoners of conscience to unconditional release was further restricted by changes to legislation on administrative surveillance. In September the Statute on Administrative Surveillance over People Released from Imprisonment was amended to empower the local militia to impose indefinite surveillance over some former prisoners of conscience without the prior approval of the Procuracy. In October the penalties for those who violate the rules of surveillance were increased. Article 198-2 of the

Russian Penal Code was amended to carry a maximum prison term of three years with no previous official warning being required. Amnesty International believed that the new laws deprived released prisoners of conscience of necessary legal safeguards against harassment and made them vulnerable to arbitrary reimprisonment.

In February Amnesty International published *Political Abuse of Psychiatry in the USSR*, detailing the cases of 110 people who had been confined to Soviet psychiatric institutions in the previous five years for peacefully exercising their human rights.

The paper analysed committal procedures facilitating the wrongful confinement of dissenters and reported specific allegations of ill-treatment received by the organization including beatings by hospital staff and the administration to patients of painful and disorienting drugs in excessive quantities and without necessary correctives. The paper also described the pressure prisoners of conscience were subject to to renounce their beliefs and the punishment they received if they refused to do so.

In 1983 Amnesty International learned of a further 28 individuals being confined to psychiatric institutions for political reasons. Most had been arrested on the charge of "circulating anti-Soviet slander" after they had written letters to newspapers or officials or had contributed information to *samizdat* (unofficial and uncensored) bulletins, and had subsequently been confined to ordinary psychiatric hospitals for indefinite periods under the criminal commitment procedure. None were known to have used or advocated violence in support of their views.

In February the All-Union Society of Psychiatrists and Neuropathologists – the official organization for members of these professions in the USSR – resigned from the World Psychiatric Association (WPA), five months before the seventh WPA Congress in Vienna. At its previous congress in Hawaii in 1977 the WPA had condemned the Soviet use of psychiatry for political purposes.

One hundred and seven Soviet citizens are known to have stood trial in 1983 for peacefully exercising the right to freedom of expression. Some were convicted of "circulating anti-Soviet slander" and sentenced to up to three years' imprisonment, but more than half were prosecuted on the more serious charge of "anti-Soviet agitation and propaganda" and given sentences of up to 12 years' imprisonment and internal exile. Both charges are incompatible with the right to freedom of expression proclaimed in the International Covenant on Civil and Political Rights, which the USSR ratified in 1973. No person brought to trial on either charge was known to have been acquitted in 1983.

The case of Sofya Belyak illustrated how broadly the charge of "anti-Soviet agitation and propaganda" has been applied by the authorities. A Roman Catholic church organist from the Ukraine, she was sentenced in October by a court in Zhitomyr to five years' imprisonment and five years' internal exile, for having allegedly circulated pamphlets on the reported appearance of the Virgin Mary at Fatima in Portugal in May 1917.

Individuals who allegedly collected information regarding human rights abuses and published it abroad were imprisoned on the same charge. Sergei Grigoryants from Kaluga and Aleksei Smirnov from Moscow were each sentenced to 10 years' imprisonment and internal exile for allegedly producing a fortnightly *samizdat* publication called *Express Information Bulletin "V"*. Citizens from non-Russian republics, accused of writing or drawing in their own national tradition, or of dissenting from Soviet Government policies, were also reportedly charged and prosecuted for "anti-Soviet agitation and propaganda". They included 14 Balts and a number of Georgians, Armenians and Ukrainians. Prominent religious activists who had consistently defended the rights of fellow believers were also sentenced to long terms of imprisonment and internal exile. They included Fathers Alfonsas Svarinskas and Sigitas Tamkevicius, two Lithuanian priests who in 1978 had formed an unofficial Catholic Committee for the Defence of Believers' Rights; and two Pentecostalists from Rostov, Galina Barats and her husband Vasily, who since 1977 had headed an unofficial Committee for the Right to Emigrate from the USSR.

The laws circumscribing freedom of expression were also applied to punish individuals who had associated together in unofficial groups whose activity, though legal, was disapproved of by the authorities. These included eight members of an unofficial "Group to Establish Trust between the USSR and the USA" founded in June 1982. In October Amnesty International published a paper on the group's nine members and supporters who had been imprisoned since its formation.

In 1983 over 100 individuals were imprisoned under two laws which punish peaceful religious activity which has not been sanctioned by the state. Unusually, five were members of unofficial yoga circles based in Sverdlovsk and Moscow, who were arrested after items such as bells and incense had been confiscated from their homes. They stood trial on charges of "violating the laws separating Church from State" and "anti-social religious activity" and were given terms of up to four years' imprisonment with confiscation of property. Most of those prosecuted under these laws, however, were "dissenting" Baptists, who reject state restrictions on their religious practices. Amnesty International adopted as prisoners of conscience a number of Pentecostalists, Jehovah's Witnesses, Roman Catholics, Russian Orthodox believers and Ukrainian Greek Catholics who were imprisoned under this legislation.

The authorities continued to prosecute and imprison citizens who sought to exercise their right to leave the country. Some were prosecuted after they had attempted to emigrate without official permission, including six young Estonians who tried to sail across the Baltic Sea in rubber dinghies and were arrested on a charge of "illegal exit abroad". They were sentenced to three years' imprisonment. Others of Jewish, German and Russian origin were imprisoned for "circulating anti-Soviet slander" or "anti-Soviet agitation and propaganda" because they had repeatedly asked for permission to emigrate. Three people were imprisoned for advocating the right of Crimean Tatars to return to their native Crimea from Soviet Central Asia where they were forcibly deported *en masse* in 1944. Amnesty International also adopted as prisoners of conscience four would-be emigrés of long standing, who were imprisoned for refusing "call-up to military service". One of them, Semyon Shnirman, had completed two years' imprisonment on the same charge in 1980.

On 1 July the Chairperson of the Moscow group of Amnesty International, Georgy Vladimov, was stripped of his Soviet citizenship while he was lecturing abroad. An internationally-acclaimed writer, Vladimov left the USSR in May after the authorities had twice searched his home and threatened to prosecute him if he continued his involvement with the organization. In April Vladimir Albrekht, who left the group in 1981, having previously been its secretary, was arrested on a charge of "circulating anti-Soviet slander". He was accused of having sent relief to the Polish trade union Solidarity, and was later sentenced to three years' imprisonment. His prosecution was not believed to be related to his previous membership of Amnesty International.

During the year Amnesty International was concerned about the reported ill-treatment of some prisoners in prisons and corrective labour colonies. Some prisoners of conscience alleged that they had been beaten, either by officials, or with official consent. Six said that they had been deliberately put in cells called "press-huts" with convicted criminals, who beat them while they were in custody awaiting trial. In October Amnesty International issued an appeal on behalf of Sergei Khodorovich, who was reportedly held in the hospital wing of Butyrka investigation prison in Moscow suffering from head injuries. He was arrested in April on a charge of "circulating anti-Soviet slander" for his part in administering an unofficial charity which dispenses relief to Soviet political prisoners and their families. In July he went on an 18-day hunger strike to protest against systematic beatings he had received. In December he was convicted and sentenced to three years' imprisonment in a strict regime corrective labour colony.

In December Amnesty International published *Information on Conditions of Imprisonment in Special Regime Corrective Labour*

Colony VS 389/36-1. The colony, which was built in Perm region in 1980, is in the harshest category of corrective labour colony, and housed 15 prisoners of conscience in 1983. Incorporating the first-hand testimony of one of these prisoners, the paper described the far-reaching powers of the colony's administration and the powerlessness of the prisoners to protect even their limited rights. Formally, for example, prisoners may receive an unrestricted quantity of letters. In practice, however, many letters are confiscated and destroyed by colony officials. The paper also described the cramped conditions in which prisoners live, work and exercise in strict isolation; their monotonous and meagre diet; and the rudimentary provisions for medical treatment.

Official reports indicated that at least 24 people were sentenced to death in 1983 and at least eight people were executed, but Amnesty International believed the actual number of death sentences passed to be much higher. The organization appealed for the commutation of all death sentences it had knowledge of. In August it wrote to the Chief Military Procurator of the USSR asking him to initiate a review of the case of Yermak Lukyanov, who was sentenced to death by a military tribunal in Elista in July. A Belgian citizen of Kalmyk origin who left the USSR after the Second World War, he was arrested in 1968 on a charge of "treason" – in the form of "going over to the side of the enemy" while visiting the USSR as a tourist. He was then confined to a psychiatric hospital for 15 years until ruled fit to stand trial. In September the Supreme Court of the USSR upheld the death sentence passed on him. By December the outcome of his petition for pardon was not known.

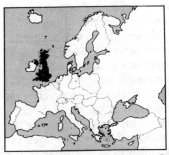

United Kingdom

Amnesty International expressed concern to the authorities about judicial procedures in political cases in Northern Ireland and publicized these concerns. The organisation sent an observer to a trial in Wales, and gave special attention to investigating a number of shootings by security forces in Northern Ireland. Amnesty International had no adopted prisoners of conscience during the year.

In August 1983 Amnesty International submitted material documenting its concern about the so-called "Diplock courts" in Northern

Ireland to Sir George Baker, an English judge who was appointed by the government to conduct an inquiry into the workings of the Emergency Provisions (Northern Ireland) Act of 1978. The "Diplock courts" differ from normal courts in several respects, the most important being that they have no jury but only a single judge.

Amnesty International submitted a detailed analysis of the legislation together with a summary of the concerns which it had submitted to the Secretary of State for Northern Ireland in December 1982, in which it had expressed concern that the proceedings in the "Diplock courts" might not conform to international standards for fair trial. The organization noted that most of those convicted in such courts were convicted solely on the basis of confessions and pointed out that several features of the system created a risk that people might be convicted and sentenced to imprisonment on the sole basis of such confessions which could have been obtained by oppressive methods and might therefore have been unreliable (see *Amnesty International Report 1983*).

In its submission to Sir George Baker, Amnesty International raised the case of Michael Culbert, a social worker from Belfast, who was arrested in 1978 and convicted in 1979 of murdering a policeman and membership of the Provisional Irish Republican Army. After his arrest he was interrogated for long periods but not physically ill-treated. He allegedly made a verbal (unsigned) confession, and this was the only evidence produced against him. He later denied having made such a confession and maintained that at the time of the alleged confession he was completely disorientated as a result of continuous interrogation, lack of sleep and being made to stand for long periods during interrogation.

At his trial by a non-jury court in October 1979, the only issue was the admissibility of his alleged verbal confession. The court held that the confession was admissible, convicted him of murder and membership of the Provisional Irish Republican Army, and sentenced him to life imprisonment. Amnesty International, believing the case raised fundamental issues of principle, had sent an observer to his appeal hearing in January 1982. His subsequent appeal was turned down.

On 3 October 1983 Amnesty International wrote to the United Kingdom Government expressing concern about the practice in Northern Ireland of bringing prosecutions solely or mainly on the basis of the testimony of former accomplices of the accused. During the previous year about 300 people had been charged with or tried for crimes involving politically motivated violence on the basis of the testimony of 20 individuals who were themselves implicated in such offences. The defendants included alleged members of both Republican and Loyalist paramilitary organizations.

In its letter, Amnesty International asked the Secretary of State for

Northern Ireland to ensure that this subject be included in the terms of reference of the inquiry into the operation of the Emergency Provisions (Northern Ireland) Act of 1978. Amnesty International sent a copy of its letter to the judge conducting that inquiry, Sir George Baker.

While noting that it was against neither international standards nor the United Kingdom's laws for the testimony of accomplices to be admitted in evidence in criminal trials, Amnesty International said that a number of features of prosecution practice in such "supergrass" cases had emerged which, taken together, raised doubts about the quality of proof in such cases. In particular:

— Many defendants were convicted solely on the basis of the un-corroborated testimony of former accomplices;

— Although in English law the normal rules of evidence ruled out testimony obtained by "hope of advantage . . . held out by a person in authority", in some "supergrass" cases testimony had been admitted in evidence which was given by people who had themselves been offered immunity from prosecution for serious crimes;

— Some such witnesses had been in custody for long periods – well over a year – before a trial, giving the police ample opportunity to influence the testimony unduly;

— Whereas in normal trials judges were required to warn juries of the dangers of convicting defendants on the sole basis of such evidence, in the "Diplock courts" in Northern Ireland there were no juries – and so judges had to "warn" only themselves.

On 21 November 1983 the Secretary of State for Northern Ireland replied to Amnesty International's letter of 30 October. He referred the organization to a statement by the Attorney-General in Parliament outlining the criteria and safeguards employed by the authorities in cases similar to those described by Amnesty International. The Secretary of State also referred to the safeguard offered by the right of appeal against sentence to the higher courts. He told Amnesty International that witnesses, held either in custody or under police protection, were not subjected to police pressure and that their right to access to relatives, friends or lawyers was respected.

The inquiry by Sir George Baker was still in progress at the end of 1983.

In September an Amnesty International observer attended the trial in Cardiff of seven Welsh nationalists accused of the bombing or attempted bombing of buildings in Wales and England (see *Amnesty International Report 1983*). (An eighth defendant failed to appear at the trial.) The defendants were charged with conspiracy and various explosives charges. Amnesty International's attendance was motivated by concern about defendants' allegations that incriminating evidence had been planted by the police and that their confessions had been fabricated or made under duress. Two defendants were found guilty of possessing explosives and were sentenced to three and nine years' imprisonment. The other five defendants were all acquitted. In his report, Amnesty International's observer expressed concern about the length of pre-trial detention (up to 17 months in one case) and about allegations of selective investigation by the police (attempts to implicate leaders of Welsh nationalism). By the end of 1983 police conduct in the case was being investigated by a senior police officer sent from another part of the United Kingdom. The Attorney-General, Sir Michael Havers was investigating whether pre-trial detention had been unreasonably prolonged.

In October Amnesty International wrote to the Secretary of State for Home Affairs, Leon Brittan, to express concern about allegations which had been published in the national press that four people in police custody in Birmingham had been subjected to ill-treatment, including suffocation with plastic bags, to induce confessions in separate incidents over the previous two or three years. The news media had reported that the police were conducting an inquiry into the allegations in one of these cases.

Amnesty International urged that all the allegations be investigated and that a full report of the findings be made public even if criminal proceedings were not undertaken. It also urged the Home Office to publicize measures taken to prevent any recurrence of the abuses, if the allegations were substantiated.

The Home Office subsequently sent Amnesty International a detailed reply saying that a police investigation would be undertaken into the two cases where the prisoners had made complaints, and that the investigating officer would seek statements from the other two alleged victims, who had not made complaints, if they were willing to see him and if he felt it would help him in his inquiries. The Home Office also said that the matter would be publicized if charges were brought and if anyone were brought to trial, and that the Home Office would also consider publicizing any disciplinary proceedings brought against police officers in connection with the allegations. At the end of 1983 Amnesty International had not learned of the outcome of the police investigations.

In July the House of Commons rejected by 368 votes to 223 a motion for restoration of the death penalty for murder. (Since 1969 the death penalty has been retained only for treason and piracy and for certain wartime offences under military law). Amnesty International had made public appeals against the introduction of the death penalty.

During 1983 Amnesty International studied a series of shootings by members of the security forces in Northern Ireland with a view to assessing allegations that there was an official government policy to have suspected members of paramilitary groups deliberately killed instead of arresting them.

These allegations had been made during the last few months of 1982 when in four incidents seven unarmed individuals had been killed by the security forces. During 1983 17 people, some of them armed, were killed by army and police personnel. The circumstances of these killings varied. In all but two cases the authorities said either that the security forces' personnel responsible had had reason to suspect that the victim was armed and threatening danger or that the victim had been accidentally killed in cross fire. In the two exceptional cases, the victims had been unarmed and were killed in front of many witnesses.

By the end of 1983 13 members of the security forces had been charged in connection with seven of the killings.

Amnesty International was continuing to gather information on the matter. By the end of 1983 there had been an inquest on only one of the killings, other inquests having been postponed pending completion of police investigations or judicial proceedings. None of the security forces' personnel charged had been brought to trial by the end of the year.

Yugoslavia

Amnesty International was concerned about the imprisonment of many prisoners of conscience and political trials in which the accused reportedly did not receive a fair trial. The organization learned of allegations by several defendants that they had been ill-treated during investigation. Amnesty International was also concerned about the treatment of prisoners held in isolation and conditions in some prisons. The organization had details of five cases in which people were allegedly held in psychiatric confinement as a result of their non-violent exercise of their right to freedom of expression. The organization learned of the imposition of 10 death sentences but did not receive reports of any executions.

In October 1983 the Public Prosecutor's Office stated that there had been a "negligible increase" in political offences in the first six months of the year in comparison with the same period in 1982, and that most of these offences were "verbal" and "committed for nationalistic motives". (According to official figures, in the first six months of 1982, 268 people were charged with political offences; the total figure for 1982 was 516). In 1983 Amnesty International learned of over 70 political trials involving more than 230 people, the majority of them ethnic Albanians from Kosovo province. Charges involving the use of violence were rare and only a relatively small number of those accused were charged with advocating or planning violence.

Nationalist activity by ethnic Albanians persisted in Kosovo province consisting largely of the dissemination of pamphlets and slogans supporting the demand that the province, which is part of the republic of Serbia, be granted its own republic status within the Socialist Federal Republic of Yugoslavia. There were, however, instances of sabotage and four bomb explosions were reported which caused material damage but no loss of life.

In June the authorities announced that 2,503 people had been sentenced for political crimes and minor offences of a political character in Kosovo over the previous two years, and that in the first nine months of 1983 seven illegal groups of Albanian nationalists had been discovered and 130 of their members had been arrested.

Amnesty International adopted as prisoners of conscience a number of ethnic Albanians, including Skender Krasniqi and nine other university or high-school students who were sentenced to between one and five years' imprisonment by the district court of Pec on 3 March. They were found guilty of having attempted to organize nationalist demonstrations in Pec and of being in possession of literature of a "hostile content". It also adopted Destan Aliu, aged 28, an ethnic Albanian from Macedonia who was sentenced to eight years' imprisonment in January for having engaged in "hostile activity". He was reported to have emigrated to the USA in 1974 and to have taken part there in anti-Yugoslav demonstrations prior to his return to Yugoslavia. Other ethnic Albanians adopted by Amnesty International included the teachers Enver Haliti and Ahmet Tahiri, who were sentenced to five and five and a half years' imprisonment respectively by a court in Titova Mitrovica on 10 May on charges of "hostile propaganda". They were accused of having made tape-recordings of broadcasts by Radio Tirana (Albania) which the court considered hostile to Yugoslavia, and of having intended to disseminate them.

Amnesty International continued to be concerned about the use of Article 133 of the criminal code dealing with "hostile propaganda" to imprison people for the expression of views which are officially disapproved of. During the year the Yugoslav press published a number of articles which reported criticism, by legal experts and others, of the provisions and formulation of Article 133. Convictions under this article, often based on the private conversations of the accused, appeared to have increased in Bosnia-Hercegovina in particular.

Amnesty International learned of some 12 such cases in which sentences of up to six years' imprisonment were imposed. It adopted as a prisoner of conscience Professor Ivan Pletikosa, aged 57, who prior to his arrest in December 1982 taught in the English department of Zagreb University. At his trial by the district court of Banjaluka in April he was charged under Articles 133 and 157 with "hostile propaganda" and "damaging the reputation of the [state]" on the basis of private remarks he allegedly made criticizing Yugoslavia's political and economic system and certain of its leaders. Professor Pletikosa reportedly denied the charges against him. The court rejected proposals to hear six defence witnesses and sentenced him to six years' imprisonment. Two observers delegated by Amnesty International to attend the court proceedings were refused access to the courtroom. In a similar case, Milan Soklic, aged 28, a sociology teacher, was sentenced to five years' imprisonment by a court in Tuzla in May. He was reportedly found guilty of having compared capitalism favourably with Yugoslav socialism and of having criticized restrictions on freedom of expression in Yugoslavia in the presence of several people at his home and in a hotel. Amnesty International also adopted Hanefija Avdagic, aged 71, who was sentenced to five years' imprisonment by a court in Zenica in May after allegedly expressing doubts about the democratic character of the Yugoslav political system, blaming the system for the country's economic problems and justifying the demands made by Albanian nationalists in Kosovo.

On 18 July the trial of 12 Muslims before the district court of Sarajevo began. The accused, who included engineers, an economist, a schoolteacher and two Imams, were variously accused of "association for the purpose of hostile activity" and "hostile propaganda" conducted from "Muslim nationalist" principles. The chief accused, Alija Izetbegovic, aged 58, was charged with the authorship of a number of texts on Islam, including one entitled "The Islamic Declaration" advocating an Islamic revival, and with propagating the views contained in this document among a group of intellectuals and Imams with the intention of "forming an association for the purpose of hostile activity". He was also accused of having initiated a visit by five co-defendants to Iran to participate in a Muslim congress there. On 12 August the court found all the accused guilty; Alija Izetbegovic was sentenced to 14 years' imprisonment, 10 other co-defendants received prison sentences of between five and 15 years' imprisonment and a 12th was sentenced to six months' imprisonment. Two observers delegated by Amnesty International were denied access to the court on 19 and 20 July but were able to attend proceedings on 21 and 22 July. The organization concluded that the charges against the accused did not include the use or advocacy of violence.

During the year, the official press criticized on a number of occasions – both in connection with this trial and with other issues – the "abuse of religion for political purposes". Charges on such grounds were brought against a Roman Catholic priest, Father Luka Prcela, aged 42, who was sentenced to five years' imprisonment by the district court of Split in May after being accused of having made critical comments about the Yugoslav League of Communists and about political leaders during sermons. He reportedly denied having made some of the statements cited in the indictment and stated that others had been distorted by being taken out of context.

In June Amnesty International wrote to the authorities raising the cases of five people alleged to have been confined in psychiatric hospitals for the non-violent exercise of their right to freedom of expression. Among these was Radomir Veljkovic, aged 58, a retired army officer who had been detained since 1973 in Belgrade Prison Psychiatric Hospital. In early 1973 he was charged with "hostile propaganda" and "damaging the reputation of the state" on the basis of documents, largely written in 1970, in which he had criticized the late President Tito and referred to abuses allegedly committed in the past by members of the state security police. In March 1973 the district court of Sarajevo reportedly found him guilty but ruled that he was not accountable for his actions at the time that he committed these offences, that he was dangerous to his surroundings, and that he should be forcibly confined to a psychiatric institution. In an appeal against this decision, Radomir Veljkovic argued that the court had not given the grounds for its ruling nor had it explained in what way he was dangerous. He stated that both he and his chosen lawyers had been prevented from attending the trial and referred to five medical certificates dated 1967/1970 diagnosing him as sane. He claimed that the psychiatric diagnosis of insanity on which the court had based its decision was false. Later in the year Amnesty International learned of the release from Belgrade Prison Psychiatric Hospital of Vjekoslav Naglic and Dusan Cetkovic, two other cases it had been investigating. In all the cases raised by Amnesty International there was no indication that any of the victims had used or advocated violence. They were all confined to psychiatric hospital after they had been charged with non-violent political offences.

Amnesty International was concerned about allegations made by some ethnic Albanians convicted of political offences that they had been ill-treated during investigation proceedings. For example, Lutvi Maqedonci, a 21-year-old student, who was tried together with 22 others by a Pristina court in February on charges of belonging to an illegal nationalist group, reportedly stated at the trial that he had been physically and psychologically tortured during investigation proceedings. He was sentenced to six years' imprisonment. In another political trial in Pristina in December, Adnan Gashi reportedly denied the charges against him and said that the statements he had made during investigation proceedings had been obtained under duress and by intimidation. He was sentenced to five years' imprisonment. There was no indication that such allegations of ill-treatment had been investigated by the courts.

Amnesty International learned of breaches of internationally accepted standards of fair trial in a number of political trials. These included restricted public access to proceedings, and the refusal by the court to allow the submission of evidence and the calling of witnesses for the defence. In the case of Alija Izetbegovic and his co-defendants (see above), the accused were denied access to their lawyers throughout the investigation proceedings. In addition, a number of the witnesses at the trial reportedly gave testimony after they themselves had been detained and interrogated by police. At the trial many were said to have withdrawn their testimony.

Amnesty International was also concerned about reports of poor conditions in certain prisons and in particular the treatment of prisoners punished with solitary confinement or isolation. One account received by Amnesty International concerned Zabela prison, where general conditions were described as fair. Solitary confinement cells, however, were described as windowless and cramped with bunks made of bare boards. Certain prisoners were said to be punished by being chained to their bunks so that they could not move. Guards reportedly often beat prisoners held in these cells.

In Frankfurt in the Federal Republic of Germany (FRG) the trial continued of three people accused of the attempted assassination in May 1981 of Rasim Zenelaj, an ethnic Albanian political emigre from Kosovo. In November, Zorica Aleksic, one of the accused, reportedly informed the court that she had been recruited by one of her co-defendants to work for the Yugoslav state security police and to kill Rasim Zenelaj. In July Stjepan Djurekovic, a Croatian emigre, was shot dead near Munich in the FRG. Amnesty International received allegations that he had been killed by agents of the Yugoslav state security police.

Amnesty International learned of the imposition of 10 death sentences during the year, nine for murder and one for terrorist activity which caused injury to a number of people and material damage. Amnesty International did not learn of any executions. In June it appealed to the Presidency of Kosovo to commute a death sentence, confirmed in final instance, imposed on Ferat Muja for murder.

The Middle East and North Africa

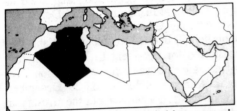

Algeria

During 1983, Amnesty International was concerned about the long-term detention without trial of individuals on political grounds, prolonged incommunicado detention and reports of the ill-treatment of detainees. To Amnesty International's knowledge, no executions were carried out during 1983.

Twenty-one leading members of Islamic movements who had been arrested in December 1982 were reportedly still in prison at the end of the year. They were arrested several weeks after, and allegedly in connection with, clashes between students at the University of Ben-Aknoun outside Algiers that led to one death and many injuries. All were charged with, among other things, plotting against the authority of the state and the integrity of national territory. However, neither they nor two others who were arrested at the same time but were provisionally released a short time later, had been tried by the end of 1983. On 29 December 1983 Amnesty International wrote to the Algerian Minister of Justice Boualem Baki, listing the names of 19 of the individuals concerned and calling for prompt and fair trials for all the detainees or their immediate release. Amnesty International feared that dozens of other individuals also arrested in November and December 1982 in connection with these and related events were still being held without trial.

Amnesty International was concerned about a number of arrests that took place in early October 1983. Former officials in governments of the early 1960s under President Ahmed Ben Bella, including Muhammad Seghir Nekkache, former Minister of Health, and the well-known lawyer Abdennour Ali Yahia, who had been active in the defence of arrested Berber activists, were among those arrested and subsequently held in Berrouaghia prison. Shortly after receiving reports of the arrests, Amnesty International sent a telex to the Minister of Justice seeking official information on the legal status of the detainees. In his response to Amnesty International's inquiry, the Minister of Justice stated that individual rights were guaranteed by the Algerian constitution, that no one could be arrested unless they had committed an offence, and that no cases could be "tried without the presence of a lawyer".

Shortly afterwards, Amnesty International was concerned about the reported state of health of one of the detainees, the lawyer Ali Yahia, who was known to be a diabetic and was said to be receiving inadequate medical treatment. On 4 November, the organization expressed its concern about this case to the Minister of Justice and in mid-December, after receiving further reports that the lawyer's condition was deteriorating, issued an urgent appeal on his behalf. In late December Ali Yahia was reported to have been transferred for treatment to Maillot military hospital in Algiers; shortly thereafter he was returned to prison.

In a letter to the Algerian Minister of Justice on 29 December, Amnesty International summarized its concerns about the arrests that took place in October and the continued detention of those arrested. Amnesty International referred to reports that the time limits on *garde à vue*, incommunicado detention by the police, had been exceeded and that detainees' families had not been told the whereabouts of those arrested.

In its letter of 29 December, Amnesty International also referred to allegations that some of those arrested in early October had been ill-treated while in *garde à vue* immediately after their arrest, before being transferred to Berrouaghia prison. Amnesty International received other occasional allegations that people held in custody had been ill-treated during the year but was unable to confirm them.

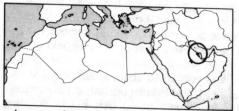

Bahrain

Amnesty International's concerns during 1983 were the long-term detention without charge or trial of political prisoners; the imprisonment of possible prisoners of conscience; the prolonged incommunicado detention and imprisonment of both untried and convicted individuals; and allegations of ill-treatment of prisoners.

During the year the organization investigated the cases of 27 political prisoners, 11 of whom had not been tried, the others having been convicted of membership of illegal organizations. Amnesty International learned of the release of 11 convicted prisoners and untried detainees.

Sixteen of those whose cases were being investigated were Bahrainis sentenced to between one and seven years' for membership of, or for forming, one of the following illegal organizations: the Organization of Islamic Unity, Movement of the Revolutionary Cell or the Constituent Committee of the Bahraini Workers' Union.

Amnesty International was also investigating the cases of 11 prisoners who had been held without charge or trial for between two and seven years, under the State Security Law of 1974 (see *Amnesty International Report 1983*). Four of these prisoners had been held since November 1981 and only came to the organization's attention during the year. They were Salam Abdul Aziz Ali, a government employee; Nader Abdullah Abu Drees, a student; his brother Abdul Aziz, who was released during the year; and Sayed Hashim al Musawi. Amnesty International asked the authorities why they had not been charged and tried, what specific acts they were alleged to have committed, whether they had been able to appeal against their detention (as provided for under the State Security Law), whether the detainees were represented by a lawyer, and where they were being held. The organization also sought assurances concerning the prisoners' state of health.

Amnesty International was concerned about 73 political prisoners – 60 Bahrainis, 11 Saudis, one Kuwaiti and one Omani – who were reported to have been held incommunicado since May 1982, when they were convicted on charges of involvement in a December 1981 plot to overthrow the government (see *Amnesty International Report 1983*). It was also reported that they had subsequently been subjected to ill-treatment and that no official information had been given regarding their place of imprisonment.

Amnesty International wrote to the authorities in May 1983 urging that all the prisoners be given immediate and regular access to their relatives and lawyers and requesting clarification about their where-abouts.

During the year Amnesty International received allegations that political detainees had been ill-treated while in the custody of the Bahrain security forces. Ja'afar Al Wardi, an electrical engineering teacher, was arrested on 26 August 1983 after being deported from Qatar. He was reported to have been ill-treated in prison while suffering from diabetes. Amnesty International urged the authorities to investigate these reports and sought assurances that he was receiving appropriate

328

medical attention. Amnesty International also received reports of ill-treatment regarding the 73 convicted political prisoners and the detainee Sayed Hashim Al Musawi (see above).

Although Amnesty International was not able to verify these allegations of ill-treatment, the reports gave rise to concern because prisoners were often subjected to prolonged periods of incommunicado detention, and the authorities were unwilling to allow the independent investigation of such allegations. Amnesty International received no reply from the authorities to its inquiries throughout the year about matters of concern to the organization.

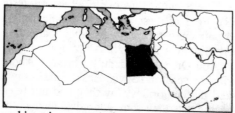

Egypt

Amnesty International was concerned about the continued use of legislation to arrest and imprison people for the non-violent expression of their beliefs, and about certain judicial procedures related to the state of emergency, which appeared contrary to internationally accepted standards for fair trial. There continued to be insufficient safeguards to protect detainees from being tortured, and Amnesty International received several allegations of torture or ill-treatment during the year. The organization appealed for the commutation of two death sentences and learned of four executions.

On 16 February 1983 Amnesty International published *Egypt: Violations of Human Rights*, based on a memorandum submitted to the Egyptian Government on 24 June 1982. The report outlined the organization's concerns in Egypt since the constitution was promulgated in 1971 and described laws under which people are arrested and imprisoned for the non-violent expression of their conscientiously held beliefs. The report featured the cases of several prisoners of conscience, including that of the journalist Hussein Abdul Raziq, who had been arrested and detained five times within a five-year period and in 1983 still faced charges in three cases, including a retrial on charges of which he had earlier been acquitted. Extracts from medical reports on injuries to detainees who claimed to have been tortured between October 1981 and March 1982 were also included in the publication. These reports concluded that the available medical evidence was consistent with the torture allegations. Amnesty International recommended that the government review the legislation used to arrest and punish prisoners of conscience, free all such prisoners, guarantee fair trials for political prisoners including the right to appeal, and take steps to put an end to torture and ill-treatment.

Amnesty International subsequently sent a mission to Cairo at the invitation of the government, and talks took place between 17 and 25 May 1983 with the Ministers of Justice and the Interior, the Minister of State for Foreign Affairs, the Prosecutor General, the Socialist Prosecutor General and the Director of the Bureau of Prisons, as well as other officials.

On 26 August 1983 Amnesty International submitted a further memorandum to the government, drawing on the talks conducted during Amnesty International's mission as well as new information related to the organization's statutory concerns. It contained a re-examination of legal issues of concern to Amnesty International, taking into consideration changes in legislation which had occurred during the preceding year. It also dealt with prisoners of conscience, political prisoners and their right to a fair trial, allegations of torture and ill-treatment and the death penalty. It acknowledged those areas where improvements had occurred but concluded by making the following recommendations:

(1) That a review be made of legislation relating to political activity, with particular reference to Articles 19, 21 and 22 of the International Covenant on Civil and Political Rights, to ensure: the protection from arrest and imprisonment of individuals non-violently expressing their human rights; the full observance of the principle of independence of the judicial function; and the right of defendants in all cases to appeal against conviction and sentence in a court of law.

(2) That all physical restrictions imposed on the Coptic Orthodox Pope Shenouda III be lifted;

(3) That an inquiry be held into all allegations of torture and ill-treatment since October 1981, and that the procedures as well as the findings be made public;

(4) That any officer found responsible for inflicting such treatment be brought to justice, and the victims compensated;

(5) That a review be made of the procedures followed for the inspection of prisons, and the investigation of prisoners' complaints of torture, ill-treatment or ill health.

On 29 October 1983 the Egyptian Ministry of Justice sent a six-page memorandum to Amnesty International in response to the organization's memorandum and recommendations. The Egyptian Government affirmed the principles of the supremacy of the law and respect for human rights as guaranteed by Egypt's constitution, as well as by international instruments to which Egypt is a party. It stated that two laws relating to political activity had recently been abolished, including Law 2 of 1977, which had been described by Amnesty International in its February 1983 publication as being inconsistent with provisions contained in Egypt's constitution as well as with the International Covenant on Civil and Political Rights. The government's response also dealt with prisoners of conscience and Amnesty International's concerns relating to political prisoners and allegations of torture and ill-treatment (see below).

This exchange of communications between Amnesty International and the Egyptian Government, following Amnesty International's mission in May 1983, was to be published by the organization in early 1984 as *Egypt: Update to 1983 Report.*

During their mission in May 1983, Amnesty International delegates raised the issue of prolonged detention without trial, following reports that some individuals had been held without charge or trial for periods in excess of one year in connection with the *Jihad* case (see below). The delegates were informed by the Minister of the Interior that, as of May 1983, approximately 40 people remained in detention, and that they had been arrested after October 1981. Subsequently, on 29 October 1983, the Ministry of Justice stated that the number of detainees had been reduced to 27.

The only adopted prisoner of conscience during the year was the Coptic Pope Shenouda III, who had been physically restricted to a monastery since September 1981. The organization raised his case with government officials during its mission in May 1983, as well as in its subsequent memorandum to the government. The Ministry of Justice, in its response, stated that Pope Shenouda was staying voluntarily at the monastery. Despite these assurances, Amnesty International remained concerned that the Coptic Pope was still being physically restricted against his will. While the conditions of his confinement were said to have improved towards the end of 1983, Amnesty International continued to regard him as a prisoner of conscience and to work for his unconditional release. The organization had insufficient information to determine whether other detainees held on political grounds during 1983 were prisoners of conscience.

Several political trials involving large numbers of defendants continued during 1983, but none had been concluded by the end of the year. One such trial involved 302 alleged members of the *Jihad* organization, the majority of whom were arrested in connection with the violent events in Assiut that followed the assassination of President Sadat in October 1981. Amnesty International was concerned that the defendants would be denied the right to judicial appeal, according to procedures applicable in trials before the Emergency Supreme State Security Court.

Two trials of alleged members of the banned Egyptian Communist Party, involving 30 and 47 defendants respectively, continued during 1983, as did the retrial of 176 defendants in connection with the so-called "Food Riots" of 1977 (see *Amnesty International Report 1983*). None of these defendants were believed to be in detention. Amnesty International was concerned about the lack of the right to appeal and the fact that convictions in all three cases may result in the imprisonment of individuals for the non-violent expression of their beliefs.

In its publication *Egypt: Violations of Human Rights*, Amnesty International quoted medical reports supporting allegations that political detainees had been tortured and ill-treated between October 1981 and March 1982. During the mission to Egypt, Amnesty International delegates discussed possible safeguards to protect detainees from such abuses with the government and other authorities, including procedures for inspecting prisons, particularly those where untried detainees are held, and for investigating prisoners' complaints of torture, ill-treatment or ill health.

On 26 August Amnesty International wrote to the government, submitting the names of five individuals who had reportedly died while in detention following their arrest in October 1981, and requesting clarification of the reports. In a detailed response on 29 October the Ministry of Justice concluded that in two cases death was due to natural causes. In the remaining three cases, however, investigations were continuing: in one case because the Prosecutor General had ordered a review of the first investigation, in the second, because a complaint had been lodged by the family that death was due to torture and beating, and in a third because of problems in identifying the body.

In another letter to the government, dated 22 September, Amnesty International expressed concern about reports that some individuals had been subjected to torture or ill-treatment following their arrest during the summer of 1983, and that at least two detainees, Ahmed Muhammad Abdul Gawad Al Touni and Mahmoud Al Farghali Mahmoud Muslim, had reportedly been hospitalized as a result. Amnesty International urged that the results of the relevant medical reports be made public, and that additional safeguards against torture and ill-treatment, such as those outlined in Amnesty International's memorandum, be introduced. No reply to this letter had been received by the end of the year.

Amnesty International learned of five cases during the year in which compensation had been awarded to people who had been tortured in the 1950s and 1960s. In April two Cairo courts awarded £E40,000 and £E25,000 respectively to a lawyer and a teacher who were tortured following their arrest in 1954 and again in 1965. In May the Cairo

Court of Appeal awarded two retired army officers £E60,000 as compensation for their imprisonment and torture during the 1960s (in one case, the officer died before the court ruling, and the compensation was awarded to his family). The Court of Appeal also awarded £E20,000 to a former army major and his family as compensation for the torture he suffered during 1962.

Amnesty International appealed to President Mubarak to commute the death sentences passed on two men, on charges of murder and robbery, in February and June respectively. Amnesty International learned of four executions during the year of people convicted of wilful murder and murder and theft. The organization was also concerned about the possibility that some of the 302 defendants in the *Jihad* case might face the death penalty. Charges against 299 of the 302 provided for the death penalty. The trial was still in progress at the end of 1983.

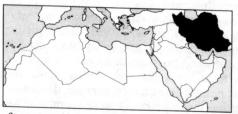

Iran

Amnesty International continued to be concerned about the large number of executions; numerous allegations of torture and other forms of ill-treatment of prisoners; the imprisonment of many prisoners of conscience; and the denial of fair trials to political prisoners. The organization recorded 399 executions during 1983, but regarded this as a minimum figure; it was concerned that executions took place after summary or arbitrary legal proceedings or, in some instances, after none. Information was received concerning both the use of torture to obtain confessions and information and whipping as a judicial punishment. The number of prisoners of conscience was not known, but many of the thousands of political prisoners were held because of their non-violent political or religious beliefs or activities, or their relationship with people who had engaged in opposition to the government. Arrest, detention and legal procedures all appeared to be arbitrary. Detainees were held for long periods before being charged and when trials did take place they lacked the safeguards which would ensure a fair trial.

Throughout the year Amnesty International frequently raised its concerns with the authorities. On 23 August 1983 in a letter to Ayatollah Ruhollah Khomeini it stated:

"Amnesty International continues to be most seriously concerned about reported human rights violations in Iran in contravention of Iran's obligations as a State Party to the International Covenant on Civil and Political Rights and of many articles of Iran's own Constitution. Amnesty International has accumulated since 1979 a large body of material documenting these violations, including personal testimonies from former prisoners and relatives of prisoners who have left Iran . . . The usual practice of Amnesty International is to support all its statements and claims with specific cases. This is not always possible in the case of Iran, because much of the information Amnesty International receives concerning individual cases is given in confidence, due to fear that the revelation of names may endanger the prisoners or their families. Amnesty International is, however, confident that the material in its possession justifies its serious concern and would welcome an opportunity to present further information to Your Excellency in person and to discuss its concern with you and members of the Government of the Islamic Republic of Iran."

No reply was received.

By the end of 1983 Amnesty International had recorded 5,447 executions in Iran since the revolution of February 1979, of which some 400 took place in 1983; the total number of executions was certainly much higher, with hundreds of executions reportedly taking place unannounced.

Those executed included members of the Baha'i faith, Kurds and members of political groups opposed to the government. In June, 59 Kurdish prisoners were reported to have been executed in Mahabad prison in retaliation for an attack by members of the Kurdish *Peshmargah* (Vanguard) forces, on the Mahabad garrison in May. Also in June, 17 Baha'is were executed in Shiraz. Among them were 10 women, ranging from 18 to 54 years of age and including a mother and her daughter. People were also executed on charges of espionage, murder, and sexual and drug offences; from September to December 1983 more than 200 people convicted of drug-trafficking were executed. On 28 June the Iranian daily newspaper *Jomhuri Eslami* (Islamic Republic) reported that a man who had killed his pregnant wife had been executed by his father-in-law in the city of Qom. The death sentence, reportedly passed by a court in Qom, was said by the newspaper to be the first to have been carried out under the Law of Retaliation, which allows injured parties to choose between financial compensation or a stipulated punishment and to carry out the punishment personally if they choose to do so.

Amnesty International was particularly concerned that the decisions to execute sometimes appeared to precede trial proceedings; that in some cases no trial at all seemed to have taken place prior to execution and that, in those cases where trials did occur, they lacked the safeguards necessary to ensure a fair trial. In May 1983 Amnesty International appealed to the Iranian authorities against the execution of members of the *Tudeh* (Communist) Party following a reported statement on 10 May by Mohsen Rezai, the head of the *Pasdaran* (Revolutionary Guards) that: "We are in no hurry to execute them, they still have much to confess, but by their confessions they have signed their own death warrants." The trials of *Tudeh* Party members did not start until December 1983.

As in previous years, some people initially sentenced to terms of imprisonment were subsequently executed, in some cases apparently without any further legal proceedings having taken place. Iraj Massali Markieh, who had not engaged in political activities himself but was related to someone actively opposed to the government, was arrested in April 1982. At his first trial he was sentenced to a term of imprisonment. He was tried again in March 1983 and executed in July 1983. The charges against him were not known. As in most other cases, his family did not learn of the execution until after it had taken place.

In some cases those executed were people under the age of 18. Article 6(5) of the International Covenant on Civil and Political Rights specifically prohibits the imposition of the death penalty for crimes committed by persons under 18 years of age.

During the year Amnesty International interviewed many former political prisoners who were living outside Iran. In every case they reported the widespread use of torture in prisons throughout the country. The most frequently reported forms of torture were whipping with woven leather whips, electric cables, hosepipes and flexible wooden strips bound with wire. Amnesty International also learned of relatives having been tortured in order to induce confessions or to obtain information from prisoners and of mock executions. One of the former prisoners interviewed was Hossein Dadkhah who was arrested in December 1982 and alleged that he had been tortured first in the *Pasdaran* headquarters in Shahrood and subsequently in Evin prison in Tehran. He escaped from custody in February 1983 and eventually arrived in Paris where he was examined on 19 March 1983 by two doctors from Amnesty International's French Section Medical Commission. In their detailed report they concluded that there was a strong likelihood that the injuries they observed were the result of the torture described by Hossein Dadkhah.

The use of torture to obtain information or to induce confessions is prohibited by Article 38 of the Iranian Constitution, but whipping as a judicial punishment is officially sanctioned and carried out on a large scale throughout the country, sometimes allegedly resulting in death.

Amnesty International regards this as cruel, inhuman and degrading punishment, as prohibited by Article 7 of the International Covenant on Civil and Political Rights. The Human Rights Committee, set up to monitor observance of the Covenant, has held that corporal punishment is prohibited under the terms of Article 7.

Among the thousands of political prisoners held in Iran during the year many had been involved in violent opposition to the government, but Amnesty International believed that many others were prisoners of conscience, imprisoned solely because of their non-violent political or religious activities, or in some cases just because they were associated with people actively opposed to the government. It was not possible to arrive at even a rough estimate of the number of prisoners of conscience, because of the difficulty of obtaining information, because of the imprecision of the charges, even when these were known, and because of the lack of fair trials, which in most cases prevented Amnesty International from assessing the validity of the charges with any accuracy. Among those prisoners the organization believed to be prisoners of conscience were Abolfazl Ghassemi, one of the leaders of the Iranian National Front and Secretary General of the Iran Party, who was elected to the Iranian parliament in the first elections after the revolution (see *Amnesty International Reports 1981, 1982, 1983*), and Mohammad Taqi Damghani, a member of the Iranian Bar Association who had been detained without trial since January 1982.

Amnesty International also appealed for the release of Esmail Movassaghiyan, a 72-year-old writer, who was arrested together with other members of his family in 1981, all having been apparently suspected of membership of, or sympathy for, *Rahe Karegar* (Way of the Worker), a non-violent left-wing party. Esmail Movassaghiyan was sentenced to death, which was commuted to life imprisonment. The date of his trial and the charges brought against him were not known. He was reported to be paralyzed in both legs, to suffer from serious stomach and kidney problems and near blindness in both eyes. Amnesty International believed that he had been ill-treated early in his imprisonment.

Following the banning of Baha'i institutions on 29 August 1983, 390 members of the Baha'i religion were arrested bringing the total of imprisoned Baha'is in the country to more than 700. The Baha'is are the only substantial religious minority not recognized under the Iranian Constitution. Those arrested were usually accused of espionage and Zionism, apparently because the Baha'i international headquarters are in Israel, but Amnesty International believed that the only reason for their imprisonment was their religious belief, which is regarded as heretical by the Iranian authorities.

The situation of most prisoners of conscience, as of all political prisoners in Iran, was exacerbated by their total lack of recourse to legal protection. Amnesty International believed that the guarantees necessary for a fair trial were lacking in cases heard by Islamic Revolutionary Tribunals, which dealt with all political cases. Defendants were not usually told the exact charges against them; they were not allowed defence counsel of their choice or to call defence witnesses or to question witnesses against them; most trials were closed to the public; there was no effective right of appeal and no effective presumption that defendants were innocent until proved guilty. Many detainees were held for long periods without charge or trial.

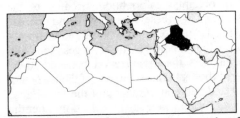

Iraq

Amnesty International continued to be concerned about the widespread arbitrary arrest of political suspects and their prolonged detention in the custody of the state security forces without charge or trial. Amnesty International remained concerned about "disappearances" and the continued detention of civilians in prisoner of war camps apparently on account of their ethnic origin and without legal proceedings. Other major concerns included the routine torture of detainees during interrogation and the ill-treatment and detention of members of their families allegedly to exert pressure on detainees to cooperate during interrogation, and the large number of executions, most of which were for political crimes.

An Amnesty International mission visited Iraq in January 1983 and discussed with various government ministers and members of the judiciary allegations of the routine and widespread torture of political detainees, the disregard of arrest and detention procedures for political suspects as laid down in the Code of Criminal Procedure, the lack of basic legal safeguards in the Revolutionary Court that tries most political detainees and the large number of executions for political offences. The delegates also inquired about the detention of people suspected of opposing the government.

On 6 May 1983 Amnesty International submitted a memorandum to the government, based on the mission's findings, which included detailed recommendations for measures to protect human rights. Amnesty International concluded that torture was routine and widespread in Iraq, that the functioning of the Revolutionary Court amounted to a breach of domestic and international law and that the long list of criminal and political offences for which the death penalty is provided and the numerous executions carried out each year in Iraq could not be reconciled with Iraq's obligations under international law. The organization urged that President Saddam Hussain issue a personal statement prohibiting torture, and that rules consistent with international standards be drawn up concerning: access to prisoners, interrogation methods, supervision of interrogators and prison warders, medical treatment and documentation, the admissibility in evidence of statements made by prisoners under interrogation, investigation of complaints of torture and the prosecution of the culprits. It also urged the government to give immediate consideration to abolishing all special courts and the death penalty.

On 28 June 1983 the government responded to the Amnesty International memorandum. It denied that gross human rights abuses had taken place in Iraq. It said that no political suspects or detainees were held and that nobody could be arrested except on a warrant issued by the court. It also stated that there had been no political executions, that the allegations of torture were false and that Amnesty International's recommendations focused on legal procedures which were already in force. The government gave its assurance that the security forces had frequently been ordered "to comply with the proper procedures on investigation, with strong warnings against abuse of their powers". It stated that cases of torture, which it said happened occasionally, had been investigated and that the perpetrators had been dealt with. The government also offered to investigate allegations of torture made in a previous Amnesty International report published in April 1981, *Iraq: Evidence of Torture*, if the victims, who had been interviewed in exile, were identified and returned to Iraq.

On 5 October Amnesty International replied to the government and on 19 October published *Report and Recommendations of an Amnesty International Mission to the Government of the Republic of Iraq 22-28 January 1983 including the government's response and Amnesty International comments*. Amnesty International reiterated its concerns and recommendations and noted that it had the names and particulars of 520 political prisoners reportedly executed between 1978 and 1981. It also disclosed the names of 22 people said to have died under torture while in custody between 1976 and 1981 and called on the government to investigate these cases and the whereabouts of a further 114 people who had "disappeared" since reportedly being arrested between 1979 and 1982. In December 1983 the government replied to Amnesty International accusing it, among other things, of prejudice and stating that the names Amnesty International had submitted were fictitious.

After the mission, Amnesty International continued to receive allegations of the arrest, detention and torture of suspected opponents of the government. In many cases arrests appeared to be carried out arbitrarily and without warrant. Individuals were often detained without charge or trial with their families being unable to establish where they were being held, despite official assurances to Amnesty International delegates in 1983 that no one could be detained without an arrest warrant issued by the court, and that suspects were detained in official police stations and were entitled to contact their relatives, appoint a lawyer and be seen by a doctor.

Amnesty International did not have sufficient information to gauge the full extent of political imprisonment in Iraq, mainly because of the authorities' disregard for legality and their frequent refusal to acknowledge, explain or record arrests.

The organization believed, however, that at least several hundred people were detained for political reasons in 1983. In one case over 130 members of the family of Ayatollah Muhammad Bagher Al Hakim, the spokesperson in Iran of an Iraqi Shi'a opposition group, ranging in age from nine to 76, were reportedly arrested in the first two weeks in May and detained by the security forces in the holy city of Najaf. Sixty of those arrested were religious scholars. On 24 May Amnesty International expressed its concern to the Iraqi authorities about the reported arrests and requested clarification of the legal status of those arrested. On 6 June an official at the Iraqi embassy in London confirmed that the arrests had taken place. He said that the three eldest members of the family had been released within two days of arrest and that releases were continuing – but that other members of the family were still being detained for interrogation.

In early June Amnesty International learned that at least six of those arrested were executed in prison in Baghdad on 19 May 1983 after being tortured: three brothers of Muhammad Bagher Al Hakim –Sayyid Ala'uddin, Sayyid Abd Al Sahib and Sayyid Muhammad Hussain – and three nephews of Muhammad Bagher Al Hakim –Sayyid Kamal, Sayyid Abdul Wahab and Ahmad Al Hakim. On 20 June Amnesty International sent a telex to President Saddam Hussain and the Minister of the Interior expressing concern and seeking clarification of the reported executions. Amnesty International also urged that no further executions take place. The organization had received no response by the end of 1983.

Five hundred suspected government opponents were reportedly arrested in August in the Kut province but Amnesty International was unable to verify this report and remained unaware of the number of detainees who continued to be held without charge or trial.

In August Amnesty International welcomed the release of 31 Ba'ath Party officials who were originally arrested in mid-July 1979 and had been tried in August 1979 by a special court in Baghdad on charges of plotting against the government. They had been serving sentences ranging from one to 15 years' imprisonment and Amnesty International had taken up the cases for investigation (see *Amnesty International Report 1980*).

A continuing concern throughout 1983 was the fate of several hundred civilians of Iranian origin including children, women and old people, who had been held in prisoner of war camps since the beginning of the Iraq-Iran war in 1980. Amnesty International was concerned that they may have been held solely on the basis of their ethnic origin and without legal proceedings. In May 1983 the International Committee of the Red Cross stated publicly that several hundred such prisoners had been "concealed" from its delegates and that among those it visited "ill-treatment has frequently been observed".

Amnesty International continued to press the Iraqi authorities to clarify the fate of at least 114 people who "disappeared" between 1979 and 1982. In many cases there was clear evidence of the involvement of the security forces in the arrest of the victims prior to "disappearance".

Allegations of torture, sometimes resulting in death, continued. First-hand testimonies of torture received by Amnesty International during 1983 were consistent with information obtained in previous years and indicated that torture was a routine practice in interrogation centres and during pre-trial detention. A former detainee held by the security forces from 30 June 1983 to 18 October 1983 described being beaten on the soles of the feet, being given electric shocks on various parts of the body, and being threatened with having his ear cut off; he was examined after his release by an independent doctor who concluded that the results of the medical examination were consistent with the alleged torture. Former detainees who had not themselves been tortured referred to the torture of fellow detainees, many of whom had reportedly been returned to the cells after interrogation with, among other signs of torture, bruises on the body, burns, broken limbs, hematomes, swollen skin, and with their toe nails having been pulled out. The wives and children of some detainees had allegedly been detained as well and held in nearby cells in order to put pressure on detainees to "cooperate during interrogation".

On 19 October Amnesty International again urged the authorities to conduct impartial inquiries into seven cases of death under torture which it had previously brought to the authorities' attention without receiving any reply. The cases documented in Amnesty International's publication, *Report and Recommendations of an Amnesty International Mission to the Government of the Republic of Iraq* included those of Reber Mulla Husain, Sayyid Muhammad Ismail, Haji Sayyid Ma'rouf, Hameed 'Ati, Adnan Abd Al Jabbar, Muzhir Hall Al Rachid and Ali Hama Salih.

340

During the year Amnesty International recorded over 300 executions but believed that the actual figure was higher. Most of those executed were reportedly army officers, army deserters and draft resisters. Many others were executed for belonging to political parties actively opposed to the government. Among those reportedly executed in May 1983 were six Ayatollahs of the Al Hakim family (see above), 12 members from the Al Zawalem tribe from Samawa and Abdel Faraoun Hussain, a student from Basrah. Reports were also received that at least 11 named doctors were executed for their opposition to the government. Barzan Al Takriti, the head of the Intelligence Service and a half-brother of President Saddam Hussain was reportedly arrested in mid-October for allegedly plotting against the government. Press reports indicated that several army officers loyal to Barzan Al Takriti were executed in November on charges of plotting against the government. Amnesty International was seeking confirmation of the reports at the end of the year.

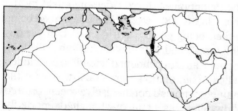

Israel and the Occupied Territories

Amnesty International's concerns were the imprisonment of prisoners of conscience; the use of administrative measures, with no judicial involvement, to physically restrict individuals without charge or trial; arbitrary arrest and short-term detention without charge or trial; allegations of torture or ill-treatment of detainees and the passing of two death sentences. Amnesty International was also concerned that thousands of detainees captured by the Israeli Defence Forces (IDF) after the Israeli invasion of Lebanon were denied the protection accorded to them under internationally accepted standards.

During 1983 Amnesty International worked for the release of 50 prisoners of conscience and investigated the cases of 41 possible prisoners of conscience. Fifty-four of these 91 prisoners were released during the year. Nineteen of the 91 cases were people convicted of security offences, 44 were conscientious objectors, and 28 were under restriction orders.

Among those for whose release Amnesty International worked were six Islamic University students from Gaza who were charged under Military Order (MO) 50 with distributing copies of a political publication in the West Bank without a permit; under MO 101 with incitement against the state of Israel (based on one of the publication's articles); and under MO 378 relating to carrying out activities against public order. The latter charges were based on their having visited and publicly supported patients in Jenin hospital suffering from symptoms of poisoning, whom Palestinians alleged had been deliberately poisoned as a form of harassment, while the Israeli authorities claimed that the symptoms were faked. They were sentenced on 8 June in Jenin to six months' imprisonment. In the organization's view, the respective MOs have been applied in these cases to facilitate the conviction of people for the non-violent exercise of their right to freedom of expression and association in the Occupied Territories.

Amnesty International received reports that other people, mainly students and journalists, were sentenced in 1983 to between one and four months' imprisonment for allegedly violating the same MOs.

Amnesty International was also concerned about the increasing number of selective conscientious objectors imprisoned for refusing to serve in Lebanon (and in one case, in the West Bank). Although some reservists have been permitted to serve elsewhere, Amnesty International received details of 81 other reservists and regulars sentenced to between 10 and 40 days' imprisonment during 1983, some of whom have served repeated prison terms. Amnesty International considered these selective conscientious objectors to be prisoners of conscience and appealed for their unconditional release.

Amnesty International investigated the cases of 13 people convicted of membership of the Palestine Liberation Organization (PLO) or, in two cases, of membership of a student organization allegedly supporting the PLO. They included students, teachers and medical personnel from the West Bank and Gaza sentenced to between eight months' and five years' imprisonment. Amnesty International asked the authorities whether there was any evidence that they had used or advocated violence. The authorities have maintained that membership of the PLO is "akin to advocating violence", but Amnesty International does not consider that membership of the PLO alone demonstrates advocacy of violence.

The detentions by the IDF in Lebanon continued to be a cause of concern to Amnesty International (see *Amnesty International Report 1983*). Those detained included Palestinians, Lebanese and other nationalities suspected of links with the PLO (most of whom had been arrested during 1982), Lebanese who refused to cooperate with the IDF, Lebanese suspected of security violations against the IDF, and

Palestinian and Lebanese women most of whom were apparently detained as hostages for male suspects.

About 12,000 individuals were reportedly detained in Al Ansar between June 1982 and November 1983 with the number held at any one time fluctuating between 4/5,000. The total number of those arrested by the IDF in Lebanon, including those held for interrogation in temporary detention centres in southern Lebanon and, in some cases, in Israel, was not known.

Amnesty International was concerned that the legal status of these detainees had not been clarified by the Israeli authorities, who declared that they were held according to "an act of state", whereby Israeli law and judicial review did not apply; and that they did not consider the detainees to be prisoners of war, although they agreed to apply provisions of the Fourth Geneva Convention with respect to them. In April 1983 Amnesty International expressed its concern to the authorities that detainees were still not being permitted to meet lawyers or relatives, were being denied the right to be confronted with, and refute, the evidence against them, and that they had been held for considerable periods in incommunicado detention.

In their reply of 20 June 1983 to Amnesty International, the Israeli authorities stated that the International Committee of the Red Cross (ICRC) had daily access to Al Ansar detainees, handled contact between detainees and their relatives and delivered letters and family parcels; and that those temporarily detained elsewhere in southern Lebanon for interrogation were seen by the ICRC "no later than 30 days after their arrest". The authorities also said that, in accordance with Article 78 of the Fourth Geneva Convention, detainees could appeal against their imprisonment to an Objections Committee, and that over 1,000 individuals had been released in this way. However, Amnesty International remained concerned that the detainees' legal status had still not been clarified; that the Objections Committee does not constitute a proper judicial instance and that in any case it only makes recommendations, not decisions. Amnesty International was also concerned that detainees still did not have access to lawyers and relatives, and that permitted periods of incommunicado detention were too long.

The issue of the detainees' legal status and their access to lawyers had earlier been brought to the Supreme Court by five Israeli lawyers representing 26 Al Ansar detainees. At the first hearing on 11 May the military authorities agreed that Israeli lawyers qualified to appear before military courts would be allowed to meet Al Ansar detainees, subject to security arrangements. The Supreme Court, in its verdict on 13 July, ruled that the IDF were empowered to detain persons about whom there was a well-defined suspicion that they had acted in a hostile fashion endangering the security of the IDF; and that detainees were subject to the rules laid down in Article 78 of the Fourth Geneva Convention, which includes the right of appeal.

Amnesty International was concerned that the ruling mentioned the applicability of only one provision of the Fourth Geneva Convention, instead of the Convention as a whole, and in particular that it did not address the applicability of Article 116 concerning family visits; and that despite the military authorities' commitment, lawyers were still not allowed access to Al Ansar detainees after the Supreme Court ruling.

On 24 November six members of the IDF held by *Al Fatah* (a faction of the PLO) in Lebanon were exchanged for 4,491 detainees, including 35 women, held in southern Lebanon by the IDF at Al Ansar camp and 100 Palestinians held in Israel, of whom 63 were convicted political prisoners and 37 were Palestinian detainees who had been intercepted at sea by the IDF in September 1983. However Amnesty International learned that around 140 Al Ansar detainees were transferred to Israel some weeks before the prisoner exchange, and detained in Atlit prison in accordance with an emergency regulation of August 1983. They were still being held in incommunicado detention at the end of the year. The organization also received reports that new arrests by the IDF had occurred in southern Lebanon, most of whom were reportedly Lebanese Shi'as.

In July the authorities confirmed the existence of a graveyard in Israel where they admitted some 44 Palestinians, Syrians and others who had died in battle, or in detention in southern Lebanon, had been buried. In a letter to the authorities on 9 August, Amnesty International stressed the importance of publicizing the names, details and cause of death of these people, particularly as large numbers of people from southern Lebanon, including some detainees, had gone missing since June 1982, as well as some detainees who had reportedly "disappeared" after being transferred to Israel. Amnesty International had received no reply from the authorities and no list of names had been published by the end of the year.

Amnesty International continued to be concerned about the increasing use of restriction orders. Under Article 110 of the Defence (Emergency) Regulations (DER) of 1945 in Israel proper, and Article 86 of the Security Provisions Order 378 in the Occupied Territories, people can be confined by administrative order, with no judicial involvement, to their town or village by day and their homes by night, and can be obliged to report regularly to the local police.

In 1983 at least 90 such restriction orders were issued, affecting 76 people including teachers, students, journalists, lawyers, trade unionists and former Mayors. Orders are initially issued for six months but can be repeatedly renewed.

The authorities in their replies to Amnesty International of 14 June and 31 October stated that restriction orders are "preventative", are used to "preserve public safety and order" and that, according to the Fourth Geneva Convention, an occupying power may take such measures for security reasons. Amnesty International believed that many people were restricted for the non-violent expression of their political opinions, and it opposed the imposition of such measures in all cases since those restricted were not charged or tried and had no effective right to refute the evidence against them.

Amnesty International was concerned that MO 378 gives any soldier in the Occupied Territories the power to arrest without a warrant, and allows security suspects to be held for up to 18 days without legal access before being brought before a court. The organization received the names of 37 West Bank high school children – although the actual number was reported to be higher – who were arrested in June under MO 378 just before or just after the start of their matriculation exams. They were held incommunicado for four to six days and were not interrogated or charged, nor told the reasons for their arrest, even though the military authorities later asserted they had been suspected of throwing stones. Consequently those that missed their exams were disqualified from matriculating. In October Amnesty International expressed its concern to the authorities that these school children may have been arbitrarily arrested and detained without having committed any specific offence, and asked for the reasons for each individual's arrest, including the date and nature of any alleged offence. No response had been received by the end of 1983.

Amnesty International was also concerned that the possession of "illegal literature" is frequently used as a pretext to arrest and detain individuals, particularly students, most of whom are then released without charge or trial. It is an offence in the Occupied Territories to possess a book prohibited under Article 88 (2) of the DER or, under MO 50 as amended by MO 862, to possess a book which, although not prohibited, is considered a risk to public order and security.

Amnesty International continued to receive allegations of the torture or ill-treatment of security suspects detained in the Occupied Territories, either on arrest or during interrogation. In one case, a civil action for assault with grievous bodily harm was brought in June against a police staff sergeant by a Jenin schoolteacher, Walid Al Arda, who was arrested on 17 May and held in the military detention centre of Al Far'a. Walid Al Arda alleged that when he refused to confess to incitement to the Jenin poisoning conspiracy (see above) he was beaten with a stick on the shoulders, back, hands and soles of the feet, and subjected to electric shocks and threats and that his family was verbally abused. The trial was pending at the end of the year.

On 28 December two Israeli Arabs were sentenced to death for the pre-meditated murder of an Israeli soldier and were seeking an appeal. Three military court judges passed the sentences contrary to a long standing practice in Israel not to impose the death penalty.

On 8 February the Kahan Commission of Enquiry, set up to determine whether the Israeli authorities had any responsibility for the Sabra and Chatila massacres in September 1982 (see *Amnesty International Report 1983*), published its findings. It concluded that Israeli forces (who had been in military control of the area at the time) had "absolutely no direct responsibility" for the massacre but that Israeli officials should have foreseen "from the information at their disposal and from things which were common knowledge that there was danger of a massacre" if the Phalange militia entered the camps without preventive measures being taken. The commission concluded also that Israeli officials did not take "energetic and immediate" actions to restrain the members of the Lebanese militia or to put a stop to their actions. The commission recommended that measures be taken against certain named officials, including the Israeli Minister of Defence.

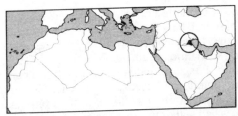

Kuwait

On 12 December bombs exploded in two foreign embassies in Kuwait, in the airport and in other installations, killing six people and injuring over 60. According to official sources, 19 people had been arrested by the end of the year and charged with carrying out the bombings. They included Iraqi and Lebanese members of *Al Da'wa Al Islamiya* (The Islamic Call), an Iraqi movement with pro-Iranian sympathies which is composed predominantly of Shi'a Muslims. The government announced that it had set up a State Security Court to try them.

Amnesty International received reports from various sources that large numbers of Kuwaiti, Iranian and Iraqi Shi'as were also arrested and detained following the bombings. Unofficial sources claimed that 3/4,000 had been arrested, while the authorities put the number at 100. Amnesty International was concerned at reports that some of those detained were ill-treated and held incommunicado. Amnesty International was also concerned that large numbers of the Iraqis arrested

346

had been deported, or had been threatened with deportation, to Iraq, where it was feared that some may have been considered opponents of the government and that as such they may have faced imprisonment, ill-treatment or execution.

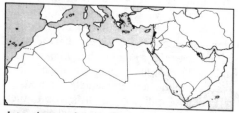

Lebanon

During 1983 Amnesty International was concerned about reports of arbitrary arrests and detentions, often incommunicado, without legal process; torture and other forms of ill-treatment of prisoners; abduction and "disappearances"; extrajudicial killings and the death penalty. There were reports of these abuses in regions of the Lebanon effectively under the control of the Lebanese government, the Israeli Defence Forces (IDF), the Syrian army and a number of Lebanese militias.

At the end of 1983 the Lebanese authorities appeared to be in control of the greater part of Beirut, having moved into West Beirut and disarmed the Muslim militias. Their control, however, was tentative since the Lebanese Forces, a coalition of mainly Maronite Christian militias of which the *Kata'ib*, Phalange militia, were an integral part, were not disarmed in East Beirut and effectively controlled an area which extended from East Beirut to the mountains of the Metn and Kesrouan. The Israeli forces had withdrawn to a line of defence on the Awali river and were in control of Lebanese territory to the south of the river. In the Shuf mountains the militia of the Progressive Socialist Party (PSP), comprising mainly Druze fighters, had defeated an attempt by the Lebanese army to replace the withdrawing Israeli forces and appeared to be in control of most of the territory. The remainder of the Lebanon –the Beka'a valley to the east and Tripoli and the 'Akkar plain to the north – was within Syria's sphere of influence, if not effectively under Syrian control. Owing to the complex military and political situation described above and to continued inter-factional fighting throughout 1983, Amnesty International was unable fully to investigate many of its concerns in the Lebanon.

During 1983 Amnesty International continued to be concerned about reports of widescale arbitrary arrests by the Lebanese army and security forces of people in West Beirut and the Palestinian refugee camps. By the end of 1982 Lebanese officials had acknowledged the detention of 1441 people, and the release of 469 over an unspecified period; the number of detainees reportedly increased during early 1983. The official justification for the arrests was that those arrested – mostly Palestinians but also Lebanese and other nationals – were criminals and illegal aliens without residence permits in the Lebanon. Amnesty International was concerned that arrests were reportedly sometimes carried out by people in plain clothes, without proper identification or arrest warrants, and that those arrested were held incommunicado, not being allowed visits by lawyers or relatives and without outside observers such as the International Committee of the Red Cross (ICRC) having access to them. Amnesty International had addressed these concerns to President Amin Gemayel on 22 December 1982 but did not receive a response from the Lebanese authorities in 1983.

Reports indicated that many of those arrested were being held incommunicado by the Lebanese authorities at the seven-storey General Security building in Badaro, at the Ministry of Defence building at Yarzeh, and at Rumieh prison outside Beirut. In March 1983 the ICRC were allowed to make initial visits to 86 detainees at Badaro. Subsequently they were only allowed to visit Rumieh prison where they registered some 700 detainees. As of the end of the year, neither families, lawyers nor humanitarian organizations had been allowed to visit Yarzeh; unconfirmed reports estimated that more than 2,000 detainees were being held there.

Amnesty International also remained concerned about reports that the Lebanese Forces continued to hold a large number of detainees, incommunicado and outside any normal legal process, in secret detention centres. Such detainees were reportedly being held at the headquarters of the Lebanese Forces at Karantina, the Adonis barracks prison near Jounieh (where over 200 women were reportedly held) and a number of camps in the Kesrouan region. On 26 April 1983 six detainees who had been held without charge or other legal process were handed over by the *Kata'ib* to the Lebanese authorities. They included Habib Shartouni, detained by the *Kata'ib* since September 1982 on suspicion of placing the bomb which killed President-elect Bachir Gemayel on 14 September 1982; Joseph Kazazian and Nazih Shaya, suspected of an attempt on the life of Bachir Gemayel which led to the death of his daughter in 1980; and three others held since 1981 on suspicion of causing explosions in East Beirut. A week later a further 11 detainees were transferred by the *Kata'ib* into the custody of the Lebanese authorities. Joseph Kazazian and Nazih Shaya were subse-quently tried, sentenced to death and executed in November 1983. Amnesty International was unaware of the fate or whereabouts of the other detainees.

In southern Lebanon Amnesty International continued to be concerned that thousands of detainees held by the Israeli forces were being denied the legal rights accorded by internationally accepted standards. (For further details see entry on Israel and Occupied Territories (page 342)). On 24 November 1983, 4,491 detainees from Al-Ansar prison were released by the Israeli authorities in exchange for six Israeli prisoners held by *Al-Fatah* (a faction of the Palestinian Liberation Organization).

During 1983 Amnesty International received a number of disturbing reports concerning conditions of detention and the ill-treatment of detainees held incommunicado by various parties in the Lebanon. Several reports, some of them from former detainees, alleged that detainees held by the Lebanese authorities at the Lebanese General Security Headquarters in Yarzeh had been routinely beaten and otherwise ill-treated during interrogation. Former detainees expressed particular concern about the brutal treatment in prison of Thuraya Rajeh, a 26-year-old Palestinian. In another case, Paola Crociani, an Italian photo-journalist, was taken from her home at 10.30 p.m. on Wednesday April 20 by four armed Lebanese security officers and detained for 36 hours before being deported from the Lebanon. While she herself did not claim to have been seriously ill-treated, she reported having heard prisoners screaming and loud music throughout the two nights she spent in detention. She also reported having seen, during the daytime, prison guards "equipped with steel whips covered with leather straps tied and hanging from both sides"; prisoners being beaten and trampled on by guards; others who had been deprived of food or water for several days; and a room with 400-500 detainees "heaped over one another for lack of space". In July 1983 five British and American journalists were detained and taken to the military security headquarters in Beirut where they were reportedly blindfolded, punched and kicked. One journalist, Ken Jobson of United Press International Television News (UPITN), reported that he was knocked to the ground and kicked in the stomach by a Lebanese soldier, "raising a large weal".

Reports also reached Amnesty International of the torture or ill-treatment of detainees held by the Lebanese Forces. In one incident a woman released by the *Kata'ib* in July 1983 reported being taken blindfold from a roadblock to a detention centre in the Kesrouan region and held with 127 other women detainees. She alleged that she had been tortured, that she had received cigarette burns on her eyelids and chest and that she had been assaulted with a stick which had been twisted inside her. She also reported that some of the detainees were pregnant after having been raped by the guards.

In another case, Ali Bajuq was detained by the *Kata'ib* for a few hours but reportedly needed 20 days hospitalization to recover from the effects of serious ill-treatment. According to the hospital's medical report he had been cut a number of times with a sharp instrument and had been injected with several drugs including heroin and a compound similar to strychnine.

There were increasing fears during 1983 about the fate of hundreds of people who had "disappeared". In July 1983 the Lebanese Prime Minister Shafiq al-Wazzan set up a special committee to investigate the situation of people "detained, abducted or disappeared" since September 1982 in West Beirut, the Shuf and Mount Lebanon. The committee, chaired by Judge Sami Yunis, was reported in the Lebanese press to be looking into a list of over 900 names supplied to it by the Committee of the Relatives of Detained or Disappeared Persons in Lebanon. Although a number of those named on the list may have been among those killed during the massacre which took place at the Sabra and Chatila refugee camps in September 1982, Amnesty International received reports that many "disappeared" individuals were being detained incommunicado by the Lebanese army and security forces or had been abducted and were being similarly held by the Lebanese Forces. There was growing concern throughout 1983 that many of the "disappeared" might no longer be alive. Relatives continued to press for information on, and access to, the many detainees being held incommunicado.

During 1983 Amnesty International was aware of reports of a number of extrajudicial executions carried out by non-governmental forces in control of territory. These included allegations that the Lebanese Forces had executed and buried detainees in a mass graveyard at their headquarters in Karantina; that "murder squads" belonging to the National Guard and to the Lebanese Forces in southern Lebanon were abducting and executing selected Palestinians living in Sidon in order to intimidate others into leaving Lebanon; and that villagers taken prisoner had been massacred by both sides during the fighting between the Lebanese Forces and Druze militias for control of the Shuf mountains.

On 8 February 1983, the Kahan Commission, the Israeli commission of inquiry into the massacre which took place at the Sabra and Chatila refugee camps in September 1982 published its final report. The commission's main finding was that "the atrocities in the refugee camps were perpetrated by members of the Phalangists, and that absolutely no direct responsibility devolves upon Israel or upon those who acted on its behalf". The commission also concluded that Israeli officials should have foreseen the danger of a massacre if the Phalange militia entered the camps, and that they did not take "energetic and immediate" actions to restrain the Lebanese militiamen or to put a stop to their actions. (See also entry on Israel and Occupied Territories

350

(page 345)). The inquiry into the same events which was initiated by the Lebanese authorities had not been completed by the end of 1983. This inquiry, led by Prosecutor General Assad Germanos, was being carried out in the strictest secrecy, without even the procedures followed being made public.

On 7 April 1983 Amnesty International sent a cable to President Amin Gemayel expressing deep concern about the execution by hanging of Ibrahim Tarraf, convicted of murder on 3 March 1983. This was the first judicial execution to have been carried out in the Lebanon since 1972. Between April and December Amnesty International was aware of 25 death sentences having been passed by Lebanese courts, many of them *in absentia*, and of over 100 cases where the Military Prosecutor had asked for the death penalty. On 6 December 1983 Amnesty International again wrote to President Gemayel expressing concern about the death sentences passed on 26 November 1983 on Joseph Kazazian and Nazih Shaya (see above). In its letter Amnesty International stated that the organization did not condone acts of violence but opposed capital punishment unreservedly. It urged the government to commute the death sentences, should legal appeals be exhausted and the cases come before the President for review.

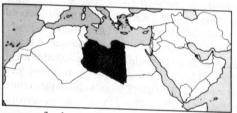

Libya

Amnesty International remained concerned about the continued imprisonment of prisoners of conscience, many of whom were serving life sentences and about the retrial of prisoners of conscience on the same charges on which they had originally been tried. The cases of those retried were heard before a revolutionary court which lacked basic legal safeguards and which handed down death sentences in some of the cases. Other concerns were the continued detention of political prisoners, including prisoners of conscience, who continued to be held after having been acquitted of charges against them or having completed their sentences; and the prolonged detention without charge of political suspects. Amnesty International was also concerned about repeated allegations of torture. A number of judicial executions for allegedly political crimes were carried out during the year, and calls for the "physical liquidation of enemies of the revolution" were renewed by the General People's Congress at its annual meeting on 17 February 1983.

It was difficult for Amnesty International to determine the exact number of prisoners of conscience being held but information reaching the organization indicated that among the hundreds of people arrested arbitrarily since 1980 were many who had been imprisoned because of their non-violent political or religious beliefs or ethnic origin, or simply because of their relationship with people who were active political opponents of the government (see *Amnesty International Report 1980, 1981, 1982, 1983*). In most cases it was impossible to establish the specific basis for detention: either the person was still held without charge, or the charges were phrased in such general terms that Amnesty International was unable to ascertain whether they included a specific offence; or the lack of fair trial by the revolutionary court made the validity and basis of convictions questionable.

Amnesty International continued to appeal for the release of 85 prisoners of conscience, nine of whom were retried by a revolutionary court during 1983 for the same offence as at their original trial and given fresh sentences, in some cases including the death penalty.

Four of those retried belong to a group of prisoners of conscience who have been in prison since they were originally arrested in April 1973 for alleged membership of illegal political parties (the Islamic Liberation Party, the Marxist Party, and the Muslim Brotherhood). They were brought to trial in June 1974 and in February 1977 and were given sentences in the latter trial ranging from four to 15 years' imprisonment. However the Revolutionary Command Council decreed that the sentences should be amended to life imprisonment or death. Amnesty International received reports that the four, Hassan Ahmad Al Kurdi, Abdullah Bilgasim Al Mislati, Salih Ali Al Zarouq Nawal and Muhammad Muhadhab Haffaf, each serving a term of life imprisonment, were retried in April 1983 before the revolutionary court and sentenced to death. Muhammad Muhadhab Haffaf was reportedly hanged in public in April 1983 (see below).

Another retrial of concern to Amnesty International involved 25 prisoners of conscience, all alleged former members of the pro-Iraqi wing of the Ba'ath Party who were originally arrested in February-March 1980 and were tried and acquitted in early 1982 (see *Amnesty International Report 1983*). However, they remained in prison following an administrative decree ordering their continued detention. During the first two weeks in July 1983 all 25 defendants were retried by the revolutionary court headed by Abdul Salam Al Zadma, a captain in the special security branch and a member of the revolutionary committees. Three of the defendants were sentenced to death: Farid Ashraf, a lawyer aged 50, Muhammad Hillal, a shopkeeper in his fifties, and Mustapha Al Nawari, a lawyer in his thirties. Two others were sentenced to eight years' imprisonment: Dr Abdulhamid Albabour, a veterinary surgeon, and Mahmoud Omar Abu Obeid, a government employee in his mid-forties. The other 20 defendants were acquitted and released. On 1 August 1983 Amnesty International appealed to the authorities not to carry out the death sentences and to release all five prisoners.

Amnesty International was concerned that normal trial procedures as laid down in the Penal Code do not apply in the revolutionary courts established according to principles of "revolutionary legitimacy" at the revolutionary committees' meeting in February 1980 (see *Amnesty International Report 1983*). Trials in these courts are summary and held *in camera*. The tribunals consist of members of the revolutionary commitees, there is no right of defence and no right of appeal to a higher court.

In December 1983 Amnesty International expressed its concerns to the authorities about the continued detention of nine prisoners of conscience, seven of whom were acquitted in 1980 when they were re-tried for the same offence for which they had previously been tried by a criminal court in 1976. They were: al-Mehdi Muhammad al-'Adl, Muhammad Muhammad al-'Adl, Oreibi 'Amr Youssef, Ibrahim Mahmoud al-Sida'iy, Abdullah Ali al-Khouja, Mansour Abdul Salam al-Majdoub, Muhammad al Makki al-Imam, Salih Inna's Youssef and Muhammad Ali al-Shridi. All nine had originally been arrested with 12 others in 1975 on charges of forming a secret political organization "with principles opposed to those of the 1969 Fateh revolution".

Sixteen other political prisoners were still being detained after they had been acquitted at their trial before the criminal court in Tripoli in February 1983, reportedly on charges of forming a political organization which called for Berber rule in Libya. The 16 belonged to a group of 40 people who were originally arrested in May 1980 and tried in February 1981: these 16 were reportedly acquitted, three others received death sentences and the rest were given sentences ranging from 10 years' to life imprisonment. No details of the exact charges against them or their places of detention were known to Amnesty International.

During the year Amnesty International learned that at least 23 political prisoners were still in prison after having completed sentences of seven to 13 years' imprisonment which had been handed down in 1969 and 1970 on charges of plotting against the government. They included Muftah Al Sharif, Muhammad Al Shairi, Abdel Matloub Azouz, Khalil Ja'afar, Attiah Al Tarwahi and Abdul Azim Kabbassa. Amnesty International was not aware of any judicial procedure which allowed the continued detention of prisoners whose sentences had expired.

Frequent and consistent allegations of torture continued to be received by Amnesty International. Torture was reportedly used most frequently to obtain confessions and information about "the enemies of the revolution" and their activities. Former prisoners interviewed by the organization said that they had been whipped while chained to the wall, burnt with cigarettes and threatened with execution. Other techniques described included whipping and sustained beatings on the soles of the feet, heavy blows to the ears and electric shocks, particularly to the head and genitals. Prisoners who had not themselves been tortured said they had frequently heard the screams of people being tortured and said that they were sometimes forced to watch fellow prisoners being tortured. The main torture centre under the jurisdiction of the revolutionary committees was allegedly in Al Hadba Al Khadra' in Tripoli.

During the year Amnesty International had access to the findings of the medical examination of one of the two people tortured on 13 November 1982 by members of the revolutionary committees at the residence of the Secretary General of the Libyan People's Bureau in Bonn, Federal Republic of Germany (see *Amnesty International Report 1983*). The findings showed that the clinical evidence was consistent with the torture allegations. Two Libyans residing in Bonn, Dr Mustapha Zaidi and Abdullah Yahia were prosecuted and brought to trial on charges of torturing fellow Libyans. However, the trial was stopped after the West German authorities decided to exchange the accused for eight West German nationals who had been detained in Libya in April. On 15 May the two accused Libyans were released and returned to Libya.

Amnesty International received reports that five political prisoners were executed in Libya in April 1983 and that 10 others were under sentence of death, all for alleged membership of illegal political organizations. Muhammad Muhadhab Haffaf (see above), was hanged in public at Al Fateh University in Tripoli on 7 April 1983. Four Palestinian teachers were also publicly executed on the same day at Ajdabia secondary school on charges of belonging to the Islamic Liberation Party. On 19 April Amnesty International sent a cable to Colonel Mu'ammar Gaddafi and to Muhammad Al Zarouq Rajab, Secretary of the General Secretariat of the General People's Congress, expressing concern about these reported executions and seeking confirmation that they had taken place but received no reply.

On 11 March 1983 Amnesty International warned that the lives of Libyans living abroad were again under threat following a decision on 17 February 1983 by the General People's Congress to hunt down and liquidate all Libyans considered hostile to the revolution: "Every citizen is responsible for the liquidation of the enemies of the revolution." This decision came after repeated urgings by Colonel Mu'ammar Gadaffi in previous months that the General People's Congress should approve the elimination of "enemies abroad".

On 23 March Amnesty International launched a worldwide campaign to expose political killings by governments. In its 131 page report, *Political Killings by Governments*, Amnesty International said that since the February 1980 call for the "liquidation of enemies of the revolution abroad" at least 14 Libyan citizens had been killed or wounded in assassination attempts outside Libya.

In December 1983 the Libyan People's Bureau in Brussels described the official policy relating to the killings of Libyans abroad as lawful action. In a written reply to Amnesty International the People's Bureau said that "many countries liquidate their political enemies secretly, only the Jamahiriya publicly announces this policy, because we are entitled to do so and all the laws support us."

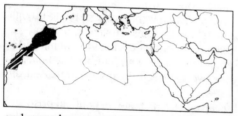

Morocco

Amnesty International continued to work on behalf of more than 200 actual or possible prisoners of conscience and was also concerned about extended periods of detention without trial and of incommunicado detention; the ill-treatment of detainees; "disappearances"; and the possibility of the execution of prisoners under sentence of death.

Amnesty International called for the release of 116 prisoners of conscience, and investigated the cases of a further 90 prisoners. One hundred and five of the adopted prisoners of conscience had been tried and sentenced to long prison terms in 1973 and 1977, for alleged membership of various Marxist-Leninist groups. During the year three such prisoners were released when their terms expired and another, Jamal ed-Din Benomar, was released before his 10-year sentence expired.

Among those prisoners whose cases Amnesty International continued to investigate were more than 80 Saharans who "disappeared" as long ago as 1976 after having been taken into custody by Moroccan security forces. The Moroccan authorities have never officially acknowledged their detention despite repeated inquiries from Amnesty International.

Amnesty International also investigated the cases of individuals who were tried and convicted in 1983 in connection with an altercation that took place in May 1983 between members of two factions of the major opposition party, the *Union socialiste des forces populaires* (USFP), the Socialist Union of Popular Forces. Four USFP members, three of whom also belonged to the *Association marocaine des droits de l'homme* (AMDH), Moroccan Association of Human Rights, were sentenced to three years' imprisonment. Abderrahman Ben Amar, a lawyer and a member of the administrative committees of both the AMDH and of the USFP; the journalist El-Yazid Barakat; Muhammad Filahi and Muhammad Bougrine. A fifth, sentenced to three years' imprisonment, was released for treatment of a serious illness.

Amnesty International feared that these prisoners may in fact have been tried, convicted and sentenced for their non-violent political views rather than for offences allegedly committed during the altercation. Amnesty International was also concerned about a number of aspects of their arrest and trial. These included the following:

1) basic procedural requirements set out in Moroccan law relating to arrest and *garde à vue*, incommunicado detention by the police, were not adhered to;

2) police interrogations were reported to have focused largely on the political views of the suspects;

3) allegations of ill-treatment during interrogation were made to the court but were not examined by it;

4) serious questions challenging the faithfulness of the police record of interrogations were not given a proper hearing in court;

5) during the trial, requests by the defence were systematically rejected – requests to have the court hear additional witnesses and requests to seek medical expertise on the treatment meted out to the detainees and handwriting expertise to determine whether signatures to the police interrogation records had been falsified.

In another case, Amnesty International issued an urgent appeal on behalf of a number of secondary-school students, including Mustapha Sabir, Fouad Abdelmoumni, Abdelkarim Marir and Abdellatif Chaiboub, who were arrested in Casablanca in January and February 1983 and were reportedly held incommunicado in police detention centres for months, during which time there were fears that they were being ill-treated. Their fate reportedly remained unknown at the end of the year despite inquiries to the authorities in Casablanca from Amnesty International and their families.

During the year, hundreds of amnesties were handed down to mark national holidays, but they did not benefit political prisoners. A separate amnesty took place on 5 May 1983, reportedly to enable the affected individuals to participate in elections planned for June. Among the 22 persons amnestied on this occasion were three officials of the *Confédération démocratique du travail* (CDT), the Democratic Confederation of Labour, and one official of the USFP, each of whom had been in preventive detention since June 1981 and had been adopted by Amnesty International as prisoners of conscience. Following their release, Amnesty International telexed messages to King Hassan II, to the Prime Minister and to the Minister of Justice welcoming the releases and requesting that the amnesties be extended to include all prisoners of conscience. In November, the two remaining prisoners in this group, also adopted by Amnesty International as prisoners of conscience, Noubir Amaoui and Mustapha Karchaoui, respectively Secretary General of the CDT and editor-in-chief of the suppressed USFP newspaper, *al-Muharrir*, were also released from preventive detention.

Amnesty International continued to receive reports of ill-treatment occurring either at the hands of the Moroccan police or, in some cases, in Moroccan prisons. The lawyer Ben Amar was allegedly ill-treated during and after his arrest in connection with the altercation between factions of the USFP (see above), and the secondary-school students referred to above were also said to have been ill-treated. Amnesty International was also concerned about the conditions which may have led to a prolonged hunger-strike begun on 5 February 1983 by five USFP militants who had been sentenced to four years' imprisonment following unrest in June 1981 in Casablanca and other Moroccan cities. In cables to King Hassan II, as well as to the Prime Minister and the Ministers of Justice and Health, Amnesty International's Secretary General urged that all appropriate medical care be provided for these prisoners.

On 2/3 December 1983, many political prisoners in Kenitra Central Prison undertook a 48-hour hunger-strike to draw attention to the serious psychiatric problems and continuing imprisonment of two prisoners of conscience, Hassan el Bou and Miloud Achdini, both of whom had been the subject of repeated appeals over the years from Amnesty International to the Moroccan authorities. Amnesty International remained seriously concerned at reports that their mental health was continuing to deteriorate.

Amnesty International was also seriously concerned about the refusal of the Moroccan authorities to clarify the fate of approximately 100 military prisoners arrested following attempts to assassinate King Hassan II in 1971 and 1972 or to acknowledge where they were held. Reports indicated that these individuals have been held since 1973 in appalling conditions – windowless, filthy and unventilated cells, extremes of temperature, solitary confinement, arbitrary punishments and beatings, inadequate food, and the complete lack of any medical care. Some continued to be held long after their sentences had expired.

Amnesty International received reports that approximately 20 of these prisoners may already have died, many at least in part because of the very bad conditions. Despite repeated appeals from Amnesty International and other sources, the Moroccan authorities continued to refuse to comment on the fate of these prisoners.

Amnesty International did not learn of any death sentences having been carried out during 1983. However the organization received information during the year that at least 58 people were being held in Kenitra Central Prison under sentence of death. One of them, Ahmed el-Khiari, had been under sentence of death since 1972 for a political murder, and was being held in a special section of Kenitra Central Prison in extremely unhealthy conditions: his small exercise area was reportedly deep under ground, receiving little natural light, and he appeared to be suffering from the cold and humidity in winter. He was also being permitted only limited contact with other prisoners. On 13 October 1983, Amnesty International wrote to the Moroccan Minister of Justice requesting confirmation of the number of prisoners threatened with execution and submitted a list of names for verification, but as of the end of 1983 had received no reply.

Finally, Amnesty International received several reports that civilians had been arrested in El Aayoun in the context of the war in the Western Sahara and had been tortured, although the organization was unable to verify them. Amnesty International also continued to be concerned about Polisario Front members reportedly held as prisoners by the Polisario Front since 1975 for having criticized the Front's policies. Amnesty International issued a statement on the subject in 1981, but was subsequently unable to obtain any information about their condition.

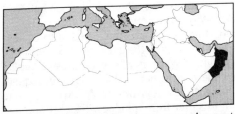

The Sultanate of Oman

Amnesty International learned, during the year, of the release of Murad Abdul Wahab whose case Amnesty International had been working on since October 1973. A customs house official in Bahrain, he had been arrested there in February 1973 with a number of others, following anti-government demonstrations and strikes. He subsequently

358

"disappeared" and Amnesty International later learned that he had been deported to Oman in March 1973, official sources in Bahrain claiming he was Omani by origin. He was tried in Oman and sentenced to 10 years' imprisonment. Since 1973, no response had been received from the Omani authorities to inquiries about his whereabouts, his well-being and the charges against him. His family were also unable to get any information about Murad, were unable to correspond with him and only received permission to visit him in prison in 1982.

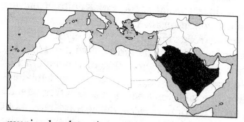

Saudi Arabia

Amnesty International was concerned about the reported detention of possible prisoners of conscience; the incommunicado detention of people apparently for political reasons and inadequate procedures which led to long delays before such detainees were charged and tried; and allegations of torture or ill-treatment of detainees. The organization was also concerned about the imposition of amputations, floggings and the death penalty as judicial punishments.

There was no response from the Saudi authorities to Amnesty International's letter of 22 December 1982, which asked for confirmation of the arrest of 128 possible prisoners of conscience and details of the charges or pending trial procedures against them (see *Amnesty International Report 1983*). Reports of the arrests were denied by the Saudi authorities in the Saudi and international press. During 1983, however, Amnesty International learned of further arrests and several releases and by the end of the year the organization had compiled a list of the names of over 170 people reportedly held incommunicado and whose whereabouts were unknown, some of whom the organization believed might be detained for the non-violent exercise of their human rights. They included Wadad al-Qumri 'Abd al-Mun'im, a 42-year-old Palestinian school teacher and member of the executive committee of the General Union of Palestinian Women who was arrested on 27 February 1982 in Riyadh while visiting her husband. Her subsequent whereabouts were unknown and there was growing concern for her state of health as she was known to suffer from a kidney disorder and had already had one of her kidneys removed. Among those reportedly released was Fawzia al-Bakr, a lecturer at the sociology department of the University of Riyadh and a journalist with the Saudi newspaper *al-Jazeera*.

At the end of 1983 Amnesty International was also investigating the reported detention in December 1983 of several Sri Lankan workers after they had tried to form trade unions on construction sites and had threatened to take strike action. Authorities in Saudi Arabia were known to have prohibited the formation of trade unions and other forms of labour organization on the grounds that official institutions existed to protect the rights of workers and to hear their grievances.

Amnesty International received a number of allegations of torture or ill-treatment from present or former detainees during the year. Most of the allegations were made by people detained for criminal offences and they suggested that ill-treatment occurred most often during the period immediately after arrest, while detainees were held in police custody awaiting trial or release. Peter Savage, a 36-year-old Briton who was detained for three months on charges of embezzlement, alleged that during his interrogation at a Riyadh police station he was beaten with a stick, told that this treatment would continue until he had signed a written confession and threatened that his wife would be arrested if he did not cooperate. Lechner Walter, an Austrian who was detained in April 1983 and subsequently convicted of smuggling whisky into the country, alleged that he was beaten with a stick and threatened with being hung up by the feet, given electric shock treatment and being beaten until he was crippled. Several former detainees complained that the risk of ill-treatment during detention increased because, in the absence of witnesses, the law requires a confession to convict for certain offences.

In at least one case the authorities reportedly carried out investigations into complaints of torture and disciplined those responsible. Keith Carmichael, a British subject, complained that he had been threatened with sexual assault and that his feet were padlocked to the back of a chair and that the soles of his feet were beaten with a cane while being held in incommunicado detention between November 1981 and 31 January 1982 (see *Amnesty International Report 1983*). Although the authorities made no direct response to Amnesty International's request for an investigation into these allegations, the organization learned that an inquiry was instituted in 1983 with Mr Carmichael being given the opportunity to identify some of those he believed were responsible for his ill-treatment. At least one prison guard was reportedly imprisoned as a result. The findings of the inquiry were not made public.

Islamic Law (*al-Shari'a*), as practised in Saudi Arabia, imposes amputations as the punishment for repeated theft where there are no mitigating circumstances. During 1983 Amnesty International was aware of one such punishment. In Mecca, on 30 December 1983, Jamil Muhammad Ahmad, a Yemeni national, had his right hand amputated from the wrist after being convicted of robbing a safe. Amnesty

International holds amputations to be a form of cruel, inhuman and degrading punishment, and thus prohibited under international law.

Amnesty International was also concerned that cruel, inhuman and degrading punishment was judicially imposed in the form of the flogging of prisoners. According to Saudi officials this form of punishment is designed to humiliate and rehabilitate rather than cause pain. The official administering the blows is meant to hold a copy of the Quran under his cane arm, using only the lower arm to wield the cane, and the strokes to the clothed back and buttocks are reportedly not allowed to draw blood. However, Amnesty International has learned that there are wide discrepancies between public floggings, which appear to be carried out in accordance with the above stipulations, and floggings which take place in prisons. In the case of the latter, former detainees reported that it was often painful, causing weals and bruising, and that the intensity of the strokes was often dependent on such factors as the detainees' relationship with the guards or whether the person being flogged was first or last in a series.

During 1983 Amnesty International learned of several cases of foreigners being sentenced to be flogged, including six British subjects who were sentenced to terms of imprisonment and an overall total of 2,700 lashes for smuggling alcohol. The Saudi press also publicized the cases of three Saudi workers who were convicted in June 1983 of negligence which led indirectly to the death of a child, and who were sentenced to terms of imprisonment and 30 lashes each.

During 1983 Amnesty International learned of 21 executions in Saudi Arabia which were carried out in public and reported in the Saudi media. In all but two cases the victims had been convicted of murder. In some cases the executions were carried out many years after the criminal conviction and imposition of sentence. Hussein bin Hassan al-Maleki was executed in Taif, on 19 August 1983, for a murder he committed in 1966; and 'Ali ibn Sa'ud Salih al-Fakieh and Munira bint 'Abd al-Talib al-Sabi' were executed on 4 November in Riyadh for a murder they committed in 1968. Under Islamic law the relatives of a murder victim may either demand retribution (*Qisas*) in the form of the death of the murderer, or they may waive such a claim freely or by settlement. In both cases the courts found it necessary to wait until the heirs of the deceased had reached the age of maturity and had all agreed on execution as the form of retribution before the sentences could be carried out. Executions are generally carried out by hanging, but stoning is the prescribed form of execution for some crimes. One case in 1983 involved Hind bint 'Ali 'Abd al-Ghani Dighna who was found guilty of committing adultery with Farouk ibn 'Ali Saytafi and of helping him to kill her husband. He was executed for murder and she was stoned to death for committing adultery. During 1983 Amnesty International

addressed several cables to Minister of Interior Prince Naif bin 'Abd al-
'Aziz expressing deep concern over the executions that had been carried
out and reiterating the organization's unconditional opposition to the
death penalty.

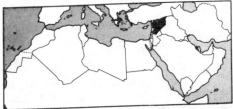

Syria

The main concerns of
Amnesty International
were the imprisonment
of over 250 prisoners
of conscience; wide
powers used by the security forces to arrest and detain thousands of
political prisoners; long-term detentions without trial; summary procedures and the lack of legal safeguards in trials by military and state
security courts; the routine use of torture by the security forces;
"disappearances" and the death penalty. Many of these human rights
violations were facilitated by provisions of the state of emergency which
had been in force since 1963.

On 26 April 1983 Amnesty International submitted a memorandum
to the Syrian government outlining practices followed by the security
forces that systematically violated human rights in Syria. The organization
concluded that there was urgent need for the government to take specific
steps with respect to the control, supervision and monitoring of the
activities of the security forces.

Among its specific conclusions Amnesty International stated the
view that a pattern of arbitrary arrests, without authorization or legal
warrants, was being carried out by the security forces in accordance
with emergency legislation introduced in 1963; that thousands of
Syrians, including non-violent critics of the government, had been
arrested and held without charge or trial, some for over 12 years; that
detainees had usually not been informed of the reason for arrest at the
time of arrest and were regularly denied their basic rights during
detention; that the extent, consistency and detail of torture allegations
received persistently over the years, some supported by medical
evidence, had forced the organization to conclude that torture was
frequently inflicted in the course of interrogation; and that documented
instances of "disappearances" and extrajudicial executions required
investigation and clarification by the government.

Amnesty International recommended:

— that steps be taken to enforce existing legislation which requires the production of arrest warrants and provides direct appeal machinery against wrongful arrest;
— that all provisions for preventive detention be revoked and current detention cases be reviewed in order to release those detained for the non-violent exercise of their human rights;
— that names of individuals arrested or released be published and relatives be informed immediately of the arrest and place of detention of a prisoner;
— that arrested individuals have immediate access to a lawyer and that close relatives be allowed to visit within 48 hours of arrest and regularly thereafter;
— that current legislation and practices designed to prevent abuses by the security forces be reviewed and an impartial investigation be initiated into allegations of torture or ill-treatment with those responsible brought to trial and adequate compensation made to the victims;
— that a full and impartial public investigation be instituted into the cases of "disappearances" or extrajudicial executions mentioned in the report, and that those responsible be punished.

Amnesty International expressed the hope that the memorandum and its recommendations would provide the basis for positive and constructive discussions and stated its willingness to send a delegation to Damascus for this purpose. Following further unsuccessful attempts to elicit a response from the Syrian authorities, the memorandum was published on 16 November 1983 in the report, *Report from Amnesty International to the Government of the Syrian Arab Republic*.

During 1983 Amnesty International worked for the release of 265 adopted prisoners of conscience and investigated the cases of 236 possible prisoners of conscience. They included officials of previous governments; members of the professions, including lawyers, doctors and engineers; members of banned political parties and a number of "disappeared" persons.

Amnesty International continued to work on behalf of 148 members of the banned Communist Party Political Bureau (CPPB) – whom the organization had adopted as prisoners of conscience (see *Amnesty International Report 1982*). They included Omar Kashash, former Secretary General of the Syrian Printers Union and also a member of the Executive Committee of the Syrian Trade Union Federation. After several arrests and a total of nearly six years in detention between 1958 and 1980 – during which he was reportedly tortured and ill-treated – he was again arrested in October 1980 and has since been held without charge or trial at al-Qala'a prison in Damascus.

In January 1983 Amnesty International learned of the release of Michel Kilo, a member of this group. A writer, journalist and member of the Board of the Union of Arab Writers, he had been in untried detention since his arrest on 5 October 1980.

Amnesty International continued to seek the release of 18 people who had served in or were connected with the pre-1970 Syrian government. As well as former president Nur al-Din al-Atassi they included Hadithe Murade, from al-Suweyda, who was a member of the Regional Command of the Ba'ath Party. They were arrested after the November 1970 coup which brought President Hafez al-Assad to power, reportedly for refusing to collaborate with the new government, and subsequently held without charge or trial in a special wing of al-Mezze military prison in Damascus.

In December 1983 Amnesty International adopted as prisoners of conscience 19 people, mainly students, who were arrested in February 1983 for their alleged membership of the illegal Party for Communist Action (PCA). Alleged members of this party were arrested at different times since the beginning of 1980 and held incommunicado without charge or trial and 50 were adopted by Amnesty International as prisoners of conscience in July and August 1982 (see *Amnesty International Report 1983*).

Muwaffaq al-Din al-Kozbari, a lawyer and President of the Prisoner's Care Association and First Secretary of the Syrian League for the Defence of Human Rights, was released in November 1983. He was among a group of 20 lawyers who were arrested in April and May 1980 following a one-day national strike by the Syrian Bar Association on 31 March 1980. The Syrian Bar Association had called for an end to the state of emergency, reforms in the emergency legislation, the abolition of state security courts, a boycott of such courts by all lawyers, and the release of all untried detainees. In 1983 Amnesty International took up for investigation the cases of 94 doctors and 68 engineers also believed to have been detained because of their support for the one-day strike.

In December 1983 Amnesty International learned of the release of Ahmad Haj Sa'eed al-'Arbu, aged 49, from Malak. He was one of a group of seven Syrian Kurds who were arrested in July and August 1973 after sending a memorandum to President Hafez al-Assad protesting against the planned displacement of Syrian Kurds from their homes in northern Syria. They were subsequently separated and transferred at different times to various prisons in Damascus and Aleppo and were adopted by Amnesty International as prisoners of conscience.

Amnesty International continued to receive a number of allegations of the torture and ill-treatment of detainees by the Syrian security forces. Although the organization was not able to fully verify these allegations they were consistent with reports received over many years which have led the organization to believe that detainees were systematically tortured by the security forces.

In July 1983 Amnesty International appealed for a public inquiry into the death in custody of Amin Nassur, a third-year student at the College of Engineering in Latakiyyah University and an adopted prisoner of conscience. Amin Nassur was among 70 other detained members of the PCA who were taken in groups of four to the Latakiyyah branches of Military Intelligence (*al-Mukhabarat al-'Askariyya*) and Political Security (*al-Amn al-Siyassi*) towards the end of April 1983. There, they were reportedly tortured in order to force them into signing declarations of withdrawal from the party and support for the government following which they would be released. Amin Nassur was reportedly beaten with canes, burned all over his body and tortured with electric shocks, following which he went into a deep coma. He was then transferred under heavy guard to a hospital in Latakiyyah, but reportedly died the same night without regaining consciousness. His guards allegedly threw his body from a third floor hospital window to make his death appear to be suicide. The coffin containing his body was handed over to his family for burial with strict instructions that it should not be opened. However, Amnesty International understands that it was opened and that the body bore the marks of severe torture.

Amnesty International also appealed urgently on behalf of two other members of the PCA who were reportedly being interrogated by Military Intelligence in Aleppo. The organization sought assurances that the detainees were being given access to lawyers and medical treatment, but there was no response from the Syrian authorities.

Amnesty International learned of 15 officially confirmed executions in 1983. Thirteen involved civilians who were hanged after being convicted for criminal offences including robbery, rape, and the torture and murder of their victims. The remaining two were army deserters, Zuhair Butros who was hanged on 10 August for deserting from the Syrian army and spying for Israel, and Zuhair Ibrahim Srour, who was convicted of murder on 7 September and was executed by firing squad. The latter was tried and sentenced by a Military Field Court. During 1983 Amnesty International addressed several cables to President Hafez al-Assad expressing concern about executions which had taken place and reiterating Amnesty International's unconditional opposition to the death penalty.

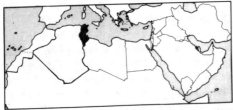

Tunisia

Amnesty International was concerned about the continued imprisonment of prisoners of conscience in Tunisia; procedures in political trials which fell short of internationally agreed standards; and continued allegations of torture and ill-treatment of political detainees. The organization learned of the passing of one death sentence during the year.

During 1983 Amnesty International continued to work for the release of over 40 adopted prisoners of conscience serving sentences of up to 10 years' imprisonment in connection with activities allegedly related to the *Mouvement de la tendance islamique* (MTI), Islamic Tendency Movement. They included Ali Ben Younes Nouir, a former secondary school mathematics teacher who was arrested in 1981 and sentenced to 11 years' imprisonment on charges of defamation of the Head of State, associating with an unauthorized organization and distributing false information. His sentence was later reduced on appeal to 10 years' imprisonment, which he was serving at Bourj Er-Roumi Prison (Nadhour Prison II) near Bizerte.

On 20 March, Tunisia's Independence Day, 16 prisoners of conscience serving sentences of between two and three years' imprisonment for alleged activities in connection with the MTI were released. Later in the year Amnesty International learned of the release, reportedly on grounds of ill-health, of two other adopted prisoners of conscience, Abdelfattah Mourou and Néjib Ben Ali El Ayari, who had both been serving sentences of 10 years' imprisonment in connection with their alleged links with the MTI. Amnesty International continued to work on behalf of Abdelfattah Mourou, after receiving reports that he remained subject to physical restrictions following his release from prison.

Amnesty International made special appeals for the release of Hachemi Ben Mohamed Hamdi, a prisoner of conscience whose health reportedly deteriorated during the year due to acute mental disorders. He was serving a three-year sentence at Tunis Civil Prison, having been convicted in 1981 of being associated with the MTI.

In January 1983 two groups of individuals were arrested apparently for non-violently exercising their rights to freedom of expression and association. One group of 56 people were reportedly arrested because of their alleged connection with the MTI. In the subsequent trial in July 38 individuals were tried on charges relating to the formation of an unauthorized organization, 16 being charged *in absentia*. Two were acquitted, two were sentenced to one year's imprisonment and 18 were sentenced to six months' imprisonment. The 16 who were tried *in absentia* received sentences of two years' imprisonment. The second group of nine people were arrested in January 1983, accused of constituting an unauthorized left-wing organization and were released at the end of February. Amnesty International knows of no related trial having taken place.

Amnesty International investigated the cases of 30 alleged members of the Islamic Liberation Party (ILP) who were tried (one of them *in absentia*) and sentenced by a military court in August 1983 to terms of imprisonment ranging from two to eight years. Nineteen of these prisoners were members of the armed forces and were charged with having affiliated to a political association, having helped to establish it and having attended its meetings. The remaining 11 civilians in the case were charged with inciting military personnel to join an underground association of a political character.

Amnesty International continued to be concerned about the conduct of political trials, including the ILP case in which all 30 defendants including 11 civilians were tried and found guilty by a military court with no right of appeal. Trial and sentencing was reportedly concluded in one day with the court rejecting all requests made by defence counsel, including requests that the trial be postponed to allow the defence lawyers sufficient time to examine their clients' files and to allow them access to books, leaflets and other printed materials allegedly confiscated by the authorities as evidence against the defendants. All but one of the defence lawyers subsequently withdrew from the hearing in protest. Amnesty International was concerned that the conduct of this trial appeared to be contrary to the provisions for fair trial contained in Article 14 of the International Covenant on Civil and Political Rights, which Tunisia has ratified.

Amnesty International was also concerned about the trial of 12 defendants before a criminal court in Tunis in July. They were charged, among other things, with forming an unauthorized association (referred to as "the secret organization") with the aim of carrying out attacks against people and property. Defence lawyers again withdrew from the hearing in protest against the lack of respect for the rights of the defence. The 12 were sentenced to prison terms ranging between two and eight years' hard labour.

At the end of the year Amnesty International was seeking further information concerning the trial in December of several people reportedly arrested in the vicinity of Ain Draham in the spring of 1983 on charges relating to the MTI.

Disturbances began on 29 December 1983 as a result of a government announcement to cut subsidies on bread and other staple foods. Hundreds of arrests subsequently took place. As of the end of the year, however, Amnesty International had not received details regarding these arrests.

Throughout 1983 Amnesty International continued to receive reports that political detainees had been subjected to torture or ill-treatment while held in pre-trial detention. During trial proceedings some detainees requested that courts permit medical examinations to ascertain whether physical marks they bore resulted from such treatment. These requests, as well as those made by lawyers on behalf of detainees, appear to have been rejected. During 1983, Amnesty International learned of no independent inquiry into torture allegations, nor of any measures taken to prosecute those responsible and to compensate the victims.

In November 1983 Amnesty International sent a cable to President Habib Bourguiba urging the commutation of a death sentence passed on a man convicted of premeditated murder. By the end of the year Amnesty International had received no information as to whether the sentence had been carried out.

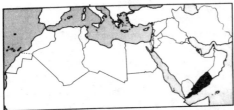

Yemen (People's Democratic Republic of)

Amnesty International was concerned about the continued long-term imprisonment of prisoners of conscience and the death penalty.

Amnesty International continued to work for the release of 20 prisoners of conscience. Most had already spent more than 10 years in prison, and some had reportedly been imprisoned for as long as 16 years because of their association with the former federal government under British colonial rule. In February, Amnesty International learned of the release of two brothers, Mohsen Saleh Bin Abdullah Al Fadhli and Muhammed Saleh Bin Abdullah Al Fadhli, both of whom had been adopted as prisoners of conscience and had been imprisoned apparently without charge or trial since 1967.

In November Amnesty International wrote to the Ambassador of the People's Democratic Republic of Yemen in London, enclosing a list of the names of 29 people whose cases had been investigated by the organization or who had been adopted as prisoners of conscience. These included several individuals whose whereabouts remained unknown and were possibly no longer alive. Amnesty International sought clarification of the prisoners' situation, including their present whereabouts and the dates when they were expected to be released. By the end of 1983 Amnesty International had received no response to its inquiries.

Amnesty International learned of one death sentence during 1983, passed on Qahtan 'Aboud Naji who was reportedly convicted of premeditated murder and other charges. On 21 December Amnesty International cabled President 'Ali Nasir Muhammad concerning reports that the death sentence had been confirmed and urged that his sentence be commuted. Amnesty International received no information by the end of the year as to whether the sentence had been carried out.

MISSIONS: JANUARY – DECEMBER 1983

Date	Country	Delegate(s)	Purpose
January	Iraq	The Secretary General, one staff member of International Secretariat and interpreter	To discuss Amnesty International's concerns with government authorities
January	United Kingdom (N. Ireland)	Staff member of International Secretariat	Research
February/March	Japan	Dr L. M. Singhvi (India) Staff member of International Secretariat	To discuss Amnesty International's concerns with government and others
February/March	Bangladesh/India	Staff member of International Secretariat	Research
March	Kenya	James Morton (UK)	Trial observation
March/April	Vatican	Franca Sciuto of International Executive Committee and the Secretary General	To discuss Amnesty International's concerns with the Pope
March/April	Uruguay	Professor Heleno Fragoso (Brazil) Staff member of International Secretariat	Research
May	Egypt	Whitney Ellsworth of International Executive Committee, the Deputy Secretary General and one staff member of International Secretariat	To discuss Amnesty International's concerns with government authorities

Date	Country	Delegate(s)	Purpose
April	Central African Republic	Robert Durst (France)	Trial observation
April	Turkey	Staff member of International Secretariat and interpreter	Trial observation and research
April	Canada	**Hélène Jaffé (France)** **Staff member of International Secretariat**	**Research**
April	Yugoslavia	Alexander Isola (Austria) Staff member of International Secretariat	Trial observation
April/May	Sierra Leone/Ghana	Staff member of International Secretariat	Research
May	Italy	Dr Ra Kurt Meier (Switzerland)	Trial observation
May	Zimbabwe	Dick Oosting (Netherlands) Staff member of International Secretariat	Research
May	Canada	Franca Sciuto of International Executive Committee	Trial observation
May	Republic of Ireland	Staff member of International Secretariat	Research
May/June	Spain	Staff member of International Secretariat	Research
June	Israel and Occupied Territories	Staff member of International Secretariat	Research
June/July	El Salvador/Costa Rica/ Mexico*	Dr Terence Allen, MD (USA) Juan María Vidarte (Spain) Staff member of International Secretariat	Research
June/July	USA	Staff member of International Secretariat	Research
July	USA	Brian Wrobel (UK)	Trial observation

*[Only staff member of IS visited Mexico]

Date	Country	Delegate(s)	Purpose
July	Yugoslavia	Professor Frits Rüter (Netherlands) Marius Broekmeijer (Netherlands)	Trial observation
August	Turkey	Staff member of International Secretariat	Research
August	USA	Steven Owen (Canada)	Preparation for trial observation
August	Ghana	Staff member of International Secretariat	Trial observation and research
September	Malawi	Professor J. Dugard (South Africa)	Trial observation
September	USA	Staff member of International Secretariat	Observe hearing on motion for new trial
September	United Kingdom	Staff member of International Secretariat	Trial observation
September/ October	Federal Republic of Germany	Douwe Korff (Netherlands)	Trial observation
October	Paraguay	Staff member of International Secretariat	Research
October	Brazil	Peter Klein (FRG)	Trial observation
October	Spain	David Lachat (Switzerland)	Trial observation
November	Jamaica	Martin Ennals (UK) Ezzat Fattah (Egypt/Canada)	To discuss Amnesty International's concerns with government authorities
November	Spain	Dr Hans Rau (FRG)	Trial observation
November	Central African Republic	Robert Durst (France)	Trial observation
November/ December	Mexico	Staff member of International Secretariat	Research
November/ December	Haiti	Staff member of International Secretariat	Research
December	Hungary	Stefan Rosenmayr (Austria)	Trial observation

Appendices

APPENDIX I

Statute of Amnesty International
Articles 1 and 2

As amended by the 16th International Council, meeting in Jouy-en-Josas, near Paris, France, 31 August – 4 September 1983.

OBJECT

1. CONSIDERING that every person has the right freely to hold and to express his or her convictions and the obligation to extend a like freedom to others, the object of AMNESTY INTERNATIONAL shall be to secure throughout the world the observance of the provisions of the Universal Declaration of Human Rights, by:

    a) irrespective of political considerations working towards the release of and providing assistance to persons who in violation of the aforesaid provisions are imprisoned, detained or otherwise physically restricted by reason of their political, religious or other conscientiously held beliefs or by reason of their ethnic origin, sex, colour or language, provided that they have not used or advocated violence (hereinafter referred to as "Prisoners of Conscience");

    b) opposing by all appropriate means the detention of any Prisoners of Conscience or any political prisoners without trial within a reasonable time or any trial procedures relating to such prisoners that do not conform to internationally recognized norms;

    c) opposing by all appropriate means the imposition and infliction of death penalties and torture or other cruel, inhuman or degrading treatment or punishment of prisoners or other detained or restricted persons whether or not they have used or advocated violence.

METHODS

2. In order to achieve the aforesaid object, AMNESTY INTERNATIONAL shall:

    a) at all times maintain an overall balance between its activities in relation to countries adhering to the different world political ideologies and groupings;

    b) promote as appears appropriate the adoption of constitutions, conventions, treaties and other measure which guarantee the rights contained in the provisions referred to in Article 1 hereof;

c) support and publicize the activities of and cooperate with international organizations and agencies which work for the implementation of the aforesaid provisions;

d) take all necessary steps to establish an effective organization of sections, affiliated groups and individual members;

e) secure the adoption by groups of members or supporters of individual Prisoners of Conscience or entrust to such groups other tasks in support of the object set out in Article 1;

f) provide financial and other relief to Prisoners of Conscience and their dependants and to persons who have lately been Prisoners of Conscience or who might reasonably be expected to be Prisoners of Conscience or to become Prisoners of Conscience if convicted or if they were to return to their own countries, and to the dependants of such persons;

g) work for the improvement of conditions for Prisoners of Conscience and political prisoners;

h) provide legal aid, where necessary and possible, to Prisoners of Conscience and to persons who might reasonably be expected to be Prisoners of Conscience or to become Prisoners of Conscience if convicted or if they were to return to their own countries, and, where desirable, send observers to attend the trials of such persons;

i) publicize the cases of Prisoners of Conscience or persons who have otherwise been subjected to disabilities in violation of the aforesaid provisions;

j) send investigators, where appropriate, to investigate allegations that the rights of individuals under the aforesaid provisions have been violated or threatened;

k) make representations to international organizations and to governments whenever it appears that an individual is a Prisoner of Conscience or has otherwise been subjected to disabilities in violation of the aforesaid provisions;

l) promote and support the granting of general amnesties of which the beneficiaries will include Prisoners of Conscience;

m) adopt any other appropriate methods for the securing of its object.

The full text of the Statute of Amnesty International is available, free upon request, from: Amnesty International, International Secretariat, 1 Easton Street, London WC1X 8DJ, United Kingdom.

APPENDIX II

Amnesty International News Releases 1983

16 February	AI reports political suspects in *Egypt* face repeated arrest and imprisonment
2 March	AI says political prisoners tortured in *Zaire*
9 March	AI reports on psychiatric confinement of *Soviet* political prisoners
11 March	AI warns of threat to *Libyans* abroad
20 March	AI urges release or trial for thousands in *Viet Nam*
23 March	AI launches worldwide campaign against political killings by governments
18 May	AI publishes evidence of torture in secret *Chilean* detention centres
19 May	AI calls on *Argentine* Government to investigate killings by security forces
8 June	AI calls on *Irish* Government to intervene in the Eamonn "Nicky" Kelly case
6 July	Political detainees denied basic rights in *Sri Lanka*, AI says
7 July	AI urges *British* Parliament to reject death penalty; releases current world statistics
14 July	AI urges release of political prisoners in *Mauritania*, cites torture
20 July	Troops in *East Timor* given secret manual permitting torture, reports AI
10 August	AI welcomes *Canadian* investigation of reported prison ill-treatment
14 September	Peaceful critics, would-be emigrants jailed under *German Democratic Republic* laws, says AI
21 September	Hundreds summarily executed in *Peru* this year, AI reports
28 September	AI cites fresh evidence of secret prison executions and torture in *Iran*
3 October	AI urges *Japan* to halt executions, criticizes official secrecy
10 October	*Chad* troops kill civilians outside battle zones, AI says
19 October	AI report on *Iraq* cites deaths under torture and hundreds of political executions
26 October	AI's annual report urges governments to stop using human rights issues for political propaganda
28 October	AI calls on *Chinese* President to halt mass executions
2 November	AI cites reports of torture by *Afghan* security police

9 November AI urges end to torture and jailing of prisoners of conscience in *Uruguay*

16 November *Syrian* security services systematically violate human rights, AI report says

8 December AI gives United Nations million signature human rights appeal

---

APPENDIX III

Amnesty International around the world

Sections

Australia: Amnesty International, Australian Section, PO Box No. A159, Sydney South, New South Wales 2000

Austria: Amnesty International, Austrian Section, Esslinggasse 15/4, A-1010 Wien

Bangladesh: c/o Amnesty International, International Secretariat, 1 Easton Street, London WC1X 8DJ, United Kingdom

Barbados: Amnesty International, Barbados Section, PO Box 65B, Brittons Hill, Bridgetown

Belgium: Amnesty International, Belgian Section (*Flemish*), Ruelensvest 127, 3030 Leuven

Amnesty International, Belgian Section (*francophone*), 126 avenue Louise, 1050 Brussels

Canada: Amnesty International, Canadian Section (*English-speaking*), 294 Albert Street, Suite 204, Ottawa, Ontario K1P 6E6

Amnistie Internationale, Section canadienne (*francophone*), 1800 Ouest, Boulevard Dorchester, local 400, Montreal, Quebec H3H 2H2

Chile: Señores, Casilla 4062, Santiago

Denmark: Amnesty International, Danish Section, Frederiksborggade 1, 1360 Copenhagen K

Ecuador: Señores, Casilla de Correo 8994, Guayaquil

Faroe Islands: Amnesty International, Faroe Islands, c/o Anette Wang, PO Box 1075, Trondargøta 47, 3800 Tórshavn

Finland: Amnesty International, Finnish Section, Munkkisaarenkatu 12 A 51, 00150 Helsinki 15

France: Amnesty International, Section française,18 rue Théodore Deck, 75015 Paris

Germany, Federal Republic of: Amnesty International, Section of the FRG, Heerstrasse 178, 5300 Bonn 1

Ghana: Amnesty International, Ghanaian Section, PO Box 9852, Kotoka Airport, Accra

Greece: Amnesty International, Greek Section, 20 Mavromihali Street, Athens 106-80

Hong Kong: Amnesty International, Hong Kong Section, 52 Princess Margaret Road, 3rd Floor, Kowloon

Iceland: Amnesty International, Icelandic Section, PO Box 618, 121 Reykjavik

India: Amnesty International, Indian Section, A26 Kailash Colony, New Delhi 110 048

Ireland: Amnesty International, Irish Section, Liberty Hall, 8th Floor, Dublin 1

Israel: Amnesty International, Israeli Section, PO Box 39032, 69103 Tel Aviv

Italy: Amnesty International, Italian Section, viale Mazzini 146, 00195 Rome

Ivory Coast: Amnesty International, Section ivoirienne, 04 BP 895, Abidjan 04

Japan: Amnesty International, Japanese Section, Daisan-Sanbu Building 3F, 2-3-22 Nishi-Waseda, Shinjuku-ku, Tokyo 160

Korea, Republic of: Amnesty International, Korean Section, 25-1 Chang Song Dong, Chong no ku, Seoul

Luxembourg: Amnesty International Luxembourg, Boîte Postale 1914, 1019 Luxembourg

Mexico: Señores, Apartado Postal No. 20-217, San Angel del Alvaro Obregón, 01000 Mexico DF

Nepal: c/o Amnesty International, International Secretariat, 1 Easton Street, London WC1X 8DJ, United Kingdom

Netherlands: Amnesty International, Dutch Section, Postbus 61501, 1005 HM Amsterdam

New Zealand: Amnesty International, New Zealand Section, PO Box 6647, Wellington 1

Nigeria: Amnesty International, Nigerian Section, 15 Onayade Street, Fadeyi-Yaba, Lagos

Norway: Amnesty International, Norwegian Section, Niels Juelsgt., 39, Oslo 2

Peru: Señores, Casilla 11080, Lima 14

Portugal: Seccâo Portuguesa AI, Apartado 1642, 1016 Lisboa Codex

Puerto Rico: Amnesty International, Puerto Rican Section, Calle Belaval 614, San Juan (Santurce), Puerto Rico 00909

Senegal: Amnesty International, Section sénégalaise, 152 Avenue du Président Lamine Gueye, BP 3813, Dakar

Spain: Amnesty International, Spanish Section, Paseo de Recoletos 18, Piso 6, Madrid 1

Sri Lanka: Amnesty International, Sri Lanka Section, c/o E. A. G. de Silva, 79/15 Dr C. W. W. Kannangara Mawartha, Colombo 7

Sweden: Amnesty International, Swedish Section, Surbrunnsgatan 44, S-113 48 Stockholm

Switzerland: Amnesty International, Swiss Section, PO Box 1051, CH-3001 Bern

Turkey: c/o Amnesty International, International Secretariat, 1 Easton Street, London WC1X 8DJ, United Kingdom

United Kingdom: Amnesty International, British Section, 5 Roberts Place, off Bowling Green Lane, London EC1 0EJ

United States of America: Amnesty International of the USA, 304 West 58th Street, New York, NY 10019

Venezuela: Señores, Apartado 5110, Caracas 1010

Groups

Netherlands Antilles	Costa Rica	Tanzania
Belize	Guyana	Trinidad and Tobago
Brazil	Mauritius	Tunisia
Colombia	Sierra Leone	USSR

Individual Subscribers or Supporters

Afghanistan	Burma
Algeria	Burundi
Andorra	Cameroon
Antigua	Cape Verde
Argentina	Cayman Islands
Bahamas	Central African Republic
Bahrain	Chad
Bermuda	China (People's Republic of)
Bhutan	Congo
Bolivia	Cuba
Botswana	Cyprus
Brazil	Czechoslovakia
Brunei	Djibouti
Bulgaria	Dominica

Dominican Republic
Egypt
El Salvador
Ethiopia
Fiji
French Polynesia
Gabon
The Gambia
German Democratic Republic
Gibraltar
Grenada
Haiti
Honduras
Hungary
Indonesia
Iran
Iraq
Jamaica
Jordan
Kampuchea
Kenya
Korea (Democratic People's Republic of)
Kuwait
Laos
Lebanon
Lesotho
Liberia
Libya
Madagascar
Malawi
Malaysia
Malta
Mauritania
Morocco
Mozambique
Namibia
Nicaragua
Niger
Oman
Pakistan
Panama
Papua New Guinea
Paraguay
Philippines
Poland
Qatar
Romania

Rwanda
Saint Kitts
Saint Lucia
Saudi Arabia
Seychelles
Singapore
Solomon Islands
South Africa
Sudan
Suriname
Swaziland
Syria
Taiwan
Thailand
Togo
Uganda
United Arab Emirates
Upper Volta
Uruguay
Vanuatu
Virgin Islands
Yemen (People's Democratic Republic of)
Yugoslavia
Zaire
Zambia
Zimbabwe

APPENDIX IV
International Executive Committee

Jan Egeland (Vice-Chairperson)	Norway
Whitney Ellsworth	United States of America
Georges le Guevel	France
Wolfgang Heinz	Federal Republic of Germany
Jan Willem den Herder	Netherlands
Edy Kaufman	Israel
Franca Sciuto	Italy
Françoise Vandale	International Secretariat
Suriya Wickremasinghe (Chairperson)	Sri Lanka

APPENDIX V

Protocol No. 6

To the Convention for the Protection of Human Rights and Fundamental Freedoms Concerning the Abolition of the Death Penalty

The member States of the Council of Europe, signatory to this Protocol to the Convention for the Protection of Human Rights and Fundamental Freedoms, signed at Rome on 4 November 1950 (hereinafter referred to as "the Convention");

Considering that the evolution that has occurred in several member States of the Council of Europe expresses a general tendency in favour of abolition of the death penalty;

Have agreed as follows:

Article 1
The death penalty shall be abolished. No one shall be condemned to such penalty or executed.

Article 2
A State may make provision in its law for the death penalty in respect of acts committed in time of war or of imminent threat of war; such penalty shall be applied only in the instances laid down in the law and in accordance with its provisions. The State shall communicate to the Secretary General of the Council of Europe the relevant provisions of that law.

Article 3
No derogation from the provisions of this Protocol shall be made under Article 15 of the Convention.

Article 4
No reservation may be made under Article 64 of the Convention in respect of the provisions of this Protocol.

Article 5
1. Any State may at the time of signature or when depositing its instrument of ratification, acceptance or approval, specify the territory or territories to which this Protocol shall apply.

2. Any State may at any later date, by a declaration addressed to the Secretary General of the Council of Europe, extend the application of this Protocol to any other territory specified in the declaration. In respect of such territory the Protocol shall enter into force on the first day of the month following the date of receipt of such declaration by the Secretary General.

3. Any declaration made under the two preceding paragraphs may, in respect of any territory specified in such declaration, be withdrawn by a notification addressed to the Secretary General. The withdrawal shall become effective on the first day of the month following the date of receipt of such notification by the Secretary General.

Article 6
As between the States Parties the provisions of Articles 1 to 5 of this Protocol shall be regarded as additional articles to the Convention and all the provisions of the Convention shall apply accordingly.

Article 7
This Protocol shall be open for signature by the member States of the Council of Europe, signatories to the Convention. It shall be subject to ratification, acceptance or approval. A member State of the Council of Europe may not ratify, accept or approve this Protocol unless it has, simultaneously or previously, ratified the Convention. Instruments of ratification, acceptance or approval shall be deposited with the Secretary General of the Council of Europe.

Article 8
1. This Protocol shall enter into force on the first day of the month following the date on which five member States of the Council of Europe have expressed their consent to be bound by the Protocol in accordance with the provisions of Article 7.

2. In respect of any member State which subsequently expresses its consent to be bound by it, the Protocol shall enter into force on the first day of the month following the date of the deposit of the instrument of ratification, acceptance or approval.

Article 9
The Secretary General of the Council of Europe shall notify the member States of the Council of:

a. any signature;

b. the deposit of any instrument of ratification, acceptance or approval;

c. any date of entry into force of this Protocol in accordance with Articles 5 and 8;

d. any other act, notification or communication relating to this Protocol.

In witness whereof the undersigned, being duly authorised thereto, have signed this Protocol.

Done at Strasbourg, the twenty-eight April one thousand nine hundred and eighty-three in English and French, both texts being equally authentic, in a single copy which shall be deposited in the archives of the Council of Europe. The Secretary General of the Council of Europe shall transmit certified copies to each member State of the Council of Europe.

APPENDIX VI

Selected Statistics

By the beginning of 1984 there were over 3,200 Amnesty International groups in 55 countries – almost 300 more groups than the year before. There were over 500,000 members, supporters and subscribers in over 160 countries and territories. Amnesty International has sections in 43 countries.

A total of 5,073 prisoners were adopted as prisoners of conscience or were being investigated as possible prisoners of conscience. During 1983, 1,339 new cases were taken up and 1,744 prisoners released.

Amnesty International issued 276 urgent action appeals on behalf of individuals or groups of prisoners in 66 countries. Of these, 95 were prompted by reports of torture, 26 were on medical grounds, 54 were issued because of legal concerns, 46 related to extrajudicial executions or "disappearances", and 38 were on behalf of people under sentence of death.